SOLIDARITY

IN A SLUM

Joseph B. Tamney

A SCHENKMAN PUBLICATION

HALSTED PRESS DIVISION

JOHN WILEY & SONS

New York — London — Sydney — Toronto

Distributed solely by Halsted Press, a Division of
John Wiley & Sons, Inc., New York.

Library of Congress Cataloging in Publication Data

Tamney, Joseph B
   Solidarity in a slum.

    1. Milwaukee — Social conditions.   2. Solidarity — Case studies
    3 Slums — Milwaukee.   I. Title.
HN80.M58T35   301.18'028   74-5353
ISBN 0-470-84485-X
ISBN 0-470-84486-8 (pbk.)

SOLIDARITY IN A SLUM

Contents

Preface

The work reported here was made possible by a grant from the United Community Services of Milwaukee for the purpose of determining which residents of an area scheduled for urban renewal needed professional help from existing government agencies. The questionnaire used in the study reflected both the needs of United Fund and my professional interest in the problem of solidarity, or involvement; this monograph was influenced more by the latter than by the former.

The first chapter sets forth a theory of involvement. Although most of the propositions stated in this chapter are not tested by the research reported here, the theory provides the framework for the entire analysis that follows. The theory is referred to from time to time, and the choice of issues studied is better understood if the reader has first read it. This monograph represents not so much a test as an expansion of the theory.

Essentially, then, this work is an attempt to elaborate a theory of involvement.

I would like to thank the graduate students who worked so hard on this research project—Mr. John Musick, who was in charge of field operations; Mr. Ronald Manderscheid and Ms. Carol Coddeta, who helped on the analysis of data; and Messrs. John Rasmann and George Gerharz, whose theses I have made use of in this monograph. To these associates I owe a great deal.

Marquette University allowed free and frequent use of their computer facilities, for which I am grateful.

I would especially like to thank Mr. Peter Sheldon of United Fund for his cooperation.

1

The Study of Involvement

It is a fact that people live and die in virtual contact with only a small part of the world around them. A mother will cry about the troubles of her son who lives thousands of miles away, but remain unaffected by what happens to the poor, lonely, man living upstairs. Many will rejoice when their favorite football team wins the championship, but remain unmoved when someone discovers a cure for cancer. A fight between our son and a neighbor's child will arouse our emotions for hours; a war between distant African peoples does not affect us even for seconds. The people around us come and go, suffer and rejoice, live and die. But we are affected by little of all this; we are involved with few of the billions who surround us. The movie documentary delineates the approaching starvation of millions—we frown; the hero dies in the last reel of a melodrama—we cry. Each of us feels a sense of oneness, or, *involvement,* with only a few of the people and objects we encounter in life. This book is concerned with mapping the pattern of involvement—the pattern of threads binding humans together—that exists among the people living in one part of urban America.

WHAT IS INVOLVEMENT?

Involvement implies a sense of oneness. The type of experience referred to might be described with words other than "oneness." Individuals might describe themselves as "close;" they might feel "dependent;" a wife might say she is "chained" to her husband, or a husband might believe himself "dominated" by his job. The words in quotes connote different degrees of acceptance of a relationship, but they share the idea of oneness.

This same idea has been significant in the history of sociology. Durkheim described solidarity as follows: "it is impossible for men to live together, associating in industry, without acquiring a sentiment of the whole formed by their union, without attaching themselves to that whole, preoccupying themselves with its interests, and taking account of it in their conduct."[1] This "sentiment of the whole" is identical to a sense of oneness. Similarly, Cooley described the primary group as a "fusion of individualities in a common whole,"[2] Weber described solidarity as a subjective feeling of belonging together,[3] and Freud described identification as a process in which children become parents. All of these authors referred to an event characterized by a sense of oneness among two or more human beings.

It might be asked why we do not use the term solidarity or primary group rather than involvement. Just about all sociological theories on the primary group and solidarity have a positive bias that this study desires to avoid. Obviously, people can be deeply but negatively involved with each other, i.e., they can hate each other. But sociologists tend to avoid this possibility. When Faris discussed the primary group, one of whose characteristics is mutual sympathy, he opposed it to institutions, which are characterized by a sense of impersonal distance.[4] There is mention of "the hostile group", but what this means is not clear, although it seems to refer to an enemy with whom there need not be much involvement. Faris's vocabulary in the article referred to does not include a concept for intense negative involvement. Similarly, Weber used solidarity to refer to the absence of conflict;[5] and in a recent work by Cousins—"The concept of solidarity... [means] the relative preponderance of favorable over hostile affects, and a similar balance of moral respect (as over against moral condemnation), among the co-participants in the concrete group...."[6] In both the primary-group tradition and the solidarity tradition there is a positive bias; it is assumed that oneness is a happy condition. Hate and conflict are avoided. By using the term involvement it is hoped that this positive bias will be minimized. A condition of high involvement can be either positive or negative.[7]

WHAT INVOLVEMENT IS NOT

Involvement is not to be equated with any concept primarily referring to norms or satisfaction or success.

For instance, consider the term anomie. This is meant to describe a situation in which people have no norms, i.e., no socially agreed upon rules for the conduct of human affairs. It is necessary to understand that anomie is not the same as alienation. Consider the condition immediately after an earthquake. Two of the most important characteristics of such occasions are the absence of any consensus as to what is to be done (anomie) and the presence of a general sense of closeness among the victims (involvement).

SOLIDARITY IN A SLUM

It will be suggested later that high involvement is more likely when behavior is spontaneous. This would mean that, in general, the social situation likely to produce the most intense involvement will be anomic, i.e., one lacking in rules and regulations.

In other situations of course anomie and alienation go together. Sommer and Osmond have described "the schizophrenic no-society," i.e., the schizophrenic ward of a hospital, where there is no leadership or interdependence and which has no status system of its own or system of justice. "If further evidence is needed that the concept of a society cannot be appropriately applied to the way of life found on the long-stay wards of the mental hospital there is the fact that patients have very little interest in one another. Patients who have lived together on the same ward for many years do not even know each other's names; sociometric studies have shown that only a handful of reciprocated friendships occur; occupational therapists have compared patients doing craftwork to seven or eight people playing solitaire."[8] No structure, no rules, no interest—the patient ward can be described as both anomic and without involvement. In short, anomie, the absence of norms, and alienation, the absence of involvement, may or may not occur together; there is no necessary relation between them such that the presence of one condition requires either the presence or absence of the other. Anomie and alienation are quite distinct problems.

Similarly, a distinction must be made between satisfaction, or concepts based on satisfaction, such as morale, and involvement. It has already been pointed out that involvement may be either positive or negative. A son may be deeply conscious of his dissatisfaction with his mother, even to the point of murdering her. Obviously, the very fact that murder, which is the elimination of a relationship, would even be considered indicates that the son felt deeply involved with his mother. This mother-son relationship, then, would be characterized by low satisfaction and high involvement. Similarly, Bettelheim has described how some political prisoners in the German concentration camps emulated their gestapo guards.[9] These prisoners certainly were involved with their guards, but we can not imagine they were very satisfied with this relationship. High involvement, therefore, does not always mean high satisfaction.

Conversely, it is also possible to have high satisfaction and low involvement. A student might ask his teacher whether he is satisfied with his academic performance. The teacher need not be very involved with the student in order to answer "yes."

Usually, satisfaction simply indicates the extent to which a situation meets our expectations. Where our expectations are met or exceeded we are satisfied. Of course we may change our expectations so that we may find ourselves in the very same situation again, and feel quite dissatisfied. But the idea of expectation is not part of our concept of involvement, which is why satisfaction and involvement are quite distinct phenomena.[10]

Finally, concepts that are based on the idea of success are not to be equated with involvement. Consider the idea of integration, which refers to the efficiency of social arrangements in accomplishing their goals.[11] An interest in integration might lead to a study of consistency among the norms held by an aggregate of people, or of the extent to which people are motivated to conform to existing norms, or of the necessity of some deviance from shared norms in order to achieve the aggregate's goals. This work is concerned with none of these problems. Efficiency and involvement are distinct problems. For instance it has been argued that governmental stability requires some apathy; it is assumed that if everyone were interested in all the problems faced by government so much time would be spent in discussing these problems with concerned citizens and so many different solutions would be put forth that government would be unable to take decisive actions quickly enough. It remains an open question whether this is true or not. However, the argument clearly assumes that success and involvement are distinct, since it suggests that continuously high citizen involvement might be inefficient. Likewise, we hear of doctors' refusing to operate on their loved ones; the assumption is that they are too involved to be able to do the job with the greatest efficiency. Success is quite distinct from a sense of oneness.

Involvement, then, is not to be equated with any concept that refers to norms, satisfaction, or success.

It is possible to ask four distinct questions of an aggregate of people: How involved are they with each other? How anomic is the aggregate? How satisfied are the people with their way of life? How efficient are they in achieving their goals? This work is concerned with only the first question.

As previously noted this work is concerned with mapping the pattern of involvement among an aggregate of people. Before doing this, however, some basic theoretical ideas about involvement will be presented. This will serve as a background for the analysis that follows in later chapters.

SOURCES OF INVOLVEMENT

Perhaps there is no stronger source of involvement than the experience of physical union with another, as in giving birth to a child or in sexual intercourse. We consider a baby to be physically part of the mother. Even after the two are separated, a recognition of having been part of the mother makes the child feel involved with her. It is important to recognize the total irrelevance of the time dimension in the theory of involvement. Spatial identity is a source of involvement, whether that identity took place in the past, is occurring this moment, or is anticipated as a future event.

SOLIDARITY IN A SLUM

It is not difficult to understand why spatial identity can produce a sense of oneness. There are laws of perception that organize or unify the field of experience. "Elements in experience are automatically and almost irresistibly grouped—other things equal—according to proximity, similarity and continuity."[12] When two objects like foetus and mother are so close and continuous we see them as one. The manner in which human beings perceive their environment makes physical closeness a source of involvement.

Our first theorem, therefore, is: *The extent of involvement depends on the physical distance between objects.* Physical union represents one extreme on the continuum of physical distance. In general as distance declines the sense of involvement should increase. However, at present the exact relation between involvement and distance is unknown. This is true in two senses: 1) We do not know how to translate units of distance into units of involvement, e.g., if A lives five yards away from C, and B lives ten yards away from C, does this mean that C is likely to feel twice as involved with A as with B? 2) We do not know the significance of the length of time a certain distance is maintained; previously it was stated that the time dimension is irrelevant, and this seems true in the sense that whether an event is associated with the past, present, or future seems irrelevant; on the other hand the duration of the event might well be important; would a person not feel more involved with someone who lived nearby for five years than with someone who lived nearby for five days? The answer would seem to be "yes," but it is now impossible to predict the size of the difference in involvement resulting from these two cases.

That we commonly express involvement in terms of distance seems meaningful. People often say about their friends—"we are very close." Conversely, we describe people who are indifferent to us as "detached" or "distant." Using the distance analogy is probably the most common means of expressing degrees of involvement. This fact certainly supports the idea that physical closeness is a source of involvement. If it were not what would explain the appeal of the analogy?

It is relevant that among other species there exist mechanisms for maintaining a relationship between distance and involvement. It would seem hazardous to suggest that *homo sapiens* has lost all sense of a relationship between distance and involvement. Carpenter has written that: "An important clue to social relations in primate societies is the observed spatial relations of individuals, sub-groups, and organized groups. The strength of the attachments between two individuals may be judged, or actually measured, by observing for a period of time the average distance which separates the two animals."[13] In general vertebrates maintain congruence between proximity and involvement.[14] Given the continued usage of the distance analogy it seems quite likely that this association between proximity and involvement is continued by *homo sapiens.*

But the discussion has really pointed our that proximity is related to involvement in two ways: as source and as symbol. To the extent that two people live close to each other or approach the foetus-mother situation, they are likely to feel a sense of oneness. But it also seems true that the closer two people live to each other the more they believe they should feel involved, since distance is supposed to symbolize oneness. To live close to someone and not be involved with them is likely to generate a sense of living a lie. But if closeness is a source of involvement how is it possible not to feel involved with, say, our neighbors? In other words, if closeness is not only a symbol, but a source, of involvement, how is it possible to "live a lie"? It is possible if closeness is more potent as a symbol of involvement than as a source of involvement. And we suspect that this is the case. The everyday use of the distance analogy suggests that closeness is a powerful symbol of involvement, while the already legendary apathy of urban neighbors indicates that closeness is at best a weak source of involvement.

It could be that the symbolic significance of distance has been lost in the urban environment. The distance analogy might be truly meaningless to urbanites—a linguistic anachronism. This is a matter for empirical study.

There are, then, two theorems relating distance and involvement: *The extent of involvement depends on the physical distance between objects. The extent to which people believe objects should be involved depends on the physical distance between objects.*

Durkheim wrote about two sources of solidarity—similarity and interdependence. Freud discussed two bases of love: 1) narcissistic—when the other person resembles us as we are or were or would be; and 2) functional—when the other person gives us what we need, such as tenderness or protection. Freud made the important point that for similarity to be a source of involvement the time dimension is not important, i.e., the similarity need not relate to us as we are now to produce involvement. On the whole, however, Freud's scheme is similar to Durkheim's formulation. Toennies in discussing human relations distinguished: 1) friendship—"the simplest fellowship type is represented by a pair who live together in a brotherly, comradely, and friendly manner, and it is most likely to exist when those involved are of the *same* age, sex and sentiment or engaged in the *same* activity or have the *same* intentions, or when they are united by *one* idea" (italics mine); and 2) the authoritative type, such as the relation between a father and son. Toennies talks more about dominance than interdependence, but all three theorists stressed that involvement is related to similarity and power (this is a broad term meant to include both interdependence and domination).[14]

Less well known, but more original, is Simmel's work on the anaysis of relationship. He emphasized that relationships are based on knowing something about another, and that differences in intensity of relationships are due

6

to differences in the degree people reveal themselves to one another.[16] Unfortunately, Simmel did not discuss the implications of his approach for the previously developed theories of Durkheim and Toennies.

It is true that Toennies frequently referred to understanding, but as his translator notes: *"Verstandnis* is translated 'understanding.' The concept ... should also carry the meaning of mutual understanding and possession of similar sentiments, hopes, aspirations, desires, attitudes, emotions, and beliefs."[17] For Toennies understanding was a consequence of similarity. The value of Simmel's work is that it stresses the independent importance of knowledge as a basis of relationship. It is true that when there is consciously recognized similarity, there is understanding. But the presence of understanding does not require similarity; people can know something about each other without being similar.

It is possible to pull together from the sociological classics, then, a third theorem: *The extent of involvement depends on the amount of similarity, power, and knowledge.*[18]

The idea of three social sources of involvement is tenable, for each is a way of being another. If two people are similar, they are, to a degree, the same. Likewise, if one person has power over another, the subordinate becomes the concrete embodiment of the purpose existing in the mind of the power-wielder; in a way, therefore, the slave is the master and vice-versa. Finally, to the extent we know someone that person exists in our minds, and we are the other. Similarity, power, and knowledge represent three ways of being another.

The willingness to communicate seems related to these same three variables. People tend not to start relationships; most communication is confirmation or elaboration of a pre-existing relation. When two sports-car owners drive past each other, they often feel free to honk their horns and wave, especially when their type of car first appears on the market; the similarity of ownership makes this sign of recognition acceptable. When a new employee reports at the job, he does not hesitate to talk to the boss; the work organization already relates them via power. It is not unusual to hear a conversation begin: "You don't know me, but I have heard a lot about you...." In this case knowledge legitimates communication. Goffman has suggested that "as a general rule... acquainted persons [i.e., people who know each other] in a social situation require a reason not to enter a face engagement with each other, while unacquainted persons require a reason to do so."[19] When people are already related because of similarity, power or knowledge then communication is legitimate and, according to Goffman, recognition of the relation is required. Under such conditions, to communicate is simply to activate a latent bond. The relative ease of communication when one of these three social sources is present supports the theorem that these are sources of involvement.

An attempt was made to test this third theorem in a study of reactions to the death of President Kennedy.[20] It was assumed that the extent to which people were affected by this event was a measure of their involvement in Kennedy. Some relationships were found between this measure and indicators of ideal similarity, power, and knowledge in the Kennedy-respondent relations. The study distinguished between real similarity and ideal similarity; this was based on Freud's distinction between people being like us as we act, or being like what we would like to be, i.e., being similar to our ideals. This is a valuable distinction not made use of by many sociologists. Although this research did produce some significant statistical associations the overall results were far from giving complete support to the theorem. For instance, the social sources of involvement worked differently for males and females, i.e., not all three sources were significantly related to the assassination-reaction measure for both males and females; power was significant for males but not females. This study does suggest, however, that the third theorem might be a useful source of empirical work.

IMAGINARY AND SENSED ENVIRONMENTS

All human beings live in at least two worlds—the internal or imaginary and the external or perceived. For all practical purposes it can be said that human beings exist in two environments simultaneously—the imagination and the perceived world.

But for many people the fact of a simultaneous existence in two environments is not a real problem. The people they think about are the people they live with. A mother might be sitting at home and at one moment talking with her daughter and in the next daydreaming about her daughter. But, on the other hand, a mother might at one moment be talking with her husband and in the next reminiscing about her last meeting with her lover. That some sense of alienation is natural and universal because man is an imaginative creature is important to know but not of primary interest to sociologists. On the other hand the extent to which objects occur in both the imaginary and perceived worlds varies considerably from person to person and culture to culture, and therefore is of interest to sociologists. Among the members of a farm family there is probably a high degree of overlap between the people perceived and the people imagined. But what happens, for instance, when a farm boy moves away to the "big city"? At least for awhile he will tend to live in two different worlds—the perceived city and the imagined farm. Or compare modern adolescents and adults. The former are more likely to be dreamers—imagining a trip to the moon, a date with a movie star, becoming famous, and so on. The adolescent lives in more "worlds" than the adult. What is the effect of this on involvement? It is probable that when people live in more than one world, or environment, they can never feel as involved in any one of these environments,

SOLIDARITY IN A SLUM

as can someone who has experienced only one locality and one set of human beings. We suggest, therefore, the general idea that: *The extent of involvement depends on the degree of overlap between the imaginary and sensed environments.* In other words alienation can be reduced either by fantasizing only about the perceived environment or by perceiving only objects from the fantasized environment (e.g., the person who becomes Napoleon).

THEORY OF DISENGAGEMENT

There is one theory of involvement that is relevant here, but which does not seem reducible to the theorems presented in this chapter—the theory of disengagement.

It has been suggested that as people become old they disengage themselves from society. What does this mean? What is the relation between disengagement and involvement?

Disengagement sounds like the absence of involvement, and this theory would seem to suggest that as people grow old they become alienated. But this is not an accurate rendition of the above theory. Cumming elaborated on the meaning of engagement as follows: "The fully-engaged person acts in a large number and wide variety of roles in a system of divided labor, and feels an obligation to meet the expectations of his role partners. ...Roughly, the depth and breadth of a man's engagement can be measured by the degree of potential disruption that would follow his sudden death."[21] There are several dimensions to the meaning of engagement: 1) the number of roles, 2) the variety of roles, 3) the degree of felt obligation to meet the expectations of others, and 4) the power and uniqueness of the individual. Moreover, Cumming makes explicit that engagement is not merely activity—"activity and engagement are not in the same dimension. A disengaged person often maintains a high level of activity in a small number and narrow variety of roles, although it is doubtful if it is possible to be at once firmly engaged and inactive."[22] There are several problems with Cumming's exploration because of the presence of unjustified assumptions. She assumes that a person's significance for a group is a measure of variety of roles, but surely this is unwarranted; a government official may "bury himself in his work" and thus be both significant and restricted regarding role variety. Moreover Cumming's assumption that engaged people are more conforming would seem to reflect more the conservative bias in favor of conformity than known facts. If we eliminate these assumptions, then, engagement can be reduced to the number and variety of roles a person plays.

Translated into presently relevant terms the theory suggests that old people become involved in fewer objects.[23] (The idea of "variety" is dropped because its meaning is not clear.)

But as Cumming elaborates her ideas she goes beyond the rather narrow description of aging as becoming involved in fewer objects. She, also, describes the change from middle to old age as a move from organic to mechanical solidarity. "Immediately after retirement, husbands seem redundant to many women who have developed lives of their own since the termination of child-raising. However, extremely old people, with no division of labor at all, become dependent upon one another to such an extent that if one dies the other is likely to follow quickly. This special case of a very binding mechanical solidarity is probably the result of these extremely old people being almost merged into one identity like twin infants."[24] Aging means a shift in the dominant basis of involvement from power to similarity.

According to Cumming, then, aging means that people are involved with fewer objects and that the dominant basis of the relationships that do exist is similarity.

Why does aging have these effects? Obviously working people are forced to retire, and this might lower the number of objects people are involved with, but this could be only a temporary condition. Retirement itself does not necessitate a prolonged decline in the number of objects in which a person is involved. But Cumming does suggest that in the American industrial society retirement is a prolonged problem because: a) many working people in such a society find no leisure-time activities that use the same skills developed by their work; there is no continuity, therefore, between work and the post-retirement leisure activities available; and b) in the American industrial society retirement tends to mean failure.[25] But why should (a) lead to prolonged disengagement? The first argument would seem to be significant only if other conditions were causing a decline in general interest in the environment; (b) might be such a condition, but let us postpone comment on this argument for a moment.

Cumming also suggested that disengagement might begin "sometime during middle life when certain changes of perception occur, of which the most important is probably an urgent new perception of the inevitability of death. ... It is quite possible that a vivid apprehension of mortality—perhaps when the end of life seems closer than its start—is the beginning of the process of growing old."[26] It seems to me that the argument suggested here is that in the face of death people begin to withdraw; but, why is this limited to disengagement, that is, why does not the fact of death produce general alienation rather than simply a decline in the number of objects involved with? The same comment can be applied to the argument already presented, that retirement causes disengagement because it connotes failure. Why do not failure and the fact of death produce alienation and not simply disengagement?

Cumming's work, as she acknowledges, is not complete. It does, however, raise interesting questions and points to relevant variables. For instance, it suggests that failure and the realization of death might lead to withdrawal. On

10

the other hand, why these should lead to only disengagement and not complete alienation is not clear. Finally, Cumming's work emphasizes the probability that as people age withdrawal in some form does occur.

This last point on aging and withdrawal is both confirmed and amended by the work of Rosenmayr and Kocheis. They write:

> The great practical and emotional significance of family relations—but at the same time old people's desire to keep at a distance—became obvious to us as early as 1957, from the initial phase of our gerontological studies in Vienna. This at first appeared paradoxical, but it soon became clear that precisely this wish *to maintain some distance but not to be isolated* was to be regarded as a typical attitude among the aged. The preference for a certain amount of segregation holds not only in the area of family relations; it can also be observed in the attitude of old people towards their local social environment. We have shown in detail that aged persons appreciate arrangements (e.g., of gardens and green spaces) where they are somewhat protected and withdrawn from their surroundings, but at the same time are able to take part in, or at least watch, what is going on. They want social contacts, but resent interference. It is a general attitude, which we characterized by the formula: 'Intimacy—but at a distance. ...'[27]

Rosenmayr and Kocheis's idea of 'intimacy at a distance' reminds us of Cumming's saying 'disengagement but not alienation.' These phrases are suggestive but lack precision. They both suggest that old age has a unique form of involvement that is somewhat short of complete involvement. Perhaps the application of the theory of involvement presented in this work might help to gain precision. The work of both Cumming and of Rosenmayr and Kocheis suggests that old people seek involvement on a basis other than physical closeness and power; so Rosenmayr and Kocheis, for instance, use the phrase "at a distance" and suggest that old people "resent interference." Cumming suggests that the desired basis is similarity, yet could it not be understanding? But the crucial question, still unanswered, is whether old people are more alienated in our sense than others.

There is another idea mentioned by Cumming which is worth noting. She writes: "a person with a store of memories is less likely to give full attention to the world around him than the person who has fewer symbolic residues to capture his attention."[28] This is interesting. Perhaps it is not that old people withdraw, but that they become less involved with objects in their perceivable environment and more involved with fantasy objects, like a dead spouse, a distant child, or an invisible God.

Studies of involvement in specific institutions tend not to support the idea of disengagement. Glenn and Grimes reported that, after holding constant the sex and education of people, just about as many aged people vote as people in their fifties. They conclude "our data provide no strong evidence that [voter] turnout typically increases after age 32."[29] Moreover, reported political interest seems to increase with age. However, the authors also note that the surveys they relied on might have missed the more senile, feeble old people; thus, their conclusions may be more positive than reality justified.

Moberg reviewed numerous studies on age and religious activity. He concluded: "Research to date seems to indicate fairly conclusively that ritualistic behavior outside the home tends to diminish with increasing age, while religious attitudes and feelings apparently increase among people who have an acknowledged religion." "In other words, religion as a set of external extradomiciliary rituals apparently decreases in old age, while the internal personal responses linked with man's relationships to God apparently increase among religious people. Thus both disengagement from and re-engagement with religion are typical in old age!"[30]

That aging people in some sense withdraw seems a worthwhile hypothesis. But what is the nature of this withdrawal—does it mean disengagement or complete alienation? Does it mean merely a change to a new basis of involvement? Does it mean a shift of involvement from the perceivable to the fantasy world? And, finally, if in some sense people do withdraw, why do they?

In review it seems that there has been presented a fairly well-developed general theory of involvement, but little understanding of how and why involvement is distributed the way it is in existing societies. The purpose of this work is to increase understanding of the distribution of involvement. Regarding the general theory of the sources of involvement, for the most part, its value will be simply assumed. Some remarks concerning this theory will be made, but the focus is on the distribution of involvement.

It should be emphasized that this work is not a study of norms about involvement. That certainly is an interesting project, but not the present purpose—which is to discover not with whom a person believes he should be involved, but with whom he actually is involved. Throughout a framework will be developed for the eventual emergence of a theory for the distribution of involvement.

The focus of this research, therefore, is on the pattern of involvement in an urban slum.

2

The People Studied

In the spring of 1966 we carried out a survey of residents in an area of Milwaukee scheduled for urban renewal. Data were collected from 748 respondents, but analysis concentrated on the 623 female homemakers who were interviewed. Question topics included in the survey related to such things as the fantasy life of the respondents as well as to their home life, their participation in voluntary associations and their involvement with the national government. These data will be analyzed in subsequent chapters,

The purpose of this chapter is to introduce the people of Kilbourntown, the urban renewal area in which the study took place. First, the physical neighborhood itself will be described. Second, some of the characteristics of the people interviewed will be discussed. The social characteristics presented in this chapter will be related in subsequent chapters to various aspects of our respondents' patterns of involvement. Third, there will be some concluding remarks on the relevance of the information presented in this chapter for a theory of involvement.

THE PLACE

Milwaukee fans out to the north, west, and south from a downtown area that begins on the shore of Lake Michigan. The inner core—the Negro area of the city—begins at the downtown area and extends somewhat west but mostly north. Figure 2-1 divides the inner core into three sections; the lowest third has the poorest families and the oldest homes; as one goes north everything gets better. Almost in the center of the poorest third of the inner core is the urban renewal area in which resided the subjects of this study. The project's

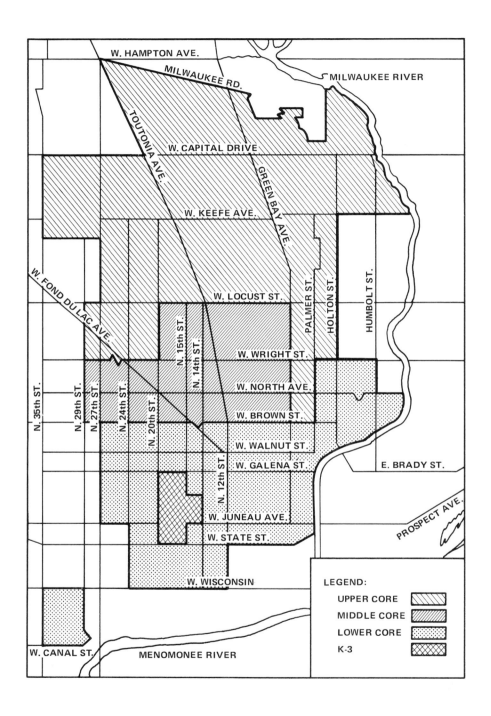

LEGEND:

UPPER CORE

MIDDLE CORE

LOWER CORE

K-3

SOLIDARITY IN A SLUM

boundaries have little intrinsic meaning; they resulted from the location of previously inaugurated projects, the location of streets scheduled for expansion, and the requirement that a renewal area contain a government-specified minimum number of deficient homes. In its artificiality the area is representative of most politically defined units in a metropolitan region. This work is based, in part, on a study financed by the city renewal agency, which commissioned an investigation of the problems that existed among the people living in Kilbourntown (or K-3 for short).

The unifying architectural theme is sidewalk-porch. The proximity of pedestrian and porch puts strollers within easy eyesight and, in summertime, easy earshot of the inhabitants. Extending back and sometimes up from these porches are homes of varying sizes, shapes, and colors. They tend to be two-stories high[1] and range from drab, decrepit masses of peeling dirty white to structures of bright, freshly-painted trim and newly re-sided walls. The condemnation of every building in Kilbourntown ignored the wide range in quality of the residences. Some homes were decaying, while others indicated mighty salvage efforts. All have been destroyed. Because of the many attempts over the years to maintain or revive the buildings there is an amazing variety of textures—stone, wood, and various kinds of modern replacements for these standard materials. Variety of quality, variety of color, variety of material— variety is perhaps the key characteristic of the K-3 physical environment.

Scattered throughout the area are businesses of many kinds, especially grocery stores, and bars. But the main business street is Vliet Street. It is not a "stroll street." For instance, on one side of the street there is: a hat store, a restaurant, a store that sells restaurant machinery, a shoe store, a bar, a plumbing-supply store, a coffee shop, and a government office. Looking across the street you would see: a restaurant, a pet shop, a barbershop, a T.V.-repair store, a dry cleaners, a fuel-company office, a private house, and a hardware store. Vliet street contains very few stores likely to attract window-shoppers; in general, there are few reasons to stroll there. However, along the six blocks that are within the boundaries of K-3 there are fifteen bars and three churches. In all, Kilbourntown contains twenty-five bars and five churches. But often adjacent to these "community centers" are businesses completely unrelated to the neighborhood—such as the plumbing-equipment outlet, a wholesale meat store and the fuel company office. The area contains two extremes—the centers of liquor and religion and the non-neighborhood businesses—with little of the in-between types of establishments.

Figure 2-2 displays the street pattern and the traffic count on those streets for which the information was available. As the counts suggest, Milwaukee seems to pass in review for the residents. It is important to keep in mind, however, that few of these cars stop in the area; they simply pass through. The heavy use of streets does not knit the neighborhood into the city, but rather

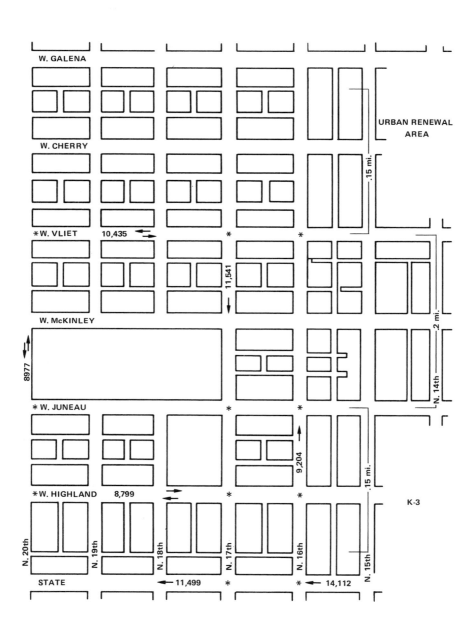

Figure 2-2. Numbers on map represent traffic counts for 24-hour periods in 1965 and 1966. Arrow indicates direction of traffic, stars indicate traffic lights. The area ends just south of Galena and north of State Streets. The dimensions of the area are indicated.

SOLIDARITY IN A SLUM

it tears Kilbourntown apart. The traffic segregates the blocks; it does not unify the city. Like many of the non-neighborhood stores the traffic pattern attracts strangers totally uninterested in the residents of the area.

Most of the low-lying buildings are dominated by over four hundred trees, which give a restful cast to the neighborhood. Unfortunately, there is an absence of pleasant spacing; it is boom or bust; some streets have no trees, others have them clustered so tightly that it is difficult for the sun to break through in summer.[2] This uneven distribution dissolves the area into patches of green and stretches of glare.

SAFETY

Of special importance if human beings are to maintain neighborhood relationships is a sense of security; residents must not fear venturing outside their homes. Most of Kilbourntown is situated in the Milwaukee police district that in 1965 had the highest number of murders, forcible rapes, assaults, and sex offences; there was no criminal category involving aggressive behavior in which this district did not have the highest incidence.

Among those persons convicted of aggressive, criminal behavior in 1965, fourteen individuals came from the households studied; thus in a single year just under 2 percent of the families to be discussed had one of their members convicted of aggressive, criminal behavior.[3]

Reprinted below is a story that appeared in the October 11, 1966, issue of the *Milwaukee Journal;* the Wells Street School is immediately adjacent to our area.

> Fear walks the streets near the Wells Street Junior High School at N. 19th and W. Wells Sts., particularly at night. It takes several forms:
> A 33 year old mother of three who says she is frightened goes from house to house seeking signatures on a petition for more police protection.
> Signers of the petition beg that their names not be disclosed lest there be retaliation from gangs of toughs who, they say, roam the area.
> The school is closed during the lunch hour. Pupils must remain inside, eating either a cold lunch brought from home or a hot one in the cafeteria.
> Every day, two or three pupils complain to school authorities that they have been punched or kicked by young hoodlums who hang around the Norris playground, just north of the school.
> A school monitor's eye is blackened by the toughs who, two or three times a week, enter the school.
> Broken glass is strewn to make "tires go, pop, pop." There is ugly profanity and open drinking on the streets.
> The petition circulator, a Negro, is waging a campaign for a tightly enforced curfew, more beat patrolmen, better street lighting and harsher punishment for the youthful offenders, who are also Negro.

"We are kind of petrified, more than scared," she said Monday. "It is like sitting on a keg of dynamite and not knowing when it is going to explode, but knowing it will if something isn't done."[4]

The present study offers no direct evidence concerning this matter; it might well be that the reporter exaggerated or even severely distorted the situation. Yet both the evidence on crime and this story do point to the absence of a degree of safety that is expected in our society and that is an important prerequisite for the development of involvement beyond a person's own household. Without safety, doors cease to be openings, and become barriers.

THE STUDY

An initial canvass made with the help of the local mailman showed that the renewal area contained 1,191 households (374 White, 730 Negro, 61 Spanish-speaking, 12 American Indian, and 4 Oriental). Because of a limited budget it was necessary to reduce the universe to 1,069 households; the dwellings north of Cherry Street (see Figure 2-2) were eliminated; this meant the loss almost exclusively of Negro families. For the 1,069 households we attempted to study, the results were as follows: completed: 748; vacant at the time of interview: 162; refused: 76; unable to contact (after 4 calls): 83. In short, one member from 82 percent of the households still occupied at the time of the study was interviewed.

To ensure as much cooperation and openness as possible we assigned an interviewer of the same ethnic background as the person to be inverviewed. The initial canvass revealed the proportion of each major ethnic group in K-3. We then gathered a staff of about twenty, which reflected these proportions; the interviewers were from the same general type of area as the respondents. They were hired through local agencies such as The Urban League, and trained by us.

Since the study was commissioned to gather information about entire households, the interviewers were instructed to always try to interview the housewife; it was assumed that she would be the single person who would know the most about an entire household.

Of the 748 people interviewed, 101 were males and 642 were females. The analysis reported here is based only on the women interviewed. Moreover, to achieve some basic similarity among the people analyzed, it was decided to eliminate the 19 cases in which the woman interviewed was not the homemaker. Usually "homemaker" meant simply the wife of the breadwinner (the respondent was asked to name the "breadwinner"). When this was inappropriate, either because there was no male breadwinner or because there was one but no wife was living with him, it was assumed that the adult woman in the household was the homemaker. If there was more than one adult women, the middle-aged woman was considered the homemaker; for instance, in a home that included a twenty, a forty, and a sixty year old woman, the forty year old was considered the homemaker. This study, then is about the households of 623 female homemakers in Kilbourntown. In the total sample of 748 households that we contacted, there was a total of 674 female homemakers. Our sample of 623 represents, therefore, 92 percent of the female homemakers in the homes contacted.[5] Remembering that we succeeded in interviewing only 82 percent of the households in K-3, this means that this study is based on a sample of 75-80 percent of the female homemakers in Kilbourntown; it is impossible to state the exact percentage because we do not know how many female homemakers there were in the households not contacted.

DESCRIPTION OF THE SAMPLE

RACE AND AGE. When we look at a large aggregate of people, there are three ways in which we can easily group them: by sex, age, or color. People are sorted out along these dimensions automatically, i.e., without thinking, because of the comparative visual obviousness of the categories for each of these three dimensions.

The multi-modal and bi-modal distributions of color and sex respectively make them "natural" dimensions for perceptual categorization.[6] Although age is more normally distributed, the obvious differences among young people, old people, and the rest of a population, as well as the frequency of the "extreme" cases, allow one to readily use these gross age-categories in grouping a population. Upon seeing an aggregate we would tend to divide them in terms of color, sex and age; it is not surprising, therefore, that social roles are frequently allocated on these same bases. Perceptual groupings on the basis of these three types of categories are "givens" upon which a society builds. One of the purposes of this study is to examine the extent to which these "perceptually given" groupings are sociologically meaningful.

Since all males were eliminated from this analysis, the interest is concentrated on color and age. Specifically, the study compares "whites" with "blacks", old people with those between the ages of twenty and sixty years. Since the sample includes only homemakers, the third age-category, children, is not relevant. Each chapter, then, begins with a comparison of whites and blacks, young and old.

Table 2–1 describes the female homemakers by color and age. As can be seen, the sample tends to be composed of old "whites" and young "blacks". There are relatively few Spanish-speaking and Indians, so our analysis will focus on the "whites" and "blacks." In comparing the latter two aggregates the differences in age distribution will have to be kept continually in mind.

Figure 2–3 shows the ratio of "whites" and "blacks" on each block in K-3.

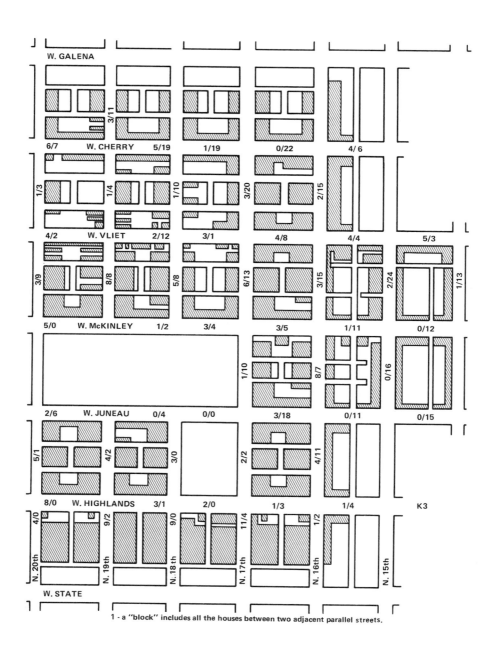

Figure 2-3. Distribution of "whites" and "blacks" by blocks (number of "whites"/number of "blacks")

1 - a "block" includes all the houses between two adjacent parallel streets.

SOLIDARITY IN A SLUM

TABLE 2–1

AGE AND COLOR OF FEMALE HOMEMAKER RESPONDENTS (N=623)

(Figures given as percentages of total sample)

	Color[1]				
Age	"White" (N=169)	"Black" (N=409)	Spanish-speaking (N=24)	Indian (N=9)	Other[2] (N=12)
17–19	2	3	4	0	0
20–29	7	33	21	33	25
30–39	15	27	50	33	33
40–49	15	17	13	22	25
50–59	20	8	8	11	8
60–74	28	9	4	—	8
75 plus	12	1	—	—	—
no response	2	2	—	—	—

1. We use "color" rather than "ethnicity," because the major part of our analysis is concerned with "skin-color aggregates." Our label, of course, is less appropriate for the Spanish-speaking or the Indians than for the rest of the sample. The respondent was categorized by the interviewer, who was given the following alternatives: White, Negro, Latin-American (Mexican, Puerto-Rican), Other (Indian, Chinese, etc.), and Indeterminate. Since we tried to ethnically match interviewer and interviewee the labelling was probably as accurate as is possible. "Black," for instance, means respondents were perceived as negroes by the interviewers.

2. Includes cases in which interviewer failed to designate ethnicity of respondent.

TABLE 2–2

LENGTH OF RESIDENCE AT PRESENT ADDRESS

Years	Percent (N=623)
1	34
2	13
3	11
4	7
5	4
6–10	11
11–20	11
21–57	6
No response	3

Neither the Spanish-speaking nor the Indians cluster on any one block. As can be seen on the map, "whites" tend to live in the western and especially southwestern part of Kilbourntown (i.e., toward the corner of 20th Street and State Street). Yet, "whites" are scattered throughout the renewal area. About 44 percent of them live on blocks that do not contain a majority of "whites." However, only 28 percent of the "whites" under forty years of age live on such blocks. The more integrated blocks tend to contain old "whites" and young "blacks." The presence of both color and age differences probably minimizes the development of involvement across racial lines, even though there is the bond of spatial proximity among those living on integrated streets.

The dominant impression of the K-3 residents is variety. There are "whites," blacks," Indians, Spanish-speaking, and a few Orientals. All the ages are represented. Both the buildings and the people of Kilbourntown lack any unifying theme.

MOBILITY.   One of the major characteristics of modern society is the extent to which people move about. But physical mobility is not a single variable. It breaks down into time-per-place and variety of places. An individual might move a great deal and thus spend little time with any one set of neighbors, but make all these moves within the same city, so that the general social and cultural atmosphere remains stable. The effects of such a pattern would seem to be quite different than if a person were a world traveller. The analysis, therefore, tries to separate the effects of time-per-place and of the social variety of places lived.

Tables 2-2 through 2-6 present the basic data on mobility. What stands out is the high mobility of the sample.[7]

Table 2-6 presents all four of the dimensions of mobility just discussed. As one reads down and to the right in the table, mobility as a significant experience declines. As can be seen in the upper left-hand corner of the table only 2 percent of the respondents are extremely mobile, that is, have lived at their present address less than five years, have moved four or more times in the last five years, have lived in Milwaukee less than ten years, and have lived in four or more different towns and cities. At the other extreme the figure is 14 percent. It is worth noting that 24 percent of the sample is very "cosmopolitan," i.e., has lived in four or more different towns and cities. Although Kilbourntown might be considered a slum, the residents are not to be thought of as individuals who have never left their block and know nothing of anything outside their own small world. Many of the K-3 residents have experienced quite different ways of life. Overall, there is no pattern in Table 2-6. The table simply documents the variety of mobility-experiences the respondents have had.

There has been some research on the relation between physical mobility and involvement. Litwak, based on a study of attitudes about involvement and not of involvement itself, concluded that mobility does not destroy extended family ties. Bott, on the other hand, emphasized that mobility pushes the nuclear family together; husband and wife depend on each other more, and have the same set of friends; they do things together. "In facing the external world, they draw on each other, for their strongest emotional investment is made where there is continuity." This idea that involvement is related to continuity is interesting. Bott's work suggests that although extended family ties exist among mobile people, they will not be very significant. In fact, although there is general agreement that such ties do exist, we do not know how much involvement these ties symbolize. Bott's idea that "emotional investment is made where there is continuity" seems worth further investigation. We shall return to this point.[3]

TABLE 2–3
YEARS LIVED IN MILWAUKEE

Years	Percent (N=623)
1	8
2–3	6
4–5	5
6–9	12
10–20	36
21–50	26
51 or more	7
No response	*

* Less than 0.5 percent.

TABLE 2–4
NUMBER OF MOVES IN LAST FIVE YEARS

Number of moves	Percent (N=623)
1	19
2	19
3	12
4 or more	12
None	30
Unusable responses[1]	7

1. The high number of unusable cases resulted, in large part, from our check on consistency between this question and an inquiry about length of residence at present address. Often the inconsistency seemed understandable, being due apparently to respondents thinking in terms of "about" five years.

This study, then, is interested in the effects of physical mobility on involvement patterns. Mobility seems to be obviously relevant. For instance, it would be understandable if as people separated spatially they lost interest in each other. Throughout this work we shall be interested in the relation between mobility and the distribution of involvement.

POVERTY   Table 2-7 presents the data on poverty. At the time of the study

TABLE 2–5

NUMBER OF DIFFERENT TOWNS AND CITIES LIVED IN

Number of Places	Percent (N=623)
1	16
2	39
3	21
4	10
Five or more	13
No response	1

TABLE 2–6

COMPOSITE OF MOBILITY VARIABLES

(Years at present address, number of moves in past five years, number of towns and cities lived in, length of time in Milwaukee, N=570[1])

Years at Present Address	Numbers of Moves in Last Five Years	Percent of Total Sample			
		Less than ten Years in Mil.		Ten or more Years in Mil.	
		Cosmopolitan[2]	Local[3]	Cosmopolitan	Local
	4 or more	2	6	2	3
One-four years	2–3	4	12	4	14
	1	2	8	2	9
Five-ten years	0	1	2	3	8
More than ten years	0	–	–	4	14

1. Unusable cases are not included in the table.

2. *Cosmopolitan* means that respondent has lived in 4 or more different towns and cities.

3. *Local* means that respondent has lived in 3 or less towns and cities.

SOLIDARITY IN A SLUM

TABLE 2-7

NUMBER OF RESPONDENTS BY FAMILY INCOME AND FAMILY SIZE[1]

(In parentheses are percentages based on those who answered income question)

Family Income Level	Family Size															Total
	1	2	3	4	5	6	7	8	9	10	11	12	13	14	15	
Below $1,000	29(6)	7(1)	4(1)	5(1)	4(1)	2*	1*		1*							53
1,000–1,999	20(4)	28(6)	21(4)	11(2)	6(1)	4(1)	1*	1*		2*						94
2,000–2,999	13(3)	20(4)	12(3)	19(4)	9(2)	14(3)	5(1)	2*		1*	2*					97
3,000–3,999	3(1)	17(4)	12(3)	8(2)	9(2)	13(3)	10(2)	11(2)	2*	3(1)	1*	1*				91
4,000–4,999	2*	7(1)	5(1)	7(1)	7(1)	8(2)	7(1)	3(1)	7(1)	7(1)	2*					62
5,000–5,999	1*	2*	6(1)	5(1)	6(1)	3(1)	4(1)	1*	3(1)	1*	4(1)	1*	1*			38
6,000 and over	0	15(3)	12(3)	7(1)	8(2)	4(1)	2*	4(1)	5(1)	3(1)	2*	1*	1*			63
Refused to answer	12	26	13	5	9	4	5	3	1	1			1			80
Didn't know	2	4	4	1	2	0	1	0	2	1	1					18
No response	2	3	3	2	0	1	0	1								12
608[2] TOTAL	84	129	92	70	60	53	36	26	21	19	12	3	3			

* Means less than .5%

1. Those within the staircase are by our minimal standards not poverty stricken; those above the staircase are poverty stricken; those below the staircase did not tell us their income.

2. The total is not 623, because the program that computed family size was performed when 15 cases were missing from our master tape; since there seemed to be no bias, we did not revise the table.

a common formula was to consider a family to be poverty-stricken if the family income was lower than the sum that would be arrived at by allowing $1,500 for the first person in the family and $500 for each person thereafter. A family of any size making $6,000 or more was not considered poverty-stricken. Our question about income was as follows: "Would you please look at this card and tell me which letter comes closest to your total family income before taxes for last year?" On the card handed to the respondent were a list of incomes in thousands of dollars, e.g., below $1,000, $1,000-$1,999, $2,000-$2,999, and so on . Since the responses were in intervals of a thousand, the aforementioned formula, which is based on intervals of 500, could not be used precisely. We chose to underestimate poverty, e.g., all families with four or fewer members and making $2,000-$2,999 are not considered poverty-stricken in this study; according to the formula using $500 intervals this would be true if the income were $2,999, but not if it were below $2,500; thus we have consistently underestimated poverty. For our female, homemaker sample, 41 percent of the households are poverty-stricken.[9]

Looking at the Table 2-7 it is once again the variety of situations that is impressive. To talk about 41 percent of the families being in poverty masks the variety of specific situations.

CONCLUSION

Kilbourntown lacks any unifying theme. There is the variety of buildings, with their different colors, sizes, shapes, conditions, and textures. And there is the variety of people-with their different colors, ages, socio-economic levels, and mobility patterns. Moreover, there is the steady stream of strangers either using the busy streets to go somewhere else or stopping temporarily at one of the non-neighborhood stores scattered about K-3. There is no obvious similarity unifying either the physical structure or the residents of Kilbourntown.

The types of establishments in the area do little to unify the neighborhood. There are the bars and churches, but these usually have a limited clientele; they are the homes for neighborhood cliques. Kilbourntown lacks the resources that would develop a multitude of casual contacts that would involve different people each day. For instance, there is no stroll street. Moreover, frequent moving from one residence to another make it unlikely that people of K-3 will develop high involvement relations with neighbors.

Our comments suggest that the physical environment plays an important role in shaping people's pattern of involvement. For instance, there is the possibly alienating effect of the variety of homes and of the poor distribution of trees. But the objection might be raised; what do we desire-"LEVITTOWN" with its repetitious and boring scenery? Perhaps disorder should be valued? But unity based on similarity does not require that objects be identical.

There is a form of unity that is aesthetical, as when objects of different sizes are all proportioned to each other. There is then a mathematical unity amid physical diversity.

Walking around Kilbourntown, one is struck by the lack of unity or harmony in the physical setting. This, in turn, leads to the thought that possibly harmony in the physical surroundings can contribute to the development of a sense of community, and to the theorem: positive involvement in face-to-face relations increases as does the aesthetic quality of the physical setting. The theorem is presented simply to suggest that there is a relation between aesthetics and a theory of involvement.

In succeeding chapters the relation between the "perceptual givens" of color and age and involvement will be examined, as well as the effects of mobility on involvement. In our analysis we examined the relation between income levels and various aspects of involvement. Little reference will be made to the results, because about all of them suggested that income level was insignificant. Because of the difficulty in getting accurate data on income through the use of questionnaires, we are not sure how to interpret these results.

3

Fantasy And Involvement

In Chapter One it was suggested that "the extent of involvement depends on the degree of overlap between the imaginary and sensed environments." The main point of this chapter is to examine the extent to which there is a lack of correspondence between the fantasy world and the sensed world among our respondents, and to suggest some reasons why there might not be correspondence.

There are at least two types of situations in which such correspondence would be absent: 1) when people think about objects that can not be seen or heard such as dead people or a deity; there are people who claim to have seen or heard spiritual beings; however, in our study it is assumed that our respondents who think about God or a dead person have not perceived or heard them; and 2) when people think about living individuals they rarely contact; it is assumed that during most of the time such living people are in fantasy, they will not simultaneously be part of the external sensed environment. Both types of situations will be discussed in this chapter.

We assume that to the extent the objects in a person's fantasy do not coincide with those in his sensed world, the individual will be alienated from his environment.

THE RELEVANT QUESTIONS ON THE QUESTIONNAIRE

There were two questions asked of the respondents that are relevant to the problem of fantasy. Both are open-ended and were meant to determine the most significant objects with which the respondent felt involved.

The first question is—"Who are the three people you think about most?"

We wanted a simple, concrete question that would reflect involvement, and that would not be biased by any preconceptions on our part. Thus, we did not inquire about people our respondents felt "close to," because this might have biased the responses in favor of people in the neighborhood. We assume that fantasy life mirrors "real" life, in the sense that the people thought about would be the most significant individuals in a persons's life. However, it must be clear that this question can be considered only a rough indication of involvement. It was hoped that although the question cannot precisely measure the degree of involvement the responses would indicate the persons with whom an individual is most involved.[1]

Questions were also asked about whether the imagined person was still alive, where the person lived, the relation of the person to the respondent, how frequently the respondent talked with the person named, and whether the respondent discussed personal problems with the individual thought about. These data will be used when appropriate.

A major weakness of the "think about" question is that it asks only about people: it is unable to find the individuals who relate to animals or who are most involved with a deity. Therefore, a second question was asked of the respondents—"What makes you feel proud?" If the respondent asked what was meant by this question the interviewer was instructed to add—"What would you tell people if you wanted to impress them?" The question was followed by five numbered blank lines. The study assumes that, if a person can feel proud about the actions or achievements of somebody or something else, he or she must be somehow involved in the source of pride. That is, the respondent must be a part of something to feel proud about it himself; we cannot feel anything about an object to which we are not related. Like the "think about" question, this inquiry about pride does not measure involvement precisely, it simply points out the objects in which a person is significantly involved; unlike our first question, however, the second is not limited to persons.[2]

THE DISTRIBUTION OF INVOLVEMENT

Before pursuing the question of the extent to which the respondents' fantasy does not reflect the sensed environment, it would be valuable to use the two open-ended questions to sketch out the respondents' overall pattern of involvement. Who are the people the homemakers of Kilbourntown think about? What are the respondents proud of?

THE "THINK ABOUT" QUESTION

In the original study the relation of the people "thought about" to the respondents was not determined. We attempted to reinterview about a 15 percent random sample of our respondents; this was done two months after the original study. In the reinterview specific questions were asked about the residential location of the persons thought about as well as the relation of these persons to the respondents. Of the 112 respondents we tried to recontact, 72 were interviewed; of the rest, 14 had definitely moved; the staff was not able to contact 24 respondents after three attempts. Of the 72 people reinterviewed, 63 were female homemakers. Obviously this subsample is biased in favor of the less mobile and more easily contacted part of the list of original respondents.

TABLE 3–1

FREQUENCY WITH WHICH DIFFERENT TYPES OF PEOPLE ARE
THOUGHT ABOUT

(Listed as percentages)

	Age and color of respondent						
	17–39 years		*40–59 years*		*over 60*		*Total*
Type of person	*White (N=6)*	*Black (N=80)*	*White (N=21)*	*Black (N=44)*	*White (N=18)*	*Black (N=9)*	*(N=178)*
mother	17	23	5	14	6	11	16
father[1]	17	10		5		11	7
spouse		11	19	11	17	11	12
son[2]	17	16	29	7	22	11	16
daughter		13	38	9	28	22	16
"child"		3		2			2
brother		4		9			4
sister[3]		9	5	14	6	33	10
grandfather			5				1
grandmother							
granddaughter				2	6		1
grandson							
aunt		3					1
uncle							
niece		1		5	6		2
nephew				2			1
cousin				2			1
godmother		1					1
godfather							
friend		8		16	2		8
miscellaneous[4]	50			2			2

1. Includes one case of father-in-law.

2. Includes one case of son-in-law.

3. Includes three cases of sisters-in-law.

4. One person listed President and Mrs. Kennedy and a local judge; another referred to his landlord.

SOLIDARITY IN A SLUM

Table 3-1 shows the relation of the people thought about to the respondents for the subsample of 63 homemakers. Of the 178 people mentioned, all but 11 percent are members of each respondents' family. One striking characteristic of the fantasy world is that it is peopled by the family.

Considering the immediate family to be parents, spouse, children and siblings, 83 percent of the people thought about belonged to the immediate family. Moreover, 68 percent of these people are blood relatives. The significance of the family is not due to the importance of a single relationship; in fact as people age it seems that some family relationships replace others; so the importance of parents declines, while the significance of children and siblings increases. But our respondents do not go outside the family for fantasy figures. The specific relations change, but not the fact that they are familial relations. Even women living alone chose family members; five isolates chose fourteen people, twelve of whom were from their families. For the types of woman living in Kilbourntown, whether she is white or black, young or old, their fantasy life is an extension of family life, and if we are to understand what is happening on the fantasy level, we must study what is happening to the family in our society.

There is a difference, however, between whites and blacks. There are too few whites seventeen to thirty-nine years old to compare the two aggregates in this age range. But among those forty to fifty-nine years old there is a clear difference between whites and blacks; 86 percent of the people thought about by whites are members of the nuclear family, i.e., spouse, son, or daughter, while the comparable figure for blacks is 27 percent. Among those sixty and above the difference diminishes, but it is in the same direction; 66 percent of the whites' and 44 percent of the blacks' fantasy figures come from the nuclear family. Black involvement is diffused among members of the nuclear and extended family; white involvement is concentrated on the nuclear family. One result of this is that when black women meet, the probability is much higher for them than it is for white women that their patterns of involvement will be different. As a consequence it may be harder for black women to understand or to feel similar to each other. When white women meet, the shared topics of interest will no doubt be spouse and children. This will not be as true for black women. This phenomenon of diffused involvement seems especially true for the black women forty to fifty-nine years of age. Even friends are important for blacks in this age range; 16 percent of those thought about are friends, which is not very high, but it is the modal response.

Table 3-2 shows the distribution of responses on the "think about" question for the entire sample of 623 homemakers. Based on the subsample of 63 respondents who were reinterviewed, it can be assumed that category 8 in Table 3-2, "Person not child or spouse and not in home," refers mainly to members of the extended family. It would probably be correct, therefore, to combine categories 5 and 8.

TABLE 3–2

DISTRIBUTION OF RESPONSES TO "THINK ABOUT" QUESTION

Person thought about	Frequency mentioned			
	Response 1	Response 2	Response 3	Total
1. God	5	0	1	6
2. National political figures	7	5	1	13
3. Local political figures	0	0	1	1
4. Civil rights leaders	0	1	1	2
5. Religious Leaders	5	6	3	14
6. Self	8	1	1	10
7. Family reference	270	245	221	736
8. Person not child or spouse and not in home	262	259	214	735
9. Blank	66	106	180	352
	632	632	632	1869

But our interest in presenting Table 3-2 is to show the significance of recognizably nonfamilial persons (categories 1-5) in the fantasy life of our respondents. No nonfamilial category was mentioned by more than 2 percent of the sample. The overriding fact remains that fantasy seems to reflect family.

Religion and politics, however, do enter into the fantasy life of Kilbourntown. Considering that the question asked about "three people" the respondent thought about, it is remarkable that six people did mention God. Although some individuals think of God as an idea, similar to an abstraction like "equality," many people tend to think of God as a person to whom they can relate. God is someone to love, fear, or worship. God is a source of comfort and command. God to most people is not an abstraction but a person and as such is a part of the personal world of the respondents. We shall return to this topic.

Not only is God important but so is the religious institution. Fourteen religious leaders are thought about.

We could only identify this category if the respondent used either "Father" or "Reverend" in naming the person; it is quite possible that in coding we missed some religious leaders who were named but for whom no religious title was given. Thirteen of the fourteen references to religious leaders were made by black people. The relative importance of religion to black people will be a recurrent theme in this work. Again, we shall return to this topic. For now, it is sufficient to emphasize the point that the homemakers of Kilbourntown, or at least some of them, extend their involvement beyond the family to God and church.

Seemingly of about equal importance with the religious institution is politics. One striking fact, however, is the absence of local political leaders. Political involvement seems to occur only on the national level. In part this reflects that truly memorable people, charismatic people, are able to make it to the top of the political ladder. So several respondents mentioned Mr. and Mrs. John F.Kennedy, and one even mentioned Franklin Delano Roosevelt. These were politicians who literally captured the imagination of the people. But Lyndon B. Johnson, president at the time of the study, was also mentioned; his existence in our respondent's fantasy would not seem due to his charismatic qualities but to the importance of the presidential office for the residents of Kilbourntown.

The almost complete absence of reference to civil rights leaders, national or local, was quite surprising. The "think about" question followed a series of inquiries about voluntary associations; one of these queries specifically asked about membership in civil rights groups, so that the respondents were reminded of this category almost immediately before answering the "think about" question. Of course our sample is mainly from the lower class, but the ratio of political leaders to civil rights leaders seems important. Given the fact that political leaders were mentioned, the near absence of reference to civil rights leaders indicates how little this movement had penetrated the black masses at the time of the study.

Ten people mentioned themselves in response to the "think about" question. This is a small number, but it points to an aspect of involvement not touched on yet in this work. A study in depth might indeed reveal that self-involvement is the most wide-spread form of involvement. As with the reference to God, it is surprising that in response to the "think about" question anyone would mention themselves.

What, then, is the pattern of involvement suggested by the "think about" question? Assuming that what is mentioned by a minority of respondents is on the periphery of involvement for the majority, the following picture emerges: a concentration of involvement on the family, with a modest degree of involvement in God, church, country, and self. But the "think about" question is of limited use, since it refers only to specific persons. It is not very useful, therefore, for measuring involvement in organizations or abstractions like "equality". Let us compare the conclusion drawn from the "think about" question, therefore, with the responses to the "proud" question. The exact wording of the latter was simply—"What makes you feel proud?" It is regretable that we did not, also, ask our respondents what makes them feel ashamed. The "proud" question reflects only positive involvement. One of the virtues of the "think about" question is that it can indicate either positive or negative involvement, people loved as well as people hated.

Table 3-3 shows the distribution of responses to the "proud" question. As compared with the "think about" question (see Table 3-2), the responses to the "proud" question are less concentrated. This is no doubt due to the greater openness of the "proud" question; quite literally, it allows people to mention anything.

There is no change, however, in the dominance of the family, which remains the modal response. It occurs twice as often as the next most frequent category. Within the family category references are scattered over a variety of family roles, though clearly children are the most frequent family member the respondents are proud of. In fact, the percentage of references to children, 15 percent, is the highest percentage given any single subcategory. Perhaps it is only lower-class people who take so much pride in their children, perhaps in part as consolation for their own frustrations. It would be valuable to have comparable studies of middle-and upper-class neighborhoods in order to determine the relative significance of the 15 percent figure. In the next chapter the parent-child relationship will be examined in more detail.

TABLE 3–3

DISTRIBUTION OF RESPONSES TO THE "PROUD" QUESTION

(Percentages based on total number of responses actually given.)

Object proud about		Percent of total responses (N=1136)	
1. Physical things (e.g., cars, flowers)		5	
2. Animals		(N=6, or less than .5%)	
3. Country or president		11	
4. Freedom or tolerance in U.S.		5	18
5. Educational opportunities now available		1	
6. War in Vietnam		1	
7. Milwaukee		1	
8. Racial reference		1	
9. Nonracial ethnic reference		1	
10. Reference to church or specific religion		2	7
11. Reference to personal religious practices or to God		5	
12. References to family		36	
spouse	7		
children	15		
parents	4		
other	10		
13. Self		20	
Personal achievements[1]	12		
Health	5		
To be alive	3		
14. Job		2	
15. Friends		1	
16. Miscellaneous		7	

1. Includes references to abilities and favourable personality traits (e.g., kindness).

The significance of political involvement as indicated by the "proud" questions is surprising. If items 2 through 6 in Table 3-3 are considered in their relation to national politics, then 18 percent of the responses indicated national political involvement. The rarity of references to Milwaukee matches the almost complete absence of local political leaders in the responses to the "think about" question. Political involvement for the homemakers of K-3 means only national political involvement.

But what is to be made of the greater significance of politics over religion, to which only 7 percent of the responses refer? This difference can probably be explained by the context in which the "proud" question was asked. It followed a series of questions intended to measure national involvement. The immediately preceding question was—"Do you agree or disagree that people who refuse to fight for their country when it is in trouble should not be allowed to live in that country?" Seven such questions preceded the proud question. That 18 percent of the responses to the "proud" question related to national concern was in part the result of the context in which the question was asked. On the other hand there were no references in these preceding questions to freedom, tolerance, or educational opportunities, which were mentioned in 6 percent of the responses to the "proud" question. Of course, the preceding questions made political events in general salient. But the references to such things as freedom and tolerance suggest a genuine and positive involvement with the country. However, the difference between the percentage for country and for religion is no doubt exaggerated due to the nature of the preceding questions.

That only 1 percent of the sample referred to race as a source of pride indicates that at the time of this study there was little sense of positive racial identity that could serve as a basis for a racial social movement. There were more references (5 percent) to the ideological catchwords of such a movement —such as freedom and equality. Remember that interviewers generally were of the same color as those interviewed; still, race remained unimportant. It could be, of course, that the respondents are more ashamed of their color than proud of it. It could also be that color is significant at a pre-conscious level and so is not thought of in response to an open-ended question. Moreover, there is the fact that the questionnaire was administered in the respondent's house, where the family was salient. But this last point does not seem to adequately explain the scarcity of references to race; for on the "think about" question many family members were named who did not live with the respondent, and on the "proud" question a majority of the responses did not refer to the family. At least at the time of this study (Spring, 1966) race did not seem to be an important source of self-identity for our respondents.

Similarly, work is not an important source of pride. About 13 percent (eighty-six) of the women in the sample said that their own job was the main source of family income; 2 percent of the responses to the "proud" question relate to our respondents' jobs. It is reasonable to assume that in light of the unattractive jobs the respondents are likely to have, it is amazing that even 2 percent of the responses refer to their work.

Friends also fall into the class of unimportant objects. Both the "think about" and the "proud" question reveal a huge gulf between family and friends. That the family is more important than friends in the lower class is not surprising, but the degree of difference makes us pause.

Consistent with the "think about" results, religion is a significant category for the "proud" question. But only a total of 23 people mentioned a specific religion or church. As will be discussed in Chapter Five, our respondents do go to church, but this affiliation is of only modest importance. The fact that more references are given to personal religious practices or to the personal relation to a deity suggests that for our sample the spiritual relationship is more important than the social relations that are a consequence of church affiliation itself.

The "self" is more significant on the "proud" question than it was on the "think about." In part this resulted from our respondents' interest in health. There is a consistent, positive relation between age and references to health; as people age they become concerned about health and proud of good health, if they are fortunate enough to have it. One consequence of the increase in concern about health, which is related to age, is that it means greater self-involvement as people become older.

The pride the respondents took in physical things should probably be considered as self-pride. A car, for instance, is often a status symbol and reflects the success of the owner. To be proud of one's flower garden is likewise to be proud of one's own achievement. It would be correct, therefore, to add together items 1 and 13, which would mean that a total of 25 percent of the references involve the self. At least to this writer this rather high percentage is surprising. One tends to associate slum areas with an absence of self-respect based on individual accomplishments. But, clearly, such self-respect exists to a significant degree in Kilbourntown.

It might be thought that Table 3-3 does not adequately reflect the relative importance of the different categories. After all it is easier to say more than one thing about some objects than others; for instance, it might be easier to list more items under family than under job. To hold constant the number of references per category, Table 3-4 shows the distribution of responses using only the first response given by the respondents. As can be seen, the results in Tables 3-3 and 3-4 are almost identical. Regarding the relative importance of different categories our comments based on Table 3-3 need no revision.

However, Table 3-4 makes an additional point. If we assume that the first response indicates what is most important to the respondent, then the results in Table 3-4 reveal a diversity of involvement patterns in Kilbourntown. For a third of the respondents the family comes first, but about a fifth begin with the country (but remember the influence of questionnaire context) and another fifth with the self. Slightly less than 10 percent begin with religion, and the rest are scattered. In a sense there are four different types of involvement patterns based on the four different starting points: family, country, self, and religion. No doubt each gives rise to a unique perspective on the world.

Tables 3-1 through 3-4, then, present a generally consistent picture of the respondents' patterns of involvement. Dominant is the family, although for whites this means the nuclear family, while for blacks it refers to the extended

TABLE 3-4

DISTRIBUTION OF FIRST RESPONSES TO THE "PROUD" QUESTION

(Percentages based on number of responses actually given.)

Object proud about		Percent of response (N=495)	
1. Physical things (e.g., car, flowers)		3%	
2. Animals		*	
3. Country or president		16	
4. Freedom or tolerance in U.S.		5	23%
5. Educational opportunities now available		1	
6. War in Vietnam		1	
7. Milwaukee		1	
8. Racial reference		2	
9. Nonracial ethnic reference		1	
10. Reference to church or specific religion		3	8
11. Reference to personal religious practices or to God		5	
12. Reference to family		35	
spouse	(7)[1]		
children	(17)		
parents	(2)		
other	(9)		
13. Self		20	
Personal achievement	(9)[2]		
Health	(7)		
To be alive	(4)		
14. Job		1	
15. Friends		0	
16. Miscellaneous		6	

* Only one respondent said she was proud of her pet.

1. The percentages in brackets are breakdowns of the major categories. So, seven percent of the total sample said they are proud of their spouse.

2. I.e., nine percent said they are proud of their personal achievements, which we classified as indicating self-pride.

family. Secondary foci for involvement are the self, the country, and religion. But there are some individuals for whom each of these secondary foci will be of primary importance. Racial or ethnic collectivities, work, friends, voluntary associations other than churches—all these seem to be of little importance. In subsequent chapters we shall further explore respondents' involvement in the family, religion, and country. We did not anticipate the importance of self-involvement; the failure to investigate this area is a serious gap in this study.

THE ABSENCE OF INVOLVEMENT

In discussing the "distribution of involvement" we considered actual responses to the "think about" and "proud" questions. But what about the blanks?

Blanks for open-ended questions are difficult to evaluate because this type of question is so demanding of the interviewer. Giving only one or two responses to the "think about" question might simply mean that the interviewer did not urge the respondent to give three answers or that the interviewer did not allow sufficient time for a third name to occur to the person being interviewed. Blanks might not tell us anything about the subject's fantasy life; they might simply reflect the interviewer's inadequacy. In an attempt to determine the significance of interviewing skills, interviewers were compared in terms of their effectiveness in eliciting responses to the "think about" question. There was quite a range of success in getting "think about" responses, but one interviewer was clearly poorer that all the rest. In sixteen out of twenty-nine cases she had no responses; this was the only interviewer who failed more than she succeeded. Her interviews are excluded from the analysis in this section. It seems undeniable, however, that to some unknown extent the presence of blanks is due to the conditions of the interview experience itself, and not to the nature of our respondents' fantasy life.

It could be argued that the presence of blanks might simply indicate difficulty in understanding the question. To check this we determined the number of blanks by age and education; there are some differences in the expected direction, i.e., the more educated had fewer blanks, but the range of the differences is not great, and the apparent effect of education differed among age aggregates; among those forty to sixty-nine years old the range across educational levels was 11 percent, while among those sixty and above the range was 1 percent. The difference did not seem sufficient to warrant further consideration of the education variable.

Some people gave collective-type responses to the "think about" question, e.g., "family," or "the children." It might be thought that such people would have more blanks. In fact the opposite was true; the 43 people who gave this type of response had a total of 5 percent blank responses; those individuals who gave at least one response of any type (N=558) had a total of 9 percent blank responses.

Since the "think about" question is used as an indicator of involvement, it might be proposed that blanks would mean an absence of involvement. But that would be inaccurate. Singer studied a "sample of 240, presumably normal, adults between the ages 19 and 50, of at least college education, who came from a fairly widespread area in the United States...." He found that "96% of the respondents reported that they engaged in some form of daydreaming daily. ..."[3] But—"The maximum daydreaming reported is between the ages eighteen and twenty-nine, with decreasing frequency in the thirty to thirty-nine group, and with lowest reported frequency in persons aged forty to forty-nine."[4] Although Singer's sample is quite different from ours, the fact that 96 percent of his respondents reported at least daily daydreaming suggests that all humans have some sort of meaningful fantasy life. Therefore, if people cannot name three people they think about, this cannot be assumed to indicate an absence or paucity of fantasy but only that the fantasy activity is not diffused among at least three *real* people. Actually there are two dimensions to consider: 1) fantasy may be focused or diffused, i.e., limited to a few or involving new people continually, and 2) fantasy may be about real or imaginary people. An inability to name three people in response to the "think about" question could occur, therefore, for the following reasons: a) the person's involvement is so diffused that it is difficult to pick out one, two, or three specific people, or b) the person's fantasy is mainly about imaginary people, or c) the person has no fantasy. According to Singer, "c" becomes more possible as people age; this might indicate a general decline of activity, and therefore, of involvement—in short, disengagement. Condition "b" would mean a lack of correspondence between fantasy life and social life, and therefore alienation. Condition "a"—a diffused fantasy—would seem to mean the absence of deep involvement—a flighty person. It is assumed, therefore, that blanks on the "think about" indicate alienation, although there are three possible reasons.

For the total sample, whites and blacks have almost identical percentages of blank responses to the "think about" question: 15 percent for the whites, 16 percent for the blacks. Even holding age constant, there are no dramatic differences between the color aggregates, the largest difference being 6 percent for those forty to forty-nine years old. Table 3-5 presents the percentage of blank responses to the "think about" question by age. The two extreme aggregates obviously deviate from the other age ranges, but the subsamples at the extremes are quite small.

As noted in the last chapter we are especially interested in the impact of mobility on involvement. Accordingly, the percentage of blanks was related to number of cities lived in, years at present address, and years in Milwaukee. By and large no pattern emerged except for those forty to fifty-nine years old, and this pattern remained regardless of household size. Table 3-6 shows the relation between the percentage of blanks and years in Milwaukee for people in

TABLE 3–5

PERCENT OF BLANK RESPONSES TO THE "THINK" ABOUT QUESTION

(By age of respondent, N=590[1])

Age in years	Percent blank	
	%	N
17–19	2	(15)
20–29	14	(147)
30–39	17	(148)
40–49	17	(101)
50–59	17	(67)
60–74	13	(82)
75–98	23	(20)
No response		(10)

1. This is our total after we removed the interviews conducted by the inadequate interviewer noted in the text. There were twenty nine interviews done by this interviewer; we also removed two other cases in which the interviewer was not identified; finally two cases were eliminated because of coding errors.

this age range who are not lifetime residents of Milwaukee. There is a curvilinear relationship (i.e., one where the relationship between the variables changes as the values change) between the percentage and the number of years in Milwaukee. But why would those mobile people who have lived eleven to twenty-five years in Milwaukee have a high percentage of blanks? If mobility

TABLE 3–6

PERCENT OF BLANKS ON THE "THINK ABOUT" QUESTION RELATIVE TO YEARS SPENT IN MILWAUKEE: AMONG THOSE WHO HAVE LIVED IN MORE THAN ONE CITY AND WHO ARE FORTY TO FIFTY-NINE YEARS OLD

Years in Milwaukee	Percent blank	
	%	N
0–5		(11)
6–10	12	(22)
11–15	27	(27)
16–20	30	(23)
21–25	23	(22)
26–55	2	(32)
[Lifetime residents	11	(21)]

SOLIDARITY IN A SLUM

itself is significant, the high percentage would have been expected among the newcomers to Milwaukee. Of course it is possible that it takes around ten years for people to forget those with whom they were significantly involved; this seems difficult to believe, yet it is a possibility. But, then, why does it take ten to fifteen years more to replace lost relationships and thus for the percentage to go down? It could be that it actually takes about ten years to feel so involved with someone that respondents would mention them in response to the "think about"question. This seems absurd in regard to a spouse, but perhaps there is some value in looking more closely into the time dimension of involvement. How long does it take to develop a deep involvement with someone? No doubt the answer is related to the significance attributed to a relationship by culture. In the United States great significance, and therefore power, is given to one's spouse, and thus he or she is likely to be thought about frequently soon after the marital relation begins. But American culture is vague about the significance of other relations, and perhaps it does take considerable time for people, even family members (other than spouses), to develop a deep involvement.

But it could also be that mobility itself is not important, and that the results in Table 3-6 are due to the effect of another, unknown variable. There were too few cases in some of the subsamples to do an analysis for those below forty. However, there was no indication of any relation between years in Milwaukee and percentage of blanks for those sixty and above. At best, then we can say that there is weak support for the idea that there is a curvilinear relation between the length of residence in a city and the percentage of blanks.

Litwak has already suggested that mobility does not undermine family involvement, so the absence of a relationship between mobility and blanks should not surprise us. Moreover, the studies of Brown et al. and Tilly and Brown have shown the importance of kin in the migration process. Speaking of migrants, Tilly and Brown wrote: "Everywhere we find more persistence and proliferation of personal relations than should be there. The very groups one would expect to find disrupted by migration, for lack of security, experience or skill in city life, show extensive contacts among kinfolk." Clearly, our finding that mobility does not seem to diminish familial involvement is supported by other studies.[5]

TYPES OF INVOLVEMENT THAT PRODUCE ALIENATION

Earlier in the chapter the point was made that involvement with certain objects is itself a source of alienation, since when those objects are thought about, the resulting fantasies cannot simply reflect in mirror-like fashion the sensed environment. To what extent were the respondents involved with such objects?

TABLE 3-7

PERCENT OF RESPONDENTS REFERRING TO DEITY ON "PROUD" QUESTION

	(By age and color of respondent)	
	Color	
Age	White	Black
17–19	(3)	(11)
20–39	3 (36)	6 (245)
40–59	5 (59)	15 (103)
60–74	2 (48)	34 (38)
75–98	5 (20)	(2)
No response	(3)	(8)

DEITY

One indicator of involvement in the deity is whether or not the respondent mentioned God as one of the three people thought about. Six people did mention God. Of course, this underestimates the significance of spiritual relations, because people do not usually think of God as simply "a person." Another indicator of involvement with the deity is whether or not people mentioned their personal religious practices or their relation to God as something they are proud of. If they did, significant spiritual involvement can be assumed. However, if people fail to mention God this does not necessarily mean the absence of spiritual involvement; it may mean that the respondent does not value her spiritual relationship as much as other aspects of her life. In spite of this, we will use the "proud" question in the discussion of spiritual involvement. The reader must bear in mind, however, that this question reflects not simply involvement, but valued involvement.

In analyzing the proud question we differentiated between responses that referred to specific churches or religious organizations and those that referred either to personal religious practices, such as praying, or to a relationship with a deity; it is the latter type of response in which we are interested. The deity (i.e., the relationship to a deity) was mentioned by fifty-seven respondents (9 percent of our sample). Table 3-7 shows the distribution of these references by age and color. Observably, pride in one's relationship to the deity is a black phenomenon in Kilbourntown; more precisely, it exists mainly among the older blacks.[6]

Marx has recently compared the religiosity of blacks and whites.

There is a popular stereotype that Negroes are a 'religious people.' Social science research has shown that they are 'over-churched' relative to whites, i.e., the ratio of Negro churches to the size of the Negro population is greater than the same ratio for whites. Using data from a nationwide survey of whites, by Gertrude Selznick and Stephan Steinberg, some comparison ot the religiosity of Negroes and whites was possible. When these various dimensions of religiosity were examimed, with effect of education and region held constant, Negroes appeared as significantly more religious only with respect to the subjective importance assigned to religion. In the north, whites were more likely to attend church at least once a week than were Negroes; while in the South rates of attendance were the same. About the same percentage of both groups had no doubts about the existence of God. While Negroes were more likely to be sure about the existence of a devil, whites, surprisingly, were more likely to be sure about a life beyond death. Clearly, then, any assertions about the greater religiosity of Negroes relative to whites are unwarranted unless one specifies the dimension of religiosity.[7]

Our research does support the "popular stereotype" that Negroes are "a religious people." At least between the whites and blacks dwelling together in an urban slum there is a clear difference regarding the deity. Blacks value the spiritual relationships in which they are involved; whites do not, either because they are not involved in spiritual relationships or because they do not value such involvements.[8]

If sociologists and others are to understand people they must clearly recognize the distinction between spiritual involvement and institutional (or church) involvement. More people in our sample referred to the former than the latter. Deities are people, or at least that is how they are considered by the majority of believers. God is not an idea, an abstraction, a belief—but a person. Jesus Christ, for instance, might be related to as a lover, a father, a friend, a helper, and so on—only he is a superlover, a superfather, a superfriend.

But spiritual involvement, precisely because it is a humanlike relationship, can be a source of alienation from our fellow man. It has already been pointed out that involvement with a deity produces alienation, because it cuts off our fantasy from the sensed environment. But spiritual involvement can alienate us in still another way. Because the Christian God is a superfather or a superfriend or a super-whatever, he can take the place of purely human counterparts. Because God is humanlike he can turn people away from involvement with the humans about them. The Christian image of God must be a great temptation leading believers to turn away from the purely human. It might be argued that, on the contrary, being a Christian leads to involvement in human affairs; for instance, it might inspire crusades for social justice. Note, however, that our discussion is not about "being a Christian" but about being involved with a deity. Someone might actively support Christian morality but give little attention to the person of God. But it is the latter on which we are commenting. The blacks of Kilbourntown, more than the whites, seemed involved with God. Possibly, this means not only that fantasy cannot mirror the sensed environment, but also that black women may turn away from human relations for the perfection of the Christian God.

But the involvement with the deity is not equally important for all black women. Rather its importance increases with age. Given the fact that approaching death does not make the elderly white women more religious, it would seem hazardous to suggest that the difference between the younger and older black women is due to the effects of different life stages. It is possible that this difference reflects generational change, i.e., perhaps the older black women have failed to pass on the value of spiritual involvement. However, it cannot be forgotten that the proud question is open-ended. Perhaps for young black women it is not that they are not involved with God, or that they do not value this involvement, but that other things such as family and children are more salient, so that they forgot about God, for awhile. Fully one-third of the older black women refered to a spiritual relationship, and it must be remembered that open-ended questions underestimate the prevalence of relationships. For older black women in Kilbourntown alienation due to involvement in a spiritual relationship would seem quite significant. It must be very hard for nonbelievers or for those whose religion is mainly a matter of morality to understand the way in which these older black women experience the world.

THE DEAD

For a discussion of the last two types of objects—dead persons and persons rarely contacted—we return to the "think about" question.

The prominence of the dead at least in some primitive societies is well known.

> It is not enough to state that the dead are constantly present to the minds of the living, who do nothing without consulting them; that the well-being, prosperity and very existence of the social group depend upon the good will of its dead members, and that these in their turn cannot dispense with the worship and the offerings of their descendants. The solidarity existing between them is yet more profound and more intimate, and it is realized in the very essence of individuals. The dead 'live with' the members of their group who are born into the world.[9]

Compared to most, if not all, primitive societies, the dead play a minor role in American society. The modern mythology is future-oriented, and so pays little homage to past commoners or heroes. If anything, our society seems to worship the young. Despite this dramatic change on the mythological level, however, the dead remain important to many modern people. For whom are the dead important? Which dead linger on in our social world? These are the questions we are presently interested in.

The "think about" question asked our 623 respondents to name three

SOLIDARITY IN A SLUM

TABLE 3–8

PERCENT OF REFERENCES TO PEOPLE WHO ARE DEAD ON THE
"THINK ABOUT" QUESTION

	(By age of respondent)		
Age	Percent of references		Percent of respondents who think about at least one dead person
	%	N	%
17–19	0	(15)	0
20–29	2	(156)	5
30–39	3	(156)	9
40–49	5	(104)	12
50–59	5	(71)	10
60–74	7	(88)	11
75–98	18	(22)	27
No response		(11)	—

people, implying a possibility of 1,869 different replies. However, only 1,520 choices were actually made. Of the actual replies 81, or a little over 5 percent are dead. Of the 623 respondents, 40 chose one dead person, 16 chose two, and 3 gave three dead persons; in short, about 9 percent of our sample mentioned at least one dead person in response to the "think about" question. The deceased are a minor, but noteworthy part of the social world even in urban America, although this characteristic might be restricted to the urban slum.

Who are these remembered dead? As noted previously, we attempted to reinterview about a 15 percent random sample of our respondents. The sixty-three female homemakers reinterviewed had mentioned 177 persons on the "think about" question, 13 of whom were dead (i.e., about 7 percent). Their relations to our respondents were as follows: Mother—5; spouse—2; sister—1; aunt—1; daughter—1; grandfather—1; friend—1; President Kennedy—1.

WHO THINKS ABOUT DEAD PEOPLE?

Table 3-8 presents data relating age to thinking about the dead. Although this phenomenon begins early in life, it obviously also increases with age. The percentages in the first column of this table are based on the total number of possible responses; if only the total number of actual responses is considered, i.e., if blanks are excluded, the percentages are: 0, 2, 4, 6, 7, and 23. Of those people mentioned by respondents over seventy-four, just about one-fourth are dead. A comparison of whites and blacks by age-aggregate showed no significant differences.

TABLE 3-9

PERCENT OF RESPONDENTS WHO THINK ABOUT AT LEAST
ONE DEAD PERSON

(By marital status[1] of respondent)

Marital status	Percent	
	%	N
Never married	10	(19)
Married	9	(360)
Divorced	11	(37)
Separated	5	(97)
Widowed	16	(80)
No response		(5)

1. N=608, because this analysis was done subdividing marital status by household size, and we have data on household size for only 608 cases.

In table 3-8 the data are presented in two ways—as a percentage of all the references that were to persons who were dead and as the percentage of respondents who thought about at least one dead person. The overall pattern is the same in both cases. To know that, at least for this lower-class sample of women, one-quarter of the elderly are significantly involved with the dead may help the rest of the population understand the perspective of those near the death side of life.

In an attempt to explore further who thinks about the dead, this type of involvement was related to marital status (see Table 3-9). As expected, widows have the highest percentage. But this could be due to the fact that having lost a spouse, they have a dead person with whom they were significantly involved while he was alive to think about. In fact, being a widow is associated with thinking about the dead only if the widow was fifty or more; none of the sixteen widows younger than this thought about the dead. On the other hand, for each age-aggregate fifty and over (i.e., fifty to fifty-nine, sixty to seventy-four, seventy-five to ninety-eight) at least 20 percent of the widows think about at least one dead person. Although the subsamples are small it does seem that there is nothing in widowhood itself that makes people think about the dead. It is far from automatic for a widow to continue being deeply involved with her spouse after he dies, especially if the widow is young.

However, this study did not gather data on how recent was the spouse's death and this is probably important. Townsend and Tunstall concluded from their cross-cultural study of old people: "Loneliness is related much more to 'loss' than to enduring 'isolation'. There is evidence not only that the recently widowed are more likely to be extremely lonely than those widowed for many years, but also that persons whose children die or who have become separated from their children, and persons who have been detached in other ways from their social circle (such as people who are moved into a house or flat in a new district), feel lonely."[10] It seems quite possible that a recent loss will have different effects from a distant one. Perhaps the percent of recent widows thinking about dead people would be quite high.

It is interesting that 'separated' women have an unusually low percentage in Table 3-9. This remained true for all age categories (data not shown). Perhaps the fact that some people separate rather than divorce indicates a casualness about social relations in general. Perhaps separated people are more flexible and find it easier to change involvements. This casualness need not mean shallow relationships. Theoretically, a person may feel very involved with another but also may easily give up that involvement and become involved with another person. It would be valuable to determine if, in fact, people can be flexibly yet deeply involved. A study of separated persons might be especially fruitful if one was interested in this question.

PEOPLE RARELY TALKED WITH

The respondents were asked how often they talked with the people they think about. The response categories used were: daily, several times a week, once a week, two or three times a month, or less than two or three times a month. We are here interested in the last category, i.e., the people our respondents talk with once a month or less; about 15 percent of the possible responses are people rarely talked with. To fantasize about people rarely seen or heard is to contribute to the separation of the fantasy world from the sensed world, and, therefore, to increase alienation.

Neither age nor color shows any consistent relation to thinking about individuals rarely talked with. Table 3-10 shows the percentage of the fantasy world given over to people rarely talked with by age and color. Two slight tendencies are noticeable, namely that blacks consistently have slightly higher percentages and that the peak period is in the thirty to thirty-nine year age-range.

Mobility is important in understanding why people fantasize about individuals with whom they rarely communicate; only 5 of the 274 people the respondents rarely talked with came from the neighborhood; it is because people move about that our sample now had relations with individuals they rarely got to talk to. For the subsample we reinterviewed about the people they think about, there were thirty cases of people rarely contacted; only four of these people then lived in Milwaukee; the rest lived in Tennessee, Chicago, Arkansas, Mississippi, and California. In their fantasy world the people of K-3

TABLE 3–10

PERCENT OF RESPONSES REFERRING TO PEOPLE WITH WHOM THE
RESPONDENT IS RARELY IN CONTACT

	Color			
	White		Black	
Age	%	N	%	N
17–19		(3)		(11)
20–29		(11)	13	(134)
30–39	15	(25)	20	(112)
40–49	6	(26)	15	(69)
50–59	10	(33)	17	(34)
60–74	12	(48)	17	(38)
75 and over	8	(20)		(2)
No response		(3)		(8)

(By age and color of respondent)

are in contact with all parts of this nation. They can not be completely provincial. This scattering of relations reflects the mobility of the American population in general.

As would be expected the more stable respondents tended to think about people with whom they are in frequent contact. For the sixty-one respondents who have lived in Milwaukee all their life,[11] only 6 percent of their possible responses to the "think about" question are individuals rarely talked with; this is half the percentage for the total sample. We also considered the length of time our respondents lived at their present address; almost all of our respondents (95 percent) under thirty had lived at their present address no more than five years; obviously, length of residence could not differentiate among them. Even among those in their thirties only 5 percent had lived in their present house more than ten years. For those in their forties and fifties, longer residence in the same house is associated with a decline in the number of references to people rarely talked with; for both age-aggregates those living at the same address more than ten years show this decline. On the other hand, those over sixty seem unaffected by length of residence. In general then, more stable people think less about people they rarely communicate with. But the degree to which this source of alienation is present reflects the mobility patterns not only of our respondents, but also the patterns of potential fantasy objects, i.e., of family members. Our respondents' stability, then, could be expected to explain only a part of the tendency to think about people rarely contacted.

SOLIDARITY IN A SLUM

SUMMARY ANALYSIS OF "THINK ABOUT" QUESTION

To get some idea of the overall degree to which respondents are involved in their sensed environment, Table 3-11 is presented. The "think about" question was used to measure: a) the absence of significant involvement (percentage of blanks), and b) the presence of involvement with objects that produce some degree of alienation because fantasy will not mirror the sensed environment (percentage of persons thought about who are dead; percentage of persons thought about who are rarely contacted). If we combine all three percentages and subtract from 100 percent we get a measure of the extent to which respondents are involved with the sensed environment. The measure of involvement is shown in the parentheses in Table 3-11.

The only subcategory that stands out is that of persons seventy-five and over; clearly, they are low in their involvement; this seems to result both from a high percentage of blanks and from relatively frequent reference to dead people. In short, the "disengagement" of the old may reflect both a decline in involvement and a shift of involvement from the living to the dead.

The major difference by color concerns spiritual involvement, and this is

TABLE 3–11

PERCENT OF RESPONSES ON THE "THINK ABOUT" QUESTION THAT ARE BLANK OR THAT REFER TO THE DEAD OR TO THE RARELY TALKED WITH BY AGE AND COLOR

(The figure in parentheses is 100 minus the total.)

Age	White				Black			
	Blank[1]	Dead	Rarely talked with	Total	Blank[1]	Dead	Rarely talked with	Total
17–19[2]	—	—	—	—	(11)	—	—	—
20–29[3]	—	—	—	—	15%	1%	13%	29%(71)
30–39	12%	7%	15%	34%(66)	17	3	20	40 (60)
40–49	12	5	6	23 (77)	18	5	15	38 (62)
50–59	18	3	10	31 (69)	18	5	17	40 (60)
60–74	16	8	12	36 (64)	11	4	17	32 (68)
75–98[4]	24	18	8	50 (50)	(2)	—	—	—

1. Percentages in this column are based on our total sample minus the cases obtained by the inadequate interviewer. We have assumed that the figures would have been the same if the entire sample had been adequately interviewed.

2. There are too few cases to justify analysis.

3. There are too few white respondents to justify analysis.

4. There are too few black respondents to justify analysis.

not reflected in Table 3-11. If we could somehow combine a measure of this variable with the others contained in this table, there would probably be a significant difference between whites and blacks, with the latter being more alienated from the sensed environment.

CONCLUSION

The point of this chapter has been to develop an understanding of alienation resulting from a divergence between fantasy and the sensed environment. We have tried to show the extent to which such alienation exists among our respondents.

But, it is one thing to lay bare the basis for objective alienation and another thing to claim that people actually experience this alienation as such. What Cortazar says about "metaphysical rivers" is meant to apply to life in general: "There are metaphysical rivers, she swims in them like that swallow swimming in the air, spinning madly around a belfry, letting herself drop so that she can rise up all the better with the swoop. I describe and define and desire those rivers, but she swims in them. I look for them, find them, observe them from the bridge, but she swims in them."[12] Sociologists are the definers, observers. But the people we study swim in reality. Scientists stand back, people dive in. It would be quite erroneous to assume that all objective alienation is simultaneously subjective alienation.

Kornhauser, among others, has suggested that the United States be considered a "mass society," one which is characterized by "(1) the weakness of intermediary relations [i.e., the local community, local press, voluntary organizations, the work group], (2) the isolation of primary relations, (3) the centralization of national relations."[13] The distribution of involvement found among our respondents is somewhat consistent with this model. Most intermediary institutions are unimportant—however, with the strong exception of the religious institution. The importance of this institution calls into question the relevance of the "mass society" model to our respondents. On the other hand, consistent with this model is the unimportance of local politics and the concentration of political involvement on the national level. But a final evaluation of this model awaits a clearer specification of what "the isolation of primary relations" means. In the meanwhile it seems to me that the importance our respondents attached to the family seriously questions the appropriateness of the label 'mass society." Family and religion are important sources of counterpressures for whatever forces are generated by the state. The model of a "mass society" is useful but cannot adequately express the richness of social life in Kilbourntown.

SOLIDARITY IN A SLUM

4

The Household and Family

Several ideas set forth in Chapter One are important for understanding our perspective on the household. For women, and especially housewives, there are probably only two universally important environments—fantasy and the household. The first question we ask, therefore, is how much overlap is there between our respondents' fantasy world and household? This represents a refinement of the analysis presented in the previous chapter.

Second, and the major topic of this chapter, we want to know some details about the pattern of familial involvement in Kilbourntown. Are wives always deeply involved with their husbands? Are mothers equally involved with all children? How does color and age affect the pattern of involvement? In this chapter we shall try to delve deeper into what the data in the last chapter suggested was the central object in our respondents' lives—their families.

OVERLAPPING SPACES

For the majority of our respondents, who do not work full-time, the "sensed environment" is for the most part limited to the home; therefore the overlap between fantasy and household is perhaps a more precise measure of the degree to which fantasy reflects the sensed environment than are the data used in the last chapter.

Our analysis is, again, based on the "think about" question. The question now is: How many of the people thought about live with the respondent?

The relevant data are presented in Table 4-1. The first column in this table shows the percentage of people thought about who also live in the household. The table divides nonhousehold fantasy figures into children (column 2) and others (column 3).

There is a general decline in overlap as people are older, until we get to those over seventy-four, for whom the figure is 7 percent. It would be quite understandable for our old people to feel lonely, since just about none of the people they think about lived with them. For young people there is fairly high overlap with about half the people thought about living with the respondent.

Comparing whites and blacks of the same age, there is a general tendency for blacks to have less overlap. This would be consistent with the data in the last chapter, which suggested that blacks give more significance to the extended family. As a result there is somewhat less congruence for black women between their fantasy and their daily sensed environment.

If we compare Tables 3-11 and 4-1 we see that in the latter table the degree of overlap between fantasy and the environment is more consistently related to age. Table 3-11 refers to the degree to which fantasy figures are not part of the sensed environment for long periods of time, while Table 4-1 refers more

TABLE 4–1

PERCENT OF FANTASY COEXTENSIVE WITH HOUSEHOLD AND
NUCLEAR FAMILY: BY COLOR AND AGE OF RESPONDENT

	(Percentages based on number of actual responses)			
Color & Age	Percent of fantasy figures living in respondents households	Percent of fantasy figures who are respondents children not living in respondents households	Percent of fantasy figures not included in previous two columns	Subsample size
White 17–19	—%	—%	—%	(9)[1]
20–29	46	0	54	(26)
30–39	34	1	65	(65)
40–49	37	18	45	(67)
50–59	28	26	46	(81)
60–74	14	23	63	(112)
75 plus	7	34	59	(41)
Black 17–19	42	0	58	(31)
20–29	34	2	64	(338)
30–39	32	5	63	(273)
40–49	30	10	60	(168)
50–59	19	11	70	(80)
60–74	7	24	69	(100)
75 plus	—	—	—	(6)

1. In parentheses is the number of persons named in response to the "think about" question.

TABLE 4–2

PERCENT OF FANTASY FIGURES WHO LIVE WITH RESPONDENT OR
ARE RESPONDENTS' OWN CHILDREN LIVING AWAY FROM HOME

Age	Color	
	White	Black
17–19	—[1]	42
20–29	46	36
30–39	35	37
40–49	55	40
50–59	54	30
60–74	37	31
75 plus	41	—[2]

(By age and color of respondent.)

1. There were only nine respondents in this category, which seemed too few to analyze.

2. There were only six respondents in this category.

to the respondents' daily experience. Is a sense of alienation more closely related to daily experience or to longer time periods? Would the results in Table 3-11 or those in Table 4-1 be more closely related to a sense of alienation? At present all we can do is point to the problem of determining what are the subjectively meaningful time intervals in people's lives.

As a minimum it is assumed that the respondent is more likely to experience some alienation if the fantasy does not mirror the environment at the time of the fantasy. Therefore, Table 4-1 would seem to present the better data, for it can safely be assumed that much of the respondents' fantasizing will take place in the home, and therefore if the fantasy objects do not live with the respondent, it would be highly unlikely that fantasy would mirror the sensed environment. But, does this objective alienation produce different amounts of subjective alienation depending on whether the respondent is going to see the nonhouseholder thought about in the next few days or weeks? It seems possible. That is, if a woman daydreams about a son who lives around the corner and whom she will see tomorrow, this would have a different effect than if she daydreamed about a dead son. It may be worthwhile to do research on the problem of whether the alienating effect of non-overlapping environments is affected by the anticipation of contact with the person thought about; if such anticipation is significant, the effects of different time intervals between the fantasy and the anticipated contact with the fantasized object should then be explored.

One obvious explanation for the decline in the overlap of fantasy and household as people become older would be the maturing of children with the result that they leave the home—at least in the United States. This would mean that columns 1 and 2 in Table 4-1, when added together, should show no change with age, i.e., if we add together involvement with household members and involvement in nonhousehold children the resulting percentages should be the same for all ages. Table 4-2 shows this combined total in relation to age and color. For whites, there is a curvilinear relationship. In the younger and older years the percentages are about the same, while between the ages of forty and fifty-nine the percentage is unusually high. For the whites, then, it can not be said that the low percentages for the older respondents are due simply to their children moving out; this cannot explain the difference in Table 4-2 between those forty to fifty-nine and those sixty and over.

For blacks there is not the curvilinear relation found for whites,[1] but there is a decline in percentages as people get older, although the decline begins earlier for blacks than for whites.

In short, as Table 4-2 shows there is still a difference by age even when

TABLE 4–3

PERCENT OF DIFFERENT CATEGORIES OF PEOPLE (OTHER THAN CHILDREN) PRESENT IN RESPONDENTS' HOUSEHOLDS WHO ARE THOUGHT ABOUT

Relation	Number thought about	Number in households	Percent thought about[1]
Roomer[2]	2	42	5
Friend[2]	1	12	8
Grandparent (or parent)[3]	6	21	29
Sibling	4	37	11
Spouse[4]	155	370	42
Other relative	4	59	7
Children at home, but not respondents' own	1	87	1

1. This percent overestimates the number thought about, since the number thought about is based on N=623, while the number in a household is based on N=608. It seemed unnecessary to refine our analysis to justify the basic conclusions stated in the text. Two adults are not included because of improper coding.

2. These categories were used by the respondent.

3. This category refers to the homemaker's parents.

4. In some cases the homemakers's parents are included. This happened because the code used was "spouse or parent," and when no grandchildren were present in the home, the homemaker's parents were coded with the same number as spouses. So, there were eight married women who were coded as having two spouses; in fact, of course, this meant simply that the homemaker's mother or father was living in the home, but there were no grandchildren at home. Such miscoded grandparents could not be separated in the analysis from spouses. But there were few such cases.

TABLE 4-4

PERCENT OF DIFFERENT AGE AGGREGATES OF RESPONDENTS'
OWN CHILDREN WHO ARE THOUGHT ABOUT[1]

Age of children	Number thought about	Number respondents have	Percent thought about
0–4	71	236	30
5–6	25	167	15
7–13	69	508	14
14–16	23	138	17
17 and above			
at home	56	138	41
other	114	310	37

1. Our respondents thought about 6 dead children; these are not included in the table.

we combine columns 1 and 2 in Table 4-1. The decline in overlap of fantasy and household that occurs for older people can not be explained simply by the fact that mature children leave home.

Another explanation for the absence of overlap is that people live alone. But this assumes that if people do live together they will fantasize abouut each other, and as will be seen in the next section this is not always true.

The main point of this section is that in our sample there is a basis for considerable alienation, since for no age-range does the overlap of fantasy and household reach 50 percent. Moreover, this overlap declines as age increases, reaching an amazingly low 7 percent for the elderly.

FAMILY INVOLVEMENT

In this section we shall analyze the nature of family involvement, still making use of the "think about" question. We assume that the objects in fantasy are the ones with whom the respondent is most involved, i.e., we use the "think about" question as a crude measure of involvement.

In Chapter One it was suggested that spatial closeness itself produces involvement. In a related discussion Adams has suggested that the effect of physical distance varies directly with biological distance, i.e., as biological distance decreases, the effects of physical distance decline. Adam's point is that biological distance is much more important than physical distance.[2] This would mean, for instance, that our respondents should be less involved with distant relatives living in the household than with close relatives living outside the household. Is this true?

Table 4-3 shows the percent of different categories of people living with the respondent who are thought about. Table 4-4 shows the percent of the respondents' own (i.e., by birth, not marriage or adoption) children who are thought about.

If the percentage for children seventeen years of age and over who are not living at home is compared with the other figure in Tables 4-3 and 4-4 we can see the relative importance of physical and of biological distance. First, note that the percentage for these children is just about the same as for children of the same age who are living at home. The fact of co-residence with the respondent seems inconsequential. Second, if we compare adult children living away from home with other categories of relatives living with the respondent, and leaving aside for a moment the case of spouses, it is clear that involvement seems more affected by the biological closeness of children than by the physical closeness of roomers, friends, siblings, and other relatives. But the relative importance of biological and physical distance is no better illustrated than by comparing adult children not living in their parent's home (37 percent of whom are thought about) and children not the respondent's own but living with the respondent (1 percent of whom are thought about). The latter category is quite mixed, including stepchildren, grandchildren, children of a sibling and the like, but the very low percentage for this category suggests that all these types of relation amount to the same thing for the respondent. In a related study, Bowerman and Irish found that stepchildren felt less affection than natural children for their parents.[3] It is quite clear that biological distance minimizes, if not eliminates, the effects of physical distance.

A closer examination of Tables 4-3 and 4-4, however, calls into question even the significance of biological distance. First, the highest percentage (42 percent) is for spouses, with whom the respondents have no biological relationship. Second, the respondents have an equal biological relation with their own parents and with their children, but the latter are more frequently listed by the respondents as fantasy objects; equal biological distance does not mean equal chances of being fantasy objects. Third, there is little significant difference between non-relatives living with the respondent such as roomers (5 percent) and friends (8 percent) and certain kind of relatives also living with the respondent such as siblings (11 percent) and "other relatives" (7 percent). As already discussed, it is assumed that fantasizing about an object is a sign of involvement with that object. Given this assumption, the results just noted indicate that social involvement does not seem simply to reflect biological distance.

The data in Tables 4-3 and 4-4, then, do not support the idea that either physical or biological distance is important to involvement. What is important is the nuclear family. Outside this unit involvement is scattered among different types of people, although parents do stand out from other categories of people. This scattering of involvement outside the nuclear family, however,

TABLE 4–5

PERCENT OF MARRIED RESPONDENTS WHO THINK ABOUT THEIR SPOUSE

Age	White		Black	
	%	N	%	N
17–19	—	(2)	—	(9)
20–29	—	(7)	42	(83)
30–39	47	(15)	48	(75)
40–49	45	(20)	63	(32)
50–59	39	(26)	60	(10)
60–74	27	(22)	17	(12)
75 plus	—	(4)	—	(1)

(By age and color of respondent[1])

1. Actually the percentages refer to the number of people coded "5" who are thought about. Code "5" refers to either spouse or parent, but for our married respondents there are only a few cases in which "5" refers to parents. Eliminating such cases would have been time-consuming and would not have changed the pattern of results.

might be affected by physical distance, i.e., the friends or sisters or aunts we become involved with might be those who are physically close to us; our research could neither confirm nor deny this.

There appears to be a curvilinear relation between the age of children and the percent who are thought about (see Table 4-4). Among nonadult children only the very young have a good chance to be thought about. This could be

TABLE 4–6

PERCENT OF MARRIED RESPONDENTS WHO THINK ABOUT THEIR SPOUSE

(By color and age of respondents and number of cities and towns lived in by respondents[1])

Number of cities and towns lived in	Age and color					
	17–29		30–39		40–59	
	White	Black	White	Black	White	Black
	% N	% N	% N	% N	% N	% N
1–2	— (7)	42 (57)	— (8)	44 (41)	33 (36)	42 (26)
3 or more	— (2)	39 (41)	— (8)	53 (31)	60 (10)	70 (20)

1. There are too few cases aged 60 and above to analyze.

THE HOUSEHOLD AND FAMILY

due to differences in family size, i.e., only the very young children in our sample are likely to be the only child in their family; all of the older children are likely to have at least one sibling at home. But it is also true that very young children do demand more attention from their parents than older children. We are assuming of course, that the frequency with which children of a certain age are thought about is a crude measure of the average degree of parental involvement with children at that age; thus, since children between five and six are less frequently thought about than children four or younger, we assume that mothers generally are more involved with the younger children. The curvilinear relation suggested by Table 4-4 between age and involvement will be made use of later on in the chapter when we discuss the natural history of familial involvement.

Although the data in Table 4-3 point to the importance of the spouse, it cannot be ignored that only 42 percent of the spouses living with our respondents were mentioned in response to the "think about" question. We attempted to explore the nature of the husband-wife relationship further. Table 4-5 shows the percent of respondents who think about the spouse by age and color of respondent. For the whites there is an inverse relation between the percentage and age; when the white women are older, fewer of them think about their spouse. For blacks, there seems to be a curvilinear relation between the percentage and age. A very high percentage of black women between ages forty and fifty-nine think about their spouse. In general, black women seem more involved with their husbands than do the white women. However, among both whites and blacks, husband-wife involvement seems less frequent among the elderly than among the rest of the sample.

The expected pattern of involvement among spouses would be similar to that found by Blood and Wolfe in their study of Detroit families. They reported the wife's mean marital satisfaction by stages in the family life cycles as follows:

Honeymoon	4.26
Preschool	3.99
Preadolescent	3.91
Adolescent Children	3.76
Post-Adolescent	
Children at Home	3.50
Postparental	3.83
Retired	3.80[4]

This pattern shows an end-of-the-cycle upsurge not found in our data. This may reflect sample differences. On the other hand, a satisfaction index, which was the measure used by Blood and Wolfe, is difficult to interpret, because it reflects both the amount of involvement and the expectations about involve-

SOLIDARITY IN A SLUM

ment. A person may be satisfied either because she is highly involved or because she is not involved with her husband very much but does not desire high involvement. A measure of satisfaction can not be used as a measure of involvement. In spite of Blood and Wolfe's work, therefore, it is possible that spousal alienation in old age, as suggested by our data, does occur.

Why might there be a turning away from the spouse in old age? We suggest this happens because the types of problems that occur as people become old are unrelated to the reasons for the choice of a spouse. For many old people, interest in sex declines. Interest in dancing, going to parties, and perhaps even a general interest in fun, diminishes. Children have left the home, so the fatherly characteristics of a husband which might have been important at the time of marriage are in old age less significant. Elderly people face new problems centering on illness, loneliness, and retirement. The strengths of a man that make him a desirable husband may not be relevant to helping wives solve the new problems of old age. As a result elderly women may have to look elsewhere—to children or to members of the extended family or to God or to themselves—for the resources needed to survive in the last stage of the life-cycle.

But even if this is true, we have hardly begun to explain why less than half of the married respondents mentioned their husband in response to the "think about" question. One possible source of light is Elizabeth Bott's discussion of mobility and family ties.

> Networks [of relationships] become dispersed when people move around from one place to another...their [i.e., spouses] external relationships are relatively discontinuous both in space and in time. Such continuity as they possess lies in their relationship with each other rather than in their external relationships. In facing the external world, they draw on each other, for their strongest emotional investment is made where there is continuity.

Mobility makes nonhousehold relationships discontinuous, but "emotional investment" follows continuous lines therefore mobile people are more involved with their spouses. Key concepts such as "continuity" and "emotional investment" are not clearly defined, but the basic prediction relating mobility and the marital bond is clear.Table 4-6 shows the relation between spousal involvement and the number of different towns and cities the respondent has lived in; the latter seemed to be the measure of mobility that best expressed Bott's idea of continuity. It can be assumed that the continuity of relations with nonhousehold members would be seriously affected by a move from one town to another. In general the data in Table 4-6 support Bott's hypothesis. Clearly, among the respondents thirty to fifty-nine years of age those who have lived in three or more places seem more involved in their spouses. The lack of significant results for those seventeen to twenty-nine does not necessarily contradict Bott; the question used in the interview did not allow us to categorize respondents on the basis of the number of places lived since marriage, but since birth; this failure would be especially crucial for the younger respondents, more of whose moves probably occurred before marriage. It is best, therefore, not to consider the young respondents. In general, then, our data support Bott's idea that involvement is related to continuity.

The problem we are discussing is why only 42 percent of the spouses are thought about by our respondents, It has been suggested that this might be due: 1) to the fact that the characteristics relevant to mate selection may be irrelevant to being able to adjust in old age, and that therefore aging wives may have to seek help from people other than the spouse who have the needed resources, and 2) if families are not mobile, then continuity is not limited to the marriage relationship. Our comments perhaps shed some light on the problem, but it is still far from clear why so many spouses are not frequently thought about. It is possible that the "think about" question, contrary to what we hoped, measured only positive involvement. Wives might have mentioned their spouses only if they were happily married. Even though people may think about people they dislike, they may suppress the memories of such fantasies. It remains a question whether the problem is why so many wives dislike their spouses or why so many are relatively uninvolved with their spouses. In either case, more research is needed that attempts to measure the involvement, as defined in Chapter One, of husband and wives with each other. Why are so few spouses mentioned in response to the "think about" question?

THE QUALITY OF INVOLVEMENT

In the last section we discussed the distribution of involvement—whether respondents are involved with people they live with, and whether they are involved with their children and their husband. The question was simply whether or not involvement existed. Now we shall begin a consideration of the quality of this involvement. In what ways are our respondents involved with their family?

COMMUNICATION

About each person a respondent thought about we asked: "Do you discuss your really personal problems with (person mentioned)?" We used this question as an indicator of the extent to which involvement is based on knowledge.

There are some problems in using the discussion question as a measure of knowledge. Besides the fact that some people will lie, a positive answer does not always mean the same thing, i.e., a person might reveal much more of herself in some discussions than in others. Moreover, this question examines a relationship from only one side; it tells us nothing about how much the other person reveals to our respondent. Finally, inter-personal knowledge is not totally dependent on self-revelation; some people will know us better than others simply because they have lived with us, and had more occasions to observe us. Still, it seems clear that a positive response to the discussion question indicates that interpersonal knowledge exists in a relationship.

Table 4-7 shows the frequency respondents discuss their personal problems with different categories of people. The distinctiveness of the marital relationship in American society is clearly indicated by the extremely high percentage of respondents who discuss their personal problems with their husbands; of course, we must remember that only half of the existing spouses are thought about. As we would expect, revelation to children increases as the children age; the fact that any revelation occurs with children under seven is surprising, and might simply indicate the looseness with which some people interpreted the question. The data do indicate the problem of children; they are objects of maternal involvement, but until they become teenagers no signifi-

TABLE 4–7

PERCENT OF TYPES OF PEOPLE WHO ARE THOUGHT ABOUT WITH WHOM RESPONDENTS DISCUSS THEIR PERSONAL PROBLEMS[1]

Type of person thought about		Percent with whom discuss personal problems	
		%	N
Spouses		91	(147)
Others living with respondents (excluding own children)		61	(13)
Others not living with respondents (excluding children)		55	(718)
Children:	0–4 years old:		
	at home	9	(56)
	other	—	(9)
	5–6 years old:		
	at home	35	(26)
	other	—	(1)
	7–13 years old:		
	at home	42	(60)
	other	—	(3)
	14–16 years old:		
	at home	57	(21)
	other	—	(2)
	17 and over:		
	at home	69	(48)
	other	64	(104)

1. We excluded persons thought about for whom there was a "no response" on the discussion question or the question asking respondents to list the members of their household. In this table we are referring only to respondents coded as either white or black.

cant personal communication takes place with most of them. Women can be involved with their environment and yet feel lonely, because often they are involved with children who are incapable of understanding them. For those women who believe that being understood as a person is a major part of personal relationships,involvement with children can be a cause of loneliness.

On the other hand more self-revelation takes place with adult children than with other adults, excluding spouses of course. However, the differences are small. Respondents discuss their problems with 69 percent of the adult children at home and with 61 percent of all others at home who are thought about; the difference of 8 percent is small. The difference between adult children not at home and other adults not living with the respondent is only 9 percent. Among people significant enough to be thought about, self-revelation does not seem more likely to children than to other types of acquaintances. Personal communication distinguishes only the husband-wife relation.

It is quite clear from Table 4-7 that the quality of the parent-child relation changes as the child ages. The older the child the more likely he or she is to be a confidant for our respondents.

It might be asked how meaningful can the discussion question be when 35 percent of the children five to six years of age are supposedly confidants for their mothers. It is possible that our respondents answered the question too hastily. But there are several other explanations. Perhaps, when children are young, mothers tell them their problems, but without expecting any answers; talking to young children who cannot help may be better than talking to four walls. It is also possible that mothers may discuss their problems in only a superficial way with young children. Again, it is possible that in some cases the mother's problems involve the children, making some mothers treat children like adults. In a study of lower-class families, Pavenstedt found that in thirty stable families parents did not seem to distinguish between children and adults—"they projected adult comprehension and responses onto the infants, sometimes even the newborn."[6] Future studies of communication should not overlook the possibility that in daily life some people may not distinguish between children and adults.

Despite the fact that children are communicated with even at a young age, the fact should not be lost sight of that one-third of the adult children thought about are not confidants for the mothers. Children, on the whole, never seem to reach the level of confidence experienced by husbands.

The very high percentage of thought-about husbands with whom respondents discuss their problems raises the issue whether the "think about" question is measuring only positive involvement. Theoretically, people who are loved or hated should be thought about. But only a loved person is likely to be a confidant. The high percentage of spouses with whom the respondents communicate could be explained, then, in two ways: 1) The "think about"

TABLE 4–8

PERCENT OF PEOPLE THOUGHT ABOUT WITH WHOM RESPONDENT DISCUSSES PERSONAL PROBLEMS

(By age and color of respondent.[1])

Age	Color			
	White		Black	
	%	N	%	N
17–19	—	(9)	57	(30)
20–29	50	(22)	47	(303)
30–39	60	&85')	57	(245)
40–49	61	(52)	64	(143)
50–59	61	(72)	67	(72)
60–74	63	(92)	54	(83)
75 and over	52	(20)	—	(5)

1. Totals on which percentages are based do not include cases in which the respondents did not answer the question about with whom they discuss their personal problems.

question reflects only positive involvement; 2) Our respondents do not continue to live with spouses they hate, so they are likely to feel either love or indifference or something in between toward their husbands, but not hate. Our data do not allow us to choose between these explanations. It is possible, therefore, that the "think about" question is biased and indicates only positive involvement.

Komarovsky has discussed the network of confidants that existed in her lower-class sample. "Two-thirds of the wives had at least one person apart from their husbands in whom they confide deeply personal experiences. In 35 percent of the cases the wife...shares some significant segment of her life *more fully* with her confidants than with her husband."[7] The evidence from our study certainly does not contradict this description. In Table 4-1 it can be seen what percent of the fantasy refers to people who are not members of the nuclear family (column 3); in fact, this percentage is an underestimation, since it does not include the nonnuclear-family people living with the respondent who are thought about. Except for middle-aged whites, it is over 45 percent. In other words, it is certainly true that our respondents are involved with many individuals who come from outside their nuclear families. If, now, we look at Table 4-7 it can be seen that respondents discuss their personal problems with 55 percent of those people who do not live with the respondents and who are not the respondents's children. Our data, therefore, support Komarovksy's point that lower class women are involved in a network of relationships outside the nuclear family in which they discuss their personal experiences.

TABLE 4–9

PERCENT OF CERTAIN TYPES OF PEOPLE WHOM RESPONDENTS THINK ABOUT, AND WITH WHOM THEY DISCUSS PERSONAL PROBLEMS

(By age and color of respondent)

	Age and color					
Type of people	40–59		60–74		75 and over	
	White	Black	White	Black	White	Black
	% N	% N	% N	% N	% N	% N
Spouse	94 (17)	88 (25)	— (5)	— (2)	— (2)	— (1)
Adult children at home	87 (15)	56 (16)	— (2)	— (2)	— (0)	— (0)
Away	48 (23)	67 (18)	86 (21)	60 (20)	67 (12)	— (2)
Other adults not living with respondents	54 (52)	64 (131)	46 (56)	50 (54)	29 (54)	— (1)

What is the quality of our respondents' pattern of involvement? Table 4-8 shows the percent of all the people thought about with whom the respondents discuss their personal problems. Overall there is a curvilinear relation with age; young and old communicate with fewer people with whom they are involved than do the middle-aged. For the young respondents the low percentage no doubt reflects the difficulty of communicating with children. Among women fifty years of age and over the main categories of confidants are spouses, adult children, and other nonhousehold adults. Table 4-9 shows the percent of people in each of these categories with whom respondents discuss their personal problems. The numbers in the cells of the table are small; moreover, it must be remembered that the cell frequencies refer not to respondents but confidants so that the number of respondents referred to in each cell is no doubt smaller than the number shown. The data can only be viewed as suggestive, but they do seem to help us in understanding the meaning of Table 4-8. As can be seen in Table 4-9 spouses become insignificant for respondents sixty and over; in part this is due to the death of spouses and in part to the apparently low involvement among old spouses in our sample. The significance of this loss is magnified among black women, because it accompanies a general decline in self-revelation; older black women in our sample seem to communicate less often with both adult children and nonhousehold adults. On the other hand, white women seem to compensate for the loss of spouse by dramatically increasing the frequency with which they communicate with their adult children who live away from home; the frequency increases from 48 percent to 86 percent. In part, then, the lower frequency of self-revelation among black women in the sixty to seventy-four age range seems due to their failure to increase communication with their adult children as they enter old age.

The low frequency of communication among the white women seventy-four and over is due to a general decline in self-revelation. It can not be forgotten that the truly elderly women who are left in a place like Kilbourn-town might never in their lives have experienced much communication. Our study has not been able to follow the same people over time; therefore we cannot conclude that the respondents, who are now sixty to seventy-four years old, when they are over seventy-four will show a decline in self-revelation. The type of person who is seventy-five or more and lives in Kilbourntown might be quite different from the type of person who is a resident of K-3 and in the sixty to seventy-four age range. But one of our purposes in this chapter is to develop a tentative model for a "natural history of familial involvement." To accomplish this we are acting *as if* we had studied the same people throughout their lives.

It is important to note that in at least one-third of the cases the people thought about are not confidants. There is ample basis for feelings of loneliness in Kilbourntown, if we define loneliness as a sense of not being known as we perceive ourselves. Our homemakers are involved in many relationships in which they do not reveal what is most important to them. Such impersonal involvements would seem highly likely to produce a sense of loneliness. It is possible that the effect of noncommunication varies depending on the social object, i.e., depending on whether a person is involved with God, a deceased relative, a young child, and so on. But the refinement of an understanding concerning the cause of loneliness suggested by this line of reasoning we leave to another time.

Moreover, our data no doubt overestimate how much communication does take place. The general point that husbands and wives in the United States do communicate is supported by the work of Blood and Wolfe. They report in their study of Detroit house-wives that 40 percent of the wives said their husbands tell them about events at work daily, 37 percent said it happened at least once a week, and only 7 percent said their husbands never tell them about their work.[8] But both our study and the Detroit study have at least two major weaknesses: 1) there was no measure of actual information transferred, and 2) there was no control on the significance of the specific events discussed. A study that did seek specific information was reported by Babchuk and Bates. They asked thirty-nine couples to name close, mutual friends. Of the 277 friends mentioned, 118 were listed by both spouses. Over half of the supposed "mutual friends" were not mentioned by both spouses.[9] No doubt other studies of husband-wife communication on specific topics would, also, reveal considerable ignorance of each other's thoughts.

Because of its vagueness and perhaps because some of our respondents thought they "should" be discussing their problems with their close relatives and friends, and therefore gave the socially right but not the true answer, the discussion question probably overestimates the amount of self-revelation that takes place. Given this fact, why did our question reveal as much noncommunication as it did? First, there is the obvious problem with children: until they mature, meaningful communication is not possible. Second, it seems likely that some people restrict self-revelation in order to differentiate the spousal relationship. In her study of working-class families, Komarovsky reported the following:

> The young woman made a deliberate effort, after her engagement, to become more reserved with her mother. "I wanted," she explained, "to feel closer to John than to Mother, so that when we are all together I would exchange a look of understanding with him and not with her."[10]

This woman regulated her flow of communication to develop a desired pattern of involvement; no doubt there are norms, however vague, that outline some rank-order of involvement, and these are reflected in the pattern of communication. Third, the pattern of communication is probably related to liking as suggested by Jourard;[11] communication, then, would be greatest in the spousal relation, because of all family relations it is the most freely chosen; it is the most voluntary relation, and therefore the one most based on liking as opposed to role-obligation. Giving information is a way of solidifying a relationship, so we would be more likely to reveal ourselves in relationships that are more intrinsically satisfying, i.e., we tend to communicate freely to the extent an object is a direct source of reward and therefore liked. The distribution of self-revelation, therefore, is likely to reflect both relevant norms about communication and the liking pattern. For our respondents the result of probably these and other processes is that between one-third and one half, depending on age, of their involvement is impersonal.

POWER

By power is meant the extent to which one person determines the life of another. No one has succeeded yet in devising an adequate measure of this concept. In our case we used two questions: "Which person do you most often go to for advice when you have money problems?" And: "Which person do you most often go to for advice when you have family problems?" The responses used by the interviewer were: "solves own problem," "goes to no *one* person," and "goes to someone." If the interviewee went to someone, we asked about the respondent's relation to her advisor.

There are some obvious problems with our measure of power. First, it is assumed that the advisors' comments will actually affect our respondents' behavior. Second, even if the question does reflect power, it fails to indicate, except crudely, the amount of power. If someone's advice about money problems is followed, to what extent does that determine our respondents' behavior? We cannot tell. Third, the questions refer only to extraordinary circumstances; they do not tell us who is shaping the everyday life of our respondents. Although true, this last criticism is not as significant as might first appear, because: (a) controlling what a person does at moments of crisis affects the total pattern of a person's life; day-to-day influences only modify this pattern; so, giving advice on whether a mother should work can result in a totally new family arrangement, which daily decisions would only modify, and b) a person's *sense* of dependence on another is probably determined more by what happens at these moments of heightened self-consciousness than by daily, often little-noticed events. We think, therefore, that from the point-of-view of both objective and subjective involvement, it is meaningful to measure power by asking about the people our respondents go to when they have significant problems.

We restricted our questions to the two types of problems most likely to be universal in a low-income area. It should be noted that our questions do not prejudge who might be significant in a person's life. One of the weaknesses of some measures of family power is that the questions assume that power resides either with the husband or the wife, i,e., within the nuclear family; we make no assumptions about the distribution of power. (It is true that the questions are worded to force the respondent to name someone; this was done because we feared that a more permissive question would have resulted in everyone saying they go to no one; however, our alternative responses did allow for such an answer, so that the interviewers did not feel compelled to force the respondent to name someone.) It is important to remember that everyone in the course of life faces family and money problems. These problems have arisen in our respondents' lives, and someone has determined their reactions. Who?

Table 4-10 shows the percentage of respondents who seek advice for either money or family problems. Regarding money matters there is some difference between whites and blacks in the middle years, with the blacks seeking advice more often. Concerning family problems the most striking fact is the small percentage (5 percent) of black women sixty to seventy-four who seek advice on family matters; among the whites there is a slight decrease among the older people. The most important point, however, is that the overwhelming majority of our respondents said they solve their own problems.

In their survey of Detroit housewives Blood and Wolfe asked: "Every wife has some days when things go so badly that she gets pretty tense and upset. After you've had a bad day, what do you do to get it out of your system?" Only 33 percent mentioned some form of interaction with others. The authors conclude: "Clearly, most housewives cope with bad days on their own. Their most characteristic device is to go to bed early, to sit down and relax, or just try to forget about their troubles. Reading and television are common distractions at home, with going for a walk the favorite way of getting out of the house."[12]

Similarly, in a study done in Cleveland with both working-and middle-class families, Sussman found that only 31 percent of the respondents reported giving or receiving advice on personal or business matters; this study gathered data only on the respondents's relation to kin, but, as our study suggests, this is probably the major source of advice.[13] When we combined responses to our two advice questions, we found that about 30 percent have sought advice from someone on at least one problem. The rough similarity of percentages from Blood and Wolfe, Sussman, and our research suggests that our results are valid.

It is usual in family research to assume that inter-personal power exists between spouses, and that what is not known is the distribution of this power between husband and wife. For instance, a researcher might select a list of topics related to family behaviour, e.g., whether to buy a home or should children work, and ask who decides these questions. Power is measured by the frequency a spouse makes a decision. There are certain obvious difficulties with

TABLE 4–10

PERCENT WHO SEEK ADVICE FROM ANOTHER PERSON ON MONEY
AND ON FAMILY PROBLEMS

(By age and color of respondent)

Age	Money problems White		Black		Family problems White		Black	
	%	N	%	N	%	N	%	N
17–19	—	(3)	76	(11)	—	(3)	36	(11)
20–29	27	(11)	26	(133)	18	(11)	24	(133)
30–39	16	(25)	24	(110)	16	(25)	26	(111)
40–49	15	(26)	22	(69)	23	(26)	17	(69)
50–59	24	(33)	33	(34)	13	(32)	21	(34)
60–74	23	(47)	24	(38)	15	(48)	5	(38)
75 plus	10	(20)	—	(2)	10	(20)	—	(2)
No response	—	(3)	—	(8)	—	(3)	—	(8)
		(168[1])		(405[2])		(168[1])		(405[2])

1. One white respondent said she talked with several different people.

2. Four black respondents said they talked with several other people or gave no response.

SOLIDARITY IN A SLUM

this approach which need not be discussed here (e.g., how to select the topics). What our results, and to some extent the results of the Detroit study, suggest is that many problems faced by adults never reach any stage requiring a dyadic or group decision. Much more than research seems to allow, people try to solve their own problems; they do not allow the matter to develop to the point that a joint decision is required. Too much sociological research assumes a complete social distribution of power; our results suggest the opposite; more than we realize, people determine their own lives.

Such statements as were just made may be called sociologically naive. It is true that to talk about a person determining his own life is to oversimplify. What we want to emphasize is that apparently a significant number of problems are solved or ameliorated without individuals believing that they had been directly dependent on the intentional acts of others.

Power requires that we be determined by acts of others, which acts, in turn, are controlled by these other people. Apparently many people do not experience this type of event, contrary to what sociologists are prone to assume. It might be argued that our respondents simply misrepresented their situations; people do not like to admit dependence, so they "forget" it. Or, perhaps people do not often seek advice, but they are in fact constantly receiving it, but in little doses, so that it goes unrecognized. No doubt people do "forget," and no doubt advice oozes through the social structures. We still contend, however, that given the overwhelming majority of respondents who said they solve their own problems, sociologists must spend more time determining the extent to which interpersonal power exists, before exploring the form of distribution for whatever social power does exist.

To whom do the respondents go for advice other than themselves? Table 4-11 presents the relevant data. Regardless of type of problem or color of respondent, a majority of advice comes from outside the nuclear family. Perhaps because the two types of problems often involve members of the immediate family, their advice is not sought. This would help us understand why so many of the respondents solve their own problems. For instance, their problems might often involve their spouse in such a way as to prevent his being used as a source of advice. In some cases, in fact, the problem might be the spouse. But since he is the person with whom our respondents are most likely to be open with, the husband's involvement in the problem might result in the wives feeling a sense of "nowhere to turn." From this perspective, the respondents' independence is the result of the absence of suitable sources of advice.

Overall, about 25 percent of the advice comes from an impersonal source, such as a welfare worker, a lawyer, or a doctor, while the greatest source is clearly the extended family: siblings, parents, and other relatives. At least one-third of the advice on a problem comes from this category, and for family problems over half of the advice sought by black respondents was from the

TABLE 4–11

RELATION OF PEOPLE RESPONDENTS SEEK ADVICE FROM ON
MONEY AND ON FAMILY PROBLEMS

(By color of respondent)

Relation	Money problems		Family problems	
	White(N=35)	Black(N=101)	White(N=27)	Black(N=85)
Spouse (or other adult in residence)[1]	31%	19%	11%	1%
Children	9	7	11	3
Siblings	14	14	4	14
Parents not living with the respondents	11	14	7	26
Other relatives	9	5	22	17
Friends	6	8	19	15
Impersonal sources	20	33	26	24

1. Our coding does not allow us to differentiate spouses from other adults in residence with respondent (children excluded); we assume most of those mentioned are spouses.

extended family. The immediate family of spouse and children is a significant source of advice only among whites in matters of money, in which case 40 percent of the advice is from the nuclear family. Table 4-12 shows the same data as Table 4-11 except that the former is limited to cases in which the

TABLE 4–12

RELATION OF PEOPLE RESPONDENTS SEEK ADVICE FROM ON
MONEY AND ON FAMILY PROBLEMS BY COLOR OF RESPONDENT

(For married respondents only)

Relation	Money problems		Family problems	
	White(N=20)	Black(N=56)	White(N=12)	Black(N=41)
Spouse (or other adult in residence)	55%	31%	25%	2%
Children	5	6	8	0
Siblings	10	10	0	7
Parents not living with respondents	5	12	8	20
Other relatives	10	7	25	24
Friends	0	4	8	22
Impersonal sources	15	30	25	24

SOLIDARITY IN A SLUM

respondent is married. The overall pattern in the two tables is the same. White women make more use of their husbands than do black women. In fact, regarding family problems almost 5 percent of the black married respondents seek advice outside even the extended family: they go to friends or impersonal sources. Although the husband-wife relation among blacks and whites does not significantly differ regarding communication, there appears to be a difference on power; black wives less often seek advice from their spouses.

If we compare money and family problems, the latter more often force respondents outside even the extended family. Almost half the help sought on family problems comes from friends and impersonal sources. There seems to be a process at work that makes involvement self-limiting. What we mean is this: As people become involved with others, say the family, more and more problems will be related to the family; but since apparently people seek advice outside the institutional source of problems, as family problems increase involvement in some other institutional area will increase. It appears as if individuals try to segregate the source of a problem from the advisor on a problem. As a result, involvement in any one institution or group will tend to be self-limiting.

For our respondents the result is a scattering of involvement outside the family.

The fact that even for whites the nuclear family does not dominate the advice pattern is consistent with Gans's comment on spouses living in a lower-class Boston district: "They take their troubles less to each other than to brothers, sisters, other relatives, or friends."[14] Similarly Komarovsky, based on an intensive study of sixty lower-class families, concluded that "these men and women do not turn to one another for emotional support. ..."[15] Not only do our respondents tend to solve their own problems, but they also tend, with the exception of white women who have money problems, to go outside the nuclear family when they do seek advice.

Table 4-13 shows the rank order for the various sources of advice. Clearly the professional sources stand out over any one familial category; only the spouse approximates the significance of professional people in guiding our slum respondents. This fact underlines the necessity, especially in lower-class families, of not assuming that significant decisions are made within the family.

The rank order on money problems is very similar for whites and blacks, but the two aggregates differ somewhat on how they solve family problems. As already noted, the spouse has an insignificant role to play for the black women who have family problems; on the other hand their parents are dramatically more important for them than for whites. A word of warning is, however, needed; this difference in the importance of parents reflects, at least in part, the different age structures for whites and blacks. The relatively small number of people who seek help made a detailed color-age analysis useless, but

TABLE 4–13

RANK ORDER OF TYPES OF PEOPLE RESPONDENTS SEEK ADVICE
FROM ON MONEY AND ON FAMILY PROBLEMS

Relation	Money problems		Family problems	
	White	Black	White	Black
Spouse (or adult in residence)	1	2	4	7
Children	5	6	4	6
Siblings	3	3	7	5
Parents not living with respondents	4	3	6	1
Other relatives	5	7	2	3
Friends	7	5	3	4
Impersonal sources	2			2

(By color of respondent)

we must not forget that the white population is much older. This no doubt accounts at least for some of the difference between whites and blacks regarding parental significance. On the other hand the similarity of rank order for the two color-aggregates on money problems suggests that age differences are not the whole explanation for differences regarding family problems. Moreover the greater significance of parents for black women fits the general finding that the black respondents are more involved with their extended family. It should be remembered, however, that this difference does not exist for money problems; greater black dependence on extended kin occurs only for the more personal family problems.

The slightly greater significance of "children" for the whites is probably explainable in terms of the greater age of the white children. It is interesting that siblings decline in relative importance as we shift from money to family problems; on the other hand, "other relatives" and friends gain importance. The sibling bond seems to have primarily "instrumental" significance. This suggests that being a brother or sister remains significant primarily for the material demands we can make on the basis of a close blood tie. This limited utility suggests that with the increasing professionalization of society the sibling relationship will decline in importance.

We note with interest that spouses are distinguished from other types of people by the frequency they are thought about and are recipients of communication, but not by the frequency they are asked for advice. What type of discussion occurs between spouses? Is it restricted to problem-expression and the elicitation of sympathy?

TABLE 4–14

PERCENT WHO SEEK ADVICE FROM ANOTHER PERSON ON MONEY
AND ON FAMILY PROBLEMS FOR BLACKS

(By age of respondent and years in Milwaukee)

Age	Years in Milwaukee	Percent who seek advice			
		Money		Family	
		%	N	%	N
17–29	1–5	31	(71)	22	(71)
	6–15	15	(55)	18	(55)
	16 or more	53	(19)	50	(18)
30–39	1–5	25	(16)	19	(16)
	6–15	29	(68)	29	(68)
	16 or more	7	(28)	21	(28)
40 or over	1–5	36	(11)	27	(11)
	6–15	27	(55)	16	(55)
	16 or more	21	(76)	11	(76)

WHO SEEKS HELP

We found it difficult to understand what determined whether a person seeks advice from someone. First, we thought that perhaps such behavior is related to the severity of the problem, but we found no consistent relation between level of income and whether or not our respondents seek advice on money problems. Second, we thought that seeking advice might reflect the degree of personal resources our respondents have; so, we anticipated that better-educated people would more often solve their own problems; no support was found for this hypothesis. Similarly, we thought that working people would be more independent; no justification for this idea was found in our analysis.

It seemed almost natural to us that mobility would be related to seeking advice. It was reasoned that newcomers to a community would not have developed confidence in the people living in the new ciy, and therefore would not seek advice as often as less recent residents. For the entire sample of 623 women the percentage seeking advice among those who had lived one to five years in Milwaukee is 31 percent; for the rest of the sample it is 22 percent; contrary to our expectations, it appears that newcomers sought more advice.

Table 4-14 presents a more detailed analysis of the relation between mobility and seeking advice. It refers only to blacks; there were too few white cases for analysis. There is no consistent pattern in the table. Our basic conclusion must be that length of residence is unimportant; it does not seem to affect the way a woman solves her problem. There are, in retrospect, some obvious reasons why we are wrong about the significance of mobility: 1) Most people solve their own problems, whether stable or mobile; 2) Most advice is sought within family relationships, which seem able to endure in spite of mobility; and 3) It is possible that the lower class in a welfare society are accustomed to seeking advice via the service structure of impersonal, formal relationships, and so is not "at a loss" when in a new city.

There are, however, a few aspects of Table 4-14 worth noting. Among the seventeen to twenty-nine year-olds, for instance, an unusually high percentage of those who have lived in Milwaukee just about all their lives, i.e., sixteen or more years, seek advice. These life-long residents are probably just continuing a pattern of dependence developed while they lived with their parents. For older respondents, length of residence seems negatively related to seeking help. It is only among the young that long-term residents more often seek advice. Perhaps for young people mobility does what time away from the parental household eventually accomplishes anyway; either mobility or time can wean young people from their dependence on their parents.

Only the youngest age category has more than twenty newcomers. Within that category there is a considerable difference between newcomers and those that have lived in Milwaukee from six to fifteen years regarding the percent who seek help on money matters. (The life-time residents in this age category have already been discussed.) The difference is 16 percent for money problems, while it is only 6 percent for family problems. It is quite possible that newcomers experience pressing financial problems that the respondent herself must solve but for which purpose she lacks the necessary resources. Thus, newcomers might be forced to seek advice on financial problems because of their ignorance of the job market, the absence of friends they can temporarily borrow money from, or ignorance about existing welfare services. But there is no evidence suggesting a similar process for respondents over thirty. However, this could be due to the greater experience of older people, which minimizes the impact of mobility.

In the last paragraph we implicitly acknowledged that people may seek help but not advice. For instance, someone when in financial need may get a job; but, if asked whether she sought advice from someone, she might answer negatively; she knew what she had to do; she had to get a job. From the point of view of power, however, the company this woman now works for has some power over her. The company will, to some extent, shape this woman's life. The advice questions, then, are in no way a complete measure of power. What these questions do give is an indication of the respondents' awareness of being very dependent on another person or organization. To seek advice is 1) to be conscious of power, and 2) to be more dependent on another than is true if one simply works for a company or the like. When we seek advice on an important problem, we give the advisor more power over us than any single person from whom we receive help is likely to have. To seek advice is to give our lives into the hands of another. Few of our respondents did this.

Finally with regard to Table 4-14, there is a tendency among those thirty and over to seek less help if they have lived in Milwaukee sixteen or more years. The respondents thirty to thirty-nine years old, who have lived at least sixteen years in Milwaukee, stand out; only 7 percent seek advice on money problems. Overall in the table there is a tendency for older, long-term residents to seek less help. It is possible that there is such a thing as a settling-in, closing-out process. When people have resided in a city for a long time, they settle in, i.e., they learn what resources are available and how to use them; moreover, fewer problems might arise, because they have developed a set pattern of life acceptable to all in the family. At the same time, both because they are more able to handle their own problems, and because they have fewer problems, these older long-term residents seek less advice from others, thereby closing out others from their lives. These people settle in, and close out others.

These ideas relating mobility and advice-seeking are very tentative. The results in Table 4-14 are distinguished mainly by the absence of any overall pattern. It is quite possible that mobility has no effect on advice-seeking.

The main point of our discussion of power is how little social power seems to exist. As already noted the advice questions probably indicate only the existence of a conscious, high dependence on another. Still, the data do suggest that sociologists have too glibly assumed the interdependence of everyone. The "advice" questions suggest we should give more attention to self-involvement; our respondents appear more dependent on themselves than any other person. This phenomenon of self-involvement is poorly conceptualized in sociology and is usually not even admitted.[16]

THE MOTHER-CHILD RELATION

The most crucial involvement in American society is that between a mother and her children. We wanted to explore this relationship in particular. But how?

We are especially interested in the variables that affect the distribution of interpersonal knowledge in a complex society. Our interest in knowledge stems from previous attempts to study loneliness. We have defined loneliness as a sense of not being known as we perceive ourselves.[17] Loneliness is a truly modern problem, yet there is little significant research examining the distribution of interpersonal knowledge in the urban world.

Previous studies tell us little about what produces interpersonal knowledge: Luckey points to the variable of length of time a relationship has lasted and Jourard suggests that self-disclosure varies with the degree to which a person likes another (which process, however, is probably countered by the tendency to romanticize people we like).[18] All in all, however, we know little about the distribution of knowledge in our society or about the conditions that affect this distribution. The centrality of loneliness to an understanding of urban society suggests the desirability of research on this subject. Our work was meant to add a little more light on this basic problem.

Especially, we studied the mother's knowledge of her child. We did not have much time in the interview to spend on this subject, and we could interview only the mother. In addition, we had the problem of how to determine the accuracy of the mother's knowledge, since we could not interview the child. It seemed that we needed a question that was: 1) straight-forward and factual so that it would be a little difficult for the interviewee to lie; 2) that was about some significant aspect of the child's life, but 3) that was not central to the American concept of motherhood so that the respondent could admit ignorance without feeling guilty. We finally asked about the child's friend-a topic that we thought best fit our criteria. Each respondent was asked: "whom does (name of child) go around with most often?" This was asked for each living child the respondent had borne. In this section we shall only be concerned about the children living at home.

In coding the answers we used a number of categories that for present purposes we have reduced to three: gave a positive answer, said did not know, and no response. The interviewers had been specifically instructed to write in "D.K.", if the respondent said she did not know, but apparently many interviewers neglected this. We had the problem, then, of deciding what to do with the blank responses. Although we believed that in the majority of cases a blank meant ignorance, it also seemed that some interviewers did not always ask the question (specifically, at least one white interviewer appeared not to ask the question for children over twenty-one). In order to avoid arbitrary decisions, therefore, we excluded blanks from our analysis. Table 4-15 presents the percent of our respondents' children by their color and age whose mother did not know about their friend; since we believe that at least for those below twenty-one a blank also means ignorance we present in brackets the percentage of children for whom we have either a "D.K." or a blank response. The bracketed figure, we believe, expresses the degree of ignorance in K-3; however, for the remainder of our analysis we shall exclude the blanks, and consider only the cases that were coded "don't know" or for which we have a positive answer. We have used only cases in which the child is the respondent's by birth; other children, even if living with the respondent, are not considered.

As can be seen in Table 4-15 there are only minor differences associated with color; the white subsamples are small, but there is a consistent trend for the whites to be somewhat less ignorant. However, the important distinctions are between age aggregates. We found no significant difference between male and female children. Regardless of color or sex of child, as the child gets older fewer mothers know their children's friends.

Overall, less than a third of the children have a mother who said she did not know the child's friend. Given the fact, however, that this information is rather elementary, our results suggest a considerable amount of maternal ignorance in Kilbourntown.[19]

While considering the data about the friends of our respondents' children, we were struck by the infrequency of these children having siblings as their friends. Table 4-16 shows how many mothers reported that their children's friends were siblings and the frequency the mothers said simply "the family" in response to the question about their children's friend. Among very young children there is a high degree of sibling solidarity, but this falls off quickly as the child's age increases. According to the mothers' reports, then, sibling solidarity seems inconsequential once children are old enough to go about the neighborhood on their own. This topic is worth further investigation. Why is it that young people who eat and sleep together seem not to "pal around" together? An investigation of this would shed light on such topics as the incest taboo and the nature of friendship and love.

TABLE 4–15

PERCENT OF CHILDREN WHOSE FRIEND IS NOT KNOWN
BY MOTHER

(By age of child and color of child)

| Age of child | Color | | | |
| | White | | Black | |
	%	N	%	N
0–4	11	(19)	17	(184)
5–6	17	(18)	18	(117)
7–13	11	(80)[23%][1]	18	(355)[26%]
14–18	26	(31)[36%]	32	(135)[35%]
19–21	31	(13)[48%]	35	(23)[40%]
22 plus	58	(12)	65	(26)
No response	—	(5)	—	(19)
		(178[2])		(859[3])

1. In brackets are the percentages of total cases for a category that were either left blank by the interviewer or in which the mother said she did not know her child's friend; these percentages are given only for the age aggregates for which a blank was most likely to represent ignorance. Before we grouped the children we examined ignorance by year of age. The aggregates we used, in our opinion, reflect either "natural" groupings (our breaking points represent significant changes in ignorance) or common sense (e.g., separation of 0–6 years from 7–13).

2. Because of blanks we had to exclude thirty eight cases.

3. Because of blanks we had to exclude seventy nine cases.

TABLE 4–16

PERCENT OF REFERENCES TO "FAMILY" OR A SIBLING AS BEING CHILD'S FRIEND

	(By age of child and color of respondent)									
	Percent "family"[1]				Percent sibling				Total	
Age of child	White		Black		White		Black		White	Black
	%	N	%	N	%	N	%	N	%	%
0–4	5	(19)	8	(184)	16	(19)	28	(184)	21	36
5–6	0	(18)	6	(117)	0	(18)	9	(117)	0	15
7–13	0	(80)	3	(355)	0	(80)	4	(355)	0	7
14–18	0	(31)	1	(135)	0	(31)	1	(135)	0	2
19–21	0	(13)	0	(23)	0	(13)	9	(23)	0	9
22 plus	0	(12)	4	(26)	0	(12)	0	(26)	0	4

1. I.e. the percent of cases in which the mothers responded to the questions about their children's friends by saying "the family."

In light of the small subsample sizes among the whites the white-black differences in Table 4-16 seem too small to comment on.

It is important to remember that in this discussion of mothers' ignorance the tables are based on the child as the unit of analysis. This means that the number of mothers being discussed is always smaller than the number of cases, i.e., children, reported in the following tables.

IGNORANCE AMONG WHITES

Although there are relatively few data on white children, a clear pattern emerges.

The mothers' age is significantly related to ignorance—the older the mothers are, the less often they know their childrens' friends. Similarly, separated white mothers more often are ignorant than either divorced or married ones. Table 4-17 shows the percent of children whose friend is not known by the mother, according to her marital status and age. Considering only the married mothers, the effect of a mother's age can be seen; considering only the young mothers, the effect of marital status can be seen. Clearly, being separated and being forty or more in age is associated with ignorance.

It is possible that the mother's age is not itself important and that the association of ignorance with older women is due to the fact that older children are less well known. In Table 4-18 the separate effect of child's age and mother's age can be seen. Among the children between the ages of nine and thirteen we can see the effect of mother's age, while a consideration of children

TABLE 4–17

MARITAL STATUS, MOTHER'S AGE, AND PERCENT OF CHILDREN
WHOSE FRIEND IS "NOT" KNOWN BY MOTHER

(For whites only)

Marital status[1]	Mother's age			
	20–39 years		40–78 years	
	%	N	%	N
Married	3	(66)	22	(59)
Divorced	0	(12)	–	(3)
Separated	42	(19)	–	(9)[2]

1. There are too few "never married" and "widowed" cases to justify presentation of these categories.

2. The percentage is 67 percent.

whose mothers are forty or more shows a jump in ignorance for children nineteen or more years of age. If we compare Tables 4-15 and 4-18, it can be seen that there is an increase in maternal ignorance for children fourteen to eighteen years old in the former table but not in the latter. In Table 4-18 mother's age is controlled; the absence of an increase in ignorance among the fourteen to eighteen years olds in this table suggests that the increase found in Table 4-15 for children of this age is due to these children's having older

TABLE 4–18

AGE OF CHILD, MOTHER'S AGE AND PERCENT OF CHILDREN
WHOSE FRIEND IS NOT KNOWN BY MOTHER

(For married whites only.)

Marital status[1]	Age of child[2]	Mother's age			
		20–39 years		40 plus	
		%	N	%	N
Married	7–13	0	(37)	17	(18)
	14–18	–	(6)[3]	19	(16)
	19 plus	–	(2)	41	(17)

1. There are too few cases of divorced or separated status to analyze.

2. There are too few cases of children below seven years to analyze.

3. There is one case of ignorance.

THE HOUSEHOLD AND FAMILY

TABLE 4–19

WORK STATUS OF MOTHER, SOURCE OF INCOME FOR FAMILY, AND
PERCENT OF CHILDREN WHOSE FRIEND IS NOT KNOWN
BY MOTHER

	(For whites)							
Respondent's work status	Main source of income for family							
	Job		Social Security		Welfare		Other	
	%	N	%	N	%	N	%	N
Full-time	0	(17)	—	(1)	—	(1)	—	(0)
Part-time	—	(2)	—	(0)	—	(0)	—	(2)
Unemployed	—	(0)	—	(0)	—	(6)	—	(7)
Retired	—	(3)	—	(2)	—	(0)	—	(0)
Not looking	15	(86)	—	(4)	37	(32)	—	(4)

mothers and is not due to any significant developments in the child's way of life in mid-adolescence. But the data in Table 4-18 do support the idea that older children, i.e., adult children, are less known by their mothers.

Maternal ignorance of their children's friends, then, is associated with living in a separated home, being an older child, and having an older mother.

But these characteristics present only part of the picture. Before we interpret our results we must get a more complete overview of the white mothers who are ignorant of their children. Ignorance is also associated with having only a grade school or no education. This variable is independent of age, i.e., among both young and old mothers little education tends to mean ignorance. Because of our small subsamples it is impossible to meaningfully subdivide our tables further. We can not determine the specific variables that are most important in producing ignorance. What we can do, however, is to present a composite profile of white ignorant mothers. So far, then, ignorance of children's friends is associated with mothers who are: older, less educated (no more then eight years of schooling), and separated from their spouses.

Table 4-19 presents data on the relation between economic factors and ignorance. One obvious conclusion is that working does not seem to produce ignorance. On the contrary ignorance is associated with not looking for a job, but especially with being welfare recipients. The results of this table remain the same when age of child is controlled. (It should be noted, however, that only one child over 19 lives in a home dependent on welfare; the ignorance associated with older children cannot be explained by the attitude of welfare mothers.) There are relatively few cases of poverty among our whites; on the

SOLIDARITY IN A SLUM

TABLE 4–20

ABSENCE OF RESPONSE TO THE "PROUD" QUESTION, AS OF CHILD,
AND PERCENT OF CHILDREN WHOSE FRIEND IS NOT KNOWN
BY MOTHER

(For whites)				
Age of child[1]	Gave some answer to "proud" question		No answer[2]	
	%	N	%	N
7–13	5	(60)	35	(17)
14–18	0	(20)	80	(10)

1. There are too few cases in the other age ranges to analyze.

2. I.e. did not acknowledge pride in any phenomenon in response to the "proud" question.

basis of what information we do have there appears to be no relation between poverty and ignorance. Working, then, is associated with knowledge; being on welfare with maternal ignorance.

If we pool our information, the image of the ignorant mother that emerges is of a woman over forty, with little formal education, separated from her husband, and living on welfare. The statistical tools available to us did not allow us to determine the relative significance of each of these variables. We suggest, however, that there are two distinct processes represented in our data: 1) maternal ageing—as mothers get old, they lose interest in their children, perhaps because they have become interested in other things, or because they have already begun to disengage or because they have become disillusioned with family life; and 2) anomic white women gravitate to the slum; these ignorant mothers seem to be societal failures—they failed to go beyond elementary school, are separated (or were deserted) rather than divorced, and they fail to support themselves; we suggest that such women are anomic, i.e., without hope of success of any kind. In Table 4-20 we show the relation between ignorance and pride, as indicated by the previously discussed "proud" question. Clearly, for the age aggregates reported (and, although the numbers are small, the same results occur for the children aged five to six), ignorance is associated with the absence of pride on the part of the mother. It does not seem far-fetched to interpret these data to mean that at times ignorant mothers are hopeless women. It should be emphasized, however, that there seem to be two hypotheses about ignorance worth pursuing-one relates ignorance to maternal ageing, the other to anomie associated with little education, separation, and living on welfare. It is possible, of course, that both the disillusionment that comes with ageing and the hopelessness that comes from repeated social

THE HOUSEHOLD AND FAMILY

TABLE 4–21

AGE OF CHILD, MARITAL STATUS, AND AGE OF MOTHER, AND
PERCENT OF CHILDREN WHOSE FRIEND IS NOT KNOWN
BY MOTHER

(For blacks)

Age of Child	Marital status and age of mother					
	Married			Separated		
	20–29	30–39	Over 39	20–29	30–39	Over 39
	% N	% N	% N	% N	% N	% N
5–6	11 (43)	29 (32)	— (2)	6 (17)	— (7)	— (4)
7–13	5 (53)	24 (154)	19 (23)	3 (32)	24 (33)	37 (19)
14–18	— (0)	32 (69)	41 (22)	— (0)	10 (10)	33 (18)

failures lead to anomie, which produces mothers ignorant of children's friends.

However, this analysis does not explain the ignorance found about the friends of the older children living at home. The variables we have discussed are unable to explain the large number of mothers who were ignorant of the friends of their children who were nineteen or over. It is possible that older children who remain at home seek ways to establish that although still at home they are now adults and no longer children. One way to do this, perhaps, is to keep parents ignorant of leisure time associates and activities. This could be a way of asserting one's independence of the family, and thereby one's adult status.

MATERNAL IGNORANCE AMONG BLACKS

Just as ignorant white mothers perfectly fit our stereotype of the slum family, so black ignorant mothers with equal clarity do not fit this pattern. Table 4-17 contains data showing that among whites ignorance is associated with mothers being separated and being older. Table 4-21 contains data for the black sample relating child's age, mother's marital status, mother's age, and ignorance. Children below five are excluded, because it could be argued that it is not meaningful to ask about the best friend of such a young child (although it should be remembered that the actual question asked the respondent about the person her child went around with most often). Children nineteen and over are excluded, because for whites the variables of mother's age and marital status are not significant in explaining ignorance about these older children living at home; moreover, there are so few adult children living at home that detailed analyses on this subsample are not possible.

TABLE 4–22

PERCENT OF CHILDREN WHOSE FRIEND IS NOT KNOWN BY
MOTHER: BY AGE OF CHILD AND AGE OF MOTHER

	Age of mother							
Age of child	17–19		20–29		30–39		40 or over	
	%	N	%	N	%	N	%	N
0–6	—	(2)	12	(189)	26	(95)	9	(11)
7–13	—	(0)	6	(94)	23	(209)	22	(51)
14–18	—	(0)	—	(0)	30	(85)	34	(47)

(For blacks)

Contrary to what is true for whites, there is no consistent difference between the children with married mothers and those with separated mothers among black respondents. Holding age of mother and of child constant, there are six possible comparisons of married and separated cases in Table 4-21. In four of these comparisons the married mothers are more ignorant, in one comparison married and separated mothers are the same, and in one comparison the separated mothers are more ignorant. No matter how the data were analyzed, married women tended to be more ignorant than separated ones. However, the data were not completely consistent, as in Table 4-21; sometimes separated mothers were more ignorant. These inconsistencies have led us to reject marital status as an important variable for understanding the distribution of knowledge among black people.

Table 4-21 does suggest that a mother's age is important. The mothers in their twenties are dramatically less ignorant. Table 4-22 presents the data on mother's age a little more clearly. Young mothers definitely are less ignorant. An exception to the overall pattern of the table is the case of very young children with mothers forty or more years old; there the percentage is only 9 percent; however, there are only eleven children in this category. It is possible, of course, that older women who have very young children represent a distinct type of person; to give birth at such a relatively advanced age might indicate real love of children or at least dedication to the role of mother. Overall, however, there is a major difference between mothers in their twenties and all others. There is also a tendency for ignorance to increase as the child's age increases, especially among children whose mother is forty or more.

Why do these young mothers seem to know more? Among the whites, also, mother's age is significant; the small number of cases we have prevents reaching any firm conclusion about how similar the white mothers in their

TABLE 4–23

PERCENT OF CHILDREN WHOSE FRIEND IS NOT KNOWN BY
MOTHER BY WORK STATUS OF MOTHER AND SOURCE OF INCOME
FOR FAMILY

	Main source of income for family						
Respondent's work status	(For blacks)						
	Job		Social security		Welfare		Other[1]	
	%	N	%	N	%	N	%	N
Full-time work	22	(167)	—	(2)	—	(2)	—	(7)
Part-time work	29	(79)	—	(1)	—	(7)	—	(2)
Unemployed	13	(54)	—	(0)	6	(43)	—	(13)
Retired	—	(8)	—	(0)	—	(3)	—	(0)
Not looking	23	(274)	48	(16)	25	(131)	—	(50)

1. This category is not analyzed, because it refers to a variety of sources of income.

twenties are to those in their thirties, but it does seem that for whites the critical difference is between those below forty and those above forty. The fact that the critical age seems to be thirty for blacks and forty for whites confuses the issue. There is a definite indication, however, that something happens to both whites and blacks as they grow old that turns their attention away from children, regardless of the child's age. This seems to occur earlier for blacks. Is this due to a general decline of interest in life? Is it due to an increase in self-involvement? Is it due to a shift of involvement to other people? Is it due to a growing disillusionment with life, which hits black women at an earlier age?

Are black mothers on welfare more ignorant than those whose families are supported by income from a job? The answer is clearly "no." In Table 4-23 ignorance is not associated with either the work status of the respondent or the main source of family income. Among women neither working nor looking for a job, there is only a 2 percent difference between those whose source of income is from a job (usually the spouse's) and those whose source of income is welfare.

Clearly, we cannot evaluate white and black families by the same criteria. At least as far as our sample is concerned, the assumption that separation and living on welfare are signs of poor home life may have some validity for whites, although even among the whites neither a majority of children on welfare nor a majority from separated homes have ignorant mothers, but such an assumption seems useless for black families. Neither source of income nor marital

TABLE 4-24

PERCENT OF CHILDREN WHOSE FRIEND IS NOT KNOWN BY MOTHER BY AGE OF CHILD AND WORK STATUS OF MOTHER

(For blacks)[1]

Age of child	Not working		Working full-time			
			Including nights and/or weekends		Not including nights or weekends	
	%	N	%	N	%	N
0–4	17	(116)	20	(15)	—	(8)
5–6	19	(72)	9	(11)	9	(11)
7–13	22	(183)	17	(42)	20	(41)
14–18	34	(65)	30	(10)	29	(14)

1. Because of too few cases we did not include children nineteen or over, (N=49).

status, on the basis of our data, are good indicators of the quality of family relations. Of course, studies of other aspects of family life may lead to different conclusions about the relation between welfare and separation and poor home life.

Nor is the reason for the failure of these assumptions about the meaning of being on welfare or of being separated due to the blacks' having a uniformly high percentage of ignorant mothers regardless of marital or income status. Compare Tables 4-19 and 4-23. Considering the welfare families, there is more ignorance among the whites than the blacks.

The fact seems to be that marital status and source of income are not indicators of maternal ignorance of children's friends among black mothers.

Looking again at Table 4-23 the only really high percentage of ignorance occurs for children whose mothers are on social security. But, of course, these would be adult children for whom ignorance is expected. More difficult to explain is why unemployed mothers seem not to be ignorant regardless of whether income is from either a job or welfare. We do not know why this is true.

Because so much is made of economic determinants in analyzing human behavior, we tried to delve deeper into the economic life of our black respondents. As can be seen in table 4-24, holding the child's age constant, whether a black woman works and whether she works on nights or weekends makes little difference. It is true that working mothers of children five to six years old appear somewhat less ignorant than mothers not working, but the subsample sizes are small. Overall, work status seems of little importance in itself.

THE HOUSEHOLD AND FAMILY

TABLE 4–25

PERCENT OF CHILDREN WHOSE FRIEND IS NOT KNOWN BY
MOTHER: BY SOURCE OF INCOME FOR FAMILY, AGE OF CHILD,
AND POVERTY

	(For blacks)						
	Children 0–13				Children 14–18		
Source of income	Poverty		Non-Poverty		Poverty		Non-Poverty	
	%	N	%	N	%	N	%	N
Job	21	(154)	15	(224)	38	(32)	31	(51)
Welfare	24	(92)	8	(36)	25	(16)	—	(8)

Table 4-25 relates source of income and poverty to ignorance; because age fourteen seems to be a breaking point in the career of a child, at least regarding the mother's knowledge, we divided the children into two aggregates: thirteen and younger, and fourteen to eighteen. In general being poverty-stricken seems slightly related to ignorance; for the younger children whose mothers are on welfare the effect of not being in poverty is quite substantial. However, there are only thirty-six cases of young children who are on welfare but not in poverty. If we consider only young children from homes dependent on a job, there is only a difference of 6 percent between those below the poverty line and those above it; what makes this comparison important is the large number of cases. Poverty, then, seems unrelated to ignorance.

We also investigated the effects of unemployment. Holding constant both mothers' and children's ages as well as level of income, and using only families whose main source of income is a job, we compared the knowledge of mothers from families in which the breadwinner has not been unemployed or laid off the previous year with those from families in which the breadwinner has experienced one or more weeks of loss of regular income. Unemployment shows no consistent effect, although there is a tendency in families earning $4,000 or more for greater ignorance to occur when the breadwinner has been unemployed or laid off. Yet no such relation appears among the poorer families. Too few cases prevented further analysis. On the whole, the economic variables are not very powerful predictors of ignorance.

Because we thought that this failure might be due to a lack of control for non-economic variables, we further analyzed our data on work status and source of income, holding constant the mothers' and children's ages. Table 4-26 presents the results. We excluded children less than five years old from our analysis, because it does not seem as meaningful to talk about friends at this age. Behavior is not as stable. When both mother and child are young, economic variables are unimportant, except that again unemployed mothers are low in ignorance. For middle-aged mothers with young children, unemployment again means knowledge, while not looking for work and relying on a breadwinner with a job is associated with ignorance. It is difficult to analyze the effects of economic variables on older children, because the different combinations have low frequencies; however, the pattern seems similar to that for younger children with mothers the same age, except for the relatively high ignorance of part-time workers. What is most interesting about Table 4-26 is the suggestive evidence that ignorance is associated with children whose mothers are not looking for a job but are dependent on some working member of the family. We expected the reverse. For mothers thirty or more, ignorance is highest among the "fat cats."

In an analysis not reported in detail because the frequencies of many combinations of the variables were too small to justify comment, we compared children in families with an annual income below $4,000 with children in families whose income was $4,000 or more. Mother's age and child's age were

TABLE 4–26

PERCENT OF CHILDREN WHOSE FRIEND IS NOT KNOWN BY MOTHER: BY MOTHER'S AGE, CHILD'S AGE, WORK STATUS OF MOTHER, AND SOURCE OF INCOME FOR FAMILY

(For blacks)[1]

Mother's age	Child's age	Mother's work status	Source of income			
			Job		Welfare	
			%	N	%	N
16–29	5–13	Full-time job	11	(35)	—	(0)
		Part-time job	—	(4)	—	(0)
		Unemployed	—	(7)	0	(11)
		Not looking	7	(60)	10	(30)
30 plus	5–13	Full-time job	16	(69)	—	(1)
		Part-time job	18	(28)	—	(4)
		Unemployed	4	(24)	8	(13)
		Not looking	32	(85)	20	(46)
30 plus	14–18	Full-time job	23	(22)	—	(1)
		Part-time job	35	(26)	—	(3)
		Unemployed	—	(9)	—	(1)
		Not looking	40	(35)	30	(20)

1. In three cases mother was retired, and these are not reported. Children less than five or more than eighteen are excluded from this table. Not reported are cases having sources of income other than job or welfare.

TABLE 4–27

PERCENT OF CHILDREN WHOSE FRIEND IS NOT KNOWN BY
MOTHER: BY MOTHER'S AGE, CHILD'S AGE, WORK STATUS OF
MOTHER, AND PRIDE

		(For blacks)				
Mother's age	Child's age	Work status	Proud of something		Proud of nothing	
			%	N	%	N
17–29	5–13	Works full-time	7	(27)	—	(8)
		Works part-time	—	(2)	—	(2)
		Unemployed	7	(15)	—	(3)
		Not looking	7	(75)	11	(28)
30–39	5–13	Works full-time	14	(36)	8	(13)
		Works part-time	—	(8)	38	(21)
		Unemployed	3	(38)	—	(7)
		Not looking	21	(84)	56	(43)

[Other subsamples are too small for analysis.]

held constant. There was one significant finding worth reporting. There were fifty-nine children between the ages of five and thirteen whose mothers were thirty or more and whose family income from a job was $4,000 or more. The ignorance-percentage for this category was 41 percent, by far the highest percentage found in that analysis. This result supports the "fat cat" theory; among the black mothers ignorance is highest among the older, relatively well-off families.

To get some indication of the mother's attitude we performed an analysis similar to that in Table 4-25, except that we dropped the variable "source of income" and replaced it with whether the respondent had given a positive answer to the "proud" question. The results are in Table 4-27. As can be seen, pride is insignificant for the children of young mothers. However, among the older mothers not interested in working, there is a difference of 35 percent between those who said they were proud of something and those that did not. The ignorant "fat cats" seem to be prideless. Ideally, of course, we should further subdivide Table 4-27 by income, but there are not enough cases to do this. It seems, however, that ignorance is associated with a mother who is: thirty or more years old, not looking for work, being supported by a breadwinner who has a job, in a family with an income of $4,000 or more a year, yet proud of nothing.

Ignorance seems associated with a combination of relative success and disillusionment. Perhaps it is among the relatively prosperous "fat cats" in black America that white racism takes its heaviest toll. It is conceivable that the older black women with some money have had to endure more frustrations resulting from the prejudice and discrimination existing in American society than poorer black women. In reaction to this these less poverty-stricken women may cease to care; they may cease to be interested in their environment, including their children. Perhaps the reason, then, why 'fat cats" tend to be ignorant of their child's friend is because they have suffered more disillusionment resulting from their encounters with white racism. Of course, this line of reasoning is only conjecture.

Considering all the analysis done on economic variables, the main conclusion is that economic conditions do not seem to significantly affect interpersonal understanding in the mother-child relationship among black people. In fact, such conditions seem totally inconsequential for black mothers in their twenties. For the older women two lines of analysis seem worth following-up. First, interpersonal knowledge seems associated with being unemployed. This label was applied to a jobless respondent if she said she was looking for a job when asked about her work status. It does not seem possible that the economic condition of being unemployed itself produces more knowledgeable mothers. There must be some non-economic characteristic associated with being unemployed in a place like Kilbourtown that accounts for this association of unemployment with knowledge. Second, some evidence was found supporting a "fat cat" theory.

But perhaps our most important conclusion is that maternal ignorance of their children's friends is associated with quite different conditions for whites and blacks. For the former, ignorance means separation and being on welfare. Neither of these conditions is indicative of ignorance in the black sample. In fact, economic conditions in general do not seem to be important determinants of black maternal ignorance. Of course, our comments are based only on a single question, which, however, was about an important area in a child's life.

FAMILY STRUCTURE AND IGNORANCE AMONG BLACK FAMILIES

Because there are relatively few whites in Kilbourntown, this section discusses only the black families. The question we are interested in is whether the kind of people living in a household influences the distribution of understanding in a family.

We have already concluded that there is no consistent relation between marital status and ignorance; moreover, an analysis by age of child that compared families with husbands and those without showed no relation between ignorance and the presence of a husband in a home. We thought that spacing might be significant; we reasoned that the closer children were in age, the more likely the mother might be forced to spread her attention, with the result that

TABLE 4-28

CHILD-SPACING AND PERCENT OF CHILDREN WHOSE FRIEND IS NOT KNOWN BY MOTHER

	(For blacks)[1]	
Spacing	*Percent ignorant*	
	%	*N*
No child within one year	22	(482)
One child a year apart— sibling older	25	(278)
One child a year apart— sibling younger	28	(268)
Two children within a year	26	(109)

1. Only children seven, eight, eleven, twelve, and fifteen years of age are included in this table.

she would know her children less well. We analyzed data only about children seven, eight, eleven, twelve and fifteen years of age. We compared children with no sibling within one year of them with those that had one sibling within a year with those that had two siblings within a year of age. The results are presented in Table 4-28 for ages, which we analyzed, combined; separate analyses for each age yielded data similar to that in Table 4-28. Obviously, child-density as we have measured it is not related to ignorance.

We also thought that the number of children under six years might be critical, because of the attention they require; no significance was found.

We also investigated family size. We were guided by the simple idea that the more people someone is related to, the less interest there is to invest in any one object. We used several ways of getting at size, but finally concentrated on the number of children. Comparing the results obtained (holding constant the child's age) by relating ignorance first with household family size and then with the number of the respondent's own children living at home and sixteen or under, we found that: 1) the two tables revealed the same pattern of results for children below fourteen; 2) the second measure, based only on the number of children, seemed more sensitive for those fourteen to eighteen. In light of the fact that household family size seemed less significant, and because the same household size could mean quite different household compositions, we decided to concentrate our analysis on the number of children.

Table 4-29 shows the effect of number of children at home on ignorance, holding constant mother's age. We used only the number of children at home who were sixteen years of age or under; this age range was used mainly because of the manner in which we coded our material. There is some meaning to this category, however; children sixteen or less are still highly dependent on the

90   SOLIDARITY IN A SLUM

TABLE 4-29

PERCENT OF CHILDREN WHOSE FRIEND IS NOT KNOWN BY MOTHER: BY MOTHER'S AGE, CHILD'S AGE, AND NUMBER OF RESPONDENT'S OWN CHILDREN SIXTEEN OR LESS LIVING AT HOME

(For blacks)

Age of mother	Age of child	Number of own children 16 or less living at home							
		1–2		*3–5*		*6–8*		*9 plus*	
		%	N	%	N	%	N	%	N
17–29	5–13	16	(19)	8	(97)	10	(41)	—	(0)
30–39	5–13	16	(19)	13	(84)	31	(32)	27	(33)
	14–18	—	(5)	7	(29)	48	(31)	31	(13)
40–85	5–13	38	(16)	17	(30)	—	(8)	—	(0)
	14–18	50	(16)	27	(22)	—	(2)	—	(0)

mothers; after sixteen, children begin to take on adult status, especially in the black community. Our measure of household composition, then, refers only to the number of nonadult children at home.

Because of the necessity to hold constant both mother's age as well as child's age some of the cell frequencies in Table 4-29 are small. The data do suggest, however, that mothers are ignorant least often not in the smallest families but in those with three to five children at home. Reading across the table this family size consistently has the least ignorance. For young mothers, i.e., those between seventeen and twenty-nine years of age, the differences are rather small; young mothers seem to know their child's friend no matter what. Also, the difference between families of one to two children and families with three to five children is rather small (3 percent) for mothers in their thirties when the children are five to thirteen years old. Overall, however, maternal ignorance is least in families with three to five children, and is highest when there are more than five children at home.

Although not reported here, different family sizes were compared holding constant the presence of pride in something, and there was still a tendency for mothers with three to five dependent children at home to most often know their child's friend.

Why does there seem to be a curvilinear relation between the number of dependent children at home and the percentage of ignorant mothers? The association of knowledge with three to five dependent children at home could be explained by saying that this is enough children so that the mother is forced to devote her time and interest to the house, but not so many that her interest

THE HOUSEHOLD AND FAMILY 91

is overstretched. This reasoning, however, does not explain why family size is generally not very significant for young mothers. It would seem realistic to assume that young women are affected by the cultural value attached to motherhood; for young women there is probably a tendency to idealize motherhood and its rewards. But as women gain experience as mothers, it is possible that they become more realistic, and see both the frustrations as well as rewards of having children. We suggest that when this disillusionment with an idealized motherhood sets in, the number of children becomes an important consideration for the development of maternal understanding. If, at this time, there are few children, mothers might feel free to become deeply involved in other relationships and tend to become ignorant of their children's lives. On the other hand, if, at the time of disillusionment, women have many children, (i.e., five or more), they are still likely to seek to develop some new involvement not centering on the children, and this involvement plus all the demands of a large family will overstretch their interest and lead to maternal ignorance.

To summarize: we have tried to uncover some of the conditions that affect the distribution of interpersonal knowledge. We suggest that the following ideas are worth more exploration: 1) Parents tend to be ignorant about the personal life of adult children at home; adult children might feel it is necessary to maintain a private life as a way of symbolizing their status as adults, especially when they continue to live with their parents; 2) Young mothers more often know about their children than old ones, although "young" means below forty for whites but below thirty for blacks; the lack of ignorance among young mothers might be due to their romantic ideas about motherhood with the result that they devote much time and attention to the family; however, this does not explain why the meaning of "young" seems different for whites and blacks; 3) At least for the black respondents (there were too few white mothers to analyze) family density does not seem to affect the distribution of knowledge in the family, but family size does; ignorance occurs least often when there are three to five dependent children at home; it was suggested that this number draws the mother's interest to the family without overstretching it; 4) Among whites, maternal ignorance seems to be part of a generally anomic life; ignorant mothers are separated, uneducated, living on welfare, and lacking in pride; ignorant white mothers seem to be people uninterested in anything; 5) The pattern associated with ignorance is quite different among the black respondents; ignorant mothers are not looking for work, are dependent on a breadwinner with a job, live in a family making $4,000 or more, but are proud of nothing. The association of ignorance and no pride is common to both whites and blacks, but the social context is quite different. Among whites pridelessness seems associated with social failure, while among blacks it seems to be part of a syndrome of variables that indicate worldly success. To explain this difference we presented the "fat cat" theory, which suggests that white racism tends to breed disillusionment among the more leisured more economically secure black women, thus bringing about the association of modest success and maternal ignorance of their children's friends.

We checked the relation between mobility and ignorance. Holding constant the age both of the mother and of the child, no relation was found between "years at present address" and ignorance. Holding constant the child's age, we also investigated the relation between "the number of moves in the last five years" and ignorance; the data suggest that frequent moving might be significant for children fourteen to eighteen years old; 23 percent of these children in families that have not moved or have moved only once in the last five years (N=48) have ignorant mothers, while 42 percent of the children have ignorant mothers in families that have moved two or more times (N=52). There was no relation between "number of towns and cities lived in" and ignorance. Overall, mobility seemed insignificant.

THE NATURAL HISTORY OF FAMILY INVOLVEMENT

Many sociologists working on the family have stressed the importance of a developmental perspective; there are events of sociological significance that occur in almost every family in a set sequence; the developmental approach suggests the question: what are the effects on family life of passing through each step in the sequence?

Reuben Hill has suggested the following developmental description of the family:

> Employing these...sets of readily available data of numbers of positions in the family, age composition of the family, and employment status of the father, several stages of the family life span can be differentiated, each representing a distinctive role complex, as follows: Stage I Establishment (newly married, childless); II New Parents (infant-3 years); III Preschool Family (Child 3-6 years and possibly younger siblings); IV School-Age Family (oldest child 6-12 years, possibly younger siblings); V Family with adolescent (oldest 13-19, possibly younger siblings); VI Family with Young Adult (oldest 20 or more, until first child leaves home); VII Family as Launching Center (from departure of first to last child); VIII Postparental Family, The Middle Years (after children have left home until father retires); IX Aging Family (after retirement of father.)[20]

There are problems with using this framework for analyzing family development. First there is a minor problem; stage II seems to assume that a second child does not come along until the first one is three years old. Second, this set of stages must be received as tentative because we can not be sure that it isolates the most important variables for understanding family life; for example, stages II-VI are based entirely on the age of the oldest child irrespective of the age and sex and total number of other children; this is obviously inadequate; for example, our analysis of maternal ignorance suggests the importance of the number of children present in the household. Similarly, stages VI-VIII do not take into account the order in which children leave the home or the reasons for leaving or the type of child leaving, e.g., the effect is no doubt different if a daughter leaves home than if a son does. Moreover, Hill's analysis does not allow for the effect of wives entering and leaving the work force.

It might be objected that the idea of a "stage" approach is all wrong. The world is made up of processes; talking about "stages" seems to unduly harden the world. There is justification for this criticism to the extent that all of life cannot be viewed as a series of stages; for example, the tendency of married couples to become disillusioned over time with their marriage seems better described as a continual, gradual process than as a series of stages. There might be a point of recognition that could be called "The Stage of Consciously Recognized Disillusion," but for some even the recognition is a slow, gradual process. To talk about stages in regard to this process of disillusionment seems to misrepresent reality. On the other hand, the family does experience discontinuity, and this is what the "stage" approach emphasizes. One day there are no children, the next day the dyad is a triad; one day the man is working, the next day he is retired. Of course it is true that humans are capable of preparing for these events. It may be asked, therefore, if there really is a significant difference between the process of disillusionment and the transition from work to retirement? There does seem to be a difference; in the former case adjustment often precedes the shock of recognition, i.e., we begin changing our lives before we fully realize how disillusioned we are; on the other hand, the shock of retirement hits before we can adjust to it. The concept of stage, therefore seems appropriate for certain events in family development.

Having said this, it must also be acknowledged that no one has proved that his list of stages completely represents all the key moments in the development of family life. For example, disillusionment with spouse might occur quite independently of the appearance of the various stages suggested by Hill. His suggested discontinuous events or stages are not equally significant for all familial characteristics.

A major weakness of our research was our failure to relate family involvement to the various stages in family development as enunciated, for instance, by Hill. To some extent we approximated them, but we could have tested the significance of each stage for involvement; unfortunately, we did not do this. Like many other studies, we talk about development, even though we have studied not the same families over time, but different families at different points of development; any statement about the development of involvement, then, can only be tentative. Our analysis, however, does suggest some comments about a natural history of involvement, which are worth future exploration.

Maternal involvement with children seems to follow this pattern. Stage

I—Child is zero to four years of age: *high* involvement based on the need of young children for a great deal of attention (Note the high percentage of infants who are thought about; see Table 4-4); Stage II—Child is five to sixteen: *moderate* involvement based on mother's dominance of the child (As children grow up they are less often thought about, and rarely do parents use children in this age range as confidants; however, mothers do know about the lives of these children, indicating high maternal dominance; See Tables 4-4, 4-7, and 4-15.); Stage III—Child is a young adult: *moderate* involvement based on the exchange of confidences (The adult child is more likely to be thought about and to be used as a confidant, but mothers seem to know less about their adult children; it should be noted that the comments about maternal ignorance of adult children are based only on the study of adult children living at home); Stage IV—Child ages, and parents enter old age: *high* involvement due to the greater concentration of involvement by parents in parent-child relations (See column 2 in Table 4-1; as can be seen in this table, whites generally concentrate their involvement on their children more than blacks. But what we are interested in is that for both blacks and whites, as the parents age, there is a jump in the importance of children in their fantasy life;[21] it is the "jump" that interests us here. We are assuming that, because the concentration of involvement increases, the actual degree of parental involvement with their children increases.)

This analysis suggests the need to investigate the significance of changes in degree of involvement within the same relationship. For instance, what is the effect of changing from high to moderate to high involvement? Will the first experience of high involvement be the same as the second? Will the fact of having experienced a decline in involvement affect children's attitude toward an increase of involvement when parents reach old age? Equally interesting to investigate are the consequences of a change in the basis of involvement from power to knowledge.

Our comments on the natural history of involvement are based on the age of the individual child, while Hill's stages are, for the most part, based on the age of the oldest child in the family. In our analysis of maternal ignorance, we did control for various structural variables, such as number of children nineteen and over in a family, number of children six years of age or less, the spacing of children, and the number of dependent children at home. Only the last variable seemed related to mother's ignorance of her child's life. On the basis of the many failures we had in using structural variables it seems doubtful to us that the age of the oldest child itself, i.e., independent of the age of the individual child we are studying, could be very significant. The value of Hill's work is that it makes us think in terms of structural effects on individual relationships; such effects need more attention in sociology. But on the basis of our work we would suggest that a structural analysis should center not on the age of the oldest child but on the number of dependent children at home. Starting with this variable sociologists can then devise more complicated structural types that make use of information on the age and sex-distribution of those children as well as the age of the parents.

FINAL COMMENT

I am struck by the hints uncovered in the research about how cut-off our respondents are. Consider these facts: 1) Most of the respondents report seeking help with their problems from no one; they solve their own problems. 2) About a third of the respondents said they do not discuss their personal problems with the people they think about. 3) About one-quarter of the children have mothers who said they did not know the person their children went around with most often. These facts suggest an aggregate of people who are in the world but not of it, of people who keep their problems to themselves —or rather, people who keep their selves to themselves. To talk of isolated people is, however, inaccurate. Our respondents work and raise families. As physical entities the women we studied are involved with their environment, but as human beings they seem alienated. They do what is necessary. Perhaps what we are searching for is the distinction between necessary and voluntary involvement. At least let us suggest that a measure of the purely voluntary involvement in Kilbourntown would reveal an aggregate of literally isolated people.

5

The Neighborhood

For the homemakers of Kilbourntown there seems little basis for doubting that the center of their world is the family. As Wilensky suggests, this is typical for urban America: "With striking consistency the recent studies of urban life underscore the nuclear family as the basic area of involvement for all types of urban populations. We find not a madly mobile, rootless mass, disintegrating for want of intimate ties, but an almost bucolic contentment with the narrow circle of kin and close friends, with the typical urbanite spending most of his leisure with the family at home, caring for the children, watching television, maintaining the home, reading. Occasionally he makes forays in the world outside, mainly to visit relatives, sometimes to demonstrate his highly held attachment to a formal organization or two."[1] There are, however, several things wrong with Wilensky's analysis. His stress on the nuclear rather than the extended family seems appropriate more for whites than blacks. Moreover, activities like television-watching and reading involve us in people and events outside the family; Wilensky seems to assume that any activity that takes place in the home increases familial involvement, but this is obviously wrong. Day-dreaming, for example, can alienate us from the family. On the whole, however, Wilensky's description can be accepted. The urban world is populated not by isolated individuals but by isolated families.

The point of this chapter and the next is to explore the nature of involvement outside the family. In this chapter we concentrate on the neighborhood, and especially the religious life of our respondents. The next chapter concerns the nation. In Chapter Three it was suggested that there were four foci of involvement in Kilbourntown: the self, the family, religion, and country. In this and the next chapter the last two of these foci will be discussed.

NEIGHBORHOOD INVOLVEMENT

City life can be defined in terms of the amount of "public activity". as Bahrdt calls it, that takes place among an aggregate of human beings. Behavior is public "where there is no all-inclusive unbroken network of intervening and negotiating connections, and where people meet constantly, enter into communication and stand in relationships to each other without the one being classified in a common social order for the other."[2] The city is the place of fleeting relationships and of individually negotiated relationships. The key to city life for Bahrdt is the absence of a "common social order" among people who interact with each other. The point is not that man is isolated, in a strict sense, but that the relations that do exist in a city are not part of some larger social structure of obligations and privileges.

What, then, is meant by a "common order"? To the exent that an aggregate of people have a set of shared beliefs about their mutual rights and responsibilities, which beliefs are conscious and relatively stable, there exists a "common order."

With some justification Wilensky has been critical of those who portray the urban man as cut off from human relationships: "Whatever the mobility of the population, intimate contacts with relatives, neighbors, and friends are a universal feature of urban life at home in the local community. ...Such contacts are also a universal feature of life at work. Even in the huge workplace where many thousands mass for the daily routine, the informal workgroup seems destined to go on performing its usual functions of controlling the workplace: initiating new members, deciding how far to go along with the boss, and making work a bit more like play. There is no evidence that human relations are any more atomized at work than in the local community and neighborhood...."[3]

Granted. Urban life does not mean isolation or atomization. But, it does mean a profound change in the nature of social relations. In the city the relationships we have are not unified or tied together; they are not part of a common structure. Rather they are experienced as discrete events. Social life lacks unity.

But does an absence of unity in our social relationships mean a sense of alienation? A man may be deeply involved in a tennis match, then deeply involved with a woman, then thoroughly immersed in a Hemingway novel, then deeply preoccupied with his job of teaching, then engrossed in the daily newspaper on the subway ride home. Is he alienated? Over time the answer must be "yes." His life lacks a unity, lacks a sense of oneness over time. Will he feel alienated? We do not know. It has already been pointed out that we do not know the relation between alienation and a person's time perspective. Perhaps some people are influenced only by immediate events, others by weekly events, and others by the degree of unity among the high points in their entire life.

It seems clear, however, that the absence of a social order uniting our various relations is at least a potential source of alienation. The question we pose in this chapter is whether there is any social order unifying the residents of Kilbourntown. These neighbors will interact with each other. Is it likely that these neighborhood relations will be experienced as part of some common social structure?

The state, of all organizations, does give a status to nearly everyone in K-3; at least most of the adults must be citizens. This source of social order will be discussed in the next chapter. In this chapter we are interested in what have been called intermediate institutions, i.e., organizations other than the family or the state. The word "intermediate" is poor because it suggests that an organization is subordinate to the state. But can this be said, for instance, of religious organizations? Can one say that the Catholic churches in Kilbourntown are subordinate to the state? The answer must be "yes" and "no". We are interested in sources of a "common order" that are not part of the state. We shall refer to these simply as nonpolitical orders.

The question we seek to answer in this chapter, then, is as follows: To what degree are the residents of Kilbourntown unified by nonpolitical sources of order? Strictly speaking, each individual has his own personal neighborhood, i.e., his own set of spatially based relationships. But we have not determined the personal neighborhood of each of our 623 housemakers. Rather, we have simply assumed that many of these spatial relationships will involve their fellow Kilbourntown housewives, and we have investigated the extent to which each of our respondents shares a "common order" with the other respondents.

TYPES OF NONPOLITICAL ORDERS

Many community studies, and especially those interested in political power, focus not on involvement but integration. The behavior of human beings may be efficiently coordinated without these people experiencing any sense of involvement with each other. The coordination may be so far removed as to be invisible. For example, workers belonging to two companies owned by the same corporation may be coordinated by that corporation without the workers in one company feeling involved with those in the other company. Similarly, coalitions of political bosses and business leaders may coordinate people without these people being aware that their lives are interrelated. Our concern is not integration but involvement.

Moreover, we are not interested in how the people of Kilbourntown are related to those living elsewhere. Our focus is on the neighborhood, on what Warren has called the "horizontal pattern."[4]

What types of nonpolitical orders exist in Kilbourntown?

The classic study of neighborhood order is the work of William F. Whyte. Not only did he find that "common orders" did exist, but he reported that, for many of the young males he studied, neighborhood structures were more important than the household.

> Home plays a very small role in the group activites of the corner boy. Except when he eats, sleeps, or is sick, he is rarely at home, and his friends always go to his corner first when they want to find him. Even the corner boy's name indicates the dominant importance of the gang in his activities. It is possible to associate with a group of men for months and never discover the family names of more than a few of them. Most are known by nicknames attached to them by the group. Furthermore, it is easy to overlook the distinction between married and single men. The married man regularly sets aside one evening a week to take out his wife. There are other occasions when they go out together and entertain together, and some corner boys devote more attention to their wives than others, but married or single, the corner boy can be found on his corner almost every night of the week.[5]

Whyte's study was done in an Italian district of Boston before World War II. Such male groups as the corner boys he describes, may, however, exist in Kilbourntown. But, more generally, Whyte's work points to the possible importance of informal groups. By informal it is meant not only that the rules regarding rights and responsibilities are not written down, but that the group is not visible to the general public. It is not open to all; rather it usually exists for a small number of people and does not seek publicity beyond that small aggregate. Basically, informal means nonpublic—not open to the public, not known by the public, not recognized by the public. For their members informal groups provide a common order.

A second form of a "common order" is a formal organization. We shall discuss three types: work organizations, voluntary associations and religious organizations. The last is sometimes considered a voluntary association. But the sense of compulsion many people feel to attend a church makes it difficult to consider church membership as voluntary. Similarly, since many people must work, it is customary to differentiate work organizations from voluntary associations.

The third and last form of a "common order" we call the advice-structures. By this we refer to the various professional individuals[6] and agencies available in our society to people seeking help with their problems; the concept refers to most welfare institutions, but it is broader than this category since it also includes psychiatrists and private charity organizations; moreover, it also refers to doctors, priests, and so on to the extent that they are sources of help to people in ways not related to their professional, special qualification; so, if people consult their doctor about family problems, which are outside his speciality, the doctor is part of an advice-structure. In general, advice-struc-

100

tures include all those professionals whose help is sought in solving what we today call "social problems."

Advice-structures fulfill what Warren has called the "mutual support function." This refers "to the type of help which is proffered in those instances where individual and family crises present needs which are not otherwise satisfied in the usual pattern of organized social behavior. Examples are illness, economic need, and problems of family functioning."[7]

To what extent do advice-structures provide "common order"? It is clear that common membership in an informal or formal organization provides a common understanding about responsibilities and rights among the members. A similar understanding exists between advisors and clients, although it may not be too clear to the clients what their rights are. But the idea of an order governing the advisor-client relation does exist in any advice-structure. On the other hand, while members of an organization are conscious of an order governing the relations among them, clients even of the same advisor are not aware of such an order. Advice-structures bind people vertically but not horizontally.

Of course, the amount of order given to a person's life by membership in an organization will vary considerably. To be a member of a religious sect could mean that all of one's life is oriented to a set of religious norms. Moreover, the sect members may live near each other and be each other's constant companions. These sect members would experience life as a meaningful whole; their religious organization would have provided them with an order that tied together all daily events. On the other hand a person might be a member of the local historical society. Compared to a sect it would order little of the person's life. Members of the historical society would find it difficult to relate most of what they did in life to the rules of the historical society. Organizations differ quite markedly, therefore, in the degree to which they provide a non-political order, but all organizations and advice-structures do provide some order.

To what extent do these sources of order exist in Kilbourntown?

INFORMAL ORGANIZATIONS

We attempted to find out if there are sociometric stars in Kilbourntown, i.e., individuals around whom our respondents cluster and through whom they are interrelated. This section is based on all 748 respondents, i.e., it includes everyone we interviewed. It became clear to us that we had found little informal organization in K-3 among our respondents, and that obviously this conclusion was also valid for our subsample of 623 female homemakers.

We used three questions to find informal leaders: the "think about" question and our inquiries about from whom the respondents seek advice on family problems and on money problems. It is true that strictly speaking the absence of leaders does not mean the absence of informal groups. However, informal organizations often lack an elaborate structure and thus are especially dependent on the relations of followers to leaders. Whyte's study of Cornerville clearly portrays the nonofficial structure as a network of personal loyalties centering on a few key leaders. We assume that without the charisma of leaders informal groupings tend to come and go and are of little significance. Our analysis of informal structure, then, concentrates on evidence concerning the existence of common allegiance to informal leaders.

On the 748 questionnaires collected, thirty-four names appeared two or more times in response to the "think about" question. Six people received more than two mentions: Presidents Kennedy and Johnson each appeared five times, God is mentioned seven times, two Protestant ministers each received three mentions, and one person unknown to us appeared three times; twenty-eight other individuals were mentioned twice. Two points are clear: 1) The most frequently mentioned are nonlocals (presidents and God); the charisma that does exist for our respondents directs their interest either to spiritual beings or to national events; and 2) There is little informal local structure among our respondents; at most 9 percent of our total sample of 748 shared a local "leader" with at least one other person, i.e., 9 percent of the sample think about at least one person who is also thought about by another person in our sample[8]. It must be clear that this 9 percent do not share a common "leader;" rather this 9 percent is composed of clusters of two to three people who mentioned the same name. The "think about" question did not reveal any local charismatic figures.

We, also, considered the specific persons mentioned in response to the two advice questions. The total sample of 748 respondents mentioned a total of 286 people from whom they seek advice. No one was mentioned more than twice, and only three names appear twice: God, a pastor, and someone else whose status is unknown to us. This total of 286 includes professional people who will be discussed in the next section.

Quite clearly there appear to be no local leaders around whom neighborhood structures could form. This does not mean that informal organizations do not exist. For instance, it is possible that some Kilbourntown homemakers get together regularly for gossip and coffee. But such contacts themselves do not produce a "common order." Simply because people regularly get together does not mean that a stable and conscious set of mutual rights and responsibilities have developed. It should be noted that our inquiry about voluntary associations included a specific question about "social clubs;" these will be discussed later.

ADVICE-STRUCTURES

Advice-structures include all the people who seek advice about their problems from professional people as well as all the professionals consulted. As already indicated only three specific people were mentioned more than once. No professionals dominate advice-giving in K-3.[9] In this section we want to discuss the significance of advice-structures as well as their nature.

Table 5-1 presents data on the type of people from whom our respondents seek advice. (For the remainder of this chapter the analysis is based on the sample of 623 homemakers.) A total of thirty-one persons seek advice on family problems from professional people; forty-five respondents seek advice on money problems from professionals. Considering both types of problems

TABLE 5–1

TYPES OF PEOPLE FROM WHOM RESPONDENTS SEEK ADVICE ON MONEY OR FAMILY PROBLEMS[1]

Advice on money	Advice on family						
	Minister or priest	Social worker	Misc. public service	Doctor	Personal relation	No help sought	Total (45)
Minister or priest	1				1	2	4
Social worker					2	5	7
Employer						4	4
Credit union			1			4	5
Loan company or bank	1				2	9	12
Landlord						2	2
Misc. public service	1					3	4
Doctor	1						1
Attorney					1	5	6
Personal relation	5				46	52	
No help sought	14	2	4	1	42	475	
Total (31)	23	2	5	1			

1. To find out how many people seek advice from any one type read down to the "total" row for family problems and across to the "total" column for money problems. "Personal relation" means advice is sought from a nonprofessional. The body of the table shows the combinations of help activities for the two problems, so the "1" in the first column in the upper left corner of the table means that one person seeks advice on both problems from a minister or priest.

a total of seventy-one respondents (11 percent of the homemakers) seek help from professionals.

It is interesting to note the types of professionals influential in Kilbourntown. The last column on the right of Table 5-1 contains the totals for the various categories used in the table with regard to seeking advice on money problems. Understandably, loan companies and banks have the highest frequency. They are composed of professionals trained to solve monetary problems and they are used. The situation is quite different regarding family problems. People with such problems make significant use of only one source of help, religious specialists. This dependence on the religious institutions reflects both a traditional closeness between religion and family and the relative absence of appropriately trained specialists. Industrial society has trained many people to handle its money problems, but few to care for personal problems. The absence of the latter type of specialist is especially flagrant in the ghettos.

One result of this is the significance of the religious institution in Kilbourntown, though use of ministers and priests as sources of advice is not limited to K-3. In a study of the Hough ghetto in Cleveland, respondents were asked to indicate from a list which sources they would utilize for help in times of personal trouble: "For help with personal problems three sources of help accounted for 76.6 percent of the first choices: clergyman first, relatives second, and lawyers or doctors third. Social agencies were mentioned as first choices by only 6.5 per cent of the respondents...."[10] Our results suggest that in fact people seek advice more frequently from relatives than professionals. But the study in Hough and ours in Kilbourntown document the importance of the religious institution in the lives of the residents of these northern ghettos. Matthews and Prothro came to the same conclusion in their study of southern politics; one-third of all leaders mentioned by black people were preachers: "No other single occupational group receives anything close to the number of leadership nominations given to preachers."[11]

The counterpart to the importance of the religious organizations is the insignificance of the "social workers" (this was the way our respondents described the advisors in question). About one out of every six respondents live on welfare. The insignificant part played by social workers in the advice-structure strongly suggests the colossal failure of the welfare program to win the confidence of the people they help.

It must be remembered that the advice questions asked about the person our respondents "most often" go to for advice. These questions did not gather information on the occasional use of professionals.

FORMAL ORGANIZATION

WORK ORGANIZATION   Data were collected on the occupation of the bread-winner. We asked about the kind of company that the breadwinner worked for at the time of the interview or, if the person was unemployed, during the last period of employment. Even though everyone did not report a specific employer, for all 748 respondents a list of 288 companies was accumulated. No further analysis was performed, since it is obvious that employment is quite dispersed. Employment of breadwinners in the same work organizations could offer a "common order" based on relations at work. But the dispersion of employment prevents such a nonpolitical order being significant in Kilbourntown.

There are, of course, community-level organizations whose purpose is to coordinate individual companies. If these coordinating agencies were effective in unifying the companies, then these agencies could provide some order even for people who work for different employers. But as Warren has said: "It is interesting to note that even where the horizontal relationship among business enterprises is formalized in such an organization [as the chamber of commerce], the ties of one local business enterprise to another within that organization are much weaker and much more peripheral than are the vertical ties of the respective branch business enterprises to their own particular national companies." "Though organizations like the chamber of commerce afford a means of horizontal integration at the community level, they characteristically coordinate these organizations only superficially."[12]

RELIGIOUS ORGANIZATIONS

Several times in our work we have noted the importance of ministers or priests in the lives of our respondents: such people seem to be the most significant local, nonfamilial sources of influence for our homemakers. The question arises, therefore, to what extent do religious organizations unify K-3? By religious organizations in this section we mean specific churches or parishes.

As with work organizations the respondents are dispersed over a wide range of religious organizations; we reviewed the specific titles of churches mentioned by our respondents and tried to eliminate any error due to different persons using slightly different titles in referring to the same churches. Whenever we believed different titles referred to the same church we pooled the respondents associated with each title. We also eliminated those individuals who gave generic references such as "Methodist" or "Congregationalist"; we still ended up with a list of 112 different churches.

The vast majority of churches (96 out of 112) attended by our respondents have five or less of the respondents as members. Table 5-2 shows the distribu-

TABLE 5–2

DISTRIBUTION OF CHURCHES RESPONDENTS BELONG TO

(By number of respondent-members[1])

Respondent-members	Number of churches
1–5	96
6–10	8
11–15	4
16–20	0
21–25	2
26–30	1
31–35	1
	112

1. For this analysis we used only the whites and blacks in our sample, N=578; of these, 415 named a specific church to which they go.

tion of churches by the number of respondent-members. The single church with the largest number of respondents as members is a Roman Catholic church; thirty-four respondents belong to it. The use of a territorial basis for defining church boundaries gives the Roman Catholic Church an edge in being able to unify neighborhoods. However, the majority of the respondents belong to churches which have few, i.e., ten or less, respondents as members.

This dispersion of church membership is matched by a dispersion of

TABLE 5–3

DISTRIBUTION OF RESPONDENTS

(By type of church they attend and by color of respondent)

Type of church	White(N=169)	Black(N=409)
Attend nonintegrated church[1]	30%	47%
Attend integrated church	39	20
Did not name specific church[2]	10	14
Do not attend church	15	11
No response noted	7	9[3]

1. "Nonintegrated" means that in our sample we found people of only one color attending these churches. Only whites and blacks were considered.

2. These people usually responded: "Baptist," "Methodist," and so on.

3. This total includes nine who gave only a general location and two who gave a minister's name that we were unable to assign to a specific church.

SOLIDARITY IN A SLUM

church location. We could locate only 19 of the 112 churches mentioned by our respondents in K-3 or within two blocks of its boundaries. Religious devotion scatters the respondents over a large area of the city.

Dispersion weakens the ability of churches to give order to life in Kilbourntown. This weakness is increased by the fact that church membership fails to significantly cut across racial lines. The whites belong to forty-four churches; the blacks belong to eighty churches. Whites and blacks share only twelve churches. Table 5-3 shows the distribution of respondents according to whether or not they attend integrated churches; "integrated" means that both whites and blacks from our sample attend the church. (Using only our sample to determine whether or not a church is integrated means that we have underestimated the number of integrated churches.) Table 5-3 gives a rather positive picture for whites; 39 percent attend integrated churches. But the picture changes when we look at details. There are only six integrated churches that have at least five respondents as members. The ratios of minority-majority (depending upon the specific church, the minority might be white or black) in the six integrated churches are - 1:6, 1:7.5, 1:10, 1:10.5, 1:12, and 1:25. These ratios take into consideration only the homemakers who participated in our study. The ratio of whites to blacks in our sample is 1:2.4; the church with the closest ratio (1:6) has only seven respondents as members, and these are mostly white, which is the reverse of the K-3 neighborhood as a whole. It would be more appropriate to write this church's ratio as 6:1, which is quite different from the white-black ratio of 1:2.4 for our sample. In all, forty-one respondents, thirty-six whites and five blacks, are members of integrated churches with a ratio of 10:1 or less (and with at least six respondents as members). It appears, therefore, that the majority of our respondents do not attend integrated churches, and that the percentage of whites in integrated churches is misleading, because these whites seem to attend churches that have only a very small black membership.[13]

Warren had noted the significance of religious organizations in American life: "more Americans are members of churches than any other type of voluntary association. ..." At the same time he recognized the importance of segmentation: "On the basis of membership and participation in one church rather than another, community people are separated from each other in an important aspect of their social participation, as they participate in one or another of the 259 religious denominations having churches in American communities."[14] It should be remembered that our figure of 112 churches refers to specific churches or parishes and not to denominations. Many of these churches are "store-front churches" belonging to no denomination. As Pinkney has noted—"The black community is noted for the number of churches it includes. Drake and Clayton enumerated some 500 churches in Chicago that served some 200,000 members. These churches represented more than 30 denomina-

TABLE 5–4

DISTRIBUTION OF CHURCH MEMBERSHIP

(By color of respondent)

Type of church	White (N=169)	Black (N=409)
Roman Catholic	37%	9%
Protestant churches	30	57
Episcopalian	(0)[1]	(.3)
Lutheran	(18)	(2)
Presbyterian	(.6)	(.6)
Congregationalist	(1)	(0)
Methodist	(5)	(5)
Baptist	(5)	(44)
Church of God in Christ	(.6)	(6)
Protestant sects	5	10
Miscellaneous	7	8
No church membership	21	17

1. In parentheses are the percentages belonging to specific Protestant churches.

tions. Seventy-five percent of these churches were store-front churches or 'house churches' with an average membership of fewer than 25 persons. A study of central Harlem in the 1960's enumerated 418 church buildings. Of this number only 122 were housed in conventional church buildings; 232 were located either in store fronts or in residential buildings; and the remainder were located in large meeting halls, private homes, or social agencies."[15] In black ghettos, generally, religious devotion scatters involvement among a large number of specific organizations. Through these organizations people interact and develop relationships with only a few neighbors. Religion can be only a weak source for a "common order" that would structure relationships among the residents of Kilbourntown.

DENOMINATIONS   By discussing only specific churches or parishes we exaggerate the amount of religious diversification. Structurally some churches are more closely linked than others. Table 5-4 shows the distribution of church membership by denomination. Among the whites 37 percent are Roman Catholic and 18 percent are Lutheran. Especially for the Catholics, the centralized religious structure suggests that there would be some meaningful coordination of the behavior of Catholics in our sample. But even if there is this coordination, will common membership in the same denomination produce an aggregate of people who know each other as members and who interact with each other in terms of a shared set of rules concerning mutual rights and responsibilities? This is not likely. Religious life is almost totally organized around the local, specific church or parish. There are, for instance, few common services. People of different Catholic parishes probably do not know each other. Catholics from different parishes remain "familiar strangers" to each other. The significance of the fact that 37 percent of the K-3 whites are Catholics lies in the potential suggested by this percentage. Both the Catholic and Lutheran churches in Kilbourntown, and in Milwaukee generally, are numerically significant churches that could do much to create a sense of a "common order." But this potential will be underutilized as long as these denominations put so much stress on individual churches.

But is it even a good policy to suggest that churches try to provide a "common order?" As the data in Table 5-4 suggest any attempt by one of the religious denominations to use membership in the denomination as a source of neighborhood structure would only unify a minority of respondents and would divide the population along racial lines. While 37 percent of the whites are Catholic, only 9 percent of the blacks are; while 44 percent of the blacks are Baptist, only 5 percent of the whites are. The religious pluralism of the United States, exemplified in Table 5-4, makes it difficult for a single denomination to serve as a neighborhood source of a "common order."

Moreover, the types of religious organization prevalent in the United States pose a special problem from the viewpoint of community-building. Despite the rise of ecumenicalism, belonging to one branch of Christianity usually implies a rejection of all other religious groups. A person can be a member of the P.T.A. without being against anyone. This is not true of most religious groups, where membership implies rejection of the denomination not joined. Such groups polarize a community, and so we call them "polarizing organizations." Since most Christian groups are polarizing organizations, their very existence creates conflict, i.e., negative involvement.

There are interdenominational organizations in Milwaukee—The Interdenominational Ministerial Alliance, The Milwaukee Associates in Urban Ministries, and The Greater Milwaukee Council of Churches. The very fact there are three such organizations suggests that the same proliferation of religious organizations is now taking place on the supradenominational level. Moreover, we doubt if the vast majority of people in K-3 are aware that these organizations exist. More important perhaps, these interdenominational organizations do not include as members many of the churches attended by Kilbourntown residents. For instance, the Lutheran and Catholic churches have not been allowed at the time of this study to join the Council of Churches. We tried to check how many of the churches attended by our black respondents belong to these organizations. The task was made difficult by our not knowing the names of all the pastors. It is our impression, however, that many of the sect-type and small Baptist churches are not associated with any of these supradenominational organizations. In all, we are sure that fourteen churches, with about one-third of our black churchgoers as members, are associated with at least one interdenominational organization. Approaching the problem somewhat differently, we found nineteen churches within K-3 or within two blocks of its boundaries; ten are not members of any interfaith organization; seven churches, six of which are Baptist, are members of the Interdenominational Ministerial Alliance. The evidence suggests that a significant number of our respondents do not belong to a church that is a member of any supradenominational organization. Because of this, and because there is a proliferation of interfaith organizations, and because about a fifth of our sample report no church membership, it is doubtful if any supradenominational religious organization could serve as a source of a "common order" in a neighborhood like Kilbourntown.

Moreover, Warren's judgement must be kept in mind, that "the local councils of churches are admittedly and deliberately weak in the sense that they do not seek organizational unification.... By no means does it approach in systemic importance the tie which most churches have to their extracommunity denominational bodies."[16] Interdenominational organizations are too weak to be significant in the life of the average person.

TABLE 5–5

DISTRIBUTION OF ORGANIZATIONAL MEMBERSHIPS

	(By color of respondent)			
	Number of memberships			
Type of organization	*White(169)*		*Black(408)*	
Church	134	(79%)[1]	341	(83%)[1]
P.T.A.	12	(7%)	76	(19%)
Union	11	(7%)	27	(7%)
Civil rights organization	1[2]		15[2]	
Other instrumental organizations	10[3]		6[·3]	
Social clubs	23[2]		29[2]	

1. This is the percent of our sample who said they attend a church. There are some cases in which the interviewer did not record a response; these are counted as "no church membership" cases. Also five black respondents did not know the name of the church they attend, and these are treated as "no church membership" cases.

2. We cannot calculate the percent of subsample, because the same individual might belong to two or three organizations.

3. Examples of such organizations are: the Democratic Party, the Lutheran Association, and the County Historical Society.

VOLUNTARY ASSOCIATION

We asked the respondents if they are members of any fraternal organizations like lodges or auxiliaries, social clubs, veterans' organizations, community improvement groups, labor unions, civil rights groups, P.T.A. (or Home and School), political organizations, church-related groups, or any other groups.

As with church membership, there is little concentration of attachment within the array of available voluntary associations. The white and black respondents belong to a total of sixty-five organizations, seven of which have members from both races. Once again, not only is membership disbursed but it divides the neighborhood along racial lines.

Our analysis does not include memberships in church-related organizations. Such memberships are especially frequent among the blacks, but since we have already discussed the significance of religious associations, church-related voluntary associations are excluded from the present analysis.[17] The importance of these organizations, however, should not be overlooked. Babchuk and Booth found in a study of the residents of Nebraska that over a four year period 45 percent of their sample had belonged at least for a while to a church-related voluntary association.[18] This underlines the importance of religious institutions in the life of Americans, an importance often overlooked by those who discuss the "mass society."

Table 5-5 summarizes the data on organization membership; information on church affiliation is included for purposes of comparison. Perhaps the most striking feature of associational life in Kilbourntown, leaving aside the churches, is that it is minimally voluntary. Eighty-eight respondents are members of the Parent-Teacher's Association; this probably refers to several different local branches of the P.T.A., but we did not collect data describing which branch members belonged to. Thirty-eight respondents are union-members; these memberships, however, are spread out over sixteen different unions. The P.T.A. and the unions are significant in Kilbourntown, but it is noteworthy that both types of organizations are minimally voluntary. If you are a parent with a child in school, pressure is applied either by the P.T.A. or the school or both to join the P.T.A. Similarly, many workers either have to join a union to get a job or are pressured into joining a union by their fellow workers. There is very little truly voluntary participation in formal organizations among the Kilbourntown residents.

The P.T.A. and the unions do offer some basis for unity. However, about 40 percent of the members of these organizations reported attending meetings only rarely. Whether this is because meetings are rare or because our respondents are not interested, we can not determine. But whatever the reason the rare attendance lessens the significance of these organizations. The P.T.A. does stand out, however, as the most significant voluntary organization in Kilbourntown. Given this fact, it is regretable that this organization plays such an insignificant role in neighborhood life. It is true, however, that since our data were collected at least a few branches of the P.T.A. in Milwaukee showed signs of taking some initiative in the formulation of educational policy. For the most part, at least in Milwaukee, the P.T.A. is a tool of the school board and the school principals. Given this passivity, membership in the P.T.A. cannot mean much to people. But the potential of the P.T.A. must not be overlooked. It does reach into many homes, and it does relate to something that is an important part of life, i.e., education. An active P.T.A. could give residents of a neighborhood a sense of common purpose and shared responsibility. An active P.T.A. could give a sense of a "common order;" it could turn "familiar strangers" into fellow committee-members or at least fellow campaigners in a good and serious cause.

The same potential resides in civil rights groups, but as can be seen in Table 5-5, only one white respondent and fifteen black respondents are members of such groups. The only organization of some numerical significance is the NAACP. It has twelve members, all black; CORE has two members, the Urban League one member; a local civil rights group has one member. All other types of voluntary organizations account for sixty-eight memberships spread among at least forty-four associations.

As Table 5-5 clearly indicates, religious organizations dominate non-household, neighborhood life in Kilbourntown.[19]

PARTICIPATION IN RELIGIOUS RITUAL

Each respondent was asked: "Do you go to church?" If the answer was "yes", the interviewee was asked whether she attended meetings "frequently, occasionally, or rarely?". These categories were used, because they allowed us to use the same predetermined responses for a variety of organizations. The church-question was part of a battery of questions about different kinds of voluntary associations. To minimize confusion we decided to use the same set of responses for each organization, and since meeting-frequencies varied from one organization to another, we could not use specific responses like weekly, monthly, and the like. Answering "monthly" for church-attendance, which is possible at least weekly, would not reflect the same involvement as attending a political club "monthly", if this organization meets only once a month. Therefore, the more subjective categories such as "frequently" were used. In this way it was hoped that the individual would alter her frame of reference for each organization, i.e., if she attended just about all the meetings, no matter how often they occurred, she would say "frequently." This is a bit idealistic. The categories used are vague, and ambiguity cannot be avoided; the middle category "occasionally" was probably especially difficult to use. However, given the limitations imposed by all the objectives we were trying to accomplish, rather subjective categories seemed to be the best set of responses available.

In retrospect it is clear we took the wrong approach. Considering only the church-attendance question, 72 out of 341 black church members do not have a frequency-response recorded for them. We are not sure why this is so, but we strongly suspect that our respondents answered in more concrete terms like "weekly" or "twice a week," and that our amateur interviewers did not know how to handle the situation. Of course we should have anticipated this problem or noticed it during the course of the study. In any case the abstract categories used appear to have been quite inappropriate for our church-attendance question. On the other hand, our respondents did not seem to have the same difficulty for all types of organizations. While roughly one out of five church members have no attendance recorded, this was true for only one social club member out of thirty-nine. We suspect that the categories seemed more inappropriate, the more regularly and frequently an organization met. And since churches meet regularly and frequently, we ended up with a large number of unusable cases; 29 white and 75 black cases were lost, because no frequency-response was recorded.

From the point of view of neighborhood involvement, church attendance is important not only because of the large number of respondents who belong to churches. Equally important is the fact that religious ritual is oriented toward solidarity-building. This is more true of the more formal churches like Catholicism and of the sects than of the sermon-oriented Protestant churches like the Congregationalist. But most of our respondents belong to the more emotion-arousing denominations like the Baptists and the Methodists, as well as to the sects and more formalized churches. The religious services our respondents attend are among mankind's most successful attempts to develop occasions for making someone feel involved with others. It is true that often today these rituals are failures. For instance, many Catholics are more annoyed than pleased at church services. But among the myriad occasions offered to man, even contemporary man, the church service remains an outstanding example of an involvement-enhancing situation.[20]

AGE, COLOR AND CHURCH ATTENDANCE

Argyle reported that once past thirty years of age, people tend to go to church more often the older they get.[21] Our data are generally consistent with this proposition (see Table 5-6). The highest percentages of nonattenders are among those seventeen to thirty-nine years of age, while frequent attendance occurs most frequently among those sixty or over. On the other hand, our data suggest that regarding attendance at religious rituals aging involves two dis-

TABLE 5–6

FREQUENCY OF CHURCH ATTENDANCE BY AGE AND COLOR OF RESPONDENT

Age	Color and frequency of church attendance									
	White					Black				
	Not a church attender[1]	Rare	Occa-sional	Frequent	Sample size (N)	Not a church attender	Rare	Occa-sional	Frequent	Sample size (N)
17–39	33%	7%	27%	33%	(30)	20%	11%	38%	32%	(213)
40–59	21	13	31	35	(48)	14	12	41	33	(81)
60 plus	25	12	12	51	(59)	13	6	22	59	(32)

1. This includes all respondents who definitely said they belong to no church as well as those cases in which the interviewer simply did not record an answer to the church question.

tinct processes: 1) As people move from youth to middle age, they cease to be outside religious institutions but do not necessarily go very frequently to church; thus, for both blacks and whites respondents over forty are more often church members than people below forty; and 2) As people move from the middle years to old age, they tend to go more frequently to church. Thus, there is a dramatic difference, for both whites and blacks, between those sixty and above and those below sixty in the percentage of frequent church-goers. The first process brings people into a church; the second makes them active members.

The idea of a two stage process as people age is consistent with the little we know about the motivation behind religious participation. As people produce a family, pressures are felt to join a church.[22] Young parents begin worrying about their children's upbringing and join a church to ensure that their children will be exposed to religion. Also, as people begin to age, it is probably more and more "expected" by family and friends that adults will attend a church. The move into the religious institution is often the result of external pressures, i.e., pressures that have nothing to do with truly personal, religious problems, so that it would be expected that such people would not be frequent church-goers. On the other hand, as people age and face death and possibly loneliness, they want to go to church; attendance is voluntary. When people reach old age, they must personally face the problems that religions are meant to solve, such as death. Frequent church attendance in old age, then, is understandable.

The differences by color are less significant than the differences by age. More whites, however, remain outside the religious institution.

SOLIDARITY IN A SLUM

MOBILITY AND CHURCH ATTENDANCE

Lee used the number of local friends and the number of organizations joined as criteria of involvement. He summarized his data on mobility and neighborhood involvement as follows: "It appears that newcomers to a locality become involved, up to a given low level, quite quickly. Thereafter, they remain more or less static for about five years. after which their involvement begins to increase steadily."[23] Lee's use of five years as a significant point of differentiation is interesting. Does his analysis apply to church attendance?

Table 5-7 presents the relevant data for blacks; there were too few whites for analysis.

Considering the "frequently" column, there is a clear pattern. Regardless of age, there is a slight tendency for this percentage to increase, the longer respondents have lived in Milwaukee.

But the data are not consistent for nonattenders. Comparing those who have lived fifteen years or less in Milwaukee with the rest, the relative newcomers are less often nonattenders among the young but more often nonattenders among the older respondents (i.e., those forty to fifty-nine years of age). The

TABLE 5–7

FREQUENCY OF CHURCH ATTENDANCE BY AGE OF RESPONDENT AND YEARS LIVED IN MILWAUKEE

		(For Blacks)				
		Frequency of church attendance				
Age	Years lived in Milwaukee	Not a church attender	Rare	Occasional	Frequent	(N)
17–39	0–15[1]	19%	13%	38%	30%	(175)
	(0–5)[2]	(30)	(16)	(29)	(25)	(73)
	(6–10)	(14)	(12)	(43)	(31)	(51)
	(11–15)	(8)	(10)	(47)	(35)	(51)
	(16–36)	26	3	34	37	(38)
40–59	0–15	15	20	33	30	(40)
	16–50	10	3	50	36	(40)
60 and over		(Insufficient cases for analysis)				(32)
						(325)[3]

1. We had sufficient cases to make further breakdowns on length of residence only among these young, mobile people.

2. The respondents seventeen to thirty-nine years old who have lived in Milwaukee fifteen years or less are further broken down into those who have lived in Milwaukee five years or less, six to ten years, and eleven to fifteen years. In parentheses are the percentages for these subcategories.

3. Seven respondents did not report age; one did not report length of residence in Milwaukee.

TABLE 5–8

FREQUENCY OF CHURCH ATTENDANCE BY YEARS
LIVED IN MILWAUKEE

(For Blacks seventeen to thirty-nine years of age)

| Years lived in Milwaukee | Frequency of church attendance | | |
	Rarely or not at all	Occasional or frequent	Sample size (N)
0–5	48%	54%	(73)
6–10	26	74	(51)
11–15	18	82	(51)
16–35	29	71	(38)

analysis is further complicated by the fact that among those seventeen to thirty-nine years of age the more detailed breakdown on years in Milwaukee suggests a curvilinear relation between years in Milwaukee and percentage of nonattenders. The percentages are: 30 percent (zero to five years in Milwaukee), 14 percent, (six to ten years), 8 percent (eleven to fifteen years), and 26 percent (sixteen or more years). Since there were too few cases to perform more detailed analyses on those over thirty-nine years of age, we will restrict our further comments on mobility to the data on the young respondents.

To get a clearer picture of what might be happening, we collapsed the church-attendance categories as shown in Table 5-8. It seems clear that, at least for our young people, newcomers attend church less often than the rest of the respondents reported in the table. The dominant fact suggested by Table 5-8 is that newcomers tend to remain outside the churches. Consistent with Lee's analysis, there does seem to be an initial period of about five years when newcomers less actively participate in religious rituals.[24]

HOUSEHOLD FAMILY SIZE AND CHURCH ATTENDANCE

The size of the household could be important in several ways: 1) Isolated people might more often go to church seeking companionship; 2) People with large households might be too busy to go to church very often; or 3) People with children might go to church often out of a sense of duty to their children. Table 5-9 presents the relevant data for black people only; there are too few white cases for analysis.

Among the young those with very large families (9 plus) clearly go to church often. The idea that some women may be too busy at home to go to church seems completely without foundation. The fact that all other

SOLIDARITY IN A SLUM

household sizes are roughly the same in church attendence suggests that household size itself is not important. It seems probable that religious people are likely to be ones who have very large households both because charity dictates that they help needy relatives and because of the high value often placed on children by Christian ministers and priests. Clearly there is no evidence among the young that household chores are a significant influence on church attendance.

Among the older black respondents there seems to be a curvilinear relation. But two warnings are necessary: 1) The subsample sizes are small, and 2) The "6 plus" category contains two size-categories ("6-8" and "9 plus") that appear to be quite distinct among the young; because of sample-size problems we had to collapse these two categories. The only tentative conclusion that seems worth making is that possibly isolates do go to church less often then other people. It may be that the reason for the increase in the percentage of people who attend church rarely or never among those respondents living in households of six or more people is that household chores may affect older people more than younger ones; it is possible that middle-aged people begin to lose interest in life so that their plans are more easily affected by inconveniences.

To check further on the significance of isolation we investigated the

TABLE 5–9

FREQUENCY OF CHURCH ATTENDANCE: BY AGE OF RESPONDENT AND HOUSEHOLD FAMILY SIZE

		(For blacks)		
		Frequency of church attendance		
Age[1]	Household family size	Rarely or not at all	Occasional or frequent	Sample size (N)
17–39	1	(Too few cases)		(4)
	2	40%	60%	(30)
	3–5	33	67	(84)
	6–8	33	67	(61)
	9 plus	15	85	(32)
40–59	1	33	67	(18)
	2	18	82	(22)
	3–5	21	79	(24)
	6 plus[2]	33	67	(15)

1. There are too few cases of black respondents sixty and over to analyze.

2. Note that the categories "6–8" and "9 plus" are combined.

TABLE 5–10

FREQUENCY OF CHURCH ATTENDANCE: BY HOUSEHOLD FAMILY SIZE

	(Among white respondents aged sixty and above)		
	Frequency of church attendance		
Household family size	*Attends rarely or not at all*	*Occasional or frequent*	*Sample size (N)*
1	48%	52%	(25)
2 plus	23	77	(31)

relation between isolation and church attendance among the white respondents aged sixty and above (see Table 5-10); this is the only age range among the whites in which there are sufficient cases for analysis. As can be seen, the isolated women attend church less often. It could be that isolated elderly women are older than the nonisolated elderly and attend church less often because they more frequently suffer from physical handicaps. But even very elderly women should be able to attend church occasionally if they really want to.

Two types of people stand out in the analysis of household size; 1) Young people with large households often go to church; and 2) Isolates tend not to be frequent church-attenders.

CONCLUSION

Sociologically speaking, the city means the dominance of public activity, and, therefore, of fleeting and individually negotiated relationships. The city is the failure to experience unity over time in one's relationships.

Kilbourntown deserves to be called part of a city. We found no truly significant source of nonpolitical order outside the family. The major characteristic of Kilbourntown neighborhood life is dispersion—there are no local, informal leaders or professional advisors around whom the sample clusters, and our respondents are associated with at least 288 employers, 112 specific churches, and 65 different voluntary associations.[25] This dispersion of social life beyond the family makes the emergence of a common neighborhood social order impossible.

Our respondents jostle against others in the stores, observe people around them going to church, watch parties gather at different houses, hear the car horns announcing new marriages, see the signs of death and sorrow, and continually pass children on the streets; our respondents are immersed in a crowd of people. At the same time that they are aware of these people, of their proximity, of their being part of the environment, still they cannot fit these people into any framework; these people remain isolated examples of people, a boy here, a screaming woman there.

Coleman has pointed out that neighborhood disorganization need not mean personal disorganization, which is true. The absence of neighborhood structure does not automatically produce mental illness. Coleman concludes: "Communities are becoming less and less the 'building blocks' of which society is composed. ... The new society emerging in the twentieth century may well have social organization without local community organization."[26] Similarly, Alexander has written that "this idea of recreating primary groups by artificial means is unrealistic and reactionary; it fails to recognize the truth about the open society. The open society is no longer centered around place-based groups; and the very slight acquaintances that do form round an artificial neighborhood are once again trivial; they are not based on genuine desire."[27] Both Coleman and Alexander see the neighborhood as doomed.

On the other hand, "The Open Group" (a group of British scholars) has recently suggested that "an attempt should now be made to base the foundations of local government on the communities to which people belong...." "Redrawing the map of local government to correspond with the maps that residents have inside their minds has obvious attractions. A system of neighborhood or urban parish councils would then be as much rooted in people's loyalties as any system could be...."[28]

In discussing the neighborhood it is important to keep distinct the ideas of intimacy and common order. A person cannot be intimate with an entire neighborhood, even if he chose to be. Neighborhood involvement can never be based on intimacy. As sources of neighborhood social order "The Open Group" has suggested local political councils; but surely religion and especially schools offer other opportunities for building neighborhood unity. For instance, if members of an area were responsible for the development of a wide range of educational facilities for themselves this would give some social meaning to the neighborhood and to neighborly relations.

But the major question is whether people themselves experience any desire for neighborhood unity. It seems evident to us that at least some people would feel alienated in neighborhoods like Kilbourntown because of the absence of unity or structure in their neighborhood social relations. The unrelatedness of social bonds would prevent some from experiencing life as a continuous oneness, as a continuous involvement. But how many people have this experience, and how great a source of alienation is it? When we know the answers to these questions, we will know the importance of neighborhood social orders.

But even though people may wish to structure their neighborhood, they are faced with a monstrous technical problem: In a world that requires integration on a massive scale, how can people produce involvement on the local level?

6

National Involvement
with George Gerharz

The residents of Kilbourntown do share one source of social order—the state[1]. Our research did not consider in detail the extent to which our respondents are involved in city or state politics. But the analyses of the "think about" and the "proud" questions presented in Chapter Three suggest that of all the political levels, the national seems to be the most significant. The nation is one of the four foci around which the lives of the respondents seem to revolve. In this chapter we are concerned with two questions: How involved are the respondents in the nation? What produces national involvement?

We must be clear, however, about the limitations of national involvement. Even if all the residents of Kilbourntown were deeply involved in the nation, this could not eliminate the source of alienation discussed in the last chapter. The modern state can not take the place of neighborhood structure. It is true that the nation provides all citizens with a set of goals and assigns to all of them rights and responsibilities, i.e., the nation does provide a common order. But for most citizens the relation of these goals, rights, and responsibilities to the daily routine of their lives is tenuous at best. It is nothing new to point out that citizenship usually means little to people beyond voting and paying taxes. The people in our daily life form an amorphous mass of "fellow citizens." Labelling each other as citizens influences our behavior but little.

On the other hand, the nation is not meaningless. It can give some unity to our lives and social meaning to our relationships. But it can do this only sporadically. The nation enters our lives at election times, during international crises, during demonstrations for social justice, and the like. The nation is neither meaningless nor a panacea for the cure of all alienation. The nation can not replace neighborhood structure, but it can give some unity to daily life.

THE MEASUREMENT OF NATIONAL INVOLVEMENT

National involvement means a sense of oneness with the nation. Our concept is similar to, but not identical with, the idea of nationalism. Weber noted that nationalism might be associated with such characteristics of a population as shared language, customs, or religion, or "memories of a common political destiny." But these conditions do not define nationalism; rather Weber referred to them as bases of nationalism. It is a sense of mission, a belief in the superiority of one's own cultural values and in the necessity of increasing the international prestige of these values that defines nationalism. Weber linked this condition to the struggle for prestige. Nationalism means that people are striving for a sense of personal value by championing their own culture. It finds expression in a missionary fervor to spread national values throughout the world.[2]

What is especially appealing about Weber's work is his separation of potential sources of nationalism from nationalism itself, a distinction that is similar to our differentiation of bases of involvement from the condition of involvement. However, national involvement is not the same as nationalism. The latter includes the former but goes beyond it. Nationalism requires that a person see himself united with a nation. But it means more. As Weber used it, nationalism also means a sense of superiority, so that people can feel justified in seeking the conversion of others to their own culture. Nationalism, therefore, means not only that people identify with the nation, but that they are proud of the culture associated with that nation, and furthermore, that they attempt to spread this culture over the face of the earth, because they believe it is superior to all other cultures.

Many discussions of nationalism lack the relative clarity of Weber's work. Boyd Shafer in his article "Toward a Definition of Nationalism" notes ten conditions often associated with the idea of nation: 1) a unit of territory, 2) cultural characteristics (including language), 3) sameness of social and economic institutions, 4) sovereign government, 5) belief in common history, 6) esteem for fellow nationals, 7) devotion to the nation and/or fellow nationals, 8) pride in the nation's achievements and sorrow in its tragedies, 9) hostility for groups threatening the nation, 10) hope for a glorious future and supremacy.[3] One or more of these elements is often used in defining nationalism. Generally, writers on this subject fail to distinguish: a) potential sources of national involvement (numbers 1 thru 5 above), b) measures of national involvement *per se* (none included in above list and none usually given), c) effects of national involvement (6-7 above) and d) nationalism (8-10 above).

In our own research we did not study nationalism but national involvement. Moreover, because of methodological problems we did not attempt to study a sense of oneness with the nation directly. Rather we studied whether or not a person showed the symptoms of national involvement. We tried to devise a measure of the extent to which a person acted as if he were involved with the nation.

Our questionnaire contained seven questions supposedly related to national involvement. Basically, these questions are: Would respondent feel ashamed if the American government admitted it was scared of Russian military power? Does the respondent feel proud when the United States is praised? Does respondent own an American flag? Does respondent get angry when she hears the United States criticized? Would respondent get angry if she saw a foreigner spit on the American flag? Does respondent believe a person who refuses to fight for his country should be expelled from the country? Does the respondent feel the war in Vietnam is not worth fighting? In our opinion too many attitude scales consist of repeating the same thought in different ways. To find that these items are interrelated only tells us that respondents are rational creatures, for the interrelations do not justify assuming the existence of an attitude independent of the test situation. Our approach was to choose seven items that appear quite different but that should be interrelated if our respondents are involved in the nation. In short, whether or not the seven items form a scale is a test to determine whether there is such a thing as a sense of oneness with the nation among our respondents. Our assumption was that if the seven items formed a scale, then a sense of national involvement really exists in Kilbourntown.

In what way are these seven questions related to national involvement? Our reasoning was as follows: a) People do not like to be criticized or admit they are scared, but they do like to be praised. Therefore, if they identify with the nation they will get angry if they hear people criticize the United States, will feel ashamed if American leaders say they are scared of Russia, but will feel proud if they hear the country praised; b) If people are involved with the nation, they will be more likely to own a flag, the symbol of the United States and they will be angry if they see someone spit on the flag; c) It is difficult for people to admit that what they are doing is wrong. Therefore, if they identify with their country, they will find it difficult to believe that people could be justified in criticizing a war in which their country is involved or that people could find a just reason for not fighting for their country. It was assumed that the seven topics covered by these assumptions would be interrelated only if there were such an attitude as national involvement.

When we considered the correlations among the seven items, it was clear that the flag ownership question was not a good one from our point of view. It is significantly related to only two of the six other questions. This is the most

TABLE 6–1

CORRELATIONS AMONG SIX QUESTIONS SUPPOSEDLY MEASURING
NATIONAL INVOLVEMENT FOR THE BLACK SUBSAMPLE (N=304)[1]

	Russian power	Praise U.S.	Criticise U.S.	Spit on flag	Refuse to fight	Vietnam war
1. Scared of russian power	—	.35	.34	N.S.[2]	N.S.[2]	.15[1]
2. Hear people praise U.S.	—	—	.42	.15	.22	.19
3. Hear people criticize U.S.	—	—	—	.25	.26	.15
4. People spit on flag	—	—	—	—	.20	.12
5. Refuse to fight for U.S.	—	—	—	—	—	.13
6. Vietnam war not worth fighting	—	—	—	—	—	—

1. Only those cases are used in which there was a usable response for the national involvement questions.

2. N.S. means the correlation was not statistically significant at the .05 level.

concrete of our questions, in which we asked the respondents whether or not they owned a flag; if they answered "no" we further inquired if they had ever thought about buying a flag. The absence of correlation with our other questions could mean that 1) owning a flag in the United States, and especially among poor people, is no indication of national involvement; flags are used so rarely that buying one just seems unimportant; or 2) the flag-ownership question, being concrete, is more revealing of national involvement than the other more attitudinal-type questions whose answers are less firmly grounded in facts and which, therefore, are more likely to reflect what the respondent thinks is a desirable response. We assumed that the first explanation was correct, but we could not rule out the second. Somewhat uneasily we simply eliminated the flag ownership question from our consideration.

Using only six questions, there were fifteen correlations only two of which were not statistically significant. The correlations for the black subsample are shown in Table 6-1. All the correlations are in the expected direction.

As the figures in Table 6-1 indicate the significant correlations are generally low. As would be expected, factor analysis revealed no single dominant factor; the first factor referred mainly to how proud respondents would be if they heard someone praise the U.S. (factor loading of .83) and how angry they would be if they heard someone criticize the U.S. (factor loading of .81). But this factor accounted for only 30 percent of the total variance. These two questions are the most "attitudinal" we have, i.e., they are very vague and general and consequently little grounded in fact. Moreover, and to our surprise, these two questions did not form a single factor for the white subsample (N=131).

Our attempt to develop a measure of national involvement must be considered a failure. It is important to ask why we failed. Four possible explanations seem worth consideration: 1) National involvement as an attitude producing human behavior does not exist: 2) The attitude does exist (at least for our black respondents) and is reflected in questions 2 and 3 (see Table 6-1); but national involvement is only one of many variables affecting reactions to specific historical problems such as the Vietnam War or conscientious objectors; 3) The instrument was poorly worded or conceived; for instance, the Vietnam question asked respondents whether they ever thought the war was not "worth fighting." Obviously, "worth" could be interpreted in several different ways, e.g., the war costs too much, the war is immoral, or the Vietnamese are not worth defending; and 4) It now seems likely to us that some of the questions were better measures of nationalism than national involvement. For instance, the Vietnam question is similar to asking people to admit they made a mistake; people can do this even about themselves provided they do not have an image of themselves as being perfect. A crusading nationalist might have such an image of the nation, and thus be unable to admit the nation erred, but someone can be involved with the nation and admit a mistake. Similarly, it seems to us that some of the other questions (especially the ones about spitting on the flag, people fighting for the country, and being scared by the Russians) are probably more related to personal maturity than involvement.

That six questions are interrelated suggests that it is possible that a sense of national involvement does really exist among our respondents. At least in part, the smallness of the interrelations reflects our inadequate reasoning as to the behavioral implications of national involvement. Future attempts to measure involvement by studying its supposed effects must be careful to sort out the effects of involvement, knowledge of specific historical events (like the Vietnam War), and the effects of respondents' immaturity. But the weakness of the correlations, also, casts doubt on the significance of a sense of national involvement in determining how the homemakers of Kilbourntown react to the events that occur around them.

The next section of this chapter will examine responses to one of the questions meant to measure national involvement: "How do you feel when you hear people say how great the United States is—angry, no different than usual, somewhat proud, or very proud?" Of the six questions just discussed this question seems closest to reflecting a sense of oneness with the nation. To feel anger would suggest negative involvement; to be proud would indicate positive involvement; to remain unchanged would suggest indifference. Although this question is obviously relevant to the topic of involvement, we cannot claim it is an adequate measure of involvement. It is too easy to give the "proud" responses. The question is biased in favor of positive involvement. On the other hand, we are not suggesting that people would lie to the interviewers. Most people no doubt believe themselves when they say they would feel proud, but probably more give this response than would actually feel proud if they heard someone praise the United States. The "nation question" is perhaps best understood as a measure of the respondent's self-perception of national involvement. As such it has some value.

FEELING PROUD ABOUT THE UNITED STATES

As noted above there were four responses to the question about how the respondent would feel if she heard people say how great the United States is: get angry, no different than usual, somewhat proud, or very proud. Only four people (two black, two white) chose "angry." This could be realistic on the level of self-consciousness; perhaps only four homemakers can readily admit to themselves that they are basically angered by the nation in which they reside. The small number could also reflect a desire to please our interviewers. At any rate we combined our first two categories into one labelled "indifference." Those who responded "somewhat proud" are labelled "moderate involvement" and those who said "very proud" are listed under "strong involvement."

When we defined national involvement as a sense of oneness with the nation we did not specify that the individual must like the nation. For us involvement can be positive or negative. Someone who loves the nation and another who hates it are equally involved with it. (On this point we differ from many "alienation" studies in which alienation is equated not with the absence of involvement but with the presence of negative involvement, i.e., involvement with a hated object). Given the fact that involvement can be positive or negative, it is especially regretable that we were not able to use our "get angry" category, which would have reflected negative involvement. It must be continually kept in mind that in this section the discussion is restricted to seemingly positive involvement. Moreover, at best our study reflects involvement at the conscious level in a form acceptable to the respondent. Given the turbulent racial situation in the United States it seems especially necessary to remember that an individual need not have only one sense of involvement. As psychoanalysts have taught us we must see the individual as having many layers of personality each of which may have its own sense of involvement. What our study reflects, assuming it is meaningful, is the sense of involvement as the person rather consciously decides to portray it in the public and somewhat formal situation of being interviewed.

AGE, COLOR, AND NATIONAL INVOLVEMENT

Table 6-2 presents the distribution of national-involvement scores by age and color. There is no consistent difference between whites and blacks. The main color difference appears among those sixty and over, in which age range the whites are somewhat more involved in the nation.

Age, on the other hand, does seem significant especially for the whites. There is a tendency for involvement to increase with age among the whites. The data are less clear for the blacks. Involvement and age seem curvilinearly related among the blacks. The percentage of "indifference," for instance, declines then rises. This is also true of the percentage of "strong involvement." A curvilinear pattern also appears in the "strong involvement" column for whites; the peak for "strong involvement" is in the fifty to fifty-nine age range. Overall, it can certainly be concluded that as people age they seem to be more involved with the nation than the very young, i.e., those in their twenties and thirties. But the data also suggest that national involvement declines in old age. The peak of involvement occurs in our sample among those in their fifties.

TABLE 6–2

NATIONAL INVOLVEMENT

	(By age and color of respondent)							
	White				*Black*			
Age[1]	*Indif-ference*	*Moderate involve-ment*	*Strong involve-ment*	*Sample size (N)*	*Indif-ference*	*Moderate involve-ment*	*Strong involve-ment*	*Sample size (N)*
22–29	36%	7%	57%	(14)	25%	18%	57%	(108)
30–39	26	8	66	(24)	25	20	55	(111)
40–49	19	12	69	(26)	13	17	70	(69)
50–59	10	10	81	(31)	15	3	82	(34)
60 and above	11	18	71	(63)	21	16	63	(38)
No re-sponse	—	—	—	(1)	—	—	—	(7)
Total				(159[2])				(367)

1. In this chapter the first age aggregate begins with age "twenty two" because we have restricted our sample to respondents who were of voting-age at the time of the 1964 national election (i.e., one and a half years prior to our study.)

2. Our white subsample in this chapter is 165, but 6 whites did not answer the national involvement question.

REGION AND NATIONAL INVOLVEMENT

We were surprised by the general lack of difference between races in terms of involvement. In all, 70 percent of the whites and 62 percent of the blacks are strongly involved in the nation. Our expectation was that blacks would be much less involved. In Chapter One we set forth the theory that involvement is a function of similarity, power, and knowledge. It seemed to us that whites would have more bases than blacks for feeling positively involved in the nation. Certainly the symbolic personalities of the nation are whites, so that blacks should feel less similar to the "nation" than whites. On the other hand there is some ambiguity regarding the power variable. Although both races are to a significant extent determined by governmental action, this process is much more direct (e.g., welfare services) for the black people, so that blacks might be more conscious of their dependence on the national government. With regard to knowledge we assumed that the whites would know more about the government (which in the United States is probably synonymous with the nation), and so be more involved. Overall, therefore, we expected whites to be more involved with the nation than blacks.

Moveover, in the case of black people it seems to us that there is some conflict between national involvement and loyalty to the black ethnic group. More and more black leaders seem to define the situation as one in which the more loyal you are to your color the less committed you should be to the national institutions and national leaders. "Black" involvement seems to militate against national involvement.

The appearance of the "black nationalism" movement has been accompanied by a renewed sense of brotherhood with black people everywhere. The self-assertion of black people has been accompanied not only by a stress on the separation of black people within the United States but also by an international orientation, at least among some of the leaders. There is a growing interest among black Americans in black people around the world. For instance, there is the use of African names and African styles of dress.

Even if the bases of involvement exist for black people, therefore, this potentiality might never be fully actualized. A prior or higher loyalty to race might prevent the growth of national involvement.

We expected black people to be less involved with the nation, therefore, both because of a relative absence of bases of involvement and because of the effects of their commitment to racial unity. We were very surprised, therefore, by the similarity of white and black respondents.

To explore racial differences further we subdivided the black population into three aggregates: those born in the northern states, those born in the border states, and those born in the southern states. There is little difference between northerners and border people; the percentages for strong national involvement are 50 percent and 49 percent respectively. On the other hand 67 percent of the southerners are high on national involvement.

Table 6-3 presents data on the relation between age, region of birth and national involvement. Considering black people only, age and region both seem significant, but region is the more important of the two. The highest percentage of people who said they would feel very proud occurs among the older black women born in the south.

Part B of the same table contains the scores for whites divided by age in the same manner as we divided the blacks. Comparing just those blacks and whites from the north and border states, there are fewer blacks high on

TABLE 6–3

NATIONAL INVOLVEMENT

	(By region of birth, age, and color of respondent)			
Region of birth and age	*A. National involvement: Black*			
	Indifference	*Moderate involvement*	*Strong involvement*	*Sample size (N)*
North and border states, 39 or below	29%	30%	41%	(59)
North and border states, 40 and above	20	24	56	(46)
Southern states, 39 or below	24	14	62	(159)
Southern states, 40 and above	14	9	77	(92)
				(356[1])
	B. National involvement: White			
North and border states, 39 or below	39%	11%	50%	(38)
North and border states, 40 and above	13	14	73	(120)
				(158[2])

1. Eleven cases were lost; four came from regions other than those reported above; seven did not report age.

2. In one case there was no response for age.

national involvement but there are more indifferent whites among those thirty-nine and below. The higher frequency of indifference among the young whites probably reflects that there are more truly alienated people among the young whites than among the young blacks in our sample. Just as in our analysis of the household we found white mothers who seemed truly uninvolved in every aspect of their environment, so now we similarly find more young white mothers indifferent to the nation. Of course, such people are a minority. We did not check to determine if the ignorant mothers are also indifferent citizens. But the evidence does suggest that the highest percentage of truly alienated people exist in our white sample.

If we compare the older whites with the older blacks from the north and border region a different picture emerges. The older whites are more involved in the nation. Clearly, among those forty and over and born in the northern and border states our expectation that whites would more frequently be highly involved in the nation than blacks is substantiated. However, the difference is not as dramatic as we might have expected.

But we must also compare the older whites with our black subsamples from the south. The older black women from the south and the older white women from the north are almost identical in their distribution of scores.

Why are older black women from the south so involved with the nation? The fact of southern origin seems important. Even among the young, black women from the south are more frequently strongly involved with the nation than young black women from the north. Being southern seems to mean being involved with the nation.

Stouffer in his study of civil liberties found southerners least tolerant of nonconformers, a fact not explainable in terms of rural-urban or educational differences among people from different regions. Stouffer writes: "There is something in Southern culture that tends to differentiate Southerners, in cities as well as rural areas, at all educational levels, from all other regional groups."[4] What is southern culture?

C. Vann Woodward believes that the distinctive history of the South gives this region a unique identity. Further, he suggests that a distinctive regional identity would protect southerners from extreme nationalism.[5] This may be true, but the evidence suggests that a part of this regional identity is national involvement, if not nationalism. Why might southerners more often be strongly involved in the nation? There is one aspect of Woodward's analysis of southern history that suggests an answer. Unlike other Americans, southerners are "concrete;" they are involved in specific places. Woodward quotes Eudora Welty as follows: "Like a good many other [regional] writers, I am myself touched off by place. The place where I am and the place I know, and other places that familarity with and love for... set me to writing my stories." "She speaks of 'the blessing of being located—contained' ".[6] It is possible that the

SOLIDARITY IN A SLUM

sense of being rooted in a certain physical place contributes to national involvement. The sense of being located and of valuing a location might move people to identify with the symbolic representations of that place—the local community, the region, and the nation.

It is also possible that part of the southern heritage is militaristic, almost Prussian-like. If so, this would certainly favor the appearance not only of national involvement but nationalism.

The important point is that, for whatever reason, southern culture seems to explain the unexpectedly high national involvement in our black subsample. Northern blacks are less involved in the nation than northern whites. Of course, it is possible that southern whites are more involved in the nation than southern blacks. We want to stress, however, the apparent role of a regional culture in producing national involvement. We shall return to discuss the significance of southern culture for black people after more data are presented.

MASS MEDIA AND NATIONAL INVOLVEMENT

Karl Deutsch has stressed the point that a nation has a unique communication system, taken in the broad sense to include language, history, and actual exchange of information. "Membership in a people essentially consists in wide complementarity of social communication. It consists in the ability to communicate more effectively. and over a wider range of subjects, with members of one large group than with outsiders."[7]

However, he also notes that "to permit the rise of national consciousness, there must be a minimum, at least, of cohesion and distinctiveness of a people; and these must have acquired at least a minimum of importance in the lives of individuals."[8] Seemingly, communication is effective only if bases of involvement are already present. From the perspective of our theory of involvement the effect of communication *per se* is ambiguous.

The most immediate effect of communication should be greater knowledge and a sense of greater understanding. In terms of our study this should mean that people who use the mass media should become more conscious of the existence of a nation, should realize they have knowledge of this nation, and therefore should be more involved with the nation.

But will this involvement be positive or negative? National leaders pictured on television, for instance, will in almost all cases be white. What will be the reaction of black people? They might realize that American citizenship means dependence on white people, and hate their nation. Or, they could see that leaders such as John F. Kennedy stood for things they valued; realizing, then, that national leaders shared their goals, black people might feel more involved in their nation in a positive way. The mass media can make people realize their dependence on nonlocal events. But will this lead to simple

TABLE 6–4

TELEVISION NEWSCAST VIEWING AND NATIONAL INVOLVEMENT

(By color of respondent)								
	National involvement							
Viewing of national television newscasts	White				Black			
	Indif-ference	Moderate	Strong	Sample size (N)	Indif-ference	Moderate	Strong	Sample size (N)
Don't watch Brinkley or Cronkite	24%	17%	59%	(41)	20%	18%	62%	(91)
Watch Brinkley and/or Cronkite	13	12	75	(118)	21	17	62	(276)
Totals				(159)				(367)

appreciation of a fact or to resentment? Will an awareness of dependence on a national government lead to positive or negative involvement?

There is no doubt that communication seems likely to increase involvement. But the fact of communication, itself, cannot tell us whether the resulting involvement will be positive or negative.

It is difficult, therefore, to predict the overall effect of mass media usage. Our expectation was that the increased information associated with such usage would lead to increased positive involvement. But especially in the case of the black people it it difficult to predict the overall consequence of media usage with any certitude.

In passing it should be noted that we studied two forms of communication: schooling and the mass media. Because it is a means of information-transmission we expected schooling to have effects similar to the mass media. Znaniecki stressed the importance of schooling in giving all children of a nation a common literature, history, set of culture-heroes, and ideology.[9] Unexpectedly we found no relation between years of schooling and national involvement, even after we controlled for age and region of birth. It could be that this outcome reflects the admitted crudeness of our national involvement measure or the absence of any measure of educational quality. The latter problem would seem especially important. But we believe that the effects of formal schooling, except with regard to the development of basic skills, is so superficial that later experience can easily modify the school experience.

Is there any relation between mass media usage and national involvement?

We asked our respondents if they had a television set, and if they did whether they usually watch several specific T.V. personalities. Among the names were Walter Cronkite and David Brinkley.[10] Table 6-4 shows the distribution of national involvement scores according to whether the respondent does or does not watch Brinkley or Cronkite. For whites there is a definite tendency toward strong involvement to be associated with newscast-watching. However, no similar relation appears for the blacks.

The same analysis was done for the black subsample, controlling for age and region of birth. But, generally the subgroups contained too few nonwatchers for meaningful analysis except in the case of the young, southern-born black people; no pattern between the two variables (i.e., media usage and national involvement) appears in this subsample. Television news seems to lack impact on national involvement for our black women.

However, the overwhelming preponderance of those who say they do watch news programs among the blacks must make us suspicious; 75 percent of our sample said they usually watch one or both of the news programs. It could be the people were simply lying. More likely it is a case of the television being on with nobody giving much attention to it as long as the news is on. It could be argued that we should have asked how often they watch news programs. But we thought that any contact with such an effective media as television would have an impact.

We also asked our respondents: "Do you have a chance to read any newspapers?" If they said "yes" we asked them which one and whether they read them "about every day, several times a week, or a couple of times a month." Note that this question puts more of a burden on the respondent than the television-news question. She must name the newspapers, and then answer the frequency question in terms of each named newspaper.

Table 6-5 presents the national involvement data according to the frequency of newspaper-reading. If the respondent read more than one newspaper, she was classified according to the highest frequency with which she read any one newspaper. Clearly, for the white people national involvement appears to be positively related to newspaper-reading. Because of sample-size problems we were not able to use all our reading-frequency categories. The analysis of the white subsample, however, does give some support to the idea that frequent involvement with the mass media is associated with positive national involvement.

The data for the black sample do not show this pattern. Newspaper-reading does not seem related to national involvement among our black respondents. Those who read a newspaper "a couple of times a month," however, deviate from everybody else; they are twice as frequently indifferent as the rest of the black sample. Of course, there are only few of these cases (N=27). But there seems to be a reasonable explanation for their relatively high frequency of indifference. It must be remembered that "a couple of times a month" is the lowest reading-frequency offered those who said they do get a chance to read the newspaper. It is quite possible that some of these respondents never read the newspaper more than two or three times a year. Still, why would they more often be indifferent than those who never read a newspaper? We suggest that those who never read a paper develop an alternative means of gathering information such as listening to the radio. On the other hand, those who chose the lowest reading-frequency category are those who do use the newspaper to find out what is happening in the world but who hardly ever bother to get this information. In short, it is possible that the people in the "couple of times a month" category do know least about the nation, so that their high frequency of indifference would be consistent with our expectation that information would increase positive involvement.

But, in general Table 6-5 suggests that frequency of newspaper-reading among black respondents is not significantly related to national involvement. To check this further we controlled for age and region of birth, then calculated the percentage that gave the "very proud" response. Table 6-6 presents these percentages for the black sample.

TABLE 6–5

NEWSPAPER READING FREQUENCY AND NATIONAL INVOLVEMENT

	(By color of respondent)							
	National involvement							
	White[1]				Black			
Frequency of reading daily newspapers	Indifference	Moderate	Strong	Sample size (N)	Indifference	Moderate	Strong	Sample size (N)
Daily	13%	13%	74%	(124)	21%	20%	59%	(170)
Several times a week					20	13	67	(106)
Couple of times a month	29	14	57	(35)	41	10	49	(27)
Don't read newspapers					19	14	67	(64)
Total				(159)				(367)

1. Because of small frequencies we combined, for the whites only all the reading categories except "daily."

134   SOLIDARITY IN A SLUM

TABLE 6–6

PERCENTAGE GIVING STRONG NATIONAL INVOLVEMENT RESPONSE

(By newspaper reading frequency, region of birth, and age of respondent for blacks)[1]

Newspaper-reading frequency	North and border region				Southern region			
	39 or below		40 and above		39 or below		40 and above	
	%	N	%	N	%	N	%	N
Daily	34	(32)	58	(26)	59	(70)	83	(40)
Several times a week	53	(15)	55	(11)	62	(50)	83	(24)
Couple of times a month	—	(5)	—	(2)	60	(15)	—	(5)
Don't read newspapers	—	(7)	—	(7)	71	(24)	65	(23)

1. There is a total sample of 356; 11 cases were lost because respondents come from different regions or did not report age.

First, let us consider age and region differences, In all but one case the older respondents are more often strongly involved in the nation; the exception occurs among the southern-born women who do not read any newspaper, among whom young and old are much alike. Consistently, the southern-born are often strongly involved in the nation. Both age and birth-place, therefore, remain related to national involvement.

Second, let us consider the impact of newspaper-reading frequency by looking down each column. Looking at the black women born outside the south, there are usually only a few cases in each cell of the table, but it is interesting to note that the young daily readers stand out from the other subgroups because of the relative infrequency of strong national involvement. Among young non-southerners, then, frequent newspaper-reading seems associated with the absence of national involvement.

A somewhat similar process occurs among the young southern-born black women. In this subgroup strong involvement occurs most often among those who do not read any newspaper, but the difference between daily readers and nonreaders is only 12 percent. On the other hand, there is a stronger tendency in the reverse direction among the older southern-born women. In this subgroup our expectations about the effect of exposure to newspapers is supported. However, among the young reading the newspaper seems associated, although weakly, with the absence of strong involvement. This suggests that the more the young women learn about what is going on, the less often they identify with the nation.

Our ideas concerning the influence of the mass media seem to fit the white respondents' behavior. But among the black women television-news watching is insignificant, and the effects of newspaper-reading are not consistently in the same direction. Yet the fact that most surprised us is the strong national involvement of the southern-born black women.

If anybody in our total sample has a right to hate the United States it is the southern black person. These people have been deprived of their civil and human rights. Yet they have high national involvement (the reader must remember that in this discussion involvement means positive involvement). For the southern negro, culture seems to drown out experience. We cannot imagine that there are more bases in the experience of southern blacks for them to feel national involvement than there are in the life of northern blacks. Southern black involvement seems artificial, something implanted by cultural agents but lacking any roots in the daily experience of the black respondents.

The argument might be made that northern black people are affected by relative deprivation. Because northerners expect more, they are more easily frustrated. As a result they have a less positive attitude toward the national government. This may be sound reasoning, but it does not tell us why southern black people should feel a strong positive involvement with the nation.

It is true that the question used to measure national involvement reflects only the respondent's conscious image of her involvement. But for whites this image seems to be meaningful, i.e., it is related in the expected manner to a possible basis in experience for national involvement. On the other hand, among the black respondents this image seems to mirror not experience with the nation but regional culture. The pattern of black involvement does not seem justified by experience; the pattern seems to be the result of a culture unthinkingly passed on from generation to generation, which has produced a people whose verbal reactions are divorced from their experience.

Our data suggest that among the black respondents there exists a subtle form of self-alienation. Southern culture seems to have produced people whose conscious image of themselves does not seem justified in their daily experience. What are the consequences of this form of self-alienation? This is a question for future research.

Since we question the meaningfulness of the involvement question for our black respondents, it seemed inappropriate to continue the analysis on national involvement using this question. If the response to this question does not seem to be justified by the black person's actual experiences, then the answer probably tells us little about the extent to which the nation serves as a source of order in the daily lives of our black respondents. If the answer is artificial, it would not be an accurate indicator of the extent to which our respondents orient their lives by national goals and by their role as citizens.

The rest of this chapter will be concerned with voting in the 1964 presidential election (Johnson versus Goldwater). Voting in an election is not an adequate measure of national involvement. On the other hand, it is a sign that a person does orient her life through her role as a citizen. We are not interested in the candidate or person supported, but whether people voted. Our concern is not to label people as "liberal" or "conservative," but as "involved" or "uninvolved." Voting is an indication that a person is involved in the nation. It is not a measure of involvement but a sign of involvement.

NATIONAL INVOLVEMENT AND VOTING

Voting is one of the most studied aspects of human behavior. In the course of all this research voting has been found to be related to a host of variables. Stokes divides these variables into three types: 1) Voting is normative, i.e., people vote because they are supposed to; voting is a good thing in itself in American culture. On the other hand, one reason women might not vote is because the norm is less applicable to them than to men; 2) Voting is instrumental, i.e., people vote because voting is a means to some desired goal. Obviously a great variety of goals might be relevant to political action, which means that the actual immediate motivations for the voting will be quite diverse, making empirical study difficult. On the other hand, people might lack self-confidence or feel that the situation is hopeless, or that the right result is assured even without their vote, and so not participate in the election; or the instrumental act might not occur because a person is pulled in different directions by different goals, and the resulting tension might be resolved by withdrawal from the situation; 3) Voting is expressive. By this Stokes seems to mean that the act of voting might become symbolically connected with nonpolitical objects; so, for instance, someone might refrain from voting because his hated father is a politician, and not voting is a means of hurting him. This brief summary suggests the variety of variables that could be considered in any analysis of voting. We shall be limited in our approach and consider only a few relevant variables.[11]

Stokes's "expressive" category refers to voting as a symbolic act. We would expect that those who are highly involved in the nation would be motivated to express this involvement by voting. One pressure to vote, therefore, would be to express national involvement.

This theory assumes that involvement seeks to express itself. As commonsensical as our argument might sound, there is in fact no truly obvious reason why national involvement must express itself in voting. However, we do think there should be such a relationship, i.e., we do suggest that if people feel involved, and if they are offered an opportunity to express this involvement, they will accept it. There are two lines of argument why this might be so. First, it might be that a sense of involvement loses its significance if not expressed

TABLE 6-7

NATIONAL INVOLVEMENT AND PERCENTAGE VOTING

(By color of respondent)

	Percentage voting			
National involvement	White		Black	
	%	N	%	N
Indifference	42	(26)	47	(79)
Moderate involvement	66	(21)	59	(59)
Strong involvement	57	(112)	57	(225)
Total		(159)		(363)[1]

1. In four cases the respondent did not answer the voting question.

in overt action. People might seek to express or concretize their involvement in order to give reality to this feeling. This interpretation suggests that people seek out opportunities to express their involvements. Second, it might be that if a person is presented with an opportunity to act out a sense of involvement, and fails to act, this abstention would imply that the person is not involved; and to avoid the tension that would result from the apparent inconsistency of being involved but acting as if not involved, the more involved people would vote. There seems ample reason, then, for suggesting a relation between national involvement and voting.

Table 6-7 presents the relevant data. There is some modest support here for our theory. Indifferent respondents vote least often among both whites and blacks. On the other hand there is little difference between the other two degrees of national involvement. That the difference between the percentage voting among the indifferent respondents and the percentages for the two categories of involvement is greater among the whites is consistent with our argument that black involvement is artificial.

The association between national involvement and voting supports the idea that voting is a sign of involvement. Some people might argue, however, that no contemporary presidential election has offered a meaningful choice, so that voting has little significance. This may be true. It follows, then, that some people who are highly involved in the nation may choose not to vote because they view this act as trivial. We assume such people are few in Kilbourntown. Our purpose in the next section is to determine through an analysis of voting which people in Kilbourntown orient their lives to a national social order. Since Americans are expected to vote only once or twice a year, someone could

TABLE 6–8

PERCENTAGE VOTING

Age	White		Black	
	%	*N*	*%*	*N*
22–29	—	(10)	36	(105)
30–39	52	(25)	56	(112)
40–49	50	(26)	61	(71)
50–59	69	(33)	64	(34)
60–74	60	(48)	78	(37)
75 plus	30	(20)	—	(2)
No response	—	(3)	—	(7)
Total		(165)		(368)

(By age and color of respondent)

Percentage voting

vote at every opportunity and spend most of his life unconcerned about the nation. Sudying voting is only a crude substitute for what is needed—a measure of the extent to which daily life or at least major decisions are influenced by national goals. Until such a measure is developed, analyses of voting may be useful in suggesting conditions that foster an orientation to the national social order.

VOTING

Table 6-8 presents the percentage voting by age and color. Two aggregates stand out: the old whites and the young blacks. That fewer young people vote than middle-aged people seems generally true.[12] But the analysis of national data by Glenn and Grimes does not support the idea that old people are less likely to vote than the middle-aged; 90 percent of the people interviewed in the research reported by Glenn and Grimes who were seventy to seventy-nine years old voted in the 1964 election.[13] Apparently the elderly white ladies of Kilbourntown are far from representative of their age cohort. They are much more alienated than the typical elderly person. Of course, the age range of the elderly women we interviewed went higher than seventy-nine; but it seems unlikely that the difference between 30 percent (the percent voting in our study) and 90 percent (the percent voting in research reported by Glenn and Grimes) can be explained by the difference in the age ranges. The elderly white ladies in Kilbourntown cannot be considered representative of people their age.

TABLE 6–9

VIEWING OF NATIONAL TELEVISION NEWSCASTS AND PERCENTAGE VOTING

(By color of respondent)

Viewing of national television newscasts	Percentage voting			
	White		Black	
	%	N	%	N
Don't own television	40	(15)	33	(18)
Own a television, don't watch newscasts	54	(28)	44	(73)
Watch Brinkley and/or Cronkite	60	(122)	58	(277)
Total		(165)		(368)

Between thirty and seventy-four years of age the pattern is different for whites and for blacks. Among the former there seems to be a curvilinear relation between age and the percentage voting, while among the black respondents there seems to be a linear, positive relationship. Such different patterns prevent any conclusion about the relation of aging to national involvement.

Generally, the percentages are higher for the black respondents. The most striking difference is among those sixty to seventy-four years old, among whom the blacks have a much higher voting percentage.

It might be argued that our failure to eliminate those who could not vote because of residency requirements might account for the low percentage of young black voters. But among those black women in their twenties who have lived in Milwaukee five years or less, 28 percent voted, while among those who have lived in Milwaukee six to ten years, 34 percent voted. If residency was a major explanation for the low percentage of voters we would expect a large difference between these two subsamples.

Using voting as a sign of national involvement, we can say that among the young and the old the nation seems of little relevance. For the rest of the sample at least the majority voted.

What influences people to orient their lives to the state?

It seems probable that those people who make use of the mass media will vote. It has been found that people with more political knowledge are more likely to vote.[14] Knowledge can motivate voting in at least two ways: 1) Knowledge is a source of involvement. Learning about the nation, therefore, would increase national involvement and people involved with the nation are likely to express their involvement by voting; 2) Knowledge helps people to understand how their goals are related to national programs, and people who have this understanding are more likely to vote. Because the mass media transmit political knowledge, especially in their news programs, and because such knowledge is related to voting, it seems probable that media involvement is also related to voting.

Table 6-9 presents data on television-news watching and voting. For both whites and blacks more of those who watch the newscasts voted. However, among the whites there is little difference between those who own a television but do not watch newscasts and those who do watch them. These two aggregates are quite different among the blacks. The evidence suggests, therefore, that news programs are more significant for blacks than whites.

Table 6-10 presents data on newspaper-reading frequency and voting. There is again a positive relation between mass media involvement and the voting-percentage, and again the relationship is stronger for blacks than for whites. The only deviance from our expectations is that the "couple of times a month" readers are lower even than the nonreaders. But this is consistent with our previous discussion of who is likely to use the "couple of times a month" response. As the reader will recall, the people choosing this response showed the least involvement in the nation on the basis of the "nation" question.

In general, mass media involvement is positively related to voting percentage, but this relationship is stronger for the black sample. This is similar to the finding of Matthews and Prothro that exposure to the mass media is associated with a greater increase in political participation among southern blacks than among southern whites.[15]

But is it that media involvement itself is important, or is it that other variables motivate people both to learn about their environment and to vote, without their being any direct connection between this learning and voting? As would be expected among the black respondent: 1) more of those born in the north (71 percent) voted, than those born in the border states (54 percent) or in the south (52 percent); 2) more of those born in a city (70 percent) voted than those born in a small city (55 percent), a town (59 percent), or on a farm (49 percent). However, when we compared our black respondents who had had one to eight years of schooling with those who had had more, we found no

TABLE 6–10

NEWSPAPER READING FREQUENCY AND PERCENTAGE VOTING

Newspaper-reading frequency[1]	Percentage voting			
	White		Black	
	%	N	%	N
Daily	59	(130)	67	(170)
Several times a week	53	(17)	53	(103)
Couple of times a month	—	(7)	30	(28)
Don't read newspapers	45	(11)	40	(67)
Total		(165)		(368)

(By color of respondent)

1. This is based on how frequently the respondent read either of the two major daily newspapers: the Journal and the Sentinel. If the respondent read both, but with different frequencies, the higher frequency was used in assigning the respondent to a category.

difference; in both aggregates 54 percent voted. We decided to form subsamples based on region of birth. urbanness (people were divided into those born in a large city and everyone else), and age. Table 6-11 presents the subsamples and the percentage of each who voted. The range of percentages (30-84 percent) is quite dramatic. The young, nonurban, southern-born stand out as nonvoters. All three variables—region, urbanness, age—seeem to be significant. Is media involvement related to voting percentage within these subsamples?

Table 6-12 shows the relation between newspaper-reading frequency and voting percentage within four subsamples. The northern and the southern urban subsamples are combined because of the small frequencies of each type. Although some of the cells in Table 6-12 are quite small, the pattern is the same as in Table 6-10. Media involvement is positively related to voting percentage.

An analysis similar to that in Table 6-12 except involving television-newscast watching showed that this variable continued to be related to voting percentage even within subsamples.

In a way our results seem to be too good. This is especially true with regard to newspaper-reading. Why is there a difference between people who read a paper "daily" and those who read it "several times a week"? Between national elections both groups must pick up plenty of information about national events. Why, then, are they different in voting percentages? Similarly, we found that more of those people who read two newspapers voted than of those who reported reading only one. Is there not a saturation point for

TABLE 6-11

PERCENTAGE VOTING, CONTROLLING FOR REGION OF BIRTH, URBANNESS OF BIRTHPLACE, AND AGE

(For blacks)

Region	Urbanness[1]	Age	Percentage voting %	N
North	——	less than 30	62	(13)
North	——	30 and above	84	(31)
South	urban	less than 30	64	(14)
South	urban	30 and above	73	(22)
South	non-urban	less than 30	30	(76)
South	non-urban	30 and above	59	(199)
Total				(355)[2]

1. All those born in the North were considered to come from an urban environment.

2. Five voters and eight non-voters are excluded from failure to report age, region, or degree of urbanness; or because they do not come from the regions listed.

politically relevant information? Can the people who read two newspapers learn that much more than those who read only one? Table 6-12 suggests that there are just 3 significant groupings from the perspective of voting: those that read papers daily, those who say they read a "couple of times a month," and the rest, i.e., the people who responded either "several times a week" or "don't read;" their voting percentages are similar in the two subsamples in which we had enough cases to compare the aggregates. It is possible that many of the "don't read" respondents simply cannot read. For them reading is out as a source of information. But it is conceivable that for some of them their level of interest is high enough that they seek out information about the world in which they live from sources other than newspapers. As already suggested the "couple of times a month" respondents would be people who could and do read, but rarely because of their lack of interest in their environment.

But why is there such a difference between "daily" readers and the others, and especially why is there such a difference between "daily" readers and those who read the papers "several times a week"? We suggest that the choice of a frequency category is related to content of what is read. "Daily" readers would be people who read all the paper, while the other readers would be more selective, reading either the sports section, or the fashion section, or certain sensational stories or the like. We do not have the data to test this suggestion. However, based on our personal experience it seems plausible.

We suggest, therefore, that we have three aggregates: 1) those who read

TABLE 6–12

NEWSPAPER READING FREQUENCY AND PERCENTAGE VOTING
WITHIN FOUR RELATIVELY HOMOGENEOUS SUBSAMPLES THAT
EMERGED FROM CONTROLLING FOR REGION OF BIRTH,
URBANNESS OF BIRTHPLACE, AND AGE OF RESPONDENT

(For Blacks)

Frequency of reading daily newspaper	Percentage voting							
	South, non-urban, less than 30		South, non-urban, 30 and above		North; South urban; less than 30		North; South urban; 30 and above	
	%	N	%	N	%	N	%	N
Daily	39	(23)	69	(98)	69	(13)	87	(31)
Several times a week	25	(24)	54	(50)	—	(9)	75	(16)
Couple of times a month	—	(8)	27	(14)	—	(3)	—	(2)
Don't read news-papers	28	(21)	49	(37)	—	(2)	—	(4)
Total		(76)		(199)		(27)		(53)

"daily" and read all the news; 2) those who read the newspaper rarely; such individuals use the newspaper as a source of information but so rarely that it does not motivate them to political participation; and 3) the rest—a composite made up of people who do not read but use other media, as well as those who read the papers but do so selectively. This third aggregate occasionally becomes aware of politically relevant information, and thus some of them are motivated to vote, depending on the interplay of a host of forces.

The television question did not ask about frequency of watching, so we can not adequately compare our different categories on the television and newspaper questions.

VOLUNTARY ASSOCIATION AND VOTING

Numerous studies have found that those who belong to voluntary associations are more politically active.[16] McClosky argues that this relation between membership and political activity occurs because: 1) experience in association makes people more articulate; 2) it increases their sensitivity to the relation between their self-interest and political events; and 3) membership means exposure to agencies of socialization, which will reinforce the sense of civic duty.[17] Seeman's work reinforces the idea that participation in associations

TABLE 6–13

MEMBERSHIP IN VOLUNTARY ASSOCIATIONS AND PERCENTAGE
VOTING

Voluntary association membership	Percentage voting			
	White		Black	
	%	N	%	N
Non-member	48	(104)	44	(185)
Membership in one association	71	(41)	63	(124)
Two or more memberships	75	(20)	77	(59)
		(165)	(368)	

(By color of respondent)

would increase self-confidence. Specifically, he found that absence of membership in organizations is associated with a general sense of powerlessness.[18] Finally, participation in associations means exposure to a greater variety of interpersonal influences than would be found among family and close friends, so that if a person has any inclination to vote, she would be more likely to find social support for this action if she is a member of formal organizations.

In this section, we shall: 1) consider whether there is evidence to support the significance of voluntary associations for our sample, and 2) try to determine if media involvement is important, after controlling for association membership.

Table 6-13 relates organization membership and number of memberships to voting. "Voluntary association" in this analysis refers to: fraternal organizations, social clubs, veterans' organizations, community-improvement groups, labor unions, civil rights groups, church-related groups (but not church membership itself), P.T.A. or "Home and School," and political organizations. Each respondent was asked if she is a member of each type of organization just enumerated; in addition, there was a general question about whether she was a member of any other organization. The data in Table 6-13 shows the expected positive relation between association membership and voting.

Among the whites the number of memberships is less important than for our black respondents. Among the latter there is a significant difference between those belonging to only one organization and those belonging to two or more. This suggests that the white respondents are more disposed to vote and require fewer additional motivating forces in their environment before they are moved to vote.

TABLE 6–14

THE FREQUENCY OF ATTENDANCE AT VOLUNTARY ASSOCIATION
MEETINGS AND PERCENTAGE VOTING

(By color of respondent)

Frequency of attendance at voluntary association meetings	Percentage voting			
	White		Black	
	%	N	%	N
Frequent	81	(26)	77	(75)
Occasional	78	(14)	64	(50)
Rare	57	(12)	55	(18)
Non-member	48	(104)	42	(187)
Total		(156)[1]		(330)[1]

1. Nine whites and thirty eight blacks did not report frequency.

We would expect that if the processes suggested by McClosky are important, then voting percentage should be related not only to membership but also to frequency of attendance at organizational meetings. For each organization the respondent was asked whether she attended meetings "frequently," "occa-

TABLE 6–15

MEMBERSHIP IN VOLUNTARY ASSOCIATIONS AND PERCENTAGE
VOTING WITHIN FOUR RELATIVELY HOMOGENEOUS SUBSAMPLES
THAT EMERGED FROM CONTROLLING FOR REGION OF BIRTH,
URBANNESS OF BIRTHPLACE, AND AGE OF RESPONDENT

(For blacks)

Voluntary association membership	Percentage voting							
	I South, non-urban, less than 30		II South, non-urban, 30 and above		III North; South urban; less than 30		IV North; South urban; 30 and above	
	%	N	%	N	%	N	%	N
Member	39	(38)	70	(92)	83	(12)	88	(33)
Non-member	21	(38)	49	(107)	47	(15)	65	(20)
Total		(76)		(199)		(27)		(53)

SOLIDARITY IN A SLUM

TABLE 6–16

NEWSPAPER-READING FREQUENCY, VOLUNTARY ASSOCIATION MEMBERSHIP, AND PERCENTAGE VOTING

	(By color of respondent)							
	Percentage voting							
Frequency of reading daily newspapers	*White*				*Black*			
	Association member		*Non-member*		*Association member*		*Non-member*	
	%	N	%	N	%	N	%	N
Daily	70	(52)	50	(78)	74	(104)	56	(66)
Several times or don't read	—	(6)	50	(22)	61	(72)	39	(98)
Couple of times a month	—	(3)	—	(4)	—	(7)	29	(21)
		(61)		(104)		(183)		(185)

sionally" or "rarely." In categorizing a respondent we used the single highest reported frequency for the organizations of which she is a member. Thus, if a respondent belongs to two organizations and attends one "frequently," but the other only "occasionally" she was categorized as a frequent attender for purposes of our analysis. Table 6-14 shows the relation between frequency of attendance and voting percentage. For the blacks especially there is a smooth, consistent increase in percentage voting as frequency of attendance increases. For the whites there is a basically similar pattern, although there is a tendency for the whites to dichotomize into frequent and occasional attenders versus the rest.

In Table 6-15 we compare members and nonmembers among the black respondents, controlling for age, region of birth, and urbanness of birth place. A difference of about 20 percent occurs within each subsample between members and nonmembers.

MASS MEDIA, VOLUNTARY ASSOCIATION MEMBERSHIP, AND VOTING

It is quite conceivable that those who read the newspapers frequently are also the people who belong to organizations. Is each of these variables independently associated with voting, or is it only one of them that affects political participation? Table 6-16 presents data on newspaper-reading frequency, as-

TABLE 6–17

NEWSPAPER-READING FREQUENCY, VOLUNTARY ASSOCIATION
MEMBERSHIP, AND PERCENTAGE VOTING FOR BLACK
RESPONDENTS BORN IN THE NON-URBAN SOUTH AND THIRTY
YEARS OR MORE OF AGE

Frequency of reading daily newspaper	Percentage voting			
	Association member		Non-member	
	%	N	%	N
Daily	75	(51)	64	(47)
Several times or don't read	69	(36)	39	(51)
Couple of times a month	—	(5)	—	(9)
		(92)		(107)

sociational membership, and voting percentage. For the white subsample, reading frequency seems unimportant, since both categories of reading frequency in the nonmember column have the same percentage of voters. However, association membership does seem important; there is a 20 percent difference between members and nonmembers among "daily" readers. It is also interesting that 85 percent of the white association members are "daily" readers. Among both whites and blacks we have an example of the 'piling on' process, i.e., those who are association members, and thus likely to vote, are disproportionately also "daily" readers. On the other hand, the percentages for the black subsamples support the conclusion that both reading frequency and association membership are significant. The lowest percentage is for the "couple of times - nonmember" category (29 percent), followed by the "several times/don't read - nonmember" category (39 percent). Appropriately, the highest percentage is for the "daily-member" cell (74 percent). Reading across the table and reading down the table, significant differences appear. The range of percentages (29-74 percent) is also impressive.

Why does reading frequency appear to be a more meaningful variable for the black respondents than for the white subsample? Among the whites 79 percent report reading the newspaper "daily," while only 46 percent of our black respondents said they read that often. Whites more than blacks are raised and live in an environment where newspapers are routinely bought and perused. Whites develop a habit of newspaper buying, but not all who buy read carefully through the paper. On the other hand, black people buy a newspaper regularly less out of habit and more because they want to read it. We are

TABLE 6–18

TELEVISION-NEWS WATCHING8 VOLUNTARY ASSOCIATION MEMBERSHIP AND PERCENTAGE VOTING

	(For blacks)			
	Percentage voting			
Viewing of national television newscasts	Association member		Non-member	
	%	N	%	N
Watch Brinkley and/or Cronkite	73	(144)	47	(135)
Own a television, but don't watch newscasts	50	(32)	41	(39)
Don't own television	—	(7)	36	(11)
		(183)		(185)

suggesting that our reading-frequency categories more faithfully represent information-absorption among the blacks than among the whites. When a white person says she reads the newspaper daily this may mean little more than she buys it everyday. From the point of view of our theory, then, our questions probably are more meaningful among the blacks, for whom both media usage and association membership appear significant.

Table 6-17 is the same as the preceding table except we have limited our sample to those black women born in the nonurban South and thirty or more years of age, which is our largest subsample. Within this subsample reading frequency seems less important, than in the previous table, among association members. However, it is quite significant among non-members. Both media usage and association membership appear significant even in this subsample.

The analysis of the combined effects of television-news watching and organizational membership also tends to support the argument that both variables are significant. Tables 6-18 and 6-19 present the relevant data; both in our total black sample (the distribution of cases did not allow a meaningful analysis of whites) and in the subsample of nonurban, southern born, older women, percentages increase if the respondent watches the news and if she belongs to at least one association.

To evaluate the relative effect of newspaper reading and television watching let us compare Tables 6-17 and 6-19. The former table reveals that reading frequency is mainly important among the nonmembers, and that association membership has a greater effect among those who are not daily readers. Table

TABLE 6–19

TELEVISION-NEWS WATCHING, VOLUNTARY ASSOCIATION
MEMBERSHIP, AND PERCENTAGE VOTING FOR BLACKS BORN IN
THE NON-URBAN SOUTH AND THIRTY YEARS OF AGE OR MORE

Viewing of national television newscasts	Percentage voting			
	Association member		Non-member	
	%	N	%	N
Watch Brinkley and/or Cronkite	75	(72)	51	(80)
Others[1]	50	(20)	41	(27)
		(92)		(107)

1. This includes those who don't own a television and those who own one but do not watch Brinkley or Cronkite.

6-19 reveals that television has a bigger inpact among association members, and that associational membership mainly effects those who watch the news. Looking at Table 6-19 it seems that television and membership have a significant impact only when they work together, i.e., among those who watch the news and belong to at least one organization. By themselves television and membership each increase voting percentage by about 10 percent only. On the other hand, newspapers seem able to have an independent effect. In fact, their main impact is among those who are nonmembers. In short, it seems as if there are two distinct processes that furnish the information that motivates people to vote: 1) watching television-newscasts and joining organizations, and 2) reading the newspaper daily.

If we might speculate further, we would suggest that these processes are associated with different types of voters. The second process, daily newspaper-reading, would suggest a more individualistic voter; someone who digests information alone. She is someone free to choose what to read and how to interpret it. Such a person might, also, change perspective less often because she is able to selectively perceive only what reinforces her present position. On the other hand, someone who receives information from television and from fellow organizational members is less able to control the flow of information and the process of interpretation. Such an individual would be more fluctuating in political behavior and more subject to social manipulation. But these ideas represent tentative hypotheses for further investigation.

Why is it that television-news watching and associational membership seems to be weak influences except when they are combined? If the effect of membership was to increase self-confidence or articulateness, we would expect this variable to have an impact independent of television, since the television-watching is not likely to increase confidence or articulateness. The most likely explanation for their weak influence as separate variables is that both are having their main impact through information-transmittal, but that neither gives sufficient information by itself for people to see the relation between their problems and political action.

It could be argued that the main variable producing voting is socialization, and that television simply reinforces the social obligation to vote, which is also supported by voluntary organizations. But it seems likely that the major part of socialization takes place through interpersonal contact, and therefore if a sense of civic duty is the main motive for voting, organizational membership should show a greater significance than it does.

If information-transmittal is the key variable affecting voting, then the type of organization a person belongs to should be related to voting. Following are several types of organizations our black respondents belonged to, the percentage of members who voted, and the total number of members in each organizational type: church-related groups—64 percent (N=65); P.T.A.—68 percent voted (N=109); civil rights groups—88 percent voted (N=19). The high percentage of voters in the civil rights groups makes sense, but we expected more P.T.A. members to vote than church-group members. However, it must be remembered that, as mentioned in the last chapter, P.T.A. members have poor attendance records. Moreover, some P.T.A. groups are no more than social clubs, while some religious leaders are political activists.

Other studies have found no relation between type of voluntary association and political behavior or attitudes.[19] There are two facts, then, that suggest that membership in voluntary associations is itself not an important variable. These facts are: 1) that type of organization is not important, and 2) in our study, that organizational membership has its main effect only in conjunction with television-news watching (see Table 6-18). On the other hand, that among television-news watchers a much higher percentage of association members voted suggests that organizations can channel the concern of people already interested in their environment into the field of politics.

To summarize: we have tried to study the political significance of the mass media and organizational membership. Our arguments have stressed that both are sources of information that, for several reasons, can motivate interest in the state. The data suggest two distinct information flows—one via daily newspaper-reading, the other via more public occasions for receiving information, such as at group meetings or from television newscasts, which often are watched with others. It is possible that these two processes are associated with two quite different types of political participants. What is most important for

TABLE 6–20

AGE OF RESPONDENT, YEARS IN MILWAUKEE, AND THE
PERCENTAGE VOTING

	(For blacks)			
	Percentage voting			
Age	*0–15 years in Milwaukee*		*16 years or more in Milwaukee*	
	%	N	%	N
22–29	35	(90)	67	(15)
30–39	51	(84)	71	(28)79
40–49	50	(34)	71	(35)
50–59	60	(15)	68	(19)
60 and over	72	(18)	86	(21)
		(241)		(118¹)

1. Nine cases were lost; eight of these failed to report age, while one did not report years in Milwaukee,

our purposes, however, is to affirm that media usage and organizational membership both are related to people using the nation as a point of orientation in their lives. The analysis of voting suggests that national involvement is related to both media involvement and associational membership.

However, it is possible that the relation, for instance, between media involvement and voting is due—not to one causing the other—but to the fact that both are related to another variable not included in our study. Only further research can eliminate this possibility.

MOBILITY AND VOTING

On the one hand, it could be argued that no matter where people move, they remain in the United States, so that mobility should not affect voting. Moreover, the mass media carry the same news all over the country, and many voluntary associations are national in scope, so that even if people move, they remain in the same national information network. On the other hand, moving poses problems such as having to reregister to vote and the like. But, more important from our point of view, the question arises whether in order for a national government to appear relevant a person must have roots and relationships in the local environment. Does a person who moves have a sense of somehow drifting above or outside of political systems? Is it difficult for someone to think of an act like voting as being personally relevant if the individual is not involved in the local community?

TABLE 6–21

YEARS IN MILWAUKEE AND THE PERCENTAGE VOTING

(For blacks 22–39 years old)		
Years in Milwaukee	Percentage voting	
	%	N
0–5	31	(62)
6–10	41	(56)
11–15	57	(57)
16 and over	70	(43)

Table 6-20 shows the difference in voting percentages between those who lived in Milwaukee fifteen years or less and the rest, controlling for age. Consistently more voting occurred among the age aggregates longer in residence.[20]

Table 6-21 presents a more refined analysis of years in Milwaukee for the black subpopulation twenty-two to thirty-nine years of age. The effects of mobility seem to wear off at different speeds for different individuals. There is no sharp dividing point below which we see the effects of mobility, and above which they have disappeared. Rather, the increase in voting percentage is gradual and continuous. The data suggest that participation in national affairs seems related to the development of local relationships.

This, of course, is consistent with our finding that voluntary association membership is a significant variable. The question arises whether the fact of membership in formal organizations or the degree to which any form of relationship has been developed is the crucial variable. To answer this question we divided our black sample into those twenty-two to twenty-nine and those thirty and over. Each subsample was further divided into those who are voluntary association members and those who are not. We then examined the relation between length of stay in Milwaukee and voting. Overall, both length of residence and association membership remained significant. In all subsamples a higher percentage of the more stable residents voted; similarly, holding constant length of residence, there still remained a difference in voting percentage, depending on whether the respondent was an association member or not. To compare the extremes, among the young, nonmember newcomers (in Milwaukee five years or less) 30 percent (N=23) while 82 percent (N=63) of the older, more stable (in Milwaukee sixteen years or more) association members voted. In the more detailed analysis, then, both length of residence and organizational affiliation retained significance.

The data, therefore, are consistent with the idea that national political participation, at least in the form of voting, is dependent on the degree of involvement in local relationships.

This evidence suggests the interesting idea that the expression of involvement in any social unit might be related to the degree of involvement in the immediate environment. Action, in general, may be affected by the degree to which we experience life as real. When does life become like reading a novel? When does the distinction between reality and fantasy become unimportant? We suggest that to the extent we are not involved in the environment of our daily life, a newspaper becomes a novel, and we lose the sense of urgency necessary for action. Perhaps involvement "in the environment of our daily life" is necessary to make life real.

CONCLUSION

We began this chapter by asking two questions: How involved are our respondents in the nation? What produces this involvement?

If we assume that both voting in the 1964 presidential election and giving the "strong involvement" response to the nation question are indicators of some national involvement, then a little over 80 percent of the sample is to some extent involved in the nation. Only 14 percent of the whites and 19 percent of the blacks neither voted nor chose the "strong involvement" response. We contacted only about 82 percent of the total number of households in Kilbourntown during our study. Possibly the people we could not reach are the less involved residents of K-3, but it is also conceivable that we could not contact these people because they were so busy outside their house in social activities like working, visiting, or going to meetings. Overall, there are surprisingly few people in Kilbourntown who do not indicate some involvement with the nation.

Certainly, it can not be said that our respondents live out their lives only in a world of personal relations. True isolation from the larger world would mean that the respondents would not vote, watch television newscasts or belong to any voluntary association. Only 8 percent of the sample fits this description. On the other hand, 29 percent did vote, watch television news, and belong to at least one voluntary association. The homemakers of Kilbourntown are generally in touch with a world that goes beyond their family.

As to what produces involvement we have stressed, following Deutsch, the importance of the flow of information. We assumed that if people receive information about national events they would be involved with the nation. Specifically, we studied the relation between mass media involvement and voting. The effect of these media seems to be greater among the black respondents. It seems likely to us that the stress on civic duty is much more important in white culture than black culture, so that information can have a greater impact among the black respondents. In other words, we are suggesting that voting among whites must be seen as not necessarily indicating anything more than artificial involvement. Whites vote and southern-born blacks have a self-image as involved people because their cultures support such behavior. Among both whites and blacks there are signs of an artificial national involvement not rooted in experience but culture.

Overall, the data support the ideas that: 1) exposure to information about national events increases national involvement, and 2) the mass media and voluntary associations seem to be significant sources of such information in Kilbourntown.

7

Conclusion

In Chapter One we elaborated on the experience of involvement. It is caused by closeness (although as previously noted, some of the data cast doubt on the significance of this variable), similarity, power, and knowledge. Moreover, the sense of oneness is heightened by overlap between fantasy and the sensed environment. In Chapters Three and Four we discussed different reasons for a lack of such an overlap. Throughout the first chapter the stress was on delineating in an abstract manner the social conditions that would produce an experience of oneness. This chapter guided our work. But a shift of focus began in chapter four. That chapter concluded with a section on the natural history of familial involvement. Time entered our analysis. The questions arose: How does the degree of involvement and the bases of involvement change over time in our relations with the same objects? What are the consequences of such changes? In Chapters Five and Six, time was important but in a different way. In these chapters we were interested in the extent of unity or oneness present in the relationships a person has. As our work progressed, then, the focus shifted to the problem of how to produce involvement over time in a person's life. The monograph began with a theory of what will produce the experience of involvement and ended with the question: What will produce an involved life?

The previous two chapters hopefully contributed to our understanding of how various forms of organizations and the mass media are overcoming the alienating effects of industrialization and urbanization and are helping people to experience their world as a unity.

In this concluding chapter we do not intend to restate points already made

156   SOLIDARITY IN A SLUM

in previous chapters. However, there were three themes running throughout the work, and it is necessary now to pull together the information contained in the separate chapters on these three topics. The questions that continually shaped our analysis are: a) Are the perceptual categories of white and black, young and old, meaningful, i.e., are whites different from blacks in terms of the variables studied in this work, and are young people different from the old in terms of involvement? and b) What are the effects of mobility on involvement?

Finally, in this chapter we want to develop further the idea of artificial involvement discussed in the last chapter. It is hoped that this discussion will pave the way for future studies of involvement.

COLOR AND INVOLVEMENT

It must be remembered that our sample is entirely female and resided in a single section of Milwaukee. To what extent are there differences between the white and the black women living in Kilbourntown?

Color does not seem to contribute significantly to the tendency to think about dead people or to the tendency to think about people rarely seen, or to the number of blanks on the "think about" question, or to national involvement.

On the other hand there are differences between the color aggregates. Of relatively minor importance are the following: 1) Blacks have slightly less overlap between fantasy and household. 2) There is a slight tendency for blacks to seek more help on money and family problems (although this is not true at all age levels), but when they seek help the black women are less likely to go to their husbands. 3) The white women are a little less ignorant of their children's friends; 4) overall, blacks voted more often in the 1964 Presidential election. Although these differences are slight, several of them point to greater alienation within the black household, e.g., to less overlap of fantasy and household, less use of spouse as problem-solver, and less knowledge of children's lives. On the other hand the black women seem more involved outside the household, e.g., they more often seek help on problems and more of them voted.

Major differences between the color aggregates relate to family and religion. The whites' fantasy is much more restricted to the nuclear family, while black women have a fantasy life populated often by members of the extended family.

Regarding religion, there can be no doubt that religion plays a more significant role in the lives of black women. The facts are these: a) Blacks mentioned religious leaders on the "think about" question; thirteen of fourteen such references are by black people; b) Blacks more often express pride in their religious involvement (this is mainly true for those forty years of age and over); and c) Blacks more frequently attend church services (if the categories of "no attendance" and "rare attendance" are combined, then among those seventeen to thirty-nine years 9 percent more whites are infrequent attenders, among those forty to fifty-nine years 8 percent more whites are infrequent attenders, and among those sixty and above the percentage is 18 percent. The relevant data is contained in Table 5-6). Overall, the data suggest that although there is only a slight difference between whites and blacks in church attendance, there is a major difference in the degree to which religion permeates the daily lives of the respondents. For black people religion seems more personally meaningful. However, this seems to be true mainly for the middle-aged and older black women.

Overall, the data do suggest that black women may be less involved in household life. But it also suggests that the black women in our sample are more involved outside the household—in the extended family, in the nation, and in religion. At least in our sample, black women seems to lead richer lives in the sense that their horizons seem to embrace a more varied environment. But our work can only be suggestive.

But perhaps what needs to be emphasized most is that in our study color itself is not a very significant variable. At times there are no differences between blacks and whites, and when there are differences usually they are slight or not consistent for different ages. Of course our conclusions refer only to the types of variables studied in this work and to our limited sample.

AGE AND INVOLVEMENT

As Table 3-13 reveals, white women seventy-five years of age and older have a relatively low degree of involvement with their sensed environment. This is measured by the importance of dead people in their lives as well as by the absence of people thought about. As would be expected the elderly experience the least amount of overlap between fantasy and household.[1] Moreover, only 30 percent voted in 1964, and few seek help on either money or family problems. It must be remembered that there are only twenty cases of elderly white women in our sample. But there seems adequate basis for describing these women as alienated or disengaged.

Townsend and Tunstall summarized their work on national samples of people sixty-five and over and living in private households as follows; "We considered whether people disengage from society in advanced old age. We found that in all three countries [Britain, U.S., and Denmark] substantially more people in their 80's than in their late 60's are living alone and say they are often alone. But the trend towards isolation with age is not steep, and on none of our measures are more than two-fifths of those in their 80's 'isolated' or alone. ... Moreover, there is some evidence that when people become widowed or infirm they move to join their children."[2] The information derived from their study, however, seems rather superficial. e.g., whether a person lives alone or not, frequency of contact with others, self-perception as a lonely person. Such indicators reveal the minimum of alienation. If variables such as those used in our study were employed, these national samples would have appeared even more disengaged.

Of course our small sample of elderly white women in no way can be considered typical of elderly people. These women are slum-dwellers, not middle-class Americans. But at least for this sample the idea of disengagement seems more appropriate than intimacy-at-a-distance. It may be true, as argued by Rosenmayr and Kocheis, that elderly people prefer social arrangements that allow both involvement and independence.[3] But whether this is true or not, our data certainly do suggest that Cumming's theory of disengagement is valid. Elderly people do seem more alienated. Moreover, the simple fact that one source of alienation is involvement with dead people suggests that elderly people in all social classes are likely to feel more alienated than younger people.

We prefer the word "alienation" rather than "disengagement," The latter adequately expresses decline in involvement, but it fails to express the problems associated with a shift of involvement from the living to the dead. Alienation, on the other hand, is a richer concept. It can refer to the two somewhat distinct processes that seem to characterize our elderly women: 1) a decline of involvement, and 2) a shift of involvement from people in the sensed environment to non-sensed objects. Both processes contribute to the alienation of the elderly.

Regarding some variables it does not do justice to the data to talk about a process of aging, because both the very young and the old are similar. Consider, for example, the percent of people our respondents think about and with whom they discuss personal problems (Table 4-9). On this variable both those in their twenties and those seventy-five and over are low relative to the middle-aged. We can imagine, therefore, that elderly people will be especially prone to feeling alienated because they may experience a decline in the amount of personal communication they have with the people they think about. The amount of communication these elderly people carry on may be the same as that characteristic of young people. But the elderly may experience a greater sense of alienation because they had gone through the richer period of middle life.

As Townsend and Tunstall wrote—"Loneliness is related more to 'loss' than to enduring 'isolation'."[4] In part, the sense of alienation of the elderly can be blamed on the degree of involvement experienced in middle life.

The alienation of the elderly, therefore, must be seen as resulting from; 1) a withdrawal of involvement, 2) a shift of involvement to non-sensed objects,[5] and 3) the loss of the relatively rich life of the middle years. Recall, also, that expressed pride in health increased as age increased. This suggests a fourth reason for the social alienation of the elderly; 4) an increased involvement in the body. Of course, not all elderly people have this bodily involvement. We mention it as one of the bases for the social alienation of old people.

In evaluating the data in our study related to age, it must be kept in mind that we have not followed the same people through the various life stages, but only studied different people of varied ages.

MOBILITY AND INVOLVEMENT

The data scattered throughout the work *suggest* three different relations between mobility and involvement: 1) It was found that women who have lived in more cities or towns more often than the less mobile women indicated they are involved with their spouse; in short, some support was found for Bott's hypothesis that there is a positive relation between continuity of association and involvement; 2) On the other hand. the data on seeking help for financial and family problems *suggest* a settling-in, closing-out process; that is, there is a tendency for fewer long-term residents to seek help from others. It is possible that lengthy residence gives people confidence and security that allows them to solve their own problems; as people settle-in, they close out others; and 3) The data support the idea that newcomers are less often involved in the institutional life of an area. More specifically, newcomers less often attend church and fewer of them voted. It was suggested that if people are not stable, much of life seems indistinguishable from a novel, and action loses its urgency.

Quite tentatively we put forward the following model of mobile women; 1) highly involved with their spouses; 2) seek help mainly from family and friends with their problems,[6] which results in important but temporary (or intermittent) relations; infrequent involvement in community institutions. It follows that stable people would be less involved with their spouse, have fewer personally important relations and more socially important relations, i.e., relations that are continuous and which, therefore, are important for the preservation of the social system of which the relations are parts. Relative to mobile people, stable individuals would be more involved with themselves, i.e., not dependent on others for help; moreover, they would participate in more relationships that, however, would tend to be less personal than the relations of mobile people. In effect, we are suggesting that the individual transition from mobile to stable is similar to the historic transition from *Gemeinschaft* to *Gesellschaft*. If this is true, it means that the more mobile the population of a society, the more *Gemeinschaft*-like becomes the experience of its members. These ideas go well beyond our data. But we believe they are interesting and merit further consideration. We might ask, for instance, if the contempo-

ACTUAL INVOLVEMENT

		LOW	HIGH
	LOW	ALIENATED PERSON	ARTIFICIAL PERSON
POTENTIAL INVOLVEMENT			
	HIGH	ROBOTIC PERSON	INVOLVED PERSON

rary interest in community is due more to a reaction by stable people against impersonal relationships or to the desire of mobile people who live in a more personal world to want to build institutions that will allow them to continue their personal world after they settle down.[7] Or, is it true that mobile people will value individualism in the sense of being free to become involved whenever and with whomever they decide, while stable people will value individualism in the sense of self-determination, i.e., in the sense of not being dependent on others? The former would accept dependence, if it is freely chosen; the latter would reject all dependence.

ARTIFICIAL INVOLVEMENT

In the last chapter the idea of artificial involvement was introduced, it refers to involvement without adequate bases for the involvement. The self-image would be of an involved person, but there would be no adequate basis for this, and, we believe, the involvement would not affect major decisions since its artificiality would be experienced at some level of consciousness. Note that artificial involvement is not the same as the situation that arises when a person's subjective involvement is not consistent with his potential involvement because of a mistaken understanding about the degree of potential involvement. Artificial involvement is not based on a mistake. Artificial involvement could result, for instance, from propaganda. The recognition that the amount of potential involvement (i.e., closeness, similarity, power, and knowledge) and actual involvement do not always co-vary in anything like a perfect way led us to construct a typology contained in Diagram 7-1. Taking the involved type as the ideal, we see that there are three problem types: the alienated, the artificial, and the robotic.

The last type is new to our discussion but not to other analyses of contemporary culture. The prototype is the "hero" of Camus's novel *The Stranger*, but analyses of psychopathic personalities also reveal this syndrome of potential but not actual involvement. Below are comments made by a woman who supposedly had been helped by a psychiatrist:

"Well I don't have any desires now. I used to want Alice to be shown up in her true colors, to have people see how wrong she was. Now I just don't think about it. I just act. I get along."

"I still may think that what she's doing is wrong at times, but it doesn't matter much. That is, well, I would defend myself if she did anything wrong to me... but, well, I wouldn't *dwell* on its being wrong. I'm just not involved. It doesn't matter in the same way."

"It's funny, but if anyone ever looked at what I've said, they'd get the impression of a very strange and quiet person without real emotion, someone who didn't care about anything. That's not a good picture of me at all. It's true it takes a lot more effort to get angry now, and yet I explode all the time. The difference is that I used to get angry all the time and never exploded. Now, when I'm angry, I explode and yell, but somehow I'm not really ever worked up about it."[8]

It is difficult to conclude anything about this person simply from these quotations. But these statements are troublesome. They suggest a person who remains objectively related but who is subjectively detached.

Why the label "robotic"? The type of person we are referring to is like a machine that experiences bases of involvement, but bases that never coalesce to form a new fact—a sense of involvement. Robots will on occasion have knowledge of people, for instance, but this information will not produce a sense of involvement. Robotic people develop the potential for involvement, but never experience a sense of involvement.

A thorough analysis then of the contemporary world must acknowledge the existence of three problem-types: the alienated, the artificial, and the robotic. Each problem-type is a deviation from the original theory presented in Chapter One. There it was suggested that involvement varies with proximity, similarity, power, and knowldege. Now, we are acknowledging that without these bases, there can be involvement (artificial) and that these bases can exist without causing involvement (robotic). Future theoretical development will have to specify the conditions under which artificial involvement or roboticism will develop.

Notes

CHAPTER 1

1. Emile Durkheim, *The Division of Labor in Society* (New York: The Free Press, 1964), p. 14.

2. Quoted in: Elsworth Faris, "The Primary Group: Essence and Accident," *American Journal of Sociology* 28 (July 1932): 41.

3. Max Weber, *The Theory of Social and Economic Organization* (New York; The Free Press, 1966), p. 136.

4. Faris, "The Primary Group," p. 50.

5. Weber, *Social and Economic Organization,* p. 120.

6. Albert N. Cousins, "The Failure of Solidarity," in *The Family,* eds. Norman W. Bell and Ezra F. Vogel (Glencoe: The Free Press, 1960), p. 403.

7. From our perspective, Maslow's work is interesting because his concern about "peak-experience" underscores the fact that modern man is relatively cut off from his environment. On the other hand, Maslow's discussion of the "peak-experience" suffers from a failure to stress the neutral quality of involvement itself, and thus to distinguish the conditions under which oneness is creative from those under which it is destructive. Abraham Maslow, *Religions, Values, and Peak-Experiences* (Columbus: Ohio State University Press, 1964).

8. Robert Sommer and Humphrey Osmond, "The Schizophrenic No-Society," *Psychiatry* 25 (August 1962): 247.

9. Bruno Bettelheim, "Individual and Mass Behavior in Extreme Situations," in *Readings in Social Psychology,* eds. Elinore Maccoby, et. al. (New York: Holt, 1958), pp. 300-310.

10. For an explicit statement of the relative aspect of morale see: Aaron J. Spector, "Expectations, Fulfillment, and Morale," *Journal of Abnormal and Social Psychology* 52 (January 1956): 51-56. Unfortunately, alienation, the opposite of involvement, has sometimes been defined relatively; for example, Levin considered that the "felt discrepancy between what is and what might be is the hallmark of one's state of being-in-the-world," and that this feeling could be considered alienation. The term alienation has become linked with industrialization and often means not only the nature of the relation between a man and his products, but also the the frustrations associated with the life of a worker in an industrialized world. It would seem beneficial, however, to reserve the term alienation for the analysis of relationships, and morale for the discussion of frustrations. Murray Levin, *The Alienated Worker* (New York: Holt, Rinehart and Winston, 1962), p. 59. See also:

John P. Clark, "Measuring Alienation Within a Social System," *American Sociological Review* 24 (December 1959): 849-852.

11. For a general discussion of "integration" see: Werner S. Landecker, "Types of Integration and Their Measurement," *American Sociological Review* 61 (January 1951): 332-340.

12. Bernard Berelson and Gary A. Steiner, *Human Behavior* (New York: Harcourt, Brace and World, 1962), p. 106.

13. C. R. Carpenter, "Societies of Monkeys and Apes," in *Primate Social Behavior,* ed. Charles Southwick (Princeton: D. Van Nostrand, 1963), p. 6.

14. Other authors have pointed out that for some species distance from a certain point of common orientation is an indication of the amount of power an animal has within the group. Robert Ardrey, "The Drive for Territory," *Life* (26 August 1966): 40-58; Edward T. Hall, *The Hidden Dimension* (Garden City: Doubleday, 1966).

15. Durkheim, *Division of Labor;* Sigmund Freud, "On Narcissism: An Introduction," *Collected Papers,* vol. 4 (New York: Basic Books, 1959), p. 47; Ferdinand Toennies, *Community and Society* (New York: Harper Torchbook, 1963), p. 252.
Frederick summarized the historical discussion of the meaning of community as follows; "first, there is the debate as to whether community in the first instance simply exists, or whether it is willed. Secondly, there is the debate over whether community, other values apart, is primarily a community of law or of love. Thirdly, there is the debate over whether community is organic or purposive." "Willed," "law," and "purposive" refer to systems based on power; the other terms are more ambiguous, but seem to imply the nonrational attraction that Toennies discussed and which occurs in groups connected via similarity or where the ethos is one of fundamental identity of the members of the group because of common blood. Carl Frederick, "The Concept of Community in the History of Political and Legal Philosophy," in *Community,* ed. Carl Frederick (New York: Liberal Arts Press, 1959), pp. 23-24.

16. Kurt Wolff, *The Sociology of Georg Simmel* (Glencoe: The Free Press, 1950), p. 307.

17. Toennies, *Community,* p.384.

18. Aristotle and, following him, Aquinas had a somewhat similar theory of relation; they clearly recognized the importance of knowledge, but merely pointed to similarity and power rather than clearly recognizing them. See: *The Great Books of the Western World* (Chicago: Encyclopedia Britannica, 1952) vol. 8, Aristotle, *Metaphysics,* 5: 15, and vol. 19, Thomas Aquinas, *The Summa Theologica,* 1: 13: 7. Hume, on the other hand, seems to have missed the significance of knowledge, but did realize the importance of contiguity, similarity, and less clearly perhaps, power. *Ibid.,* vol. 35, Hume, An Enquiry Concerning Human Understanding, p. 458.

19. Erving Goffman, *Behavior in Public Places* (New York: The Free Press, 1963), p. 124.

20. Joseph B. Tamney, "A Study of Involvement: Reactions to the Death of President Kennedy," *Sociologus* 19 (1969): 66-79.

21. Elaine Cumming, "Further Thoughts on the Theory of Disengagement,' *International Social Science Journal* 15 (1963): 377-378.

22. *Ibid.,* p. 380, footnote 3.

23. In the terms of Back and Gergen, old people have a smaller "effective life space." By this phrase these authors mean "the extent to which the person is willing to accept something as relevant to his conduct (including any facts about the world—past, present, and future)." Kurt W. Back and Kenneth J. Gergen, "Ageing and Self Orientation," in *Social Aspects of Ageing,* eds. Ida Harper Simpson and John C. McKinney (Durham: Duke University Press, 1966), p. 292.

24. Cumming, "Theory of Disengagement," p. 391, footnote 3.

25. *Ibid.,* p. 387.

26. *Ibid.,* p.381.

27. Leopold Rosenmayr and Eva Kockeis, "Propositions For a Sociological Theory of Ageing,"

International Social Science Journal 15 (1963): 418.

28. Cumming, "Theory of Disengagement," p. 382.

29. Norval D. Glenn and Michael Grimes, "Ageing, Voting, and Political Interest," *American Sociological review* 33 (August 1968): 565-571.

30. David O. Moberg, "Religiosity in Old Age," in *Middle Age and Ageing,* ed. Bernice C. Newgarten (Chicago: University of Chicago Press, 1968), p. 508.

CHAPTER 2

1. About 40 percent were two stories high, 8 percent were two and one-half stories, 21 percent had only one floor and 16 percent had one and one-half floors. A few buildings had three or four floors; there was inadequate information on about 13 percent of the buildings. Kilbourntown probably had much more variability in building size than a typical middle-class neighborhood. This variety contributed to the visual breaking up of the area.

Moreover, about 11 percent of the buildings had commercial enterprises; 77 percent were residential units. (There was inadequate information on about 12 percent of the buildings.) Again, this contributed to a sense of variety and a lack of unity.

2. This part of the city averages about 550 trees per quarter-mile; the city average is 1200; the desired average is 900. Data from Department of Parks and Streets, City of Milwaukee.

3. Data from Police Department and Office of the Clerk of Courts, City of Milwaukee.

4. Alex P. Dobish, "Young Hoodlums Rule by Fear in Area of Wells Street Schools," *Milwaukee Journal,* 11 October 1966.

5. Included in the study are female breadwinners; their main sources of income are as follows: job—86 (36 percent), social security—34 (14 percent), welfare—89 (37 percent), pension—2 (1 percent), other government programs—11 (5 percent), miscellaneous private sources—7 (3 percent), no response—9 (4 percent).

6. For a discussion of this see: Kenneth J. Gergen, "The Significance of Skin Color in Human Relations," *Daedalus* 96 (Spring 1967); 390-403.

7. As one would suspect for a mobile population, few, about 14 percent, owned the building in which they lived. (There was inadequate data on 12 percent of our sample. Our information on ownership is only approximate. The question was not asked in the interview. Our information comes from the city taxroll, which listed ownership as of December, 1966, i.e., about six months after the interviews were made. We compared the surname of respondent with the person taxed for the property. Our percentage is probably fairly accurate, however, because at the time of the interviews the buildings were "condemned" for renewal, and the owners were waiting to sell their property to the government.)

8. Eugene Litwak, "Geographical Mobility and Family Cohesion," *American Sociological Review* 25 (June 1960) 385-394; Elizabeth Bott, "Urban Families: Conjugal Roles and Social Networks," *Human Relations* 7 (1954); 372; Marvin B. Sussman and Lee G. Burchinal, "Kin Family Network: Unheralded Structure in Current Conceptualizations of Family Function," *Marriage and Family Living* 24 (August 1962): 231-240.

9. The percentage is based on the number of respondents who told us their income. The data on income cannot be considered precise information. Total family income is difficult for anyone to state precisely. On the other hand, the categories used are fairly broad. We assume that people were able to pick the right category even if they could not state their family's precise income. There is the additional problem, however, that people tend to overestimate their income, we could do nothing about that in our study.

CHAPTER 3

1. It is difficult to determine the reliability of open-ended questions. In this case, however, about

forty black women in our sample were interviewed, as part of another study, some two months after the first interview. They were asked—"Name the three people whom you think about most." About 40 percent of the individuals named were also named in our study. In the reinterview the "think about" question followed a long series of questions on the respondent's household. As could be expected, the main reason for the differences in the people named on the two occasions was that in the reinterview the respondents named more household members. In short, it appears that the "think about" question was influenced in the reinterview by its location in the questionnaire. We believe that the list of people named in our study is a more valid indicator of involvement because the question appeared in a more neutral context. In our study, the "think about" question followed questions on whether the respondent was born in a rural or urban area, her mobility and her memberships in voluntary associations. Admittedly, no context is completely neutral.

2. We have already noted the reliability problem with regard to open-ended questions. There is also the problem of interviewer differences in pursuing answers, especially for our study, which used indigenous personnel. Analysis of the frequency of "no response" by interviewer revealed some clearly abnormal frequencies. Since respondents were not randomly distributed among interviewers, these differences might be "real". But we cannot overlook the problem of interviewer differences; obviously the analysis of the distribution of involvement must be considered crude.

Another problem with open-ended questions concerns the ability to verbalize; "no responses" might reflect difficulties in communicating with the interviewer. We did relate "no responses" on the pride question with the years of schooling; there was no significant relation except for those with thirteen years of schooling or more, few of whom did not respond; however, there are only twenty-five such cases in our sample.

3. Jerome L. Singer, *Daydreaming* (New York: Random House, 1966), p. 57.

4. *Ibid.,* p. 59.

5. Eugene Litwak, "Geographical Mobility and Family Cohesion," *American Sociological Review* 25 (June 1960): 385-394; James S. Brown et. al., "Kentucky Mountain Migration and the Stem Family: An American Variation on a Theme by La Play," *Rural Sociology* 28 (March 1963): 48-69; Charles Tilly and C. Harold Brown, "On Uprooting, Kinship and the Auspices of Migration," *International Journal of Comparative Sociology* 8 (1967): 164.

A failure to answer the "proud" question does not mean the same thing as not answering the "think about" question. The latter can mean the absence of involvement in valued objects. A person may not be proud of anything because: 1) He is not involved in anything, 2) He does not value anything, or 3) Although he is involved, he is not involved in anything that is also valued. Clearly, involvement and pride are related but are independent. Therefore, we have not used the absence of pride as an indicator of the absence of involvement.

6. There are twenty-three respondents proud about a specific church; three of these are whites in their sixties. The remaining twenty responses are spread evenly among the various black age aggregates. In every respect, religion appears to be more central to the lives of black people.

7. Gary T. Marx, "Religion: Opiate or Inspiration of Civil Rights Militancy Among Negroes," *American Sociological Review* 32 (February 1967): 68.

8. But what is the effect on black people that the God of Christianity is almost always portrayed as white? Will the "black is beautiful" idea weaken or destroy the significance of Christianity for black people?

9 Lucien Levy-Bruhl, *The Soul of the Primitive* (New York: Frederick A. Praeger, 1966), p. 340.

10. Peter Townsend with the assistance of Sylvia Tunstall, "Isolation, Disolation and Loneliness," in *Old People in Three Industrial Societies,* ed. Ethel Shanas et. al. (London: Routledge and Kegan Paul, 1968), p. 276.

11. This was determined by taking those who said they have lived in only one city; this was double-checked by matching their reported age and their reported years lived in Milwaukee; since

we used five year intervals for the last two variables, a few cases might have been inappropriately considered life-time residents; if there was a discrepancy between age and years in Milwaukee, the cases were excluded.

12. Julio Cortazar, *Hopscotch* (New York: Pantheon, 1966), p. 96.

13. William Kornhauser, *The Politics of Mass Society* (London: Routledge & Kegan Paul, 1960), p. 75.

CHAPTER 4

1. The fact that middle-aged white women appear more deeply involved in their children could be an artifact of the wording of our question. The "think about" question limited respondents to only three people. If middle-aged black women were involved with many people including their children very deeply, because the question limited them to only three people, there would be times when these mothers would not mention their children despite their high involvement with them. As a matter of fact, however, middle-aged black women have a rather high percentage of blanks (18 percent) on the "think about" question; the percentage for whites is about the same. There seems no basis for believing, then, that middle-aged blacks are involved with more people than middle-aged whites.

The higher percentage of white children who are fantasy figures could be due not to the fact that white mothers are involved with more children, but to the fact that they have a lower total of fantasy figures. In fact, however, the middle-aged whites have a higher total that their black counterparts. (See Table 3-11).

2. Bert N. Adams, *Kinship in an Urban Setting* (Chicago: Markham, 1968), p. 169.

3. Charles Bowerman and Donald P. Irish, "Some Relationships of Stepchildren to their Parents," *Marriage and Family Living* 24 (May 1962): 113-128.

4. Robert O. Blood and Donald M. Wolfe, *Husbands and Wives* (Glencoe: The Free Press, 1960), pp. 159-161.

5. Elizabeth Bott, "Urban Families: Conjugal Roles and Social Networks," *Human Relations* 7 (1954): 372.

6. Eleanor Pavenstedt, "A Comparison of the Child-Rearing Environment of Upper, Lower and Very Low Lower Class Families," *American Journal of Orthopsychiatry* 35 (January 1965): 95.

7. Mirra Komarovsky, *Blue-Collar Marriage* (New York: Random House, Vintage Book Edition, 1967). p. 208.

8. Blood and Wolfe, *Husbands and Wives,* p. 149.

9. Nicholas Babchuk and Alan P. Bates, "The Primary Relations of Middle-Class Couples: A Study in Male Dominance," *American Sociological Review* 28 (June 1963): 379.

10. Komarovsky, *Blue-Collar Marriage,* pp. 112-113.

11. Sidney Jourard, "Self-Disclosure and Other Cathexis," *Journal of Abnormal and Social Psychology* 59 (1959): 431.

12. Blood and Wolfe, *Husbands and Wives,* p. 186.

13. Marvin B. Sussman, "Relationships of Adult Children with Their Parents in the United States," in *Social Structure and the Family: Generational Relations,* eds. Ethel Shanas and Gordon F. Streib (Englewood Cliffs: Prentice-Hall, 1965), p. 77.

14. Herbert Gans, *The Urban Villagers* (New York: The Free Press, 1962), p. 51.

15. Komarovsky, *Blue-Collar Marriage,* p. 338.

16. If the "think about" question is at all meaningful, there should be significant overlap between the people in our respondents' fantasy life and the people they seek advice from. For blacks, 34 percent of the people they seek help from are thought about; if we eliminate the nonpersonal sources of help (who would be more peripheral to our respondents' lives, i.e. who although sources of advice would probably exercize this power less frequently) the figure is 48 percent. For whites,

45 percent of their advisors are thought about, and if we eliminate the nonpersonal sources it is 58 percent. Clearly, this does suggest that the "think about" question is meaningful. It is, also, evident that there is more unity in the white world; more of their advisors are part of their fantasy world.

17. Our approach is similar to that of Fromm-Reichman who views loneliness as a lack of interpersonal intimacy. She also notes that loneliness is "one of the least satisfactorily conceptualized psychological phenomena, not even mentioned in most psychiatric textbooks." Frieda Fromm-Reichman, "Loneliness," *Psychiatry* 22 (February 1959): 1-16.

18. Eleanore Luckey, "Number of Years Married as Related to Personality Perception and Marital Satisfaction," *Journal of Marriage and the Family* 28 (February 1966): 44-48; Jourard, "Self-Disclosure."

19. Among the blacks there are ten handicapped children, i.e., children whose illnesses incapacitated them. For such children, ignorance is low; only one handicapped child's mother does not know the friend's name.

20. Reuben Hill, "Decision-Making and the Family Life Cycle," in *Social Structure*, eds. Shanas and Strieb, pp. 116-117.

21. This occurs earlier for blacks. The explanation might be as follows: a) for whites, nonhousehold children jump in importance when the spouse and siblings are dead; b) for blacks, children might become important when parents and aunts and uncles are dead; and since older members of the extended family die before spouses and siblings, the jump in importance of children occurs earlier for blacks.

CHAPTER 5

1. Harold L. Wilensky, "A Second Look at the Traditional View of Urbanism," in *Perspectives on the American Community: A Book of Readings*, ed. Roland C. Warren (Chicago: Rand McNally, 1966), p. 141.

2. Hans Paul Bahrdt, "Public Activity and Private Activity as Basic Forms of City Association," in *American Community*, ed. Warren, p. 83.

3. Wilensky, "A Second Look," p. 138.

4. Roland L. Warren, *The Community in America* (Chicago: Rand McNally, 1963), p. 240.

5. William F. Whyte, *Street Corner Society* (Chicago: University of Chicago Press, 1965), p. 255.

6. On this point the concept of advice-structure differs from Warren's idea of the "mutual support function". Bartenders can fulfill this function, but they would not be considered part of an advice-structure. The bartender-customer relation would be considered, by us, as part of the informal organization of Kilbourntown.

7. Warren, *The Community*, p. 196.

8. The figure of 9 percent assumes that a pair of respondents do not share more than one name on the "think about" question. But this did happen, so that the actual percentage of people sharing one or more names on the "think about" question is less than 9 percent.

9. In a few cases, the respondent mentioned not a name but a role, like "my social worker." Even if these roles all referred to the same person it would not affect the validity of our general conclusions.

10. Marvin Sussman and R. Clyde White, *Hough, Cleveland, Ohio: A Study of Social Life and Change* (Cleveland: The Press of Western Reserve University, 1959), pp. 91-2; quoted in Warren, *The Community*, p. 197.

11. Donald R. Matthews and James W. Prothro, *Negroes and the New Southern Politics* (New York: Harcourt, Brace and World, 1966), p. 180.

12. Warren, *The Community*, p. 172.

13. Suttles studied an ethnically mixed neighborhood in Chicago, and reported: "In all there are

SOLIDARITY IN A SLUM

ten separate places of worship in the area. None of them brings together different ethnic groups." Gerald D. Suttles, *The Social Order of the Slum* (Chicago: University of Chicago Press, 1968), p. 42.

14. Warren, *The Community,* p. 192.

15. Alphonso Pinkney, *Black Americans* (Englewood Cliffs: Prentice-Hall, 1969), pp. 112-113.

16. Warren, *The Community,* p. 194.

17. Religious voluntary associations that drew members from more than one church, however, were included in the analysis.

18. Nicholas Babchuk and Alan Booth, "Voluntary Association Membership: A Longitudinal Analysis," *American Sociological Review* 34 (February 1969): 31-45.

19. An important omission in our field work is the absence of information on the contribution of neighborhood bars to life in Kilbourntown. We know there are plenty of them, and we know from observation that they are frequented both day and night. These bars may not be too important, however, to female homemakers. But the important question is whether bar-life really changes anything. All forms of what Simmel called sociability produce temporary occasions of involvement with others. But does sociability in K-3 produce any lasting sense of a "common order" that could give a continuous sense of involvement? People who drink together can still remain "familiar strangers." In fact the impersonality of sociable events noted by Simmel contributes to experiencing others as "familial strangers." Do the bars in neighborhoods like Kilbourntown produce any lasting sense of involvement with others? Georg Simmel, "The Sociology of Sociability," in *Theories of Society,* eds. Talcott Parsons et.al. (Glencoe: The Free Press, 1961), pp. 157-163.

20. For further discussion of this see: Joseph B. Tamney, "The Prediction of Religious Change," *Sociological Analysis* 26 (Summer 1965): 72-81.

21. Michael Argyle, "Religious Observance," in *International Encyclopedia of the Social Sciences,* ed. David Sills (New York: Macmillan and The Free Press, 1968), vol. 13, pp. 421-428.

22. Dennison Nash and Peter Berger, "The Child, The Family and The 'Religious Revival' in Suburbia," *Journal for the Scientific Study of Religion* 2 (October 1962): 85-93.

23. Terrence Lee, "Urban Neighborhood as a Socio-Spatial Scheme," *Human Relations* 21 (1968): 259. Similarly, Nohara found that length of residence is related to neighborliness (as measured by number of best friends in the neighborhood, number of neighborhood homes visited, frequency of such visits, and number of neighbors' names known).

Specifically, he found that people living in the same dwelling unit three years or more are more often high on neighborliness than those who have lived in the same dwelling unit less than three years. Shigeo Nohara, "Social Context and Neighborliness: The Negro in St. Louis," in *The New Urbanization,* ed. Scott Greer et. al. (New York: St. Martins Press, 1968), pp. 179-188. See, also: Joel Smith et. al., "Local Intimacy in a Middle-Sized City," *American Journal of Sociology* 60 (November 1954): 276-284.

Recently, Litwak and Szelenyi have suggested that "short tenure can be partially compensated for by rapid means of indoctrination." They argue that "where the group norms state newcomers are to be welcomed and newcomers have norms that long-term residents are friends, speedy indoctrination is encouraged...." The authors seem to assume that if there are norms stating that a certain behavior is desirable, then that behavior will occur. But this is not always true. For instance, perhaps it takes people years to break old ties, and so be willing to become involved in a new neighborhood. Or, perhaps it takes years to collect enough information about others to consider them close friends. But the article by Litwak and Szelenyi points to a key issue: the extent to which the effects of mobility on involvement are controllable by social policy. Eugene Litwak and Ivan Szelenyi, "Primary Group Structures and Their Functions: Kin, Neighbors, and Friends," *American Sociological Review* 34 (August 1969): 467.

24. Jitodai in an analysis of over 3,000 white residents of Detroit found no relation between migratory status and frequency of church attendance after controlling for several key variables. However, in a subsample of Southern-born, white, non-Catholic females (this was the subsample closest to ours), there was a tendency for those who had lived less than twenty-five years in Detroit to attend church less frequently than those who had lived twenty-five years or more in Detroit; but some of the cells in this subanalysis are quite small. Jitodai's work, the results of which are not consistent with ours, implies that it is impossible yet to be certain about the effects of mobility on organizational participation. Ted T. Jitodai, "Migrant Status and Church Attendance," *Social Forces* 47 (December 1960): 241-248.

25. Our interest in voluntary associations has been from the perspective of whether or not they are significant sources of neighborhood structure. There is, of course, some research that suggests that not belonging to voluntary associations is associated with a general sense of powerlessness, which some authors call alienation. It should be noted, however, that these authors differ from us in their meaning of "alienation." Arthur C. Neal and Melvin Seeman, "Organizations and Powerlessness," *American Sociological Review* 29 (April 1964): 216-226; Joel I. Nelson, "Participation and Integration: The Case of the Small Businessman," *American Sociological Review* 33 (June 1968): 427-438.

26. James S. Coleman, "Community Disorganization," in *Contemporary Social Problems,* eds. Robert K. Merton and Robert A. Nisbet, 2nd ed. (New York: Harcourt, Brace and World, 1966), p. 709.

27. Christopher Alexander, "The City as a Mechanism for Sustaining Human Contact," in *Environment for Man,* ed. William R. Ewald. Jr. (Bloomington: Indiana University Press, 1969), p. 65.

28. The Open Group, "Social Reform in the Centrifugal Society," *New Society* 363 (11 September 1969): 389.

CHAPTER 6

1. In this chapter we have equated nation and state. This is not always legitimate. The assumption would probably not be valid for many South American countries, for instance, but we believe it is reasonable for the United States at this point in time.

2. H.H. Gerth and C. Wright Mills, *From Max Weber: Essays in Sociology* (New York: Oxford University Press, Galaxy Book, 1958), pp. 171-179.
Louis Wirth similarly linked nationalism with the struggle for status. Louis Wirth, "Types of Nationalism," *American Journal of Sociology* 41 (May 1936): 723-737.

3. Boyd C. Shafer, "Toward a Definition of Nationalism," in *Nationalism and International Progress.* ed. Urban G. Whitaker (San Francisco: Chandler, 1961). pp. 4-5.

4. Samuel A. Stouffer, *Communism, Conformity and Civil Liberties* (Gloucester, Massachusetts: Peter Smith, 1963), p. 130.

5. C. Vann Woodward, *The Burden of Southern History* (Baton Rouge: Louisiana State University Press, 1960), p. 15.

6. *Ibid.,*pp.23-24.

7. Karl W. Deutsch, *Nationalism and Social Communication,* 2nd ed. (Cambridge: M.I.T. Press, 1960), p. 97.

8. *Ibid.,* pp. 173-174.

9. Florian Znaniecki, *Modern Nationalities* (Urbana: University of Illinois Press, 1952), p. 22.

10. There also was a fictitious name, "Allen Garmon," on the questionnaire. Only twenty-eight people reported watching him, and for some of these a positive answer could be the result of an honest mistake. The other names were Red Skelton, Jack Benny, and Dean Martin.

11. For further discussion of some of the points raised in this paragraph see the following articles

in the *International Encyclopedia of the Social Sciences,* ed. David Sills (New York: Macmillan and The Free Press, 1968): Donald E. Stokes, "Voting," vol. 16, pp. 387-395; Herbert McClosky, "Political Participation," vol. 12, pp. 252-265.

12. Norval D. Glenn and Michael Grimes, "Ageing, Voting, and Political Interest," *American Sociological Review* 33 (August 1968): 563-575.

13. *Ibid.,* p. 575.

14. Angus Campbell et. al., *The American Voter* (New York: John Wiley, 1960), p. 139.

15. Donald R. Matthews and James W. Prothro. *Negroes and the New Southern Politics* (New York: Harcourt, Brace and World, 1966), p. 253.

16. See, for instance: Philip K. Hastings, "The Voter and the Non-Voter," *American Journal of Sociology* 62 (November 1965): 302-307; William Erbe, "Social Involvement and Political Activity: A replication and Elaboration," *American Sociological Review* 19 (April 1964): 198-215. This relation was also found to hold for a sample of black people in urban South Carolina: John B. McConaughy and John H. Gauntlett, "The Influence of the S Factor upon the Voting Behaviour of South Carolina Urban Negroes," *The Western Political Quarterly* 16 (December 1963): 973-984.

17. McClosky, "Political Participation," p. 257.

18. Melvin Seeman, "On the Personal Consequences of Alienation in Work," *American Sociological Review* 32 (April 1967): 273-286.

19. Erbe, "Social Involvement"; Joel I. Nelson, "Participation and Integration: The Case of the Small Businessman," *American Sociological Review* 33 (June 1968): p. 431, footnote 9.

20. Similarly Sharp found in a random sample of Detroit residents that the percentage voting increased continuously as the years lived in Detroit increased. Harry Sharp, "Migration and Voting Behavior in a Metropolitan Community," *Public Opinion Quarterly* 9 (Summer 1955): 204-209.

CHAPTER 7

1. Also among those 60-74 (there were insufficient cases of people over 74) there is a decline in the percent of married women who thinks about their spouse. In short, spousal involvement seems to decline among the old respondents. And, of course, maternal ignorance of the child's friend decreases at an early age (30 for blacks, 40 for whites).

2. Peter Townsend with the assistance of Sylvia Tunstall, "Isolation, Disolation and Loneliness," in *Old People in Three Industrial Societies,* eds. Ethel Shanas et. al. (London: Routledge and Kegan Paul, 1968), p. 286.

3. Leopold Rosenmayr and Eva Kockeis, "Propositions For a Sociological Theory of Ageing," *International Social Science Journal* 15 (1963): 410-426.

4. Townsend and Tunstall, "Isolation," p. 285.

5. The only form of involvement that significantly increases with age besides involvement with the dead is church attendance. This suggests the increasing importance of spiritual involvement which is a form of involvement with nonsensed objects.

6. What we mean is that more of the mobile women than of the stable women will do this; a majority of both types might never seek help.

7. This, in turn, leads to the larger question—does change come from those who are forced to endure inhuman lives or from those who experience a new life and are seeking to make it endure?

8. Herbert Fingarette, "The Ego and Mystic Selflessness," in *Anxiety and Identity,* eds. Maurice Stein and Arthur Vidich (Glencoe: The Free Press, 1960), p. 554.

Bibliography

Adams, Bert N. *Kinship in an Urban Setting.* Chicago: Markham, 1968.

Alexander, Christopher. "The City as a Mechanism for Sustaining Human Contact." In *Environment for Man,* edited by Willian R. Ewald, Jr., pp. 60-102. Bloomington: Indiana University Press, 1969.

Ardrey, Robert. "The Drive for Territory." *Life* (26 August 1966): 40-58.

Argyle, Michael. "Religious Observance." In *International Encyclopedia of the Social Sciences,* edited by David Sills, pp. 421-428, vol. 13. New York: Macmillan & The Free Press, 1968.

Babchuk, Nicholas and Bates, Alan P. "The Primary Relations of Middle-class Couples: A Study in Male Dominance.' *American Sociological Review* 28 (June 1963): 377-384.

Babchuk, Nicholas and Booth, Alan. "Voluntary Association Membership: A Longitudinal Analysis." *American Sociological Review* 34 (February 1969): 31-45.

Back, Kurt W. and Gergen, Kenneth J. "Ageing and Self Orientation." In section IV of *Social Aspects of Aging,* edited by Ida Harper Simpson and John C. McKinney. Durham: Duke University Press, 1966.

Bahrdt, Hans Paul, "Public Activity and Private Activity as Basic Forms of City Association." In *Perspective on the American Community: A Book of Readings,* edited by Ronald L. Warren, pp. 78-85. Chicago: Rand McNally, 1966.

Berelson, Bernard and Steiner, Gary A. *Human Behavior.* New York: Harcourt, Brace and World, 1962.

Bettleheim, Bruno. "Individual and Mass Behavior in Extreme Situations." In *Readings in Social Psychology,* edited by Elinore Maccoby, et al., pp. 300-310. 3rd ed. New York: Holt, 1958.

Blood, Robert O. and Wolfe, Donald M. *Husbands and Wives.* Glencoe: The Free Press, 1960.

Bott, Elizabeth, "Urban Families: Conjugal Roles and Social Networks." *Human Relations* 7 (1954): 345-384.

Bowerman, Charles and Irish, Donald P. "Some Relationships of Stepchildren to their Parents." *Marriage and Family Living* 24 (May 1962): 113-128.

Brown, James S., et al. "Kentucky Mountain Migration and the Stem Family: An American Variation on a Theme by La Play." *Rural Sociology* 28 (March 1963): 48-69.

Campbell, Angus. "The Passive Citizen." *Acta Sociologica* 6 (1962): 9-21.

Campbell, Angus, et al. *The American Voter.* New York: John Wiley, 1960.

Campbell, Angus. *Elections and Political Order.* New York: John Wiley, 1966.

Campbell, Donald T. "Common Fate, Similarity, and Other Indices of the Status of Aggregates of Persons as Social Entities." *Behavioral Science* 3 (June 1958): 14-25.

Carpenter, C.R. "Societies of Monkeys and Apes." In *Primate Social Behavior,* edited by Charles Southwick. Princeton: D. Van Nostrand, 1963.

Clark, John P. "Measuring Alienation Within a Social System." *American Sociological Review* 24 (December 1959): 849-852.

Coleman, James S. "Community Disorganization." In *Contemporary Social Problems,* edited by Robert K. Merton and Robert A. Nisbet, pp. 670-722. 2nd ed., New York: Harcourt, Brace & World, 1966.

Cortazar, Julio. *Hopscotch.* New York: Pantheon, 1966.

Cousins, Albert N. "The Failure of Solidarity." In *The Family,* edited by Norman W. Bell and Ezra F. Vogel, pp. 403-416. Glencoe: The Free Press 1960.

Cumming, Elaine. "Further Thoughts On The Theory of Disengagement." *International Social Science Journal* 15 (1963): 377-393.

Deutsch, Karl W. *Nationalism and Social Communication.* 2nd ed. Cambridge: M.I.T. Press, 1966.

Dobish, Alex P. "Young Hoodlums Rule by Fear in Area of Wells Street Schools." *Milwaukee Journal,* 11 October 1966.

Durkheim, Emile. *The Division of Labor in Society.* New York: The Free Press. 1964.

Erbe, William. "Social Involvement and Political Activity: A Replication and Elaboration." *American Sociological Review* 19 (April 1964): 198-215.

Faris, Elsworth. "The Primary Group: Essence and Accident." *American Journal of Sociology* 28 (July 1932): 41-50.

Fingarette, Herbert "The Ego and Mystic Selflessness." In *Anxiety and Identity,* edited by Maurice Stein and Arthur Vidich, pp. 552-585. Glencoe: The Free Press.

Frederick, Carl. "The Concept of Community in the History of Political and Legal Philosophy." In *Community,* edited by Carl Frederick. New York: Liberal Arts Press, 1959.

Freud, Sigmund. "On Narcissism: An Introduction." *Collected Papers.* vol. 4. New York: Basic Books, 1959.

Fromm-Reichman, Frieda. "Loneliness." *Psychiatry* 22 (February 1959): 1-16.

Gans, Herbert. *The Urban Villagers.* New York: The Free Press, 1962.

Gergen, Kenneth J. "The Significance of Skin Color in Human Relations." *Daedulus* 96 (Spring 1967): 390-403.

Gerth, H. H. and Mills, C. Wright. *From Max Weber: Essays in Sociology.* New York: Oxford University Press, Galaxy Book, 1958.

Glenn, Norval D. and Grimes, Michael. "Ageing, Voting, and Political Interest." *American Sociological Review* 33 (August 1968): 563-575.

Goffman, Erving. *Behavior in Public Places.* New York: The Free Press, 1963.

Hall, Edward T. *The Hidden Dimension.* Garden City: Doubleday, 1966.

Hastings, Philip K. "The Voter and the Non-Voter." *American Journal of Sociology* 62 (November 1965): 302-307.

Hatch, Robert. "Films." *The Nation* (September 22, 1969): 274-275.

Hill, Reuben, "Decision-Making and the Family Life Cycle." In *Social Structure and the Family: Generational Relations,* edited by Ethel Shanas and Gordon F. Streib, pp. 113-139. Englewood Cliffs: Prentice-Hall, 1965.

Hutchins, Robert Maynard, ed. *Critique of Pure Reason in Kant,* vol 42. *Aristotle,* vol.8. *Thomas Aquinas,* vol.19. *David Hume,* vol. 35. *Plato,* vol.7. The Great Books. Chicago: Encyclopedia Britannica, 1952.

Jitodai, Ted T. "Migrant Status and Church Attendance." *Social Forces* 47 (December 1960): 241-248.

Jourard, Sidney, *The Transparent Self.* Princeton: D. Van Nostrand, 1964.

Jourard, Sidney, and Lasakow, Paul. "Some Factors in Self-Disclosure." *Journal of Abnormal and Social Psychology* 56 (1958): 91-98.

Komarovsky, Mirra. *Blue-Collar Marriage.* New York: Random House, 1964. (Some references are to Vintage Book Edition, 1967.)

Kornhauser, William. *The Politics of Mass Society.* London: Routledge & Kegan Paul, 1960.

Landecker, Werner S. "Types of Integration and Their Measurement." *American Sociological Review* 61 (January 1951): 332-340.

Lee, Terrence. "Urban Neighborhood as a Socio-Spatial Scheme." *Human Relations* 21 (1968): 241-267.

Levin, Murray. *The Alienated Worker.* New York: Holt, Rinehart and Winston, 1962.

Levy-Bruhl, Lucien. *The Soul of the Primitive.* New York: Frederick A. Praeger, 1966.

Litwak, Eugene. "Geographical Mobility and Family Cohesion." *American Sociological Review* 25 (June 1960): 385-394.

Litwak, Eugene, and Szelenyi, Ivan. "Primary Group Structures and Their Functions: Kin, Neighbors, and Friends." *American Sociological Review* 34 (August 1969): 465-481.

Luckey, Eleanore. "Number of Years Married as Related to Personality Perception and Marital Satisfaction." *Journal of Marriage and the Family* 28 (February 1966): 44-48.

Maslow, Abraham. *Religions, Values, and Peak-Experiences.* Columbus: Ohio State University Press, 1964.

Marx, Gary T. "Religion: Opiate or Inspiration of Civil Rights Militancy Among Negroes." *American Sociological Review* 32 (1967): 64-72.

McConaughy, John B. and Gauntlett, John H. "The Influence of the S Factor upon the Voting Behaviour of South Carolina Urban Negroes." *The Western Political Quarterly* 16 (December 1963): 973-984.

McClosky, Herbert. "Political Participation." In *International Encyclopedia of the Social Sciences,* edited by David Sill, pp. 252-265. vol. 12. New York: Macmillan and The Free Press, 1968.

Nash, Dennison, and Berger, Peter. "The Child, The Family and The 'Religious Revival' in Suburbia." Journal for the Scientific Study of Religion 2 (October 1962): 85-93.

Moberg, David O. "Religiosity in Old Age." In *Middle Age and Ageing,* edited by Bernice C. Neugarter, pp. 497-508. Chicago: University of Chicago Press, 1968.

Neal, Arthur C., and Seeman, Melvin. "Organizations and Powerlessness." *American Sociological Review* 29 (April 1964): 216-226.

Nelson, Joel I. "Participation and Integration: The Case of the Small Businessman," *American Sociological Review* 33 (June 1968): 427-438.

Nohara, Shigeo. "Social Context and Neighborliness: The Negro in St. Louis." In *The New Urbanization,* edited by Scott Greer et al., pp. 179-188. New York: St. Martins Press, 1968.

Orum, Anthony. "A Reappraisal of Social and Political Participation." *American Journal of Sociology* 72 (March 1967): 32-46.

Pavenstedt, Eleanor. "A Comparison of the Child-Rearing Environment of Upper, Lower and Very Low Lower Class Families." *American Journal Of Orthopsychiatry* 35 (January 1965): 89-98.

Pinkney, Alphonso. *Black Americans.* Englewood Cliffs: Prentice-Hall, 1969.

Pinter, Frank A. "Cross Pressure." In *International Encyclopedia of the Social Sciences,* edited by David Sill, pp. 519-522. vol. 3. New York: Macmillan and The Free Press, 1968.

Rosenberg, Morris. "Some Determinants of Political Apathy" *Public Opinion Quarterly* 18 (1954-55): 349-366.

Rosenmayr, Leopold, and Kockeis, Eva. "Propositions For a Sociological Theory of Ageing." *International Social Science Journal* 15 (1963): 410-426.

Seeman, Melvin. "On the Personal Consequences of Alienation in Work." *American Sociological Review* 32 (April 1967): 273-286.

Shafer, Boyd C. "Toward a Definition of Nationalism." In *Nationalism and International Progress,* edited by Urban G. Whitaker. San Francisco: Chandler, 1961.

Sharp, Harry. "Migration and Voting Behavior in a Metropolitan Community." *Public Opinion Quarterly* 9 (Summer 1955): 204-209.

Shils, Edward. "Color, the Universal Intellectual Community, and the Afro-Asian Intellectual." *Daedulus* 96 (Spring 1967): 279-295.

Simmel, Georg. "The Sociology of Sociability." In *Theories of Society,* edited by Talcott Parsons, et al. pp. 157-163. vol. 2. Glencoe: The Free Press, 1961.

Singer, Jerome L. *Daydreaming.* New York: Random House, 1966.

Smith, Joel, et al. "Local Intimacy in a Middle-sized City." *American Journal of Sociology* 60 (November 1954): 276-284.

Sommer, Robert, and Osmond, Humphrey. "The Schizophrenic No-Society." *Psychiatry* 25 (August 1962): 244-255.

Spector, Aaron J. "Expectations, Fulfillment, and Morale." *Journal of Abnormal and Social Psychology* 52 (January 1956): 51-56.

Stokes, Donald E. "Voting." In *International Encyclopedia of the Social Science,* edited by David Sill, pp. 387-395. vol. 16. New York: Macmillan and The Free Press, 1968.

Stouffer, Samuel A. *Communism, Conformity and Civil Liberties.* Gloucester, Massachusetts: Peter Smith, 1963.

Strauss, Anselm, *The Social Psychology of George Herbert Mead.* Chicago: University of Chicago Press, 1956.

Sussman, Marvin B., and Burchinal, Lee G. "Kin Family Network: Unheralded Structure in Current Conceptualizations of Family Function." *Marriage and Family Living* 24 (August 1962): 231-240.

Sussman, Marvin, and White, R. Clyde. *Hough, Cleveland, Ohio: A Study of Social Life and Change.* Cleveland: The Press of Western Reserve University, 1959.

Tamney, Joseph B. "The Prediction of Religion Change." *Sociological Analysis* 26 (Summer 1965): 72-81.

———. "A Study of Involvement: Reactions to the Death of President Kennedy." *Sociologus* 19 (1969): 66-79.

Tilly, Charles, and Brown, C. Harold. "On Uprooting, Kinship and the Auspices of Migration." *International Journal of Comparative Sociology* 8 (1967): 139-164.

The Open Group. "Social Reform in the Centrifugal Society." *New Society* 363 (11 September 1969): 387-395.

Toennies, Ferdinand. *Community and Society.* New York: Harper Torchbook, 1963.

Townsend, Peter with the assistance of Sylvia Tunstall. "Isolation, Disolation and Loneliness." In *Old People in Three Industrial Societies,* edited by Ethel Shanas. et al., pp. 258-287. London: Routledge and Kegan Paul, 1968.

Warren, Roland L. *The Community in America.* Chicago: Rand McNally, 1963.

Weber, Max. *The Theory of Social and Economic Organization.* New York: The Free Press, 1966.

Whyte, William F. *Street Corner Society.* Chicago: University of Chicago Press, 1965.

Wilensky, Harold L. "A Second Look at the Traditional View of Urbanism." In *Perspectives on the American Community: A Book of Readings,* edited by Roland C. Warren, pp. 135-147. Chicago: Rand McNally, 1966.

Wirth, Louis. "Types of Nationalism." *American Journal of Sociology* 41 (May 1936): 723-737.

Wolff, Kurt. *The Sociology of Georg Simmel.* Glencoe: The Free Press, 1950.

Woodward, C. Vann. *The Burden of Southern History.* Baton Rouge: Louisiana State University Press, 1960.

Znaniecki, Florian. *Modern Nationalities.* Urbana, University of Illinois Press, 1952.

INDEX

A MANIFOLD VOICE

STUDIES IN COMMONWEALTH LITERATURE

A
MANIFOLD VOICE

Studies in Commonwealth Literature

WILLIAM WALSH

PROFESSOR OF EDUCATION
AND DOUGLAS GRANT FELLOW
IN COMMONWEALTH LITERATURE
IN THE UNIVERSITY OF LEEDS

1970

CHATTO & WINDUS

LONDON

Published by
Chatto & Windus Ltd
40 William IV Street
London WC2

★

Clarke, Irwin & Co. Ltd
Toronto

S.B.N. 7011 1580 7

© William Walsh 1970

Printed in Great Britain
by T. & A. Constable Ltd
Hopetoun Street
Edinburgh

TO
THE UNIVERSITY OF LEEDS
AND
THE AUSTRALIAN NATIONAL
UNIVERSITY

Acknowledgments

I am indebted to the following for permission to quote from work protected by copyright: to R. K. Narayan, William Heinemann and David Higham Associates; to Nirad C. Chaudhuri, John Farquharson and Chatto & Windus; to the literary estate of Olive Schreiner and Hutchinson & Co.; to Chinua Achebe, William Heinemann and Heinemann Educational Books; to V. S. Naipaul and André Deutsch; to Patrick White and Curtis Brown; to A. D. Hope and Hamish Hamilton; to the Katherine Mansfield estate and The Society of Authors; to Morley Callaghan and Mac-Gibbon & Kee.

Contents

Preface

IN this book I start from an assumption of the intimacy of language and literature, an intimacy so close and active that I see language as the co-partner with the author in producing a given work. The existence of a work of literature depends not on the writer alone but also on the degree of maturity the language it is written in has attained to, just as its complexity and fineness depend on the range of resources within that language. The practice of criticism, consequently, is not limited to the immediate analysis of the work in question but it also involves a telling-over of the powers latent in the language. A belief of this kind is the ground of the double intention in *A Manifold Voice*. First, I seek to explore some of the less familiar resources—less familiar to the British reader, that is—existing in the English language by pointing, as precisely and concretely as I can, at a number of writers who have worked in traditions outside those of Britain and the United States. The amazing capacity of English to express such a span of sensibility, whether West Indian, Canadian, Australian, African, New Zealand, Indian, testifies not only to the gifts of individual authors but to the genius of the language.

Secondly, my intention is to offer an answer to a question implicit in this undertaking: which of the authors writing in English outside Britain and the United States of America have made a significant use of the resources of the language? Which of them are of more than simply local importance? My answer is my choice. These are the writers who, judged by appropriate standards, have added to the canon of literature in English: who have realised, that is, in a creative way capacities implicit in the language. I do not claim for all these writers an equal significance. Some are without doubt more important than others. All are serious writers, all are genuinely representative; but there are some who are more important representatively than intrinsically. In fact, in one or two—as, I hope, my treatment shows—the representative quality, the capacity to embody a national identity and sensibility, shades and limits the pure literary worth. Nor can one overlook the great differences in context in which these writers operate. Patrick White, for example, writes straight from the heart of the British tradition, even though it may be given his own national modification and even though he may do it at immense physical distance; R. K. Narayan and Nirad C. Chaudhuri work against the background of their own powerful and very different civilisation and in a second language learnt at school; Chinua Achebe also writes in a second language but against a much more strongly oral tradition; the Canadian, Morley Callaghan, works under the influence, and suffers the pressure, of both English and American literature; much of the best work of Katherine Mansfield and V. S. Naipaul was actually composed in England although the life it deals with may belong to remote and different worlds.

I speak of this book as a set of studies in Commonwealth Literature, and I am very much aware how much this is a term of art. I have no desire to justify my use of it by arguments which it would take a constitutional lawyer to appreciate and probably to frame. I use the term because it is short, much employed and useful. It may be objected to by those who take a more exact political view of the Commonwealth than I do here, and, more strongly, by writers who rightly feel themselves to be Australians or New Zealanders or Canadians, writing against a particular historical tradition and in a particular national context, and not writers contributing to the literature of an amorphous Commonwealth. I sense the justice of these feelings, but I still use the term, which has now become widespread in Britain, the United States and other countries, as a convenient, shorthand indication and because it represents, in a reasonably uncontentious though perhaps clumsy way, a fact of history and substance about the situation of the writers I have chosen to consider.

I owe much to conversation on these subjects with three close friends: Professor D. J. Enright of the University of Singapore, Professor George Russell of the Australian National University, and the late, and deeply lamented, Professor Douglas Grant of the University of Leeds. I am greatly indebted to the University of Leeds which enabled me to undertake this work and the Australian National University which made it possible for me to complete it in Canberra.

CHAPTER I

I R. K. NARAYAN

INDIANS were writing in English before Macaulay's Minute. There has always been a remarkable quantity of first-rate Indian work in English in scholarship, philosophy, autobiography, religion, and especially in politics. Gandhi and Nehru themselves were both in their different styles masters of an oratorical idiom. And, of course, the Indians have had, and still have, their poets. But it was not till the 1930's that a number of novelists began to write in English—genuine novelists, that is, for whom fiction is an end in itself and not a means for communicating other kinds of truth. Some thirty years later it is clear that this was a form peculiarly suited to the Indian sensibility, and one to which Indian writers have made a distinct and significant contribution. So significant, indeed, that it is odd at a time when we give more and more attention to Commonwealth writers that a group like this should have received so little notice. Odd, too, that writers should have appeared during the years when the place of English in India as well as its condition should have been the occasion of endless, intense disagreement.

Without question the most individual and remarkable of these writers is R. K. Narayan. Narayan's preoccupation is with the middle class, a relatively small part of an agricultural civilisation, and the most conscious and anxious part of the population. Its members are neither too well off not to know the rub of financial worry nor too indigent to be brutalised by want and hunger. They may take their religion more easily than the passionately credulous poor, but even in those with a tendency towards modernity one is always aware under the educated speech of the profound murmur of older voices, of 'Lakshmi and Vishnu, the protector of creatures'. It is the members of the middle class who are psychologically more active, in whom consciousness is more vivid and harrowing, that Narayan chooses for his heroes—modest, unselfconfident heroes, it is true. They have some reason for independent existence; but there is always a tension between this and that deep source of power, the family where the women rather than the old represent 'Custom and Reason' and know 'what is and what is not proper'. The family is the immediate context in which his sensibility operates, and his novels are remarkable for the subtlety and conviction with which family relationships are treated—that of son and parents and brother and brother in *The Bachelor of Arts*, of husband and wife and father and daughter in *The English Teacher*, of father and son in *The Financial Expert*, and of grandmother and grandson in *Waiting for Mahatma*.

The action of Narayan's novels is centred in the small town of Malgudi in Mysore—small by Indian standards, that is—and one comes to have a strong feeling for the place's identity. The detail suggests, surely and economically, the special flavour of Malgudi, a blend of oriental and pre-1914 British, like an Edwardian mixture of sweet mangoes and malt vinegar. It is against the presence of this town and amid a net of family relationships that Narayan's heroes engage in their characteristic struggles. The conditions of the struggle vary from novel to novel. One still discerns beneath the diversity a common pattern. What is so attractive about it is the charm and authenticity of its Indian colouring; what makes it immediately recognisable is that it seems to belong to a substantial human nature. The primary aim of these characters is to achieve what Chandran in *The Bachelor of Arts* calls 'a life freed from distracting illusions and hysterics'. At first the intention is obscure, buried under the habits of ordinary life, personal responsibilities and—since this is India—a heavy, inherited burden. The novels plot the rise of this intention into awareness, its recognition in a crisis of consciousness, and its resolution, or resolutions, since there are more often than not several mistaken or frustrated efforts at a resolution. If the analysis of the subject's struggle to extricate himself from the habitual, dreamy automatism of his Indian past shows Narayan's gift for serious moral analysis, then the various solutions adopted by his *personae* in the search for another, more conscious life, exhibit his marvellous comic talent. (Not of course that the fiction offers a neatly logical division just like this. The serious and the comic flow in and out of one another throughout in an intricate, inseparable alliance.) Tracts of human experience are looked at with an affectionately ridiculing eye, and with that kind of humour in which the jokes are also a species of moral insight. Such treatment brings out the note of the bizarre, of human queerness, in the activities of many sorts of people, business men, printers, teachers, holy men, press agents, money-lenders. At our most commonplace we are all exotic if scrutinised by a fresh eye. The range is impressive but it follows naturally on Narayan's reading of the key experience at the heart of his novels. It is always a meeting which precipitates the crisis of consciousness. It is the intervention of human difference, human otherness, into the hero's narcissistic world which shatters it for him, and he feels in response that he has to break out of his solipsistic circle into a new, better still an alien, field of action. To evoke so much variety with such casual, convincing authority and to make it also organic and functional testify to an original talent of the finest kind.

I have written at length on Narayan's fiction elsewhere[1] and I will concentrate here on two novels which appeared since I wrote that essay, *The Man-Eater of Malgudi* (1961), and *The Sweet Vendor* (1967). *The Man-Eater of Malgudi* begins on a note of modest self-mockery. The protagonist, Nataraj, runs a seedy print-shop in Kabir Street next to—in fact almost in an ante-room of—the prosperous Star Press where there is an amenable proprietor as well as a large staff and 'an original Heidelberg' printing press, with groaning double cylinders. Nataraj, with the help, or really under the direction, of his one member of staff, the learned Mr Sastri, does pretty well everything in the shop, from printing on an ancient treadle machine to sewing up the sheets; he is particularly expert in printing coloured labels for lemonade bottles, the ink of which in his view is often much more drinkable than the contents of the bottle. He keeps the line between his own place and the Star Press deliberately vague and has a habit of passing through importunate and curious customers to the more important establishment, particularly if they want to be assured about the machinery on which their orders are to be printed. This is one of his ways of

[1] *A Human Idiom*: Literature and Humanity. Chatto & Windus, London, 1964

conserving his privacy and liberty even at work and enables him to go on using one of his rooms, with its roll-top desk, Queen Anne chair and deep cane basket-chair, as a local club where his friends, the journalist and the poet, can endlessly analyse the state of the town and the nation. Nataraj is both a gay and melancholy man, protected by routine which he can slough off at a moment's notice. He is nervy, imaginative, friendly, unambitious in external things but with a vivid inner life. He, his family, his friends, the district, the enveloping tissue of history and the delicate film of relations among them all, are established by means of a patient accumulation of detail, each point of which, whether common or odd, is seen with a child's freshness of eye and organised with an adult's experienced subtlety. Everything is concrete, manifold, multiplying backwards and forwards so that the reader has a sense of life elaborated with infinite patience and completeness. The society is formal but the relations are quick and spontaneous. Into this world composed of shades and subtleties of relationships, of traditions, of complex feelings, of hallowed objects, of modes of conduct and habits of thought which are both ritualistic and homely, there intrudes the abstract and brutal will of 'H. Vasu, M.A., Taxidermist' as he is described on his card.

So easily and fully is this Indian world summoned into existence, so delicately are its primary assumptions insinuated and their intrinsic worth indicated, that the reader, like Nataraj and his friends, feels the affront of Vasu's intervention and the way in which his words and actions violate both accepted manners and every tradition implicit in them. 'The man's curiosity was limitless and recognised no proprieties,' Nataraj says of him; and 'proprieties' in Nataraj's phrase mean more than the small-town blenching at anything outside the accepted canon of monogamous chastity which is shown in, and shown up in, Nataraj's own blend of puritan horror and sensual attraction towards the prostitute Rangi. 'Proprieties' here also mean a style of life and a whole habit of sensibility sanctioned by the experience of generations, the whole complex of practice, feeling and memory which makes Nataraj a person who is a product of history. It is this propriety which is abolished by the presence of Vasu. His will is unqualified by any impersonal past.

It simply, absolutely, initiates action. He is a form of abstract causality, and he is maddened by any whiff of what is established or unquestioned because that makes him to some degree an effect.

Vasu's self-exclusion from the world of familiar intercourse—invitation after invitation is extended to him but always abruptly rejected—gives him a nihilistic and menacing air which becomes, in the Indian context, somehow ominously superhuman—a force not negotiable on human terms. This is how he bursts into the novel:

> Now an unusual thing happened. The curtain stirred, an edge of it lifted, and the monosyllabic poet's head peeped through. An extraordinary situation must have arisen to make him do that. His eyes bulged. 'Someone to see you,' he whispered.
> 'Who? What does he want?'
> 'I don't know.'
> The whispered conversation was becoming a strain. I shook my head, winked and grimaced to indicate to the poet that I was not available. The poet, ever a dense fellow, did not understand but blinked on unintelligently. His head suddenly vanished, and a moment later a new head appeared in its place—a tanned face, large powerful eyes under thick eyebrows, a large forehead and a shock of unkempt hair, like a black halo.

This quiet passage represents Narayan's manner very well. He is an even writer, not much given to the purple passage or the set piece. The basic unit of his narrative, if one can use the term, is the incident, the event happening, and this accounts for the impression of mobility his novels invariably give. Complex action, even if it is of the most muted kind, goes on all the time. The exploitation of incident, a blend of event, action, motive, memory, feeling, cause and effect, is a perfect strategy for Narayan. Its mobility conveys that sense of flux in human life which he is so conscious of, and the transparency of surface which is characteristic of his writing draws the reader's attention down to deeper levels, a middle level of motivation and individual psychology and a deeper level of poetic myth and communal awareness.

In the description of Vasu's entry the reader will be struck by the concreteness of the whole undertaking, by the sharp sensory observation upon which it is based, the simplicity of the line and the delicate focussing upon significant points of motion in the incident. The effect of these and of the extreme clarity of the language is to bring home to the reader the silky, on-going suppleness of any human action. It carries with it, too, a sense of its complexity in that it glancingly suggests the nervy, responsive psychology of Nataraj and the unclogged, custom-free directness of Vasu. The symbol of the denying curtain means nothing to him. More than this, the last phrase, 'a black halo', a submerged almost silent paradox, hints that Vasu may constitute a more obscure and profound threat to the system by which Nataraj and his neighbours live. It is a hint taken up at other sensitive places in the novel and it gives the tale of the taxidermist-hunter, who goes from stuffing dead animals to killing live ones, a more general and religious significance.

Narayan has a special gift for pressing a mild significance from the common events of ordinary life without puffing into the ineffable or collapsing into the wambling because he works with the lightest of touches and because of the discipline and accuracy of the detail. Each incident is presented with the firm objectivity produced by intimate familiarity. And all the incidents together, each smoothly articulated with the next, glide into an elegant comedy— in *The Man-Eater of Malgudi*, a comedy of contrast. The movement is so natural and living that the various incidents—the details of the printing trade, Vasu's harassing of Nataraj, Vasu's preying on the domestic animals in the town and the wild ones in the jungle, Nataraj's mission to cure and then to protect the sick temple-elephant and Vasu's own grotesque self-destruction while he waits to destroy the sacred beast—all these incidents carried on an unbroken buoyant current become a mobile pattern or dance; and the almost dialectical opposition of character and significance posed by the antagonism of Nataraj and Vasu appears as the necessary outcome of the material, offering that combination of logic and indeterminacy we are used to in everyday life, but also hinting at the presence of obscurer and greater forces than we are normally aware of.

So that Narayan's fiction operates at one level by the candid reproduction of surfaces and manners and behaviour, the consequence of direct and unfaked perception, while at a much deeper

level, because his sensibility is saturated with the Indian tradition
and sensitive to the experience implicit in the Indian myth, it
operates through an oblique and tentative poetry. Each of these is
an effect of the receptive part of his talent, its capacity to register
the outward world and what is latent in it. In between there is
another area in which he brings to bear a more active and analytic
talent for psychological dissection and moral analysis.

It is his nimble curiosity in this sphere together with his unruffled
acceptance of what it discovers ('discovers' because what is seen is
there, happening in front of one) which exempts Narayan from the
charge levelled at Indian writers by V. S. Naipaul. 'There can be
no effective writing. The ritual of Indian life smothers imagination,
for which it is a substitute, and the interpretation of India in the
Indian novel, itself a borrowed form, is at a low, unchanging level.'[1]
It is true that Narayan writes within a settled scheme. The mode of
belief, the pattern of life, the method of thinking and feeling, the
historical inheritance and the characteristic reaction to the social
and physical environment—all these recur in his novels. But why
not, since they are the conditions of the civilisation which Narayan
seeks to interpret? It is true, too, that the central predicament of his
characters re-appears in novel after novel, the subject struggling to
extricate himself from the dreamy automatism of his past. But the
solution adopted by his protagonist, and by 'solution' I mean the
concrete escape and the specific conditions in which it takes place,
is different from novel to novel, and continually exhibits the shock
of self-discovery, an experience which is inexhaustible in its content
and endlessly capable of suspense and surprise.

The crisis of consciousness which extricates Nataraj from his
tranquil routine, the odd humanity of which is observed with
Narayan's characteristically detached and tolerant eye, is precipi-
tated by the violent taxidermist-hunter, Vasu, who is not so much
a character as the other half of a collision. His motiveless enmity
towards Nataraj leaves the latter distraught. Nataraj was not constructed to sustain hostility. 'I could never be a successful enemy to
anyone. Any enmity worried me night and day. As a schoolboy I
persistently shadowed around the one person with whom I was

[1] *Magic and Dependence*, V. S. Naipaul, *Weekend Telegraph*, 18th August 1967

B

supposed to be on terms of hate and hostility. I felt acutely uneasy as long as our enmity lasted.' Nataraj had been brought up in a house where he had been taught never to kill, where his grand-uncle gave him a coin every day to buy sugar for the ants, and where he even swatted flies secretly so that the elders wouldn't know. In any event, Vasu's effect is too absolute and negative to allow a purely personal response. He is terrifying because he abolishes, by brutally refusing to acknowledge their existence, the values implicit in the life which Nataraj and his friends live. To detonate the spiritual ground in this way, and Vasu has all the impact of a bomb, is to apply an annihilating force precisely at the point on which Nataraj most depends for ultimate support.

Some of the best of the spry and mellow comedy of *The Man-Eater of Malgudi* depends on Nataraj's increasingly frantic effort at rendering the oppressive presence of Vasu at least tolerable. On the face of it he is working purely in the field of action to circumvent Vasu's persecution of the animals and the harassment of himself. But these external acts, which anyway fail in their direct purpose, are hopelessly inadequate to effect the deeper reconciliation that Nataraj's nature and indeed the character of the community call for. Nataraj cannot convert Vasu into a friend, and he finds open hostility insupportable. Both his friends and the community at large blench at the effort to enfold in an acceptable embrace the malevolently unclaspable Vasu. Men as tough as the police inspector and the game-warden, strong voices of the community's outraged authority, recoil at Vasu's combination of ferocity and legal know-how. All his friends can do is to copy the poet and develop 'the art of surviving Vasu's presence'. The problem is to assimilate a wholly alien force, and neither Nataraj himself nor his immediate circle nor the community, whether in the town or the village, is capable of solving the problem. As a result they all feel to some degree what becomes almost unbearable in Nataraj, the emotion of panic, that special resonance of disordered feeling which accompanies the disintegration of the premises of thought and action.

The climax of the comedy and the resolution of the problem of assimilation come together in Vasu's grotesque death. He has an overwhelming loathing for mosquitoes and he has made himself

over many years a man of superhuman strength, with hands
trained to batter thick panels of teak and iron. In crushing a
mosquito on his forehead with his own fist while he waits in the
dark to shoot the sacred elephant, he slaughters himself. The fantasy
of this has been carefully prepared for and it fits without friction the
final 'explanation' of Vasu. He becomes explicable, as well as dead,
when it is realised that he is really somebody for whom 'the black
halo of hair' was wholly suitable. The Maneater of Malgudi finally
takes his place in the community as a 'Rakshasa', a demon, the other
side of life. All his enormities now fall into place; his absolute
rejection of everything Nataraj and his friends live by now makes
sense and indeed testifies to the sanity of the assumptions they had
begun to doubt; and everyone takes comfort, especially Nataraj,
from grasping that even had he not died he could be certainly relied
upon to bring about his own destruction. That it was the frailest of
animals, the mosquito, which helped him, the exterminator of
animals and the eater of men, to his own death clinches the lightly
drawn parable.

> 'He had one virtue, he never hit anyone with his hand, whatever the
> provocation,' I said, remembering his voice.
> 'Because,' said Sastri puckishly, 'he had to conserve all that might
> for his own destruction. Every demon appears in the world with a
> special boon of indestructibility. Yet the universe has survived all the
> *rakshasas* that were ever born. Every demon carries within him,
> unknown to himself, a tiny seed of self-destruction, and goes up in thin
> air at the most unexpected moment. Otherwise what is to happen to
> humanity?'

Sastri's remark, contingent, interrogative, plaintive but not
querulous, offering a modest word of hope about the possibilities of
human survival, indicates the quality of the quietly complex tone of
Narayan's fiction. His novels make no large claims, assert no tremendous faith. Sastri's words indicate pretty well its measure and
character. But as Narayan's work has matured, or perhaps simply
as he has grown older, the manner in which he expresses his belief
in the nature of whatever it is that supports a hope for humanity
becomes less diffident. What at the end of *The Guide* is only the
most feathery intimation has become in *The Man-Eater of Malgudi*,

in spite of the fantasy of its context, a less oblique statement of his belief in the sustaining role of some other influence—the blessings of the gods or just the stubbornness of life itself. Certainly an explicit notation of this kind appears in the conclusion of *The Sweet Vendor* where Jagan, the protagonist, suddenly determines to detach himself from 'a set of repetitions performed for sixty years' in order to spend the rest of his life helping a stonemason to carve a pure image of the goddess for others to contemplate. His decision, which is of course in the classical Indian line, requiring that 'at some stage in one's life one must uproot oneself from the accustomed surroundings and disappear so that others can continue in peace', is in Jagan's case charmingly blemished with an appealing human flaw. He doesn't neglect to take with him his cheque book. This touch is characteristic of Narayan's sensibility. His concept of spirituality is as precise and as stained with human fallibility as is his notion of the rest of life. The servant of the goddess with whom Jagan proposes to finish out his days explains that the perfection in stone which he is aiming at must still contain a deliberate fault.

'I always remember the story of the dancing figure of Nataraj, which was so perfect that it began a cosmic dance and the town itself shook as if an earthquake had rocked it, until a small finger on the figure was chipped off. We always do it; no one ever notices it, but we always create a small flaw in every image; it's for safety.'

Jagan's decision to retire from the world is not only part of the national tradition: 'It would be the most accredited procedure according to our scriptures—husband and wife must vanish into the forest at some stage in their lives, leaving the affairs of the world to younger people'. It also follows the bias of his own nature. He is high-minded, pious, attentive to the scriptures, observant of custom, scrupulous about ritual, a follower of Gandhi, and he has evolved a number of prim theories about diet, footwear, toothbrushes and hygiene. But his character also includes the 'small flaw' making for safety. The largeness of his spiritual ambition is clipped a bit by a measure of mercantile flexibility which enables him to count some of the money taken over the counter 'as free cash . . . a sort of immaculate conception, self-generated, arising out of itself and entitled to survive without reference to any tax'. Moreover, he is—

'protected' is the word Narayan's account suggests—protected from too much voyaging into the ineffable by a certain appealing simplicity of intelligence. ' "Conquer taste, and you will have conquered the self," said Jagan to his listener, who asked, "Why conquer the self?" Jagan said, "I do not know, but all our sages advise us so." '

Jagan's renunciation of the world, then, is of a piece with the Indian tradition and the radical disposition of his own character in so far as it is a reflection of that tradition. But, of course, for Jagan himself his renunciation is a very big decision, too big in some ways for his surface or immediate personality which is dry, fussy, narrow, commercial and self-regarding. What is necessary to make this Jagan into the world-renouncing Jagan is supplied by the Indian religious tradition. Even a nature as thin as Jagan's, it becomes clear, is able to be fed from deep and more than personal sources. Part of Narayan's gift as a novelist of a more inclusive life is the delicacy and firmness with which such depths are convincingly implied in the structure of his characters. This gift depends partly upon the power and inclusiveness of the Indian tradition, partly upon Narayan's own profound acceptance of it, partly, and as far as the reader is concerned, most, on Narayan's beautifully executed evocation of the actual presences and concrete specifications of the life of the town. The suggested halo of significance follows naturally on the meticulously defined detail.

Three areas of the life Jagan is to renounce are drawn with the crispest line and shade in *The Sweet Vendor*. First the steady encircling routine of the community of Malgudi which laps Jagan round with the certainties of history and the stability of current relationships, and which, while testing and proving him in a dozen ways, still validates his function and confirms his identity and value. Next, there is his work as the proprietor of an establishment making and selling sweets. Narayan is much drawn to the truth of character shown in a person's work in which the stretched personality submits itself to impersonal ends and he describes with tender and precise care the style and method, the rituals and satisfactions of Jagan's work. Then there is the ambiguous and dangerous ground of his relations with his son, the sullen Westernised Mali whose

American-Korean wife turns out to be—dumbfoundingly to the conventional Jagan—only his mistress, and whose contemptuous explanations to his bewildered father of a scheme for manufacturing a fiction-writing machine include all the divisions which so maddeningly separate the two of them, the division of East and West, of young and old, of child and parent.

This triple structure makes a composition marked by the combined ease and authority of an artist in full control of his instrument; and it supports a world which has a background, a context, an immediate presence and a nervous individual centre, a world which impresses the reader with the quality of its completeness. Whatever happens in India, the reader feels, happens in Malgudi, and whatever happens in Malgudi, he is persuaded, might well happen in his own life. Malgudi is an image of India and a metaphor of everywhere else.

When Jagan retires from life—'I am going to watch a goddess come out of a stone'—he does so unromantically, practically, like a sound business man, arranging for his shop to be open and deciding where he should leave his keys. He seems to be doing so for comparatively external reasons because of the hell which his son Mali has made of his life at home, or because he can no longer face the incomprehensibility of action deriving from motives beyond his grasp. 'Puzzling over things was enervating. Reading a sense into Mali's actions was fatiguing like the attempt to spell out a message in a half-familiar script.' But the real reason is a more inward one. His life, or that part of it, he realises is complete. It has achieved whatever shape it is capable of. Enlightenment means realising that one has come to the point at which struggle, and all the comedy of friction, are irrelevant: it means recognising and accepting the bitter conclusion of an early novel, *The English Teacher*, that, 'a profound and unmitigated loneliness is the only truth of life'. This 'law' comes home to one with force and clarity as one shares in a life like Jagan's, so warmly surrounded by a community and so totally involved in work and family. Mobility, shape and the significance of completeness—these are the values— and they are not only Indian ones—which animate Narayan's pure, disinterested art.

As readers of the Indian novel we in this country have our deficiencies. It is hard for us to take up the references—to the Indian scene, the agricultural tradition, the vast distances, the terrible poverty, the profoundly significant religion. We live in utterly different conditions where nobody's grandmother could hand down to her grandchildren as a legacy an image of the god Nataraja, which had been found in a packet of saffron—as happens, for example, in Narayan's novel *Mr Sampath*. As readers we are almost certainly in the position of the young man Srinivas in the same novel and 'grasp the symbols but vaguely'. And yet as we read these novels, as we contemplate the proportions of the god Nataraja and think of the packet of saffron, we are not deceived, I think, in detecting through all the appearance of strangeness a familiar rhythm, the common and extraordinary rhythm of life.

II   NIRAD C. CHAUDHURI

I want now to turn to a writer of a wholly different kind from any I have so far considered in this chapter. As I remarked early on, it is in fiction that Indian writers have shown themselves peculiarly gifted, and to the novel that they have made a significant contribution, particularly through the work of Narayan, a writer of exceptional quality. The fact that these writers worked in English is admittedly a large, though implicit, recognition of the fact and influence of British civilisation in India; but it is remarkable how little the explicit recognition of the British connection counts in them. Nirad C. Chaudhuri is not a novelist. His work evinces a most conscious and detailed recognition of the fact and consequence of Britain in India and he contrasts strikingly with many of the novelists, with the self-effacing Narayan in particular, in displaying with outrageous frankness the structure and qualities of a personality which is confidently positive to the point of arrogance and cracklingly irascible to the point of bloody-mindedness. Not, as his work reveals, that he has not a good deal to be irascible and bloody-minded about. Chaudhuri is the author of *A Passage to*

England,[1] *The Continent of Circe*[2] and *The Autobiography of an Unknown Indian*,[3] the book on which I shall concentrate.

A Passage to England is the record of Chaudhuri's first, short visit to Britain. It shows a learned, lively mind, steeped in European culture, a vivid personality of distinct and unaffected charm—the violently aggressive side of Chaudhuri's nature gets little provocation in this visit—remarkable freshness of response and acuity of sense impression, together with some highly subjective analysis of the British Welfare State. It is a graceful, unusual travel book, though slight by the standard of *The Autobiography*. Its main interest for the English reader lies in its being an Indian version of that sensibility of *recognition*, which one sees in Henry James's autobiographical writings, by which something known in literature is now known in life, by which life, in fact, verifies literature and corroborates imagination.

First the travel book, next the thesis. The core of the doctrine of *The Continent of Circe* is that the Hindus are of European stock, immigrant Aryans from Mitannian-Mesopotamia, who colonised the Indo-Gangetic plain and parts of South India. The Aryans were a complete society originally with a triple structure: an aristocracy composed of priests and fighters and then the general body of the community carrying on normal economic activities as peasants, traders, cattle-raisers, artisans, to which they added a caste of workers, the Sudras (who were not however the primitive dark autochthonous population) to make the four-caste society the Hindu community has remained ever since—at least in theory. The Aryan settlement was complete in its essential form by the end of the seventh century B.C., and with it the basic ethnic pattern of India firmly established—the outstanding feature of which is the ferocious opposition between the civilised community of the Aryans and the indigenous dark population or any other which threatened it. This Aryan civilisation was affected by later invasions of Persians and Greeks, which were culturally though not ethnically important, and later by incursions of barbarian nomads from

---

[1] Chatto & Windus, London, 1960
[2] Chatto & Windus, London, 1965
[3] Macmillan, 1951

Central Asia. These latter invasions meant that the Hindus had to fight for the survival of their society on two fronts, against the internal proletariat of the indigenous, 'the primitive darks' (Chaudhuri's term) and an external proletariat of Asian nomads. The Hindus in consequence became a closed society based on birth, aggressively self-conscious, violently xenophobic and intensely colour-conscious—as, Chaudhuri claims, they remain today.

The evidence for, or perhaps I should say the source of, Chaudhuri's theory or conviction or intuition about the immigrant Aryan civilisation is first the undoubted fact of the diffusion of Indo-European languages, and secondly his own interpretations of the early Indian epics, supported thirdly by a method of extrapolating backward into history and pre-history the logic of his observations of contemporary Indian society. It will not be necessary, I am sure, for me to explain that I am not qualified as a scholar to have a view on Chaudhuri's theory on the origins of Indian civilisation. But what strikes me as a reader is the intensely personal and even passionate quality of his doctrine, scholarly in material, fanatic in manner. He hurls idea after idea with tumultuous vitality and he has the disconcerting habit of attaching to some abstract conception or erudite theory a petty personal irritation like a slight he received at a concert or a women's club. He is a man lacerated by the present, scalded by scorn for the misery, poverty, degradation and inner and outer disorder which he observes in every corner of contemporary society and powerfully impelled to find in the past a coherent explanation for the chaos and despair which surround him.

The Islamic expansion in India, gradual in its first phase, overwhelming in the second, brought into India the propagators of a new aggressive culture who had both an absolute conviction of the superiority of their culture and a religious duty to spread it. It was a well established and mature society with a fully developed way of life. In the North it displaced the Hindu ruling class and lodged in the Indian consciousness the conviction of an irreconcilable conflict between Hindu and Muslim. There could be no question whatever of absorbing the Muslims, and Hindu Society on its side lost whatever power of assimilating and adaptability it had once possessed. The bulk of the new Islamic population were Hindu converts but this fact made no difference at all to their sense of solidarity among themselves and their feeling of oneness with the Islamic world outside. 'Here is the case,' says Chaudhuri, 'of a true ethnic relationship being completely broken by a new cultural and social association.'

The psychological experience of the British in India closely repeated that of the Hindus. A people of a temperate climate, at a period of great vitality in their national life, with a strong disposition in favour of the fascinating, richly promising East, became, under the brutalities of a tropical climate and among a potentially hostile population, horribly denatured. Their sense of proportion broke down. They lost their usual equability in human relations. They became extreme and strident. They were outraged by the lack among the Hindus of the European virtues of 'reason' and 'measure'; everything appeared inconsistent and extravagant, lush and awry. They were continually oppressed by the possibility of submergence in a lower culture. Their pride in race intensified. They became increasingly unwilling to share their culture and they became neurotically arrogant. '... The British in India ... paraded a racial arrogance whose mildest form was a stony silence. ...'

In mirroring the psychological development of the Hindus, the history of the British in India helped to harden the Hindus in their own radical bias as confirmed believers in blood and birth. The repetition strengthened the original disposition. The Hindus remain a people divided against themselves, suffering an exhaustion of vitality and an ever-present maladjustment with the tropical environment. What had happened to the Hindus happened to the British, and what had happened to the British made any modification of the Hindu nature still more unlikely. It was the excruciatingly cruel country which had the same effect on both people. 'Western scholars have sometimes made Buddhism or Vedanta responsible for the apparent indifference of the Hindus to the things of the world, especially for their disinclination to mental and bodily exertion, and attributed to us a world-negation which we never had. The philosophies did not make our life what it is, it was the life which made the philosophies what they are.'

A Passage to England showed Chaudhuri as a writer with a gift for registering fresh and exact impressions of what he observes about him. *The Continent of Circe* shows him as a social analyst who has evolved, as much from imagination as from history, a theory of Indian development which provides him with a causal explanation for the failures of his society. He can therefore with a steady mind and complete conviction, as well as a high degree of Bengali fury, mercilessly expose the wounds of India. Whatever one may think of his fairness, no one can question his courage. No subject is too delicate or too sacred to be attacked, whether it is Indian mysticism or Indian militarism or the Indian attitude to sex or colour or religion, or Indian relations with China or Pakistan or the West, whether it is political or social or individual morality. If we add to the sharp eye and natural audacity a buoyant intellectual vivacity and an intense fascination with himself, we can see that gifts which might not qualify him to be an impartially objective critic of national life might help to make him an autobiographer of a rare kind.

Which indeed they do. *The Autobiography of an Unknown Indian* is one of the finest examples of this *genre* to appear in English in this century, and the most significant, single discursive work to be generated by the love and hate of Indian-British relationships. I have spoken of Chaudhuri's fascination with himself in *The Continent of Circe*. Naturally, the same thing appears in *The Autobiography* but, paradoxically, in a much more disciplined way. Here Chaudhuri sees himself as an object in a landscape or as an impulse in a more inclusive and controlling rhythm, and the whole presentation of the self is impressively tranquil and objective. Chaudhuri was born in 1897, and the book which begins in the early nineteen hundreds takes him to the end of his university career, its substance being the treatment of his childhood and youth. It is written in a masculine, confident English of long, balanced sentences, which combine a degree of formality with considerable ease and lissomness, and its only oddity is a curiously Celtic use of continuous tenses. It is an idiom which is distinctly late-Victorian in flavour, with all the positive strength and assurance of that, and it is wholly consistent with the period and sensibility of the writer.

The Autobiography is organised round a conception of place, which is shown as the great means by which embodied history is brought to bear upon growth. The significance of place in Chaudhuri's life is the principle of composition in *The Autobiography*, and its development through the sequence of places, Kishorganj his country birthplace, Banagram his ancestral village, Kalikutch his mother's village, Shillong the Assam hill station, an imagined England and a more than actual Calcutta, is handled with imaginative tact which makes the book a genuine composition obeying an inward initiative: except for the final part where it comes to an end in a huddled and clumsily inappropriate conclusion in a long, theoretical essay on the course of Indian history.

The life of the places Chaudhuri lived in is revived with a kind of creative thoroughness. There is, to begin with, the fully pictured actuality of the town, the villages, the hill station, the city of Calcutta—everything in their physical presence from the quality of the dust and the shape of the trees, to the design of the houses, the material of the roof, the layout of the neighbourhood, the character of the rivers and the configuration of the land; next, displayed with lucidity and warmth, there is the intense, enfolding family life with its routine, stresses and rituals; and then the complications of the social world outside the family with its severely functional divisions and its absolutely arranged organisation; and all of these are supported and surrounded by a massive fund of anthropological and historical learning and penetrated by sensitively intelligent sociological speculation. This intricate treatment gives the reader a double insight. He has a sense of the young Chaudhuri's life picking its way through a variety of densely detailed locations and assuming definition and individuality as it goes; and he catches, too, glimpses that steady into a vision of an extraordinary society, which combines something from the Victorian past of our own history, a high-minded, ethically serious, self-improving middle class with another universe as old and strange as *Lear*, in which priests with scimitars sacrifice goats and garlanded buffaloes to the music of drums, cymbals and gongs while the worshippers smear themselves with the animals' blood and pelt each other with a dough made of blood and dust.

Each of the places Chaudhuri lived in has a particular meaning in his development—not meaning in the sense of anything emblematic or mystical but, more straightforwardly, meaning as a special and precise twist in the shaping of his character. The town of Kishorganj, which came into existence as a municipal township in the 1860's, was the constant in the family existence. Life there was solidly based, plain, industrious, but also on occasion exciting, when enlivened by feasts, fairs, gypsies and the attractions of the river and the rains, or perilous during the season of cholera, when a workman would pass along the road swinging a censer full of sulphur. The family house stood on a plot of two acres and was composed of an intricate collection of buildings around an inner courtyard. It was furnished with beds and chests, baskets, books and trunks. The simplicity of furniture and the complexity of structure of the house corresponded to the life lived in it. There were innumerable traditions and customs, a whole complex of habits, rituals and disciplines but at the same time great simplicity and directness of feeling. The father was a liberal 'protestant' Hindu, monotheist and enlightened and mainly concerned with educating his children in a rational way of life and encouraging them in what were thought of as the English qualities of energy and self-reliance. It was a calm, regular life for the elders absorbed in their profession and for the children occupied in learning. Colour and movement broke into it only at rhythmic intervals. There was a remarkable feeling of equality among the citizens but, of course, the idea of citizenship was a restricted one, excluding the workers and peasants and indeed government officials and wealthy landowners. It was a town ruled by some hundred families. There were few old people in the population of the citizens and a large number of children. Profession and education were two serious concerns of these people and they all worked unremittingly at them. The children were in touch through their father and his clients (as well as being vice-chairman of the municipality he was a lawyer with a wholly criminal practice) with the world of human violence. Murder, robbery, rape, arson were common events in the town and outside it. But these things were balanced by two other forces. Around them there seemed to be an immutable sphere of justice and order presided over by an organisation the ordinary people still called the 'company' and the educated the 'government'; and underneath they felt the unquestioned foundations of religion and morality, 'things in which everyone believed and things to which in the last resort everybody returned'.

Life in Kishorganj made for a rational habit of mind. It offered stability but it also encouraged, largely because of the influence of an admirable, level-headed father, moral and intellectual independence. Parental connections led back to the villages, the ancestral village of Banagram and the mother's village of Kalikutch—'so self-effacing in bamboo and cane greenery'. Here the children's experience fed a rich emotional life. The rhythms of the country, the feeling for blood and family, the living Bengali tradition of drama and folk-poetry, the intimate connection of family life and art deepened and refined the children's feelings. *The Autobiography* presents, through the minutely detailed round of daily life, a portrait of a highly civilised society, in which drama, poetry, religion and ordinary life were intimately united.

> We always had these plays at the time of religious festivals and weddings, and at times also for their own sake. The repertory, though large, was almost exclusively drawn from either of the great epics, the *Ramayana* or the *Mahabharata*, and the stories were thus familiar to the audience. From this followed that the watching of the plays was even for young people like us not a passive gulping down of a story but an appraisal, in the light of a critical code which was never crude, of points of composition and acting, and, at times, even of doctrine.[1]

At the same time this is not an idyll of lyrical nostalgia. Chaudhuri makes very clear the claustrophobic atmosphere, the suspicions and distrusts and the envies and meannesses which this patrician society was capable of, particularly for women. His mother felt imprisoned in it and she was sure that her own health—she was subject to some pathological, mental condition—was ruined by her sojourn in Banagram. His father felt that to live permanently in the way the gentry did in the villages would be to live without work and without purpose. He had the deepest possible conviction of the sanctity of the present and the future and he hated the spirit of Byzantism that he saw expressed in this society.

Shillong, the paradisal Assam hill station, with its pure, cool air and pine trees, where the children visited an uncle who collected

[1] *The Autobiography of An Unknown Indian*, p. 60

orchids, makes a natural bridge to another place which exercised a profound influence on Chaudhuri's nature—England—for it was in Shillong that the amazed children saw the English in the flesh, men and women and doll-like babies. England had been a living presence in Chaudhuri's imagination from his early days, partly because of his father's care that he should learn English and the good sense of the teaching methods he adopted to this end, partly through the books and pictures in the house, and partly through the poems he read and the history he studied. Nor could any educated person escape the influence of England that came through the political administrative system imposed on India by the British, an influence which was recognised and supported (even if it was rejected on patriotic grounds) by great names of Hindu and Bengali thought like Michael Dutt, Bankim Chandra Chatterji, Tagore, Rammohun Roy. Chaudhuri's feeling for England was a more explicitly conscious attraction than any English boy could have had, but it was added to a personality which had the strongest natural affinity for English civilisation. He saw it vaguely at first and more precisely as he grew older as a necessary penetration of the East by the West in one of its most beautiful and worthwhile forms. It was of course England and the English civilisation, it should be stressed, which influenced Chaudhuri, not the English in India. He was the last person alive to be impressed by colonial insolence. If one asks why Chaudhuri should have had this extraordinary understanding of and sympathy with English civilisation, the answer seems to be that he saw in it an essential corrective to certain Indian qualities. He was fascinated by the vitality and pragmatism of English character, by the genius for the concrete shown in English art, by the English capacity to give form and solidity to its insight, and by the English gift evident at every point and in all its production for the differentiated and particular.

Chaudhuri, himself a man with a relish for the specific, loved the quality of concreteness in English civilisation. And it was the absence of this in Indian civilisation to which he gave a measured philosophic expression towards the end of *The Autobiography*.

I think there is even in the highest and most characteristic teaching of Hinduism (apart from the layer on layer of infinitely varied primitiveness which constitutes its buried foundation), something impelling a Hindu towards the simpler in preference to the more complex, towards the unemerged in preference to the emergent, and towards the general in preference to the particular. According to some of the noblest teaching of Hinduism, the manifested universe is an illusion, the ultimate reality attribute-less, and man's supreme happiness lies in putting an end to the cycle of births and deaths, or, in other words, in eliminating precisely those particular forms possessing sensible attributes which confer qualities and values on reality, and clothe it with attractiveness for us. With such a philosophical background it is not surprising that a Hindu should tend to ignore distinctions. To me, however, Hinduism appears to be swimming against the current. Although its penchant for the undifferentiated and attributeless is undoubtedly due to its anxiety to bite on the rock of truth and reality lying underneath the flux of changes, I would still say that in actual fact it is retrograde and out of sympathy with reality. For I believe in change and hold all reality to be a process, a process which is justifying itself, as well as making itself more significant, by becoming more particular and differentiated and by endowing itself with ever more new values.[1]

Kishorganj, Banagram, Kalikutch, Shillong and the implied presence of England, together with the vast and terrible city of Calcutta, which I shall come to in a moment—these, with one exception, complete the pattern of influences which inaugurated Chaudhuri's fundamental sensibility and fixed the scale and organisation of his interests. The exception is his parents. The Chaudhuri family was a real family in the Western sense and not, as was common form in Bengal, a joint family. It enjoyed its own forceful identity and not merely the passive existence of a cell in an amorphous clan. Chaudhuri's father and mother asserted their parental authority and responsibility against their relatives so that their children were brought up by them and not by a set of surrogates in some vague, impersonal community *crèche*, a system which eliminates the influence of mother and father by abolishing parental exclusiveness, and one which in Chaudhuri's view Plato would certainly not have recommended so strongly had he seen the results it produced in Bengal. The father was physically robust, conscientious in his work in court and afterwards in business, liberal, intelli-

[1] *The Autobiography of an Unknown Indian*, p. 439

gent, disinterested, concerned to develop the initiative and the independence of his children, and a solicitous nurse of his wife during her bouts of melancholy madness. The mother was ferociously honest and emotionally grasping, at once intensely self-centred and cool and objective towards the children, and deeply afflicted by her mental disease. Chaudhuri shows himself to have the courage, the ethical and intellectual values of his father and the honesty and the impassioned egocentricity of his mother. The life of the family in the places he lived in as a child was the source of everything positive and committed in Chaudhuri's nature. Calcutta, when he came to it as a student and undergraduate, opened to him the possibilities of detachment. The context of his childhood was one into which he fitted naturally and happily, that of the next part of his life one in which he was to feel himself at more and more painful odds with his environment.

> Kishorganj, Banagram, and Kalikutch are interwoven with my being; so is the England of my imagination; they formed and shaped me; but when once torn up from my natural habitat I became liberated from the habitat altogether; my environment and I began to fall apart; and in the end the environment became wholly external, a thing to feel, observe, and measure, and a thing to act and react on, but never to absorb or be absorbed in.[1]

His treatment of Calcutta, where he was to spend thirty years, although *The Autobiography* takes him only to the beginning of his career, is as full, as positively thick with information, as ever. His inquisitive, analytic eye turns upon everything from architecture to social relationships, from the method of garbage disposal to nationalist politics, from his own intellectual history to the current taste in furniture. But the tone is increasingly less cordial, the attitude more antagonistic. Place in his early life focussed the paradisal Indian light; Calcutta was a prism breaking it into its component and colder parts. He was of course a failure in a worldly sense. He was a brilliant undergraduate but he collapsed during his graduate studies, and the academic life which would surely have been his natural habitat was shut off from him. Perhaps it needed a near lifetime of failure and poverty to prepare him for writing this book

[1] *The Autobiography of an Unknown Indian*, pp. 257-8

C

because behind it burn not simply events but a life and character. He shows himself bitterly forging a will capable of resisting an overwhelming environment. The powerful intellect is the servant of the will and the theoretical speculation is the necessary instrument for making the action of the will rational and defensible. Sometimes he suggests—not altogether mischievously—that the troubles of India are caused by an exclusive diet of carbohydrate sprinkled with chilli, or by a belief, as he puts it, in a pantheon of gods as corrupt as the Indian administration. But at the centre of his work is an attempt to account for the destruction of a spirit originally strong by an appalling external world. He fiercely cherishes what most people would find intolerable, the identity of the alien, but that again he makes coherent—at least for himself—by a theory which involves making half the population of India foreigners in their own country.

If I say that in the end the theories do not count, this is not to dismiss an intellectual framework raised on the basis of great learning and experience; nor is it to reject the force and relevance of Chaudhuri's criticism of Indian society—although I believe that one would really need to be an Indian to be able, and to have the right, to judge this question. But it is to claim for *The Autobiography of an Unknown Indian* a different existence and significance—literary rather than philosophical or sociological. Its achievement rests less on the correspondence of its theory with actuality and much more on an inward life and coherence. It is not the doctrine propounded but the presence evoked which justifies and supports the book. *The Autobiography* depends on a fully realised rendering of the growth of a character of genuine and singular individuality, by turns arrogant, despairing, nervy, complacent, melancholy, but always faithfully Indian and saltily himself. Through the lucid agency of this convincing portrait we see an age-old society, with a powerful disposition towards inertness, in the state of being penetrated by Western concepts of God, nature, personality, nationalism and freedom. The formation of Chaudhuri's character is the means by which we are enabled to observe the transformation of Bengal society, and to watch the fundamental categories of thought and the modes of sensibility altering before a silent onslaught more significant and lasting than the public action of governments or any change imposed on the physical scene of India by the work of administrators and engineers.

The development so exhaustively detailed in *The Autobiography of an Unknown Indian* is not just an evolutionary one in which a Western protestant astringency displaces the warm appeal of an Indian past—although it certainly *is* that. It is also a more personal and strenuous achievement which involves, on the one hand, hacking out an area of freedom and manœuvre from a choked jungle of inheritance; and on the other, constructing a fresh identity which would join a questioning Western mind to a temperament laced with Bengali fury. The instruments of demolition and of building, and the elements out of which the new self was to be made, were concepts and principles, usages and styles, which Chaudhuri found, not in the imaginatively cramped local British population, or the restricted Anglo-Indian tradition, but in the immensely more inclusive source of the English language and its literature. It was an undertaking which required on the part of Chaudhuri not only intellectual energy and analytical skill, but also courage, will, stamina and a quite unabashed interest in himself. The psychological composition or structure which results is a triumph of self-education and a model of the formative power of language, of its capacity to disturb and rearrange at the depths of the personality. It is also—like *The Autobiography of an Unknown Indian* itself—a monument to the creative clash of two civilisations.

CHAPTER II

I OLIVE SCHREINER

THE *Story of an African Farm*, published in 1883 when the author was 28, was written by a small, plump, asthmatic South African, an ex-governess of missionary stock. It is the only thing of note Olive Schreiner produced. It seems that it should belong to that ruck of works which though they may affect the reader at one time, usually when he is young, are happily and rapidly discarded. It is structurally a jumble and emotionally a chaos. It is in many ways thoroughly provincial. It is disfigured by some of the most unpleasant qualities of Victorian sentimentality and self-delusion about motives. It is weighed down with explicit argumentation and debate and littered with the material of youthful essays and solemn parables. But while each of these comments is just, the effect the book makes on the reader is not at all what they would lead one to expect. It is a novel which stays with one—not harmoniously and consciously—but embedded in the cells of one's memory. It is the product of a powerful personality, of strongly neurotic tendencies, self-educated and markedly deficient in intellectual discipline, but with a distinctive and ferociously assimilative sensibility. It is the intense, suffering consciousness of the author which gives the book its undoubted unity, penetrating every corner of its universe, and not primarily the African farm (marvellously observed though this is with a child's clear glance) which is the geographical location and the physical image of the cramped, ugly Boer life, nor the story, the events of which compose not so much a plot as a pattern of memories of an individual's painful emotional growth.

The author's essential interests and manner are present from the start. The novel begins with the farmhouse and its sleeping occupants, the house blanched in the moonlight, appearing as a physical object in a mineral landscape. First there is the owner Tant' Sannie, the Boer-woman, who goes to bed in the clothes she has worn all day, rolling heavily in her sleep and dreaming not of her first and

second husbands, the young Boer and the consumptive Englishman, but of the sheep's trotters she had eaten for supper. 'She
dreamed that one stuck fast in her throat, and she rolled her huge
form from side to side, and snorted horribly.' In the room next to
her slept the two children, the homely, freckled Em and the
exquisite Lyndall. In one of the outbuildings jutting from the
waggon house the German overseer lay sleeping soundly, a
Messiah-like figure, his great arms folded and his bushy black
beard rising and falling on his breast. In the box under the window
his small son lay awake listening to his father's great silver hunting
watch and seeing in terror 'a long stream of people, a great dark
multitude, that moved in one direction; then they came to the dark
edge of the world, and went over'. These three classes of people—
with one exception—make up the world of the novel. Tant' Sannie
embodies the uncouth, grossly superstitious, densely physical folk-
life of the Boer farmer. The two children express two elements of
the author's nature, Em the homely and settled and Lyndall the
intelligent and exotic. They act out in the novel a tension which
clearly exists within the author herself. Together they represent
that feminine nature which is misunderstood and persecuted by the
crudity of Boer society, just as its aspirations are betrayed by the
world outside. It draws its strength from the other kind of nature
present in the house, that of the German overseer and his son. In
them we see the gentlest and most innocent goodness, simple and
untroubled in the old man, more conscious and agonised in the son.
It is German rather than Dutch, and shines with a quietist and
mystical quality. It is something that Olive Schreiner is deeply
appreciative of and extraordinarily successful in re-creating, although she finds the religious element in it finally unacceptable.

The other characters—the exception I spoke of just now—who
make up the novel's population (the Kaffirs are hardly individualised at all; only the German overseer seems to have a truly human
relationship with them) are those who come from outside. They
bring to the farm opportunity and a loosening of its tight bonds but
they also carry with them danger and evil. For while the life of the
farm is shut in and primitive, it also encloses a standard of human
goodness, tranquil in the German overseer Otto in the first part of

the novel, more tortured and tentative but just as strong in his son Waldo in the second part, superior to anything the intruders from the outside can offer. They are shown as comic-sinister, Bonaparte Blenkins; silly-snobbish-unstable, the Englishman Gregory Rose, who transfers his affection from his fiancée Em to Lyndall; Byronic-mysterious—the stranger whose mistress Lyndall becomes. The situation therefore is more complex and interesting than a simple opposition between the prison farm and the free world. The sensitive Lyndall, in whom consciousness is most developed, cries for the moral and intellectual freedom she supposes to exist outside the farm. In fact she is disappointed by the education she receives in the world beyond and finally betrayed by the values upheld there. It is the mild, ungifted Em, a Martha-like figure, and not the brilliant Lyndall, who attains a measure of modest serenity and only Waldo, another citizen of the inner world of the farm, 'an uncouth creature with small learning and no prospect in the future but that of making endless tables and stone walls', who finally finds 'life . . . a rare and very rich thing'.

The rareness and richness of life are certainly things substantiated by the novel, although frequently only in ways which are incidental to the author's explicit purpose. High-minded feminist preaching and shrill agnostic propaganda too often muddle and muddy the real strength of the book. Olive Schreiner's gifts are for the evocation of the concrete, both of natural substance and human feeling. She has great skill, used with a fine functional discretion, for conveying the nature of the country, a strange blend of bleakness and warmth. Amid the stoniness, the heat and the brilliance of the light, the farmhouse, the outbuildings, the walls, the carts, the furniture, the food, the personal belongings are all presented with a countryman's respect for things and a sense of the value and interest of the palpable. The novel is heavy with the weight of physical stuff which gives the necessary solid basis for its more aspiring side. And heavy not only with physical material but with the kind of character close to the nature of matter itself. Two fully successful characterisations of this sort are the Boer Widow Tant' Sannie and Bonaparte Blenkins, the visiting confidence man. Tant' Sannie is a gross, stupid, greedy, wallowing creature, immersed in flesh and superstition. The other, Bonaparte Blenkins, like Tant' Sannie has a powerful physical presence, peculiarly ugly where hers was hugely abundant. Each has immense vitality and each is observed by the writer with a harsh sardonic accuracy. They belong to the tradition of humours as revivified by Dickens and they bring to the first half of the novel, where they are most prominent, the supple strength and humanity of this tradition.

Olive Schreiner's habit, when writing in this mode, is to slide in a terse illustrative physical detail but to allow the exposition of character to proceed through the varying run and turn of the language. Personalities and attitudes become apparent through the mobile expressiveness of speech. Here is a passage from early on in the novel, thick with the material quality she is so good at evoking, which brings together Tant' Sannie and Bonaparte Blenkins and irresistibly suggests the clash of cunning and stupid temperaments, and incidentally the contrast of 'cold' and 'hot' humours!

On the door-step stood the Boer-woman, a hand on each hip, her face red and fiery, her head nodding fiercely. At her feet sat the yellow Hottentot maid, her satellite, and around stood the black Kaffir maids, with blankets twisted round their half-naked figures. Two, who stamped mealies in a wooden block, held the great stampers in their hands, and stared stupidly at the object of attraction. . . .

'I'm not a child,' cried the Boer-woman, in low Cape Dutch, 'and I wasn't born yesterday. No, by the Lord, no! You can't take *me* in! My mother didn't wean me on Monday. One wink of my eye and I see the whole thing. I'll have no tramps sleeping on my farm,' cried Tant' Sannie blowing. 'No, by the Devil, no! not though he had sixty-times-six red noses.'

There the German overseer mildly interposed that the man was not a tramp, but a highly respectable individual, whose horse had died by an accident three days before.

'Don't tell me,' cried the Boer-woman; 'the man isn't born that can take *me* in. If he'd had money, wouldn't he have brought a horse? Men who walk are thieves, liars, murderers, Rome's priests, seducers! I see the Devil in his nose!' cried Tant' Sannie, shaking her fist at him; 'and to come walking into the house of this Boer's child, and shaking hands as though he came on horseback! Oh, no, no!'

The stranger took off his hat, a tall battered chimney-pot, and disclosed a bald head, at the back of which was a little fringe of curled white hair; and he bowed to Tant' Sannie.

'What does she remark, my friend?' he inquired, turning his cross-wise looking eyes on the old German.

The German rubbed his old hands, and hesitated.

'Ah—well—ah—the—Dutch—you know—do not like people who walk—in this country—ah!'

'My dear friend,' said the stranger, laying his hand on the German's arm, 'I should have bought myself another horse, but crossing, five days ago, a full river, I lost my purse—a purse with five hundred pounds in it. I spent five days on the bank of the river trying to find it—couldn't. Paid a Kaffir nine pounds to go in and look for it at the risk of his life—couldn't find it.'

The German would have translated this information, but the Boer-woman gave no ear.

'No, no; he goes to-night. See how he looks at me—a poor un-protected female! If he wrongs me, who is to do me right?' cried Tant' Sannie.

'I think,' said the German in an undertone, 'if you didn't look at her quite so much it might be advisable. She—ah—she—might—imagine that you liked her too well,—in fact—ah—'

'Certainly, my dear friend, certainly,' said the stranger, 'I shall not look at her.' . . .

Upon this the new-comer fixed his eyes pensively on the stamp-block, folding his hands on the head of his cane. His boots were broken, but he still had the cane of a gentleman. . . .

'You might not be a Scotchman or anything of that kind, might you?' suggested the German. 'It is the English that she hates.'

'My dear friend,' said the stranger, 'I am Irish every inch of me—father Irish, mother Irish. I've not a drop of English blood in my veins.'

'And you might not be married, might you?' persisted the German. 'If you had a wife and children, now? Dutch people do not like those who are not married.'

'Ah,' said the stranger, looking tenderly at the block, 'I have a dear wife and three sweet little children—two lovely girls and a noble boy.'

This is a scene in which the comedy contains a note of chastise-ment and moral severity—comedy, with an edge as well as a laugh. It is by no means the best of the several comic scenes in which these two figure. Bonaparte Blenkins's rôle as 'predikant' and his sermon on the text, 'All liars shall have their part in the lake which burneth with fire and brimstone, which is the second death', are nearly as good as the performance of the confidence men at the wake in

Huckleberry Finn. It is the richness of Olive Schreiner's comic sense which we see in the passage I have quoted above. There are, however, certain notes in each character omitted in this picture of their first encounter: on the one hand, the slightly more appealing folk-sagacity in Tant' Sannie which comes out in her reflections on her inexpressively glum and unenthusiastic new young husband, 'nineteen, weak eyes, white hair, little round nose' (' "It's a strange thing," she said, "but you can't love a man till you've had a baby by him" '); and on the other there is missing in the sketch of Blenkins the strain of cold cruelty we see in his relationship with the children and particularly with the boy Waldo. This is how he welcomes Waldo back from a journey as the boy rushes in carrying gifts for each member of the family.

> 'Good-morning, my dear boy. Where are you running to so fast with your rosy cheeks?'
> The boy looked up at him, glad even to see Bonaparte.
> 'I am going to the cabin,' he said, out of breath.
> 'You won't find them in just now—not your good old father,' said Bonaparte.
> 'Where is he?' asked the lad.
> 'There beyond the camps,' said Bonaparte, waving his hand oratorically towards the stone-walled ostrich-camps.
> 'What is he doing there?' asked the boy.
> Bonaparte patted him on the cheek kindly.
> 'We could not keep him any more, it was too hot. We've buried him, my boy,' said Bonaparte, touching with his finger the boy's cheek. 'We couldn't keep him any more. . . .'

Bonaparte Blenkins and Tant' Sannie are, then, strikingly individual and thoroughly realised in their own right. They also contribute to the design of the novel, filling out and sharpening the pattern of relationships among the half-dozen principal characters of the book. Their thick fleshy quality sets off the intensely intellectual ardour of Lyndall, while the sottishness of Tant' Sannie and the malevolence of Blenkins are balanced by the New Testament sweetness of the old German and the more troubled spirituality of his son. There is also concentrated in them—and with peculiar force in this peasant and almost biblical household—the authority of the adult world which the growing children, even the commonplace, compliant Em, find constantly uncomprehending and indifferent, and on key occasions menacing.

It is in her treatment of Em, Lyndall and Waldo as children that we see most clearly Olive Schreiner's characteristic talents; it is in her treatment of them as adults that we see her deficiencies. I have referred to her gift for establishing solidly the physical presence of the South African countryside. She also places the children in a convincing social context with the deftest assurance. The life of the farm, harsh and narrow but also full, is conveyed with the raciest gusto, its disciplined dreariness pointed up by the rare, glittering festival, like the brilliantly painted Boer wedding. She shows the endless interest and excitement implicit in the commonest things for children growing up in these conditions. The children's behaviour and the adults' reactions to it, the assumptions and expectations of both—these together project a whole manner of living, thin certainly, repellent in many ways, but undeniably positive and confident and backed with all the force of Dutch Calvinism. Each of the children is nicely discriminated from the others, although the Martha-Mary contrast between Em and Lyndall is unduly neat.

Olive Schreiner has in addition a deep intuition of the organic unfolding of the child's nature and she perfectly grasps the transition from the young child's moments of disconnected, startling clarity of perception, standing out from a shadowy background of forgetfulness, to a state in which images and the subtler stabilities of words become continuous and connected. She understands the serious function of play and the significance of a child's questioning as a means by which he tests out, and then explains to himself, the teasing and often bruising complications of reality outside himself. She has a quick feeling for children's suffering, both for its piercing intensity and the healthy way in which it is rapidly thrown into discard. Not that its apparent transience leaves it without influence. 'The troubles of the young are soon over; they leave no external mark. If you wound the tree in its youth the bark will quickly cover the gash; but when the tree is very old, peeling the bark off, and looking carefully, you will see the scar there still. All that is buried is not dead.' She has, too, a delicate perception of the strange metaphysical promptings which in the most familiar surroundings come with complete naturalness to children.

It is through her construction of Waldo's character that Olive Schreiner elucidates the spiritual gropings of the young child. Waldo is a boy tortured by a desire for God which is contradicted by the emptiness he feels in his own nature as well as by the loveless horror of human life surrounding him, both as a child on the African farm and as an adult working in the world outside. In Em the author stresses the passive, imitative element in the psychology of the young, the desire to fit in without friction, and even without notice. But it is Lyndall who is the main focus of consciousness in the novel and Lyndall's, I am sure, the voice which speaks closest to the author's own. Olive Schreiner feels in an acute way the condition of these children which is never to be nourished by an individual and personal affection. When they have anything at all, it is not much more than a gruel of generalised goodwill; more frequently they have to put up with coldness and even calculated cruelty, as when Bonaparte tramples on the small wooden machine the boy invents or whips him unmercifully. Em's reaction to this emotional environment is a self-deprecating, mousy acceptance. The miseries of reality only correspond to her grey expectations. Waldo floats off into a spiritual ambiance, losing touch more and more completely with other human beings. But it is Lyndall's response which is most finely elaborated. In dealing with her Olive Schreiner shows something of that fine faculty, half analytic intelligence, half identifying empathy, which D. H. Lawrence uses so powerfully in revealing the developing nature of Ursula in *The Rainbow*, a child in very different circumstances, too much rather than too little loved, but one with a similar intelligence and blighted capacity for love.

Character in the child, as Coleridge explained and Olive Schreiner so finely understood, is generated by a tension between the child's concern to protect its frail but real individuality and its other concern to enlarge this individuality by entering imaginatively into many other forms and images of existence. Hence the intelligent child's sensitivity to bossiness, that neurotic species of authority; hence too its passion for otherness and for playing at alien experience. In Lyndall's circumstances the concern to protect became a fierce anxiety, almost an abstract passion, for self-preservation against the encroachment of an unfeeling environment. She developed an extreme, violent force of the will, which imposed itself on the other children and which also obscurely frightened even Tant' Sannie and Bonaparte Blenkins. At the same time she suffered a hardening of feeling, a kind of petrifaction of the self, which made the entrance into other forms of life increasingly difficult, and finally impossible. '. . . there is life, there is warmth,' she wailed, 'why am I alone, so hard, so cold. I am weary of myself! It is eating my soul to its core—self, self, self! Will nothing free me from myself?' Education which she was determined to have meant for her above all the possibility of other kinds of life. As she put it when she grew up, '. . . I like to realise forms of life utterly unlike mine. . . . When my own life feels small, and I am oppressed with it, I like to crush together, and see it in a picture, in an instant, a multitude of disconnected unlike phases of human life. . . .' But the force of self-will enclosed her and shut her off from what she most required. 'I will do nothing good for myself, nothing for the world, till someone wakes me. I am asleep, swathed, shut up in self; till I have been delivered, I will deliver no-one.'

Olive Schreiner is a writer in whom the artist is balanced against the egotist. She is as successful as she is with Lyndall, Em and Waldo as children at least partly because childhood is a state in which remoteness and difference make for a measure of detachment even on the part of a novelist as intrusive as she is. The children show themselves to have what Henry James called 'a truth of resistance' capable of standing up to her strongly absorptive faculty. I hope I will not be read as seeming to imply that Lyndall, Em and Waldo are real children distinct from the artist whose creation they are. Obviously not: but in work of art—and *The Story of an African Farm* is a genuine work of art for all its flaws—the intentions of the writer are stayed from overwhelming the material by what one can only describe as its independent, relatively 'objective' life. When the children are adults, which they are fairly summarily presented as in the second part of the novel, they are much more susceptible to the personal domination of the author. Their separate life thins out to become a more attenuated symbolic existence. They are less themselves and proportionately more projections of the author and her time.

As Lyndall, Em and Waldo, grown up, are emptied of intrinsic significance, they tend increasingly to perform a representative function. Waldo, who keeps more of his original vitality than the others, expresses a standard of unqualified, persecuted goodness, based, it appears from her husband's devout memoir of her,[1] on Olive Schreiner's admired father; Em is the simple, domesticated victim-woman, passively putting up with the conditions the braver Lyndall rejects; Lyndall is the intelligent, agnostic, free woman who campaigns against the domination of men, the superstitious tyranny of a debased Calvinism and the philistine ugliness of South African rural life. What Lyndall stands for (one cannot help thinking of it like this) is in many ways admirable, certainly infinitely preferable to what she is fighting against, and it undoubtedly called for reserves of courage and independence even to express such views in Victorian South Africa, which was obviously in these matters even more provincial than Britain. But the communication is so explicit, self-satisfied and sermonising, so uncontrollably tumbled out without regard for structure or the concreteness of the fable, that the merit of the idea is lost in the stridency of the advocate.

The novel often exhibits those defects of taste and that feebleness of artistic control which were common among much greater Victorian writers. Olive Schreiner has a horribly incoherent sense of structure and the narrative line is clumsily entangled in all kinds of theoretical irrelevancies. The two main parts of the book, for example, are separated by a number of set pieces on human growth which, while they are frequently acute in detail, simply do not belong. She shows an unabashed and almost sensuously caressing sentimentality towards the Franciscan Waldo. She has the peculiar Victorian habit, when she is dealing with love, of diminishing the physical size of the woman and faintly etherealising the body, so that Lyndall tends to be both elfin and child-like. The result is to inject a morbidly incestuous note into the relationship. She swerves wildly from too much theory into the sultriest melodrama. Lyndall, deserted by the lover with whom she has been living, is nursed for

[1] S. C. Cronwright-Schreiner, *The Life of Olive Schreiner*, London, 1924

a considerable time through her last illness by Gregory Rose, Em's ex-fiancé, closely shaved and powdered and disguised as a woman! (Lyndall's lingering death has for all Olive Schreiner's progressive highmindedness something about it of the doom appropriate to the fallen woman.) Gregory Rose himself, a silly and snobbish Englishman, as unreal as Bertie Wooster but decidedly more unpleasant, is less of a cartoon than two other men in the novel, who bear many of the features of the men in women's magazine fiction. There is the mysterious, cosmopolitan stranger who carries in his bag 'a bright French novel and an old brown volume' (the bright French novel is meant to have irresistible implications of a naïvely provincial sort), who unfolds, like some immensely long-winded and humourless La Fontaine, an interminable parable to comfort Waldo. Or there is the sophisticated, 'wicked' aristocrat who makes Lyndall his mistress when for reasons of principle she refuses to become his wife. He has a tall, slight figure, delicately pencilled drooping eyelids, a heavy flaxen moustache and he fills his glass from a silver flask. Here is how he and Lyndall are seen at the decisive meeting at which Lyndall, who has in the meantime taken over Gregory Rose from the stricken Em, agrees to become his mistress.

> From under their half-closed lids the keen eyes looked down at her. Her shoulders were bent; for a moment the little figure had forgotten its queenly bearing, and drooped wearily; the wide dark eyes watched the fire very softly.
> It certainly was not in her power to resist him, nor any strength in her that made his own at that moment grow soft as he looked at her.
> He touched one little hand that rested on her knee.
> 'Poor little thing!' he said; 'you are only a child.'

And yet I cannot feel the account I have given, fair as I believe it to be, explains the intense, lasting effect this strange novel makes on the reader. Certainly the incoherence of structure and the defects of taste and of overmanipulation are there. Just as certainly they fail to muffle the brooding influence the book exercises. Nor do they nullify the considerable reflective intelligence and the remarkable evocative power shown in it, gifts admirably served in the better parts of the book by Olive Schreiner's clear lithe prose. I have pointed out the imperfections of design and the marked intrusiveness of the author's personality, and I might have made a good deal more of both. But while these are inescapable and limiting facts, bound to qualify one's response, they are also evidence of something else one is aware of going on in the depths of the book. I put it neutrally like this because it is by no means wholly under the author's conscious control. It appears cloudily and jerkily under the agitation of the surface and obscurely informing the structure of character and scene, only assuming a precise and realised form at those times when the author is less feverishly under the influence of one or other of several obsessions. When I try to define for myself what it is I am aware of, what other theme is feeling its way into the life of the novel, I find myself associating it with a flow of feeling which is painful and checked and seldom fully articulated. There are two conditions modifying Olive Schreiner's basic experience and her insight into it. One makes it possible for her, the other important for us. One is a knotty, difficult honesty, the positive side of her personal domination of the material. She is wholly faithful to herself, even when that self is pushed and distorted by private neuroticism or Victorian prejudice or crankiness or blindness. The second condition is the belief under which she always works of the unity of human experience.

What is microscopic in one is largely developed in another; what is a rudimentary in one man is an active organ in another; but all things are in all men and one soul is the model of all. We shall find nothing new in human nature after we have once carefully dissected and analysed the one being we ever shall truly know—ourself.

What gives the book its life—and in a quirky, clumsy way, it *is* alive—is a bitter, forlorn experience of the necessity of human participation, and a desperate sense of its difficulties and its final impossibility. The development of consciousness and the refinement of natural gifts of intelligence and sensibility have placed Lyndall, who most exactly dramatises the personal engagement and predicament of the author, beyond the point at which she could accept the immemorial, unconscious rhythms of the agricultural community and the Boer farm (just as in her personal life these things had raised Olive Schreiner beyond the level at which she was able to accept the simple religious fervour of her father). The rejection of the beliefs of the family and the community forces on Lyndall a strained, angry individuality and the use of her will as a weapon both of defence and attack. Consciousness, which breaches for her the rationality of the communal pattern, works to prevent her entrance into a life of mutuality and hardens her in her solitary fate. 'Perhaps she thought of the narrowness of the limits within which a human soul may speak and be understood by its nearest mental kind, of how soon it reaches that solitary land of the individual experience, in which no fellow-footfall is ever heard.'

Explicit here, the submerged, pervasive presence of this theme in the rest of the book brings the other struggles and tensions into a common system: both the general ones like that of dependent woman against a male world, child against an adult world, agnostic against a religious world (all, be it noted, situations in which the solitary one is opposed to a compacted mass); and again, the particular conflicts in the lives of Em and Waldo. In Em a resolution is possible both because she exists at a lower level of consciousness and because she is willing to put up with a humdrum substitute for a genuine personal life. For Waldo there is no resolution. His passionate attachment to a divine reality, like Lyndall's to the value of consciousness, cannot be reconciled with the life of human mutuality he despairingly desires. The voice of God is also silent in the solitary land of individual experience. The effect of *The Story of an African Farm* comes from the co-existence of an authentic communal life, in all its colour and vivacity, together with a concentrated sense of the terrible remoteness of the individual—from their co-existence and their mutual, clawing destructiveness.

II   CHINUA ACHEBE

To turn from *The Story of an African Farm* to the novels of the Nigerian writer, Chinua Achebe, the author of *Things Fall Apart* (1958), *No Longer at Ease* (1960) and *Arrow of God* (1964), is to move from a world of Victorian and feminine anxiety to one which is masculine, coherent and in a curious way classical. The sense of the classic which the novels provoke comes, I think, from two things. One is that the Ibo life pictured in them is not so much adapted to, since that implies a kind of servitude, as in perfect balance with, the natural world. The rhythms of both run together without jarring or contradiction. The second is that the fiction creates a society in which life is rounded and intricate and sensitively in correspondence with a range of human impulse. It admits both the aristocratic and the democratic principles. It is a life lived by a dignified clan of equals who meet together in an Athenian way (with one grievous exception) to make critical communal decisions. At the same time it allows for an exceptional man and for an organisation based on achievement. Age is respected but achievement revered. It is a universe which embodies a traditional and living morality and an order of reference by which the actual is comprehended and judged. Its religion is both mysterious and homely, answering to the instinct for the numinous and the need for practical good sense. Its vitality calls upon the sincerity of its followers and they support it with the conviction of living action. It produces impressive and beautiful artefacts in music, dance, decoration and, above all, in conversation. 'Proverbs are the palm oil with which the words are eaten.' The limitation of its products, however, is their transience. They all exist in an essentially fleeting medium. They do not succeed in recording themselves for the future, and while they may gain in spontaneity and vitality they fail in permanence. The tragedy of the civilisation, indeed, which as it appears in these novels is remarkably inclusive and humane, is that it is unable to achieve a right or appropriate relationship with time.

So that a satisfying concreteness of existence is accompanied by a deficiency in power of abstraction. The society of the nineteenth-century Ibo is one which exists in a kind of trance, perfect in the present. It could retain only bits of the immediate past, those which could be encompassed by an individual memory or those which were embodied in the modes of social intercourse. It had not within it the resources for assuming new intellectual postures, so that when the context which supported it began to be altered by the intrusion of missionaries and the imposition of British law and

D

administration, the nucleus itself was modified and quickly enfeebled. Whether the vision of Ibo society given in the novels is
justified by history is almost irrelevant. What we have in this
work is a conception of civilisation which has a root in reality. It
includes a world and a group with a coherent anatomy of standards
and beliefs and a solid convincing body. This is a universe perfectly
suited to a novelist. It is complete but small. It incorporates a standard and it expresses itself in a characteristic mode of living, which
is yet sufficiently flexible to allow both for the outstanding success
like Okonkwo in *Things Fall Apart* or a wretched failure like his
father Okoye in the same book. Everything in this universe is saturated with significance: not only every act and motive, which can
be related to the inherited system of reference, but also every person
and thing, which have a meaning because what belongs to the
spiritual and moral order of existence flows in and out of the physical. It is not interrupted either by any enclosing sense of private,
separate individuality or by any impermeable material surface.

I said earlier that the tragedy of Ibo society as displayed by
Chinua Achebe lay in its failure to achieve a workable relationship
with time. The personal tragedy of Okonkwo, the protagonist of
Things Fall Apart, has its own intimate temporal dimension. It is
initiated by his total rejection of the immediate past, dramatised
for him in the person of his father (after all parents *are* the past for
their children) in favour of standards established in a more remote,
more heroic time. His motive is negative, his purpose positive. His
father Okoye was cowardly, improvident, idle, womanish, frivolous, a man without title or respect; and Okonkwo, driven by a
deep fear of a similar fate is, consequently, industrious, severe, rich,
brave, honourable, a modern instance of ancient virtues. He is just
about to take the third highest title in the tribe (this taking of titles
in an ascending order of dignity by exposing oneself to increasingly
difficult tests is another example of that classical blend of the aristocratic and the democratic so characteristic of the world of these
novels). Okonkwo's error, the Aristotelian flaw, for this is the kind
of hero he is, is to suppose that the present is wholly susceptible to
his governing, moulding will. He treats the present and life itself as
something wholly subject to arrangement, or as a disposition of

forces which is completely rational. In this he is beginning to desert the central understanding of his tribe. The tribe, in its collective wisdom, allowed in its system of beliefs for the intrusion into the world of wild, irrational freaks of chance. Anyone, for example, could be without reason suddenly named as an outcast and scape-goat, condemned utterly for nothing at all. Okonkwo's reading of life depended on the present's never throwing up the unforeseeable, irrational disaster, whereas the tribe understood that even at its most obedient the present was capable of sliding away from human control. Okonkwo who has shown himself ruthlessly determined to maintain every observance of tribal law because he understood the idealism it expressed—he even hunts down and kills a boy he loves as a son when he is enjoined to do so by the priests—suddenly and absurdly causes an accidental death and is accordingly exiled for seven years by the law, the spirit of which he wishes most passionately to preserve. He is trapped by the cunning of his most treacherous opponent, the present.

Okonkwo completes his exile in his mother's village, and returns home, subdued but unchangingly concentrated on making himself a great man according to the historical criteria of the tribe, and still failing to realise the slippery nature of time and the present. He is faced by a situation which shows that ironic parallelism we are familiar with from classical drama. Okonkwo's son, Nwoye, now rejects his father, and rejects him because of qualities which the young man discerns obscurely as belonging to the future. The sensitive son, always a disappointment to Okonkwo, is converted to Christianity, which it is clear will, with its attendant British administrative structure, and from the best of motives, ruin the collective integrity of the clan. The whole arrangement has a formal classical character, but it is a formality which is implicit in the material, the formality of a set of crystals, or the elegant structure of a leaf, which is determined from within. Nothing could more natu-rally be the issue of the combination of temperament and event, of individual purpose and historical process, than the converted son's disavowal of all his father stands for. Okonkwo grew up under a stable system, within which the individual person could certainly exert himself for his own good and in doing so might well clash with others; but the supporting system survived and was accepted both by the successful and the defeated. Now Okonkwo finds the conditions of life itself, the context within which decisions are made, beginning to crumble under the influence of what cannot be opposed since it has both the inevitability of fate and the unopposable impalpability of what is to come.

At the climax of the novel, time present and time past do not come together in any point of intersection but define themselves clearly as lines of opposition. One of the District Commissioner's Court Messengers, who have already intolerably affronted the dignity of the leaders of the tribe and now come to forbid their assembly, is killed by Okonkwo. The mass of the people have already insensibly accommodated themselves to an alien domination and they break up into tumult instead of action. Okonkwo, finally realising that the past has been defeated, withdraws, and splendid in his finest warrior's raiment, with a more than Roman dignity, puts himself to death, achieving with this final stroke the heroic status which the treacheries of time had forbidden him even during the most successful phases of his life.

Things Fall Apart is a short novel, not much longer than a *novella,* but it gives a remarkably massive impression. This, I think, is because of the fine balance drawn between a whole society and an impressive individual, and because of the way in which the fundamental predicament of the society is lived through in his life. It also has to do with the equilibrium established by the novelist between the formality of the structure and the accuracy with which he reproduces individual motive and feeling. And it has to do, too, with the author's manner which is plain, calm, confident and vigorous. Achebe's attitudes are quite uncoated with sentimentality, and uncontorted by anything neurotic or morbid or vengeful. His manner, like the life he deals with, has an air of wholesome sanity and a natural human centrality. His narrative method has the character of speech, the deceptively simple and vividly flexible speech of the formally uneducated who live still by some powerful traditional vision. Its plainness and simplicity allow at relevant moments the touch of muted and unassertive poetry, as when he pictures a flicker of thought in a boy's mind:

Gradually the rains became lighter and less frequent, and earth and sky once again became separate. The rain fell in thin, slanting showers through sunshine and quiet breeze. Children no longer stayed indoors but ran about singing:

> '*The rain is falling, the sun is shining,*
> *Alone Nnadi is cooking and eating.*'

Nwoye always wondered who Nnadi was and why he should live all by himself, cooking and eating. In the end he decided that Nnadi must live in that land of Ikemefuna's favourite story where the ant holds his court in splendour and the sands dance for ever.

Or again, when he presents the unsuccessful, musical grandfather, Unoka:

... Unoka was never happy when it came to wars. He was in fact a coward and could not bear the sight of blood. And so he changed the subject and talked about music, and his face beamed. He could hear in his mind's ear the blood-stirring and intricate rhythms of the *ekwe* and the *udu* and the *ogene*, and he could hear his own flute weaving in and out of them, decorating them with a colourful and plaintive tune. The total effect was gay and brisk, but if one picked out the flute as it went up and down and then broke up into short snatches, one saw that there was sorrow and grief there.

The effect of *No Longer at Ease,* Achebe's second novel, is quite different from that of *Things Fall Apart.* It has little of the latter's massiveness and tranquility. It is febrile and edgy, and its unsettled, uneasy atmosphere suits the story of a bright young man (eight distinctions in the Cambridge School Certificate) newly returned with an Honours Degree in English from the University of London to take a senior administrative post—a 'European' post—in the Nigerian Civil Service. The young man, Obi Okonkwo, is the grandson of the Okonkwo in the first novel, a fact which keeps the contrast of character and context steadily operating for the informed reader. Obi is an appealing, limited modern creature, a blend of self-confidence and self-ignorance, of sophistication in taste and moral simplicity, whose problems belong to a different category from those of his grandfather. They are those appropriate to a seedy capital, a money economy, an education wrenching him from one set of values to another, a society which still has its root, though a weakening one, in the villages, and which is now withering into something deracinated and indifferently suburban.

But while *No Longer at Ease* contains few of the positive, poetic murmurations which enriched *Things Fall Apart,* the novel is still a sharp and honest account of the dilemma of an educated, high-minded young man suddenly put into a respected, well-paid position in the impersonal capital where the tribe still tries spasmodically to assert its claim for fellowship, and in which venality itself is a kind of submerged tribal bond. Obi's scholarship to England has been paid from the funds of the Umofia Progressive Union, whose members tax themselves mercilessly to find the necessary £800 in the hope of getting one of their own people into a position of influence, preferably a legal one (though once in England Obi, showing an inadmissible independence, had read English, a course which now qualified him to become secretary to the government's Overseas Scholarship Committee). Obi is a rich man by the standards of his benefactors, with fine clothes, a grand flat, a car and a huge salary, and the Union expect him to repay the loan out of his own huge resources. But he has also to support an ageing father and a dying mother as well as a young brother in grammar school; he has to find money to procure an abortion for his fiancée; and all the time keep up his expensive way of living. But Obi's financial crisis is only part of his predicament. He is seriously in love with Clara who is also one of the magic class of 'been to 's', i.e. those who had been educated abroad. She is an *Osu*, one of those whose ancestors had been dedicated to a god and who were forever afterwards condemned as outcasts. Each side of the equation trembles at the sacrilege of the proposed marriage, the horror of which is acknowledged even by Christopher, Obi's knowing friend from the London School of Economics. His parents, even his devoted Christian father, are appalled. It is a tribute to Achebe's wholeness of grasp of the Ibo world and of the force with which his imagination penetrates its every corner that the reader too genuinely shares in this horror.

In two-thirds of Obi's predicament he is an angry victim, mutinously subject to external influences: in the one, affected by a monstrous piece of the detritus of the primitive past; in the other, by the imposition of a money economy on a people untrained to manage it. The remaining third affects him more subtly, although, paradoxically, it is related to his professional rather than his personal life. He had returned from Britain convinced that the old gang of Civil Servants who had worked their way up and were almost religiously committed to bribery should be replaced by a new class of university-trained public officials who would show themselves free of the despotism of the past and who, strong in their inward resources, would be able to resist the corrupting persuasions of their society. Obi acted in this belief at the beginning of his career, refusing the bribes of money offered by Mr Mark to help his sister get on to the scholarship list, and the bribes in kind offered by the good-looking Miss Mark herself. Obi's error was to suppose that he could continue to live in a kind of abstract, untethered way in a society in which bribery offered the only recognised way of getting to the top and in which the idea of corruption was supported by the claims of tribal relationships, so that private advantage was consolidated by an admirable warmth of acknowledged obligation. This is the context in which poor Obi's ruin, which is not very dramatic or very tremendous, is prepared for. He goes down, still charmingly young and appealing, keeping his conscience straight by insisting that the candidates he favoured had at least the minimum qualifications. He is not perhaps quite so much the victim as the moral by-product of an incoherent system: or of one which has not succeeded in keeping its connection with the past straight or its route forward open.

Things Fall Apart and *No Longer at Ease* show the characteristic pattern of Achebe's novels: a vivid central figure—in *No Longer at Ease* an appealing rather than a strong one; a ground which is cleanly defined and densely occupied; a background from which we hear the confused mutter of social and historic complexities; and a narrative method which is syntactically plain and direct but which also engages the muscular poetry of the commonplace, a common sense and concreteness of feeling generated by traditional experience and crackling in the multitudinous proverbs with which both speech and exposition are strewn. In *Arrow of God* Achebe returns to an earlier period, to the time when the British were pressing the comforting (to them) device of indirect rule; he turns back, too, from the capital to a rural scene, in which six villages constitute a kingdom and the priesthood of Ezeulu, the chief priest of Ulu, the supreme god of the Umuaro people, is comparable to the Papacy. At the same time the key character is now the powerful and richly orchestrated Ezeulu, an altogether more impressive and enigmatic figure than the puppyishly charming Obi. Where Obi was the jelly-like nucleus of his novel, and is sensitive and stricken, Ezeulu has a stony force of endurance and a positive will, as well as greater skill in manipulating people and events. Obi was the victim and recipient of influence but Ezeulu, while he is supple and responsive to what happens, is a forceful director, a man who arranges—or since he is a traditionalist—re-arranges the patterns of life.

When the novel opens we see Ezeulu, an ageing but vital man, solidly seated among his family, friends and clan, intimately a part of and yet above the traditional, almost biblical, life of the people, the feel and texture of which is conveyed with palpable authenticity. Ezeulu's life moves easily between familiar homely things and the mysteries of his priestly vocation. At one moment he is shouting to two quarrelling wives to be quiet as they prepare bitter-leaf tea; at the next he is engaged in an impressively solemn rite in honour of the god, Ulu. Being at home simultaneously with the sacred and the profane in the way Ezeulu is, that is in a conscious, sophistic-ated way, argues for a certain inclusiveness and scope of personality, and Achebe is remarkably successful in the unforced manner in which he evokes the intelligence, or rather the intellect and maturity of a remote African priest. Ezeulu's grasp of manifold types of experience marks his priestly life too. He is both the posses-sor of a religious authority, although by no means an unquestioned one (there are protestants among the people), and also possessed by the mysteries of his religion, a religion which itself stretches up from the house and farm to what is numinous and unspeakable. The energy of Ezeulu's nature, and the force it exerts on the reader, come from the tension between the religious authority which he exercises and the spiritual power which he represents. Ezeulu is deeply assured of the reality and validity of this power, but it requires analysis and questioning on his part to be sure of its application in any given set of circumstances, just as it needs undoubted political skill to bring the god's intentions into existence. He has simultaneously to open himself to become the transparent medium of the god's will while employing all his managerial capacity in dealing with the men whom it is to affect. This is the permanent dilemma of spiritual authority and the character created by Achebe beautifully satisfies the artist's appetite for the illustrational, as Henry James called it, in making him the natural vehicle of a fundamental human complexity.

The events which constitute the novel (one thinks of it in this way rather than as something plotted and calculated, the themes being so wholly submerged in the material) slide into one another with that continuity, original but unsurprising, which suggests not so much cause and effect as living and rhythmic process. These events have to do with three spheres of Ezeulu's existence: with his private family life, with his political struggles, and with his function as religious leader and repository of the spirit. In the first we see him presiding over a numerous and complicated family or clan, a man of insistent will, gruffly overbearing, irritable about the *minutiae* of belief and decorum, with disguised preferences and secret antipathies for his own children, and constantly enigmatic in his response to their attitude towards him, which is a blend of awe for his mysterious powers, attachment to the father, shoulder-shrugging tolerance for his irascibility and a dim awareness of being used by a political manipulator. Ezeulu is by nature a reticent man but he is also expert in the devious communication practised to some degree in every family. The given wife or child may seldom be expressly told, but he is never left in doubt as to Ezeulu's intention for him. Ezeulu looks upon the family, particularly the boys, as members of his political organisation, counters to be skilfully deployed in his political game. One son, Oduche, is even bidden to join the new Christian religion, partly to please Ezeulu's friend CaptainWinterbottom, the District Officer, but even more to give Ezeulu an eye and an ear among one division of his potential enemies. The children are also intimately affected in their personal prospects by Ezeulu's sacred office, since the priestly succession must go to one of them, but while the eldest may expect or fear it, and while Ezeulu's hidden partiality is for the youngest, Nwafo, who has the gifts for it and who is strongly drawn to the god's ritual, this is one of the things in which all are helpless, waiting for the god to reveal his choice.

The reality and the richness of the family relationship are established with the confidence of complete intimacy and by a method which is largely conversational, where the speech is laced with the tough, disillusioned apothegms of those living directly in touch with natural rhythms and processes. Not that this society, nor its most expressive art, its speech, gives any hint of primitive clumsiness. The sophisticated application of developed standards based on a wide scope of experience is a cultivated art, and this is what one is aware of in the speech, in the relationships of family life and even in the political management of men to which I turn now, as well as in the profounder religious experience I shall deal with next.

In an old—not a primitive—society braced by a set of received assumptions and expectations and formed into an intricate social organisation, anyone like Ezeulu who inherits a responsible office inherits also strong hostility. A recognised system of opposition is part of the transmitted social order. The possessor's power is checked by that of others, his ambitions impeded or thwarted by other elements in the system he exists to sustain. Add to this the suspicion generated by the conflict of temperaments, and one sees how the possession of power is inescapably relative and how the possessor, moving among obstacles set up by the system or by personalities, rules by combining force with accommodation. Ezeulu's power is not exercised in an abstract emptiness, and not directed simply from the top down. He operates quite as much by sidling sideways, taking into account the palpable world and the blocks and barriers of a traditional society, thick with custom and differentiation. Ezeulu has a sure feeling for this necessary proportion and a mastery of the craft of control through a balance of intervention and retreat. Silence and surprise and the unlooked for appearance are the instruments with which he keeps in place (not just down) his enemies in this complex society, the most prominent of whom are professional antagonists like the priests

of other inferior gods, and again the civil leaders jealous about the
expansion of ecclesiastical authority, which Ezeulu, by temperament a Gregory, is vigilant for opportunities to extend. He has,
too, to be alert for the threat of the swelling British civil government and the more intimate menace of the Christian religion, which
unlike the lay authority represented by Captain Winterbottom,
seeks to administer men's minds and beliefs. Ezeulu has the gift, the
dangerous tact of not acting when he is expected to and of turning
back upon others the force of their own expectations. He counsels
his own people against a war they are certain he would be in favour
of. He recommends an accommodation with the British which
astounds them. He deliberately obeys a summons to appear before
a British court although his followers are appalled by the sacrilegi-
ous affront to his dignity. But his greatest stroke—a negative one—
is to refuse in an unprecedented fashion to name the date for the
New Yam Feast, which is something reserved to himself alone, and
without which by immemorial custom the planting cannot begin;
the renegade people are left to face the horror of starvation so that
by simply doing nothing Ezeulu brings home to them their absolute dependence on him. He re-establishes his authority, after a
period when his star has fallen, by a tactic of passivity and omission
which has an immense positive force: the technique of a Machiavelli
with religion.

For all Ezeulu's suppleness in manœuvre and his adroitness in
retrieving failure, Achebe leaves us in no doubt that political and
ecclesiastical management of the obvious kind is subordinate in
Ezeulu's mind to the mysterious demands of his vocation. He has
an analytic bent which loves to play with alternative courses of
action, 'to dissolve his resolution and to form it again'. He often
reflects on the nature of his power, questioning its scope and
validity. Does he possess it, or is he possessed by it? At what point
does the agent become the patient? How is he to define this middle
ground between action and suffering to which so much of his
spiritual activity belongs? This is a riddle he cannot solve, and his
fascination with the enigma makes him strange to his neighbours,
unknowable even by his closest friend Akuebe, whom his talk
renders 'uneasy and afraid like one who encounters a madman

laughing in a solitary place'. Towards the end of his life in moments
of spiritual crisis he seemed to live enclosed in total silence. 'He was
used to loneliness. As Chief Priest he had always walked alone in
front of Umuaro. But without looking back he had always been
able to hear the flute and song which shook the earth because it came
from a multitude of voices and the stamping of countless feet. . . .
But never until now had he known the voices to die away altogether.' The remoteness of this side of his life ('. . . one half of you
is man and the other half spirit', his friend tells him) and his
prophetic, preparatory office has in it something of the dried-up
integrity of John the Baptist, and even his appearance as he sets out
on a journey recalls the striding image of the precursor in the
wilderness.

But neither Ezeulu's powerful self-discipline nor his restless
intelligence helps him to unravel the small knot of self-ignorance
at the centre of his nature and to recognise the source of his personal
tragedy. (He sees very clearly the imminent dissolution of his
people's mode of life under the impact of an alien civilisation.)
That is the product of his very force of character. His strong intellect
and will push him on into an area which should be wholly free of
personality and emptied of everything but the god. The sudden
inexplicable death of his son, as the young man performs in a most
sacred rite, shakes his reason because it takes place just at the time
when Ezeulu had deceived himself into seeing his dispute with his
people as something else. 'It was a fight of the gods. He was no more
than an arrow in the bow of his god.' But Ezeulu's identification
of his will with the god's was to prove presumptuous. He was not
the arrow but the victim.

At any other time Ezeulu would have been more than equal to his
grief. He would have been equal to any grief not compounded with
humiliation. Why, he asked himself again and again, why had Ulu
chosen to deal thus with him, to strike him down and cover him with
mud? What was his offence? Had he not divined the god's will and
obeyed it? When was it ever heard that a child was scalded by a piece
of yam its own mother put in its palm? What man would send his son
with a potsherd to bring fire from a neighbour's hut and then unleash
rain on him? Who ever sent his son up the palm to gather nuts and
then took an axe and felled the tree. But today such a thing had

happened before the eyes of all. What could it point to but the collapse and ruin of all things? Then a god, finding himself powerless might take to his heels and in one final, backward glance at his abandoned worshippers cry:

> If the rat cannot flee fast enough
> Let him make way for the tortoise.

In *Arrow of God*, his most mature novel, Chinua Achebe has produced something which is strong, sure, telling. He has created an African world, the conditions of which are absolutely foreign to us, but he has done so with such intelligence and fullness of sympathy, and with such a lively grasp of what is humanly signifi-cant that we are easy with it and unstrained by it, and at the same time seized of its essential sensibility and values. The vulnerable virtues of the minutely elaborated Ibo society are lucidly displayed in a variety of characters, and most thoroughly in the splendidly realised figure of Ezeulu, who is both an authentic priest and a stubborn, nimble-minded, cross-grained, haughty old man, con-tinually lacerated by his people and by his time, and formidably willing to wound them both in return. Chinua Achebe's is the natural imagination of the novelist which works through particular events and personalities and discriminated shades of being and feeling. It is not surprising, therefore, that the general event is involved in the particular, and that the reader takes without any feeling that he or the structure of the novel is being manipulated, the sense in which the collapse of the whole society is implied in the priest's fall. Towards priest and people, the figure and the ground, Achebe shows—to use his own figure—'the senstivenesss of a snail's horns', joining a fine exploratory skill to an unsentimental, accurate tenderness. This attitude, evidence of a capacity for whole-ness of experience, lifts him from the ruck of novelists in whom analysis proceeds from negative emotions, which are themselves very often the inverted from of sentimentality. Achebe's emotional maturity, his masculine force in narration, his calm objective out-look, his fastidious sense of genuine tradition, the deeply particular-ising, palpable quality of his imagination, make his a talent of a rare and significant sort.

CHAPTER III

V. S. NAIPAUL

V. S. NAIPAUL is the author of six novels, two volumes of short stories and two other books which can be variously described as—what?—travel books or documentary or autobiography or exploration. He has not had to wait long for recognition. His travel books have been described extravagantly as being on the same level as D. H. Lawrence's, his novels as Caribbean masterpieces. After a career stretched over not more than half a dozen years, he received the distinction of a uniform edition, which is more usually a monument to someone dead and gone. He has been awarded a whole clutch of literary prizes, which might well have sunk a less buoyant talent.

Naipaul was born in Trinidad of a Hindu family, educated at Queen's Royal College, Port of Spain, and University College, Oxford, and has for a long time now lived and worked in Britain. At one time this might have been thought an unusual and distinctive background; in fact it now is decidedly a more representative one and Naipaul himself strikes the reader as being in a significant way a combination of a scrupulously private soul and a public and social rôle. He is not simply *a* but *the* writer, all his private nature absorbed in his function as artist. He is not only a natural writer but a natural novelist. Themes for him assume the forms of action and ideas appeal to him only in so far as they satisfy, for him as for Henry James, 'the appetite for the illustrational'. He never, as some other West Indian writers do, gives the impression that he is writing from the will or that he is preaching a party line or some ethical imperative. His vision is his own, unenervated by contemporary social clichés or political routines. He is independent but also relevant. He is engaged with the stresses and strains we recognise as crucial in our experience now. His writing is nervous and present. This, together with the mixture in him of creeds, cultures and continents, with his expatriate career, his being able to practise an art in and of totally dissimilar worlds, all gives him a peculiarly contemporary quality.

I should like to begin, then, in what is rather an unconventional way of dealing with a novelist, by commenting for a moment on one of the books which isn't a novel, *An Area of Darkness*, where we see written out pretty explicitly at least one clue to the nature of Naipaul's sensibility. If that gentle liberal genius E. M. Forster had to give advice to travellers today, it ought to be, I think, 'Only disconnect!' Cut yourself off from your own past. Unbolt your fierce identity. Dismantle your driving national force, and become something altogether quieter and more passive, a faithful recording instrument. Good but impossible advice as *An Area of Darkness* makes only too clear. The relationship between a travel writer and the country he writes about is generally clear enough. Here he is, bold and assured, nationally and personally organised and quite often in arms, and there, before him and at some distance, is the observed, sometimes detested object, the country he is visiting. But the India of *An Area of Darkness* is within Naipaul. His Trinidadian grandfather was from Uttar Pradesh, and though two generations became saturated in West Indian life, the secret premises of family action were in word and image profoundly Indian. So that Naipaul's return to India is as much a research into himself as into another country. He is crawling on sensitive naked feet up through the tunnels of his own self. Or perhaps one could say this book is a detailed investigation of one side of Naipaul's nature by another, the Indian supplying the data, the Western the microscope. Naipaul is a very significant writer indeed and *An Area of Darkness* has the richness and point of any disturbed experience suffered by a writer with so genuine, so pure a talent. Naipaul's grandfather went West, Naipaul came East, and a cold coming he had of it. He endures within himself Indian agonies. The friction of the two sides of his nature produces not warmth but despair. He is aware that in savaging India he is savaging himself. Although this book shows on every page the novelist's double discernment, which is able to fix the subtlest nuance of individuality, and with an equal assurance, an equal skill, to establish it solidly in a social world, it is valuable very much more as a report, inward and tremblingly exact, of the nature of Naipaul than as an undistorted chronicle of India. It is the subject, not the object, which counts here.

Naipaul's revulsion at so many aspects of Indian life, his almost Swiftian horror of dirt, his novelist's fierce rejection of the Indian sense of non-reality, his suspicion, even his fear, of the way in which the brutality of fact in India can slide away into formless diction—all these things quiver on every page. But they never qualify or muffle his astonishing sense of detail. The book is lightened and sharpened by this extreme clarity of vision. Even his disgust with the functionalism of caste, which keeps a man gaoled in his private gaol of duty, doesn't stop him from describing with singular precision four men washing down the steps of an unpalatable Bombay hotel.

> The first pours water from a bucket, the second scratches the tiles with a twig broom, the third uses a rag to slop the dirty water down the steps into another bucket, which is held by the fourth. After they have passed, the steps are as dirty as before; but now above the blackened skirting-tiles the walls are freshly and dirtily splashed. The bathrooms and lavatories are foul; the slimy woodwork has rotted away as a result of this daily drenching; the concrete walls are green and black with slime. You cannot complain that the hotel is dirty. No Indian will agree with you. Four sweepers are in daily attendance, and it is enough in India that the sweepers attend. They are not required to *clean*. That is a subsidiary part of their function, which is to *be* sweepers, degraded beings, to go through the motions of degradation.

Perhaps it is this dissolving of action into being which most appals him. But perhaps there is also something Indian in his fascinated horror with such detail. He is, it seems, rejecting not only India but trying to bleach out part of his own nature. His book is a kind of metaphysical diary of the effort to shine a Western novelist's light into an interior area of darkness. It reconstructs, it doesn't simply record, this experience, and it is deeply disturbing.

In his other travel book *The Middle Passage*, an acute but less personally engaged study of a return to a post-colonial West Indies, Naipaul uses as an epigraph a passage from John Anthony Froude's *The English in the West Indies* (1887).

> They were valued only for the wealth which they yielded, and society there has never assumed any particularly noble aspect. There

has been splendour and luxurious living, and there have been crimes and horrors, and revolts and massacres. There has been romance, but it has been the romance of pirates and outlaws. The natural graces of life do not show themselves under such conditions. There has been no saint in the West Indies since Las Casas, no hero unless philonegro enthusiasm can make one out of Toussaint. There are no people there in the true sense of the word, with a character and purpose of their own.

This is the life without natural graces, heroes, saints, without a national identity or a social purpose, inherited by the people of *Miguel Street*, Naipaul's first book. It is a society based upon 'the degrading fact of the Colonial society; it never required efficiency, it never required quality, and these things, because unrequired, became undesirable'. This is the world without 'scientists, engineers, explorers, soldiers or poets', without tradition or standards which shapes the people of *Miguel Street*, Bogart, B. Wordsworth, Eddoes, Man-man, Errol, Titus Hoyt I. A. London (External), and Popo who called himself a carpenter but never built anything except a little galvanised iron workshop under a mango tree at the back of his yard, and who occupies himself incessantly making 'the thing without a name'. Miguel Street is a place where the past also is blank, a thing without a name. All the impersonal elements in civilisation are missing or they are supplied in the tawdriest form by films, radio stars, pop singers, and in their most exalted form by cricketers and the game of cricket, which is itself a kind of history, poetry and art. But there is one great exception. These are people of immense vitality, of great nimbleness of wit, of a vast and disillusioned tolerance, given to the life of feeling, responsive to rhythm, riddled by uncertainty—it is true—but also quick and shrewd, and they have one splendid instrument for ordering their sad, comic, muddled universe, their language.

Naipaul himself writes a prose that is limpidly anonymous and quite free of any personal quirks or distortions. It is decent and direct, syntactically simple and clear, and as it combines curiously an air of civilised restraint with a mischievously deadpan quality, it makes a very elegant instrument for ironic dissection. In this transparent medium the speech of the inhabitants of *Miguel Street* stands out with peculiar colour and density. It is a folk-speech, and

E

intimate therefore, sly and allusive. It also carries with it a curious suggestion of 'objectivity' and passivity. Impersonal verbs abound. Turns of speech deviously suggest the limitations of the agent. Each man carries within him a kind of secret impotence and his life and conduct are made up of his simultaneous acceptance and mockery of it. Because the myths are so thin, the social code so derivative, the people pour their energy into individuality. Each one is a formed identity, without a past, maybe, but with an astonishingly vivid present. These people are not derivations of some rich history of which they are part the inheritance and part the function. They are wholly here and now and there is in each of them an extraordinary concentration of life.

In *Miguel Street* it is the place, public, graceless, huddled, but brilliant with human oddity which is both the ground and the background of the people. The street is also the one permanent relationship uniting them. Their other relationships are intense and transient. They appear and disappear like fish or birds. Suddenly they are here, suddenly gone. People come and go, they are dramatically present, but there are long intervals of silence and absence. In *The Mystic Masseur* the place is enlarged, the protagonist Ganesh Ramsumair more centrally positioned, the other characters Leela the wife, Ramlogan the father-in-law, Beharry the friend, Basdeo the printer, are disposed in relation to him. The story is a decidedly Indian one in feeling, the translation of a masseur into a mystic. It recalls R. K. Narayan's *The Guide*, one of the most distinguished of Indian novels in English, in which Raju the railway guide and near confidence man is transformed into Raju the man deserving of confidence, and in the end the holy man and martyr.

In *The Guide* the organised theme is the complex association of sincerity and self-deception: how these conditions grow out of one another, how they co-exist, disagree, supplant, and in the long run re-attract one another. In *The Mystic Masseur* the theme is less serious than this. It is Ganesh's failure as a teacher that turns him into a masseur, his lack of success with rubbing away ordinary pains that nudges him towards mysticism. Raju in *The Guide* starts out self-conscious and embarrassed by his journey towards sainthood;

he is in fact pushed into the rôle because he cannot disappoint the expectations of the pious Indian villagers. He is one of those whose character is composed by the expectations of others. Ganesh in *The Mystic Masseur* starts from nothing but a clear consciousness of his own potential greatness, and his career is made up of his efforts, dutiful, devious, unscrupulous—each where it is necessary—to give this greatness a chance to shine out. He imposes himself upon his family and neighbours in the honest service of himself. Not that Ganesh is simply a straightforward gangster. There remains about him always, even in his final apotheosis as G. Ramsay Muir, M.B.E. a distinguished Colonial statesman, something enigmatic and inexplicable. Even his crookery is the means for realising his *virtus*. Moreover, Naipaul's attitude to his subjects, though it is as modest and self-effacing as Narayan's, is considerably more malicious. He delights in his mild way when his characters act out in their conduct the truth of Coleridge's assertion, 'cunning is circuitous folly'; morality in these lives is much more a style than an ethic. But his malice is not merely negative because of the tenderness with which he regards every expression of human individuality. Even cruelty, even the beating of wives and children becomes acceptable as it is absorbed into the style of behaviour proper to this or that individual.

Perhaps these last comments may suggest that Naipaul is the possessor of a delicate, attractive talent, at once gentle and mischievous, feeling and unsentimental. And Naipaul's gift clearly is all of this. But there are both in *Miguel Street* and *The Mystic Masseur* hints of deeper resonances, insinuations of less tractable disasters. There is a kind of sadness folded into the quick lines of the sketches in Miguel Street. It is unemphatic and never despairing because neither author nor characters take up any indignant stance about what happens to them. They accept it. And they do so because of a conviction, or if that is too explicit and articulate, because of a profound attitude or a posture in the bones and nerves, that one part of being human is simply hopelessness, and another part is practising a ritual to make that tolerable. There is an image of this cool tragic sense even in the tumultuously farcical career of Ganesh the Mystic Masseur in the death of his father.

When he had closed the door behind him the wailing sounded far away. The coffin rested on a table in the centre of the room and he couldn't see the body from where he was. To his left a small oil lamp burned low and threw monstrous shadows on the walls and the galvanised-iron ceiling. When he walked nearer the table his footsteps resounded on the floor-planks and the oil lamp shivered. The old man's moustache still bristled fiercely but the face had fallen and looked weak and tired. The air around the table felt cool and he saw that it came from the casing of ice around the coffin. It was a room of the dead, strange with the smell of camphor balls, and there was nothing alive in it except himself and the squat yellow flame of the oil lamp, and they were both silent. Only, from time to time, the water from the melting ice plopped into the four pans at the feet of the table and punctured the silence. . . . Ganesh didn't sleep that night and everything he did seemed unreal. Afterwards he remembered the solicitude of Ramlogan—and his daughter; remembered returning to the house where no fire could be lit, remembered the sad songs of the women lengthening out the night; then, in the early morning, the preparations for the cremation. He had to do many things, and he did without thought or question everything the pundit, his aunt, and Ramlogan asked him. He remembered having to walk round the body of his father, remembered applying the last caste-marks to the old man's forehead, and doing many more things until it seemed that ritual had replaced grief.

These possibilities, which in any case are no more than shadowy innuendoes in the West Indian sunlight, are kept in suspense throughout *The Suffrage of Elvira*, in which the target is the representative machinery of an abstract democracy without a sanction in tradition or understanding. And target does seem an appropriate word when one thinks of the aimed and focussed intensity of Naipaul's observation. The special flavour of his work indeed comes from blending the high spirits that could be productive of farce with a most delicately exact sense of detail, and not only the detail of objects but the details of conduct, of feeling, motivation and purpose. This means on Naipaul's part a distrust for conceptual abstractions and vague codes, but a sympathetic acceptance of the most outrageous behaviour when this wells up naturally from traditional or personal sources.

Things were crazily mixed up in Elvira. Everybody, Hindus, Muslims and Christians, owned a Bible; the Hindus and Muslims looking on it, if anything, with greater awe. Hindus and Muslims celebrated Christmas and Easter. The Spaniards and some of the negroes celebrated the Hindu festival of lights. Someone had told them that Lakshmi, the goddess of prosperity, was being honoured; they placed small earthen lamps on their money-boxes and waited, as they said, for the money to breed. Everybody celebrated the Muslim festival of Hosein. In fact, when Elvira was done with religious festivals, there were few straight days left.

The faces and colours are various here; what is common is human concern for a symbol which will guarantee one's safety and be the endorsement of one's action by the gods. Or as black Haq the Muslim puts it in his homely way. 'In God we trust, as the saying goes. In man we bust. *As* the saying goes.' As with the Bible so with democracy: 'Democracy had come to Elvira four years before, in 1946, but it had taken nearly everybody by surprise and it wasn't until 1950, a few months before the second general election under universal adult franchise, that people began to see the possibilities'. When the people include a candidate like the timid dyspeptic lacrymose Hindu Harbans, the tiny, dry formidable local boss Chittaranjan, the goldsmith, who wants the candidate's daughter for his son, the hard-drinking philoprogenitive Muslim leader Baksh and his vast wife prophesying universal disaster and beating the children with regretful relish, a campaign manager like their sunglassed, slogan-bawling son Foam—short for Foreman—and his rival Lorkhoor another 'fust-class loudspeaking man' whose eccentricity it is to speak correct English on every occasion, as well as the proprietor of the rum-shop Ramlogan, swinging instantaneously from chilling ferocity to tear-dissolving cowardice; and when the possibilities include sweetening everybody with dollars, lacing them with rum, terrifying them with obeah and magic, not to speak of baffling them with the intervention of two Jehovah's Witnesses, a pair of prim hygienic witches, and all in the service of democracy and the modern world, then the resultant brew is entrancingly strange. And yet there is a kind of wild logic in the tumult of 'the election bacchanal'.

Harbans steadied his hands. 'Is that self I come to talk to you about. The modern world Baksh. In this modern world everybody is one.

Don't make no difference who you is or what you is. You is a Muslim,
I is a Hindu. Tell me, that matter?' He had begun to coo again.
   'Depending.'
   'Yes, as you say, depending. Who you for Baksh?'

'Depending': There is a nice dependence at every point between
action and character and between character and community. Crazy
as the behaviour of the characters may be by any soberer standards,
each acts according to the coherence of identity, something which
is established by the clash or mating of his personal stamp with
the style of the society. And this inward control falls in with another,
the instinctive control of a fastidious mind. So that the extravagance
never becomes a mere romp. For a more than Irish eccentricity
in the population—to take an analogy which seems highly suitable
to a multi-racial society—is matched by an almost Latin elegance in
the writer.

The combination of peasant sagacity and cultivated intelligence,
of muscle and nerve, in *Miguel Street*, *The Mystic Masseur* and *The
Suffrage of Elvira* makes the books which are fed from regional
springs and realised in regional detail more than simply regional.
There are murmurations in them all of a more inclusive humanity.
And yet, and yet... These novels communicate an air of capability,
of sinewy resource, which seems more extensive than the matter
being dealt with. Their richness, after all, resides in minute perfections and their force is a limited and contained one. The reader is
aware of considerable powers put to rather too markedly a parochial
purpose. There is perhaps a shade too much emphasis on charm.
One begins to long for something more severe and more testing.
One wants to feel not just powers in the author but power in the
work. And here in *A House for Mr Biswas* it is. If one wanted to
specify one's uneasiness about the first three novels it would have
to do, I think, with one's sense of a certain discrepancy between
the perfection of the surface and the inclusiveness of the theme.
The surface connects, it seems, only with a vague depth whereas
one feels it requires to be supported with something more powerful
and profound: 'requires', that is, if the significance of the work is
to be level with the capacity of the author.

In the three early novels there is an idea floating about, though impalpably and without assuming definition (I do not mean abstract definition), which hints at a more significant and inclusive organising theme. It is the idea of slavery. The members of this community, even those parts of it like the Indian which were exempt from historical slavery, carry about with them the mark, in their attitudes and sensibilities and convictions, of the slave, the unnecessary man. The urgency of the characters comes from their efforts, desperate or ridiculous, to get others to acknowledge, so as to have it validated for themselves, their human necessity. In the comic books this may only amount to doing one's best to leave a dent in an indifferent universe, which often results in a hurt foot and an untouched world. But slavery is one of those ingathering, creative metaphors which have in them both strength and universality. It is this metaphor which initiates and sustains *A House for Mr Biswas*. 'How terrible it would have been,' Mr Biswas reflects as he lies dying in his mortgaged house. 'How terrible it would have been, at this time, to be without it: to have died among the Tulsis, amid the squalor of that large, disintegrating and indifferent family; to have left Shama and the children among them, in one room; worse, to have lived without even attempting to lay claim to one's portion of the earth; to have lived and died as one had been born, unnecessary and unaccommodated.'

Dying in a mortgaged house is just what is happening to poor Mr Biswas, a journalist of Sikkim Street, St James, Port of Spain, aged 46, with a wife and four children. But it is happening too, the novel makes us realise, to his healthy family, to his next-door neighbour, to the community and to all of us. And not simply because of a general metaphor which can be unfastened from its loose attachment to a particular context, but because all of us in Trinidad and everywhere else are indeed dying in mortgaged houses, mortgaged bodies, mortgaged minds and feelings. We are all, all our lives, 'stiffening in a rented mansion'. Mr Biswas—this is his name throughout the novel even when he is a small child, and how can one call anyone with a name like that a hero?—Mr Biswas, the protagonist, is not a bad model of man, the anonymous ordinary man that is. He was born to a family of sugar-estate workers, a scrawny, pot-bellied baby who had six fingers and was born the wrong way at an inauspicious hour. The midwife prophesied 'whatever you do, this boy will eat up his own mother and father'. And his horoscope appalled the pundit.

He undid his red bundle and took out his astrological almanac, a sheaf of loose thick leaves, long and narrow, between boards. The leaves were brown with age and their musty smell was mixed with that of the red and ochre sandalwood paste that had been spattered on them. The pundit lifted a leaf, read a little, wet his forefinger on his tongue and lifted another leaf.

'What about the six fingers, pundit?'

'That's a shocking sign, of course. The only thing I can advise is to keep him away from trees and water. Particularly water.'

'Never bath him?'

'I don't mean exactly that.' He raised his right hand, bunched the fingers and, with his head on one side, said slowly. 'One has to interpret what the book says.' He tapped the wobbly almanac with his left hand. 'And when the book says water, I think it means water in its natural form.'

'Natural form.'

'Natural form,' the pundit repeated, but uncertainly. 'I mean,' he said quickly, and with some annoyance, 'keep him away from rivers and ponds. And of course the sea. And another thing,' he added with satisfaction. 'He will have an unlucky sneeze.'

When Mr Biswas was nine days old the sixth finger fell off and it had to be buried secretly behind the cow-pen at the back of the house. A little unnecessary bit of him died almost before he was under way. The events of Mr Biswas's life might have been arranged to make the structure of his slavery explicit. But he began, of course, as a baby with that warm half-conscious certitude that the way things were was the absolute and perfect way. Life for a child is always brilliantly present and not conceivably other than it is. As an infant he was treated with attention and respect. His limbs were oiled and exercised. He caught cold easily and he had to be watched because his sinister sneeze brought disaster: threepence would be lost, a bottle would be broken, a dish upset. But he grew in spite of malnutrition, though he was always breaking out in eczema and sores. He was never allowed to go near water and to look after the buffaloes as the other children did. But he was given the responsibility for a calf belonging to Dhari the next-door neighbour. Mr Biswas loved the calf and he took it for walks. It was on one of these that he discovered the stream which he visited secretly to play. One day he lost the calf. He couldn't find it although he mooed for it, quietly of course so as not to attract the attention of adults. He decided that it was gone for good. He slunk home, crept into the house, and hid under the bed, where 'the smell of old cloth, dust and old thatch combined into one overpoweringly musty smell'. While Mr Biswas lay, passive but alert, events outside which were remote and dramatic were under way. He was found to be lost and assumed to be at the bottom of the pond. His father dived again and again for him, refusing help partly out of pique, because after all it was his son that was down there. But Raghu, Mr Biswas's father, still steadfastly diving and refusing help went down again and again.

> Lakhan said, 'Something has happened.'
> A woman said, 'No stupid talk now, Lakhan, Raghu is a great diver.'
> 'I know, I know,' Lakhan said. 'But he's been diving too long.'
> Then they were all still. Someone had sneezed.
> They turned to see Mr Biswas standing some distance away in the gloom, the toe of one foot scratching the ankle of the other.
> Lakhan was in the pond. Pratap and Prasad rushed to hustle Mr Biswas away.
> 'That boy!' Dhari said. 'He has murdered my calf and now he has eaten up his own father.'
> Lakhan brought up Raghu unconscious. They rolled him on the damp grass and pumped water out of his mouth and through his nostrils. But it was too late.

Mr Biswas had indeed eaten up his own mother and father. The rapacious peasant neighbours closed in, harassing the widow and children and searching the garden at night for money Raghu was supposed to have hidden. The family was broken up among relatives, and the small sum of Mr Biswas's hugged certainties and tiny stabilities crumbled away. From now on life was to point out to Mr Biswas with increasing degrees of ferocity how less and less necessary he was. He was always peripheral. He belonged nowhere. He got in people's way, at his aunt's, at the pundit's where he was sent as a novice, partly, no doubt, because of the curious air of disaster he carried about with him, and where he was bullied in a high-minded way and finally expelled in disgrace because he couldn't control his bowels. He worked in a rumshop where the manager distrusted him as a spy of the owner. He became a sign-writer and lovingly decorated palings and walls in honour of Pluko, a hair tonic, Anchor cigarettes and the candidates for the local Road Board elections. It was while painting signs in the Tulsis' shop on the High Street at Arwacas that he was enlisted into the household—though medieval words like retinue or meinie might be more suitable—of the Tulsis, who had some reputation among Hindus as a pious, conservative landowning family. Their house was dedicated to Hanuman, the benevolent monkey-god, but he was the only benevolent one there. The family combined seediness and ruthlessness. It was governed by Mrs Tulsi, who worked through oriental mystery and passivity, and her brother-in-law Seth, a large, moustached, overpowering man, who used more active methods.

Mr Biswas made a gawky advance to a pretty girl in the shop. Immediately the smooth Tulsi organisation purred into action. Before he knew where he was he was accepted as the girl's official suitor, and before he could understand what that meant he found himself married to her. Mr Biswas was now not only naturally a slave but officially one. The Tulsi menage worked on simple principles. There was one servant, a Negress called Miss Blackie; but the real and many servants were the daughters and their children who swept and washed and cooked and served in the store, while their husbands under Seth's supervision worked on the Tulsi land and looked after the Tulsi animals for which they received food, shelter, and little money, and had their children looked after. But Mr Biswas, though he was a weak man and indeed a victim, was not the suave classical kind of victim who accepts his fate in courage and silence. He had a weak man's capacity for spurts of revolt and querulous malice. He was an irritable, jerking victim, a bit of grit in the oiled machine of the Tulsis. When it was necessary to be solemn he was a clown, when pious he was blasphemous, when appreciative he was ungrateful.

The Tulsis could stand just so much and it wasn't long before they put Mr Biswas out to service. He was put to keep a village shop where he showed himself both incompetent and uncaring. It was true it was not much of a shop, a short narrow room with a rusty galvanised iron roof, with concrete floors and sagging walls which shook and staggered but somehow stood up, and a house attached to it smelling of kerosene and bedbugs. Mr Biswas was cheated and despised by his customers, and frequently deserted by his wife who took off every so often and returned to Hanuman House. He had innumerable bad debts. He was swindled by the lawyer he employed to recover them. Clearly the Tulsis had to rescue what they could.

Seth sighed. 'So what we going to do with the shop?'
Mr Biswas shrugged.
'Insure and burn?' Seth said, making it one word: *Insuranburn*.

Insuranburning took care of the shop, and Mr Biswas, now at once more actively frantic and more passively a utensil than ever, was sent as a sub-overseer at the sugar estate at Green Vale at twenty-five dollars a month. The labourers, sensing the victim in him, mocked and swindled him, and Mr Biswas, who began by wondering how they lived on three dollars a month, soon wondered why they got so much. At Green Vale two things happened to him. He was a man whose salvation depended upon his becoming something, or someone. He might, with his nervous plastic nature and his love of reading Marcus Aurelius, have been saved by developing a style. He might have been held together by a kind of modest elegance. But what style or elegance could he develop in a society where a fine meal meant a tin of sardines and a bottle of soda-water? And what was open to him (for his emptiness might have been supported by the rôle a profession gave) in a community where all he could hope for would be to be a barber or a bus conductor? He decided to become a house-owner. He poured his hope and passion into the queer square structure raised for him by Mr McLean, the carpenter. A house-owner is a man with an identity and a place, a character and a context. But while the miserable little house assumed its one-room solidity, the residue of Mr Biswas's self and sanity began to dribble away. Slavery, a total lack of necessity, being simply a function and a thing turned Mr Biswas from a subject into an object. Human reality crumpled. He became afraid, then terrified of the labourers, and finally every man and woman he saw, even at a distance, gave him a twist of panic. And then every object became sullied by his fear. Objects, as real as he who was simply another object, stared at him menacingly.

> . . . he thought of the power of the rockers to grind and crush and inflict pain, in his hands and toes and the tenderer parts of his body. He rose at once in agony, covering his groin with his hands, sucking hard on his teeth, listening to the chair, as, rocking, it moved sideways on the cambered plank. The chair fell silent and stopped. He looked away from it. On the wall he saw a nail that could puncture his eye. The window could drop and mangle. So could the doors. And the castors of the dressing-table. The drawers.

The only strength in his life seemed to be his past which now became 'a miracle of calm and courage'. He felt the darkness lapping about this. The place itself was losing definition as each day the lucidity of his mind lessened. He had been a mere nobody and now he was threatened absolutely with being no body. His inward emptiness no longer had the reassurance of the external world.

> When he got to Green Vale it was dark. Under the trees it was night. The sounds from the barracks were asserted and isolated one from the other: snatches of talk, the sound of frying, a shout, the cry of a child: sounds thrown up at the starlit sky from a place that was nowhere, a dot on the map of the island, which was a dot on the map of the world. The dead trees ringed the barracks, a wall of flawless black.

The rest of Mr Biswas's life was spent striving to keep at least that much lucidity in his head and that amount of coherence in his life which would save him from being buried under 'a wall of flawless black'.

The account of Mr Biswas's dissolution, which is both evocation and analysis and each shading into the other, is, although but half-way through, the climax of the novel and perhaps the high point of Naipaul's art. The shape of the novel is like a great V with Mr Biswas's collapse at the point of the V and with the lines alive and shifting, like rivers. The analysis is clinically exact, the evocation tenderly human. The insight has grace and the grace acumen. The balancing part of the novel details with a more positive presence of the comic but with an equally exquisite touch the stumbling and bumbling progress of Mr Biswas upwards from insanity and despair. The second part of his life, some fifteen years, is spent mostly in the city, in Port of Spain. He charms his way into a job as a journalist, where his fantasy and facetiousness appeal to a harum-scarum editor, though they rub rather awkwardly against a soberer, more professional successor. He specialised in stories that combined shape and scandal. His job gave Mr Biswas some small measure of independence and his purpose—to achieve the dignity of a house-owner—gave his life form. There were of course hectic periods, moments when he appeared to be sliding helplessly back into disaster. He never separated completely from the squalor and disintegration of the Tulsi family: he was always liable to be involved in their intense intimacies and incomprehensible hostilities. But he had his measure of good fortune: he was never out of work, his children turned out to be intelligent, and he finally got his house—although naturally he was swindled by the seller. But this being cheated is in keeping with the bias of Mr Biswas's nature. He could never cease to be a victim (any more than the rest of us). But at least he was an irritable and suspicious one, and in his turn he succeeded if not in swindling fate at least in cheating it a little. He became to some degree, which is perhaps the most that any of us can hope for, an unaccommodating victim and an accommodated man.

Naipaul's next novel, *Mr Stone and the Knights Companion*, sustains the theme of slavery but in a delicately subdued, fantastic manner. The English setting is solid and palpable, genuine in feeling and authentic in detail, but the vision brought to bear on it is so idiosyncratic, so wry and curious, that the reader feels he is moving in a dream where objects and events have an unnatural prominence and clarity but the universe enclosing them is cloudy and magical. Mr Stone himself has dreamlike fantasies: he sees himself gliding up and down on his private moving strip of pavement or flying along the corridors at work, indifferent to the stupefaction of the onlookers. Mr Stone's slavery is an individual and intrinsic condition. He is the slave of his past, of his habits, of a fixed identity and its ritualistic priorities. 'Life was something to be moved through.

Experiences were not to be enjoyed at the actual moment: pleasure in them came only when they had been, as it were, docketed and put away in the file of the past, when they had become part of his "life", his "experience", his career.' This is the problem, the form 'slavery' takes, in a society unravaged by the savagery of extremes, and within that society the peculiar problem of the most settled, the middle aged, who inhabit a world which hardens on the one side into routine and falls on the other into despair. And it is this area of sensibility which is plotted with a kind of tender accuracy in *Mr Stone and the Knights Companion*. The wild folk-gaiety of the earliest novels is muted into an urban, and urbane, comedy, the turbulent Caribbean nonsense into metropolitan and pointed wit. But under the elegant surface there is an edge of grimness in place in a work which for all the slightness of its proportions has great thematic richness. 'And he had a realisation', it is said of Mr Stone, 'too upsetting to be more than momentarily examined, that all that was solid and immutable and enduring about the world, all to which man linked himself . . . flattered only to deceive. For all that was not flesh was irrelevant to man, and all that was important was man's own flesh, his weakness and corruptibility.'

The Mimic Men was published in 1967 and confirms the impression given by *A House for Mr Biswas* that Naipaul is an artist whose work contains within itself large possibilities of growth and development. *The Mimic Men* bends away in several new directions. It brings together West Indian and British themes and sets alongside one another the landscapes of London and Trinidad, of Isabella as the island is called in the story. It is a much more personal work than *Mr Stone and the Knights Companion* in which there is a hint not of the academic but of a rather deliberate 'study'. It is like *A House for Mr Biswas* in its complexity and inclusiveness but the temperament of this novel is more pinched and melancholy. *A House for Mr Biswas* celebrates the fineness of humanity implicit in the feeblest of us. The more clinical eye of *The Mimic Men* discovers the failure in the best, like the worn little pornographic booklet discovered in the desk of the hero's father, and while there are splendid comic touches they are dispersed and rare. The hilarity of the early novels has been turned into something bordering on despair and all that quality of wild high spirits is quite bleached away. Certainly there is no occasion to worry here, as there was in those novels, about too much emphasis on charm. *The Mimic Men* begins with Ralph Singh, an exiled politician—fatigued by disillusion rather than failure—writing his memoirs in an aseptic, *placeless* suburban London hotel. The novel dramatises his reminiscences. The framing effect of the reminiscences, the distancing of exile and the sieve of memory give form to the novel and enable us to grasp the quality of detachment in the protagonist (just as they also remind us of that contemplative constituent in Naipaul's own sensibility which begins to assume a more important place in his fiction).

The nature of Naipaul's hero, an ex-public unsmiling forty-year-old man, Hindu by birth, with a schoolteacher father and rich connections on his mother's side, is marked by a certain icy remoteness unmelting since childhood. An acute intelligence and minute sensitivity to what he sees make him a magnificent observer—but of the kind Coleridge called *spectator ab extra*. His consciousness of self is always kept at a certain critical point, his feelings never blend wholly with those of another. An intellectual and moral distance always persists. He is an aristocrat lacking an order he can submit to. His dreams are cold and distant. '. . . I had visions of Central Asian horsemen, among whom I am one, riding below a sky threatening snow to the very end of an empty world.' He speaks with hauteur of the English politicians he found when he came to England at a time of reform. '. . . Politicians proclaim the meanness of their birth and the poverty of their upbringing and describe themselves with virtuous rage as barefoot boys. On Isabella, where we had the genuine article in abundance, this was a common term of schoolboy abuse; and I was embarrassed on behalf of these great men.' During his seedy, promiscuous London student's life at a college off the Aldwych he plays 'the dandy, the extravagant colonial, indifferent to scholarship', a part in keeping with his schoolboy rôle of brilliant idler at Isabella Imperial. Even on his return to Isabella, now married to a gritty North London undergraduate from the college, where he makes a fortune out of land deals, he does so with an indifferent detachment. 'I did not feel responsible for what had befallen me; I always felt separate from what I did.' Nor was he separate only from what he *did*. The society of Isabella was quickened by one organic and binding relationship, a relationship which was also an appalling violation. It was that—or rather the modern version and relic of it—between masters and slaves. From the mutual and complete comprehension of these Singh was by origin and nature excluded. So that at the very centre of this world he feels himself to be no more than a picturesque Asiatic born for other landscapes.

But which? Ideal landscapes like other ideals glimmer in his imagination, though when approached they pall and disappoint.

> How right our Aryan ancestors were to create gods. We seek sex, and are left with two private bodies on a stained bed. The larger erotic dream, the god, has eluded us. It is so whenever, moving out of ourselves, we look for extensions of ourselves. It is with cities as it is with sex. We seek the physical city and find only a conglomeration of private cells. In the city as nowhere else we are reminded that we are individuals, units. Yet the idea of the city remains; it is the god of the city that we pursue, in vain.

The god of the city is the image of an order which this classically minded man—Brahmin by inheritance, Greek in sympathy and Roman in his scholarly interests—is desperately conscious he lacks. 'To be born on an island like Isabella, an obscure New World transplantation, second-hand and barbarous, was to be born to disorder.' His family offered no locus for the god, split as it was in his early years between his father's weakness and failure and his mother's vaguely wealthy vulgar connections; and in later years between the grossness of great wealth—of possessions, women, drink, swimming-pools—and the hysteria represented by his father's sudden assumption of a crazed Messianic rôle as the leader of the deprived, a movement which was no more than 'a gesture of mere protest, a statement of despair without a philosophy or a cause'.

The achievement of order through the pursuit of political power is the theme of the middle or active part of his life which he later calls a parenthesis. This part of the novel communicates with great strength and depth a sense of outward participation and inward

absence; or to put it as it appears to Singh, a sense of personal
reality and public illusion. On the face of it Singh is perfectly
prepared for a political career. Elegant, wealthy and cultivated, he
is an admirable partner for his schoolboy friend Browne, the Negro
folk-leader. But he lacks 'the frenzy, the necessary hurt' which
alone makes politics real. They become for him a set of dream-like
motions performed by an intruder into a society in which people
were linked by no internal connection, except the one, slavery,
from which he is excluded. His account of the growth of Browne's
political movement is both aromatic and analytical, a genuine
novelist's blend of diagnosis and evocation. There is the insensible,
almost innocent transformation from the sincere artificiality of the
politician on the make to the artificial sincerity of the minister in
power. What was happening in Isabella was happening tumultuously in twenty different colonies and territories. Singh sees it not
as the pace of post-war political change, neither the pace of creation
nor destruction, but the pace of chaos on which strict limits had
been imposed. Their movement was left-wing, socialist. It stood
for the dignity of the working man and of the island. But it was a
matter of feeling rather than doctrine, of borrowed phrases and
escape from thought. And what it offered above all was drama—a
sense of an explosion of life and the composition of a pattern of
justice. The marks of success increased: the public meetings, the
tours of dusty country roads, the lengthening reports of speeches,
the policemen in heavy serge shorts becoming less aggressive and
more protecting, the atmosphere of dedication and mutual loyalty.
There was also the vanity of those who believed they had the power
to regulate what they had created, together with wonder at the
suddenly realised concept of the people who responded and could
be manipulated. The speeches became more brilliant and more
dishonest, the success more dazzling, the sense of inevitable historical process more certain and finally, election night—the sobering
moment of triumph, when play-acting turns out to be serious. And
then the anxious concern with legality and ritual to consecrate
power, and the realisation that power needed a more solid base
than applause and the smell of the people's sweat. Finally there
was the manœuvring, corrupt or passionate, to hang on to this airy

F

gift which might at any moment be withdrawn. But in Singh, underneath the public dandy, underneath the political mover and organiser there was only a negation. The one prize of politics for him was that he had helped to bring drama to the island. 'Drama, however much we fear it, sharpens our perception of the world, gives us some sense of ourselves, makes us actors, gives point and sometimes glory to each day. It alters a drab landscape.' When the drama failed the landscape returned to its drabness and the images of disorder to his imagination.

> My sense of drama failed. This to me was the true loss. For four years drama had supported me; now, abruptly, drama failed. It was a private loss; thoughts of irresponsibility or duty dwindled, became absurd. I struggled to keep drama alive, for its replacement was despair: the vision of a boy walking on an endless, desolate beach, between vegetation living, rotting, collapsed, and a mindless, living sea.

The final phase of Singh's career is one of withdrawal into privacy and anonymity. This freeing oneself from events and attachments is surely part of that classical Indian tradition one can't help harking back to in thinking about Naipaul himself. In spite of his explicit and wholesale rejection of India, his work, like Joyce's, is saturated by what he, as a person, revolts from. Singh's detachment gives him the satisfaction, he says, of fulfilling 'the fourfold division of life prescribed by our Aryan ancestors. I have been student, householder, and man of affairs, recluse.' It gives him too a negative peace: 'I no longer yearn for ideal landscapes and no longer wish to know the god of the city'. Singh's life had been spent in an attempt to bring under the gods the different areas of his experience. Politics had been the effort to impose order upon a society in disarray, just as his marriage had been an effort to bring discipline to his shabby, promiscuous, emotional life, and the Roman house he built in Isabella, with a swimming-pool instead of an *impluvium*, an attempt to impose a pattern upon the physical chaos of the place. In every case the material had been impatient of, and finally made fraudulent by, the discipline put upon it. The essential struggle of Singh—and isn't it also the central human endeavour?—had been one in which he had attempted to discover instruments of mediation between his private self and the world outside, or in which he had attempted to make the enlargement of himself which was his experience more truly coherent with his nature. He had always failed.

On every occasion, that is, but one: the bleak aftermath of Singh's public life, in the empty context of a suburban hotel, provides him, in the composition of his memoirs, with the chance to discover an instrument of mediation between self and experience which is both appropriate and effective. The contemplation of memory ceases to be merely passive or lapsing and becomes an active management of experience. '. . . this became my aim: from the central fact of this setting, my presence in this city which I have known as student, politician and now as refugee-immigrant, to impose order on my own history. . .' It is explicitly his *own* history now, it should be noted; no longer that of the external world. The recording of his life becomes an extension of his life. Here, as in the Indian ambivalence I have mentioned, we seem to find again the touch of Naipaul the writer as well as the presence of Singh the character. 'So writing for all its initial distortion, clarifies, and even becomes a process of life.' Not that the discovery of the discipline of art disturbs the logic—no, that is too harsh a word—the coherence of the wavering, complex character which is in the end offered to us by the novel. I say 'offered to us', but I mean, painfully, honestly, submitted to us. More than once in the book Singh is struck by the way that personality is created by the vision of others: it seems to be no more than the answer in action to questions and clues proffered by others. But at the conclusion of his career he sees character as having a kind of intrinsic coherence—not the kind he expected, certainly, but a sort of pattern flowing from an inner initiative— which makes him question whether personality *is* merely manufactured by the vision of others. 'I begin to question this, I doubt whether any action, above a certain level, is ever wholly arbitrary or whimsical or dishonest . . . personality hangs together. It is one and indivisible.' This statement applies, I believe, to the character of Singh himself that we finally grasp in the work.

Singh's character becomes one and organic because of the strict honesty, painfully achieved and continually renovated, which controls the relationship between his self and his experience, or because self in him is gradually educated to be accessible to what is authentically his own experience. And this is also true, I believe, of the literary character of Naipaul himself, which has matured to the point where it hangs together and is one and indivisible, where it manifests, as it were, one soul in every part of the body. The narrative technique of *The Mimic Men* is dissolving and non-linear, in correspondence with the starts and swerves of the recovering memory itself. As the reader traces the folded themes of this intricate novel, he is conscious of a constellation of capacities, serious, witty, analytical, evocative and creatively intelligent, unified by the intention to bring into definition, or rather into that degree of it which is possible and appropriate, exact, unmisted actuality together with its trail of vaguer, deeper implication. Not, naturally, that even this considerable equipment, employed with disciplined honesty and rigorous clarity, is equally effective throughout the novel. Sometimes the clarity thickens, the discipline flags. There remains, for example, in Ralph Singh himself a certain acquiescence or passivity at key junctures in his personal or political life which leaves him just a shade too enigmatically impermeable. And the analysis of the character of Browne, the political leader, gives insufficient warrant for the force attributed to him in action. The women in the book, with the exception of the wife, though they are not perfunctory, are seldom treated with Naipaul's characteristic tense energy.

But in so many things in *The Mimic Men* we see an independent and fastidious talent fully engaged and brilliantly successful: in the treatment of the second-hand violated colonial and post-colonial society; in the understanding of the psychology of the sensitive young, appalled by the sight others have of their secret life; in the rendering of political and social ideas, not as untethered formulations but living activities; in the evocation of place and physical context—the London light, the cocoa valleys, houses, weather, hotels—all, we often feel, so much more constant, so much more faithful to themselves than devious, impotently treacherous man; in the general composition and suppleness of tone and the scope of concretely realised experience; and above all in the penetration and vitality with which he develops the novel's central, constitutive theme—one of profound human meaning—an exploration of the ways in which the conscious individual in a given society establishes modes of mediation between himself and his experience.

The Mimic Men reveals the features of a talent of great scope and perhaps of even more promise since it is endowed with what is perhaps the most significant artistic quality of all, the gift of growth.

CHAPTER IV

I PATRICK WHITE

PATRICK WHITE is so different a writer, or so much himself as a writer, that he requires of any reader, and perhaps particularly of the British reader, an unusual steadiness of application. Genuine and stubborn difficulties have to be faced before the reader is at home in a fiction in which the idiom is often opaque and the narrative conducted through choking thickets of imagery. As well as the perplexities provoked by the manner there are those provided by the character of the time and space in which most of Patrick White's work is located. It is not the more extended past, the nineteenth century as in *Voss* which is hard for the reader to grasp but, oddly, the nearer past—say from 1914 to 1939—the period from which so many of White's characters take their habits and assumptions. The sensibility of that time, possibly because of its relative nearness, because it is something we ourselves have shed, seems almost totally gone and bafflingly hard for a contemporary British reader to grasp with spontaneous understanding. Then there is the mystery of Australian space, that beautiful and positive emptiness, which envelops the community and overwhelms the individual. Difficulties of access, however, in the long run diminish, even if they never disappear; and certainly they come to seem less important against the reader's increasing conviction that he is in the presence of a true creative power. It is a power which derives its strength from inner resources. It is free of 'cleverness' and remarkably unaffected by fashion. It has great ease and flow—not facility—of conception, a kind of creative insouciance, which finds subjects and themes both urgent and permanent, lying waiting to be exposed in situations of the seediest simplicity and among characters of quite humdrum mediocrity.

A miniature of that power is displayed in *Down at the Dump*, one of eleven short stories published in *The Burnt Ones* in 1964. The scope of these stories is naturally more confined than in the novels, but the shape and proportions are the same. There is a similar sense of the depth of human nature and the same strikingly individual sensibility, giving off a mixed odour of sweat and spirituality. The people in *Down at the Dump* are drab, the events few and ordinary, the context sleazy and down-at-heel, the whole air wretched and deprived, and yet from these unpromising constituents Patrick White constructs a celebration of human possibility which is at once lyrical and quite unsentimental. White has an eye which is gluttonous for detail. Each passage is firm from the presence of discriminated actuality. But all the solid objective existence, convincing in surface, sure in implication, is submissive to the initiative of the writer. It is as much the result of reflection as observation, and it is composed of detail which is both authentic in its own right and quick at every point with the highly individual quality of the author's mind. This is particularly evident in the pace with which details follow one another. They tumble out with unforced vivacity, products of an endless energy. And they exhibit the peculiar violence of White's imagination which is capable of informing the mildest symptom of character or the most delicate indication of place with a strange intensity. Perhaps this intensity is the effect of a Manichaean habit of sensibility which throws everything, moral situations, place, character, age, the whole of his subject-matter into a powerful system of polarities and antinomies.

Growth from a cell or centre, an organic 'biographical' line of movement—rather than plot or a more formal arrangement—is the favoured kind of progression in White's fiction. Discipline as a self-created order, and love, even when it manifests itself as sexual feeling, as a form of charity and tenderness, are the positives offered —embodied rather—and the grounds of hope in White's most achieved work. It shows a powerful self-confidence in a novelist of this age to take so unabashed a stand on a morality as traditional as this. White's is a profoundly moral art but its vitality comes from an attitude to morality different from that prevalent in most contemporary novelists. The modern writer, when he does not wish to reject, wants to advance and refine accepted morality. He is in a strict sense progressive. But Patrick White's disposition and method are to go back, to investigate, or rather since he is not at all a lucid analyst, to uncover the sources of morality. He is drawn to the depths and wells of human nature. This is an aim at once simpler and more difficult than most writers now propose to themselves. White's fascination with the sources—or at least always with the level of significance below the level that appears—makes him, in this respect, a decidedly traditional, almost a classical, writer.

The classical effect, or the sense the reader has of an art conducted according to traditional categories, is confirmed by the universal and humane forms morality assumes in Patrick White's work. He adds to this effect, however, a peculiarly intense and personal vision of a morality which has at its heart a religious quality, religious in the sense of something accepted not constructed, something present not invented. Morality exists on the plane of action. It is a matter of things done or undone, of intentions realised or thwarted or forgotten, of act and realisation. But it depends on, and it is only alive when it issues from, a quality of being, or something comparable to what a religious person might call a state of grace.

At least this observation will bring home to the reader the range of Patrick White's sensibility. It springs from a pure sense of existence, which—in the short story I have referred to—stretches in its sympathy from the dense and dirty embodiments of existence in the haphazard gear of the rubbish dump through every kind and modulation of life up to a level of experience which is spiritual in its candour and fineness. I have called Patrick White a traditional artist. But this is not to declare that in discriminating grades of existence he freezes them into any falsely static posture. He is not in that sense a hierarchical writer. On the contrary there is a constant touching of different worlds. a Lawrentian sort of mobility and flow. A point of contrast becomes a point of connection. The rubbish dump in *Down at the Dump* runs into the cemetery. The voice of goodness from the grave calls out to the devious town councillor. It is among the heaving rubbish of the dump that the young lovers make their first tender enquiries of one another. The mystery of existence, the mystery of self, the mutuality of experience and self—this 'metaphysical' theme, no more than hinted at here—rolls like a profound current all through Patrick White's work. This depth of preoccupation is the animating presence which quickens the multiplying details and orders the vast range of material (but also, and not infrequently, which clouds the clues the artist offers to what he is about with too large and unmanageable a significance).

Just as *Down at the Dump*, simple and brief as it is, involves in undertone and suggestion Patrick White's preoccupation with being, so too it is constantly in touch, at least in hint and intimation, with the other sustaining theme of his fiction—the exploration of self. His precise interest in this short story is one that a distinction of Coleridge lights up: '. . . self—i.e. the image or complex cycle of imagination . . . which is the perpetual representative of our Individuum . . .'.[1] Patrick White is concerned in miniature here, *in extenso* in the novels, with the relations between individuality and the self.

I turn at once to the novels since neither White's poetry (a juvenile volume *The Ploughman and other Poems*, 1935) nor his play (*Return to Abyssinia*, 1946) is at all comparable with his fiction. And among the novels I shall begin with *The Aunt's Story*, 1948—the history of 'this thing a spinster which, at best, becomes that institution an aunt'. His two early novels *The Living and the Dead*, 1941, and *Happy Valley*, 1939, seem to me to be decidedly apprentice work. If they have any interest now it is historical not intrinsic. *The Aunt's Story* begins with the inescapable air of authority and assurance of a writer who has arrived. He has a distinctive manner, a personal idiom, a sense of purpose and pattern, confidence in his theme. Even the first page will, I believe, be found to justify these claims, and perhaps I could quote it here.

But old Mrs Goodman did die at last.

Theodora went into the room where the coffin lay. She moved one hairbrush three inches to the left, and smoothed the antimacassar on a little Empire prie-dieu that her mother had brought from Europe. She did all this with some surprise, as if divorced from her own hands, as if they were related to the objects beneath them only in the way that two flies, blowing and blundering in space, are related to a china and mahogany world. It was all very surprising, the accomplished as opposed to the contemplated fact. It had altered the silence of the

[1] *Inquiring Spirit*, ed. K. Coburn, p. 68

house. It had altered the room. This was no longer the bedroom of her
mother. It was a waiting room, which housed the shiny box that
contained a waxwork.

Theodora had told them to close the box before the arrival of
Fanny and Frank, who were not expected till the afternoon. So the
box was closed, even at the expense of what Fanny would say. She
would talk about Last Glimpses, and cry. She had not lived with Mrs
Goodman in her latter years. From her own house she wrote and
spoke of Dear Mother, making her an idea, just as people will talk of
Democracy or Religion, at a moral distance. But Theodora was the
spinster. She had lived with her mother, and helped her into her
clothes. She came when the voice called.

At moments she still heard this in the relinquished room. Her own
name spilt stiff and hollow out of the dusty horn of an old phonograph,
into the breathless house. So that her mouth trembled, and her hand,
rigid as protesting wood, on the coffin's yellow lid.

Here in a single page as in a moment of conception, the nature
of the novel is predestined, its frame set up, its area mapped, its
personae admitted, its development projected, even its method
hinted at. The first word, that wrong-footed 'But' (one of Patrick
White's more successful uses of an imaginatively dislocated
syntax), is a pivot with all the weight on one side. It establishes
something of the awkward tension which preceded Mrs Goodman's death. Theodora, moving the hairbrush, smoothing the
antimacassar, is shown at the moment of her entrance with the
significant symptom of dissociation—'with some surprise, as if
divorced from her own hands'. At once too, the imagery which is
to be the sustained mode of narration appears. Her hands 'are
related to the objects beneath them only in the way that two flies,
blowing and blundering in space, are related to a china and mahogany world'. The flies meaninglessly crashing into the china and
mahogany world, the mind wildly careering into the cool order
of sanity: this is the kind of balance proposed at the very beginning.
The ritual of Theodora waiting for her sister Fanny and her family
to join in the mourning, the Empire prie-dieu, the mother from
Europe, and all that is involved in 'the china and mahogany', point
back precisely to her well-bred—well-bred but somehow nervously attenuated—background. Fanny, extrovert, weeping, selfish
and so clearly different from the inwardly focussing Theodora

makes Theodora seem all the more remote, just as Fanny who is able to soften any painful experience into a vague abstraction, turning the diseased woman into her Dear Mother, makes us feel how utterly exposed Theodora is to what is concretely there— what is there being almost certainly an occasion for suffering.

In a few lines then, a situation is presented, a character conceived, possibilities of development are foreshadowed, a method of exploration held up: and all done with an art which is generous and full but not—at least not here—extravagant. More than this. *The Aunt's Story* is not the history but the rendering in terms of art of the process of mental collapse, and one is conscious from the first, in the tone, in the nuance of word and image, of some disturbing irregularity in the substance of Theodora's experience. Its sound rustles in the 'surprising' friction she finds between the accomplished and the contemplated fact, in her excessively heightened sensitivity to the objects around, in the strange distancing of subject and object, in the sense of menace and trap offered by the physical things—in the room, in the shiny box, in the imagined summoning voice from the dusty phonograph. In the last sentence there is almost a complete reversal of normality in which feeling and subjectivity are attributed to the thing, the protesting wood of the coffin itself, and passivity and the status of object to Theodora, the person.

But the story of mental decay, the fiction which constitutes the material of the novel, is itself a means in the development of a profound and powerful theme, which will be an ordering and clarifying force in the novel and the current managing the drift of event and detail. Fundamentally it is a theme of the same sort as that in *Down at the Dump* which is why I began with that story. It has to do with the nature of the self and more particularly with the release from the self and even indeed with the obliteration of the self. In the story release was achieved I pointed out by giving or accepting; in the novel release, or rather a total obliteration of the self, is achieved through *becoming*. It is this complication, this further resonance, which turns what might have been a clinically exact account of mental disintegration into a richer and more humanly significant composition.

Before I attempt to elucidate the notion of *becoming* which works through this novel, perhaps I could say a word about the shape of it. *The Aunt's Story* falls into three divisions which are temporarily successive as phases in a development but markedly distinct in nature and treatment. The first, which begins and ends formally with the death of Mrs Goodman, is a reconstruction of Theodora's life up to middle age: 'A woman of fifty, or not yet, whose eyes burn still, under the black hair, which is still frizzed above the forehead in little puffs'. The second pictures a mind burning fiercely and melting away the restraints and disciplines of distinction, and particularly the distinction of I and otherness. The third is a concluding phase of contemplation and detachment in which Patrick White allows himself a degree of explicitness not permitted elsewhere in the novel.

Each of us has that in his nature which is incommunicably unique, some small knot which is obscurely impervious and resistant. In Theodora this element is diffused much more generally throughout her nature. She was brought up at Meroë, an old plain 'honest' house, surrounded by ancient trees and hills of black rock which had for all its beauty something marred and unpromising about it. Things were always tumbling down; it was called 'Rackan'-Ruin Hollow' by the neighbours. The prevailing note of her childhood was awkwardness. She was awkward in her relations with the family, particularly with her self-centred mother and with the pretty 'normal' sister, Fanny. To her mother she was odd and difficult. She could not stitch a sampler neatly or play the piano brightly like Fanny. She had a kind of inarticulate intimacy with her father, in which there were moments of exaltation. But she was puzzled and hurt by his moody incomprehension. 'She was oppressed by a weight of sadness, that nobody would lift, because nobody would ever know that she was shouldering it. Least of all Father, who was thick, and mysterious as a tree, but also hollow. . . .' She was thin and sallow as a little girl, strange to her confident family, peculiar to the strong and wholesome servants. Away at school she began to get used to contempt and to distance. 'The long dark slommacky thing in the striped dress? That is Theodora Goodman.' There was no natural flow of communication between her and others. People seemed to her to group themselves into the arbitrary positions of statues. 'But sometimes a silence or a presence seemed to emanate a will of its own, and this was what she resented. The militant will in an intake of breath. Then she could hate the cut of a nostril, the droop of an eyelid above an eye.'

Negation in Theodora's life was almost a routine. But there were in it moments, if not of illumination, at least of escape from the prison of self. Even to call them moments of release may be too strong. Perhaps they were moments trembling on the brink of release. They occurred in her relationships with the very young, with Lou her niece at the beginning of the novel, with the boy Zack at the end of her life, with certain persons whom she met only glancingly and whose contact with her seemed exempt from the painful, spiny conditions of ordinary life, like an odd, casual tramp who was given his dinner on the verandah, or the enigmatic Syrian pedlar.

Once when the Syrian left, Theodora went with him some of the way. In the white-lit winter evening her legs grew longer with the strides she took. Her hair flew. She had increased. She walked outside a distinct world, on which the grass quivered with a clear moisture, and the earth rang. In this state, in which rocks might at any moment open, or words convey meaning, she stood and watched the Syrian go. His silence slipped past. The hills settled into shapelessness. She was left with the trembling of her knees.

Sometimes the moments occurred in an activity, when she shot with her father, listened to music, or when she touched the children. 'Since her mother's death she could not say with conviction: I am I. But the touch of hands restores the lost identity. The children would ratify her freedom.'

But mostly humanity failed either as the occasion or the means of release, even those who seemed most apt, like her friend Violet Adams at school, or the rich, urbane Huntly Clarkson with whom she almost had a kind of muted love-affair in later life. Things helped more: things like the filigree ball which filled with subtle fire when the children rolled its distorted hollow sphere across the drawing-room carpet. Or other things, for example the rose. 'Because she felt her own awkwardness. After she had hidden in the garden, she looked at her hands, that were never moved to do the things that Fanny did. But her hands touched, her hands became the shape of rose, she knew it in its utmost intimacy.' Throughout this phase of the novel the reader is conscious of how vividly present things are to Theodora—or perhaps better how vividly present she feels herself to be to them; and simultaneously aware of the powerful poetic sense of concrete existence with which the novelist conveys not only the outline but the bulk and grain and energy of things. Patrick White in this part of the work is the poet of the physics of things. But the intrinsic energy of the things which he communicates is a physical energy. Things do not, like persons, protect themselves by keeping others at 'a moral distance'. They are open. They lie there, full of a secret life and ready to be entered into. 'I shall never overcome the distances, felt Theodora, and because she was like this, she felt consolation in the deal mirror in the room for four.' But with things she could overcome the distances. She could become the stick drifting in the water or the hawk tearing its prey.

Once the hawk flew down, straight and sure, out of the skeleton forest. He was a little hawk, with a reddish-golden eye, that looked at her as he stood on the sheep's carcass, and coldly tore through the dead wool. The little hawk tore and paused, tore and paused. Soon he would tear through the wool and the maggots and reach the offal in the belly of the sheep. Theodora looked at the hawk. She could not judge his act, because her eye had contracted, it was reddish-gold, and her curved face cut the wind. Death, said Father, lasts for a long time. Like the bones of the sheep that would lie, and dry, and whiten, and clatter under horses. But the act of the hawk, which she watched, hawk-like, was a moment of shrill beauty that rose above the endlessness of bones. The red eye spoke of worlds that were brief and fierce.

What we see in such episodes is *becoming*, that kind of knowledge which Coleridge described as 'the coincidence of an object and subject'. The human mind craves to know, and the closer its knowledge is to being, the better. Knowledge in this sense for Theodora was impossible in respect of other people, even those in her own family and household. But the possibility of union with things was endless and neither she nor they ever stood back from it. This view of Theodora is fixed in the snapshot—a curiously static moment between the mobility of the first and the tumult of the second part of the novel. Theodora is sitting with her niece Lou 'her own arm round the child . . . a formal gesture of protection, scarcely flesh', and the child speaks to her:

'I wish . . .,' said Lou.
'What do you wish?'
'I wish I was you, Aunt Theo.'
And now Theodora asked why.
'Because you know things,' said Lou.
'Such as?'
'Oh,' she said, 'things.'

'Things' continue to figure in the second part of the novel, *Jardin Exotique*, still pressing on the reader their dense and positive existence. But they are solid splinters in a melting universe. They are objects which do not carry with them any strong suggestion of an objective world. Here is a passage in which objects, sharply individualised and palpably present float in a vaguely moving medium. The system of relations which might connect them to a world that includes more than Theodora is abolished.

It was perhaps *plus modeste*, but recognisable, from the objects she had put there in the morning as a safeguard, the darning egg, the dictionary, and the superfluous leather writing case. Hearing the fainter slippers of Henriette, listening to her own silence form in the small room, Theodora loved her sponge. There are moments, she admitted, when it is necessary to return to the boxes for which we were made. And now the small room was a box with paper roses pasted on the sides. Theodora walked across the carpet, frayed by similar feet in modest circumstances, with arches that have a tendency to fall, in shoes that soon must be mended. She took off a garnet ring which had been her mother's but which had changed its expression, like most inherited things. She put it on the dressing table, inside the handkerchief sachet, which was the garnet's place. I am preparing for bed, she saw. But in performing this act for the first time, she knew she did not really control her bones, and that the curtain of her flesh must blow, like walls which are no longer walls. She took off one shoe, with its steel buckle and its rather long vamp. Standing with it in her hand, her identity became uncertain. She looked with sadness at the little hitherto safe microcosm of the darning egg and waited for the rose wall to fall.

Although the narrative is packed with things and persons (but persons who have become a kind of thing, a projection of Theodora's past, of her reading, of her fantasy and of her desperation), the action retreats more and more into a subjective, and finally a solipsistic world. Everything is consumed in Theodora's private passion to know, or rather to become, since that is the only kind of knowledge she is now capable of, knowing in any other sense implying an inadmissible detachment in Theodora and an intolerable independence of existence on the part of another. I may have suggested that this is the result of a concentrated activity on Theodora's part, but in fact, just as the content is more like a dream, so the state is more like a sleep, a letting go.

> 'You must relax, Theodora Goodman,' said Mrs Rapallo. 'You must relax and float. You will find that figures will evolve, squares, chains, and galops. Sometimes you will place one hand on your hip, sometimes you will feel the hand of your partner in the small of the back. But believe me, the essential is to relax.'

At the end of this delirium sequence Theodora has lost even the minimum grip on the outside world. There is an absolute coherence in the whole and in the parts, but it is the logic of the utter loneliness of madness. Theodora herself at the end has become only one more object among a mass of other objects. She has at last escaped from the prison of self which is now simply an empty cell.

At the start of the concluding phase of the novel, Theodora is discovered drifting passively across the Middle West of the United States. The tone is quiet and withdrawn and a welcome change after the frantic and sometimes strident agitation of the too long and rather repetitive scenes of Theodora's mental disintegration. This part of the novel serves three purposes. First, it completes the simple narrative line which had made her leave Australia to travel after her mother's death and which now sends her on her way home after her breakdown in Europe. This final part links up in sobriety of manner with the first part of the novel and offers a realistic setting for the hallucinatory experiences of the middle section. Secondly, it completes the reconstruction of mental collapse which is the psychological material or theme of the novel. Theodora is now simply something prolonged by various external bits of circumstantial evidence like sheaves of railroad and steamship tickets. Her relationships with others are flat and external except, perhaps, for a fleeting moment of 'rare alliance' with someone constitutionally like herself, her father in childhood and the little boy Zak when she is forty-five. There is a continuity between her child's awkwardness with others and her adult's immeasurable remoteness.

Thirdly, the novel's conclusion suggests not a solution but a partial resolution of the spiritual experience which is central to it. Suffering or the acceptance of suffering pares away everything gratuitous and merely selfish and leaves the sufferer with a special quality of wholeness and unity, like the fundamental unity of bone. Such lucid and simple wholeness is necessary for those who will come to possess a sense of the purity of being. Theodora has now become capable even of hearing 'the difference between doing and being. The corn could not help itself. It was. The man scrabbled on the surface of life. . . .' Theodora, disordered and insane, is utterly herself. Through the abolition of her personal identity, or perhaps of her personality as it is understood by others, she has come 'a little closer to humility, to anonymity, to pureness of being'. Or to use the Coleridgean terminology with which I began, every image which the personality might assume has been cancelled and she is left simply with her totally unalloyed individuality which is something deeper and more valuable even than reason itself. 'In the house above the disintegrating world, light and silence ate into the hard, resisting barriers of reason, hinting at some ultimate moment of clear vision.'

This last quotation is perhaps a clue to an explanation of one's final feeling of dissatisfaction with the novel. Because *The Aunt's Story* is a novel, not a spiritual treatise, and one cannot but suspect that the author himself is looking for some 'ultimate moment of clear vision'. It is a novel, I think, which is a failure when judged as a novel and by the highest standards—standards which Patrick White's own work make appropriate. It is certainly a serious and powerful production, it takes in a great span of experience, it has the most perceptive insight into neurotic psychology, and it at no

G

point backs away from a difficult, important theme. Its deficiency lies in the too prominent presence of the author and in the excessively positive interference by him with the natural significance of his material. He himself is too personally engaged in racking his fiction into the shape of spiritual truth. His hand is too clearly evident on too many occasions forcefully conferring upon character and scenery the status of symbolism. These weaknesses are more serious I think than an occasional clumsiness of diction or an uncontrolled rioting of imagery or unimaginative and ugly uses of syntax. *The Aunt's Story* is a brilliant and daring novel but one in which the art is too submissive to the author's will.

The sense the reader has—the intermittent sense I hasten to emphasise—of the author manipulating the material from the outside in the interest of an idea—is wholly absent from the novel I turn to now, *The Tree of Man*. Here the intention is sunk in the art, the will quite submerged in the fiction. The author's design is gradually composed by what is latent in the situation, and it appears in the end with the flawed clarity and stumbling incoherence which belong to the pattern of a living art, and which are ultimately much more powerfully convincing than any application of an *a priori* design. There is a biblical simplicity and universality about the situation in which a man establishes not simply a home but a place, and constructs it out of the wilderness; in the way in which he first appears as the unnamed man, an anonymous representative of a future race; in the way he takes a wife and founds a family; in the way in which what is wrong in the original pair works itself out in the corruption of the children. What is wrong lies, generally, in the connection of husband and wife; it is the product—must we not say the inevitable product?—of any real relationship. But if it is to be located more precisely, it lies in the wife. The husband is a good man, with the special dignity of those whose life and work are part of a more inclusive natural rhythm. He is a man in whom sturdy, ordinary decency is raised to the level of virtue. He is a peasant, but a peasant in a land which had never known, never been subjected to, an aristocracy. The wife, on the other hand, is a sharper, neater intelligence and has a much higher degree of self-limited interest. She is the wiry, nervy cockney Eve, quick, strong and narrow. The man's is a concrete goodness, the expression of a style of character and life. His whole being is manifest in every action and relationship. The wife is more reflectively self-conscious; there is a greater discrepancy between herself and her conduct, and that, given her upbringing and background, implies, when she is not pressed by the urgencies of life, a disposition towards dreamy romanticism, a characteristic which brings about her lapse into sensuality and infidelity. Concupiscence in her case is as much a matter of discontent as of passion. It is provoked by the romanticism which is part of her nature and which contrasts with the strong and humble realism of her husband. *Her* romanticism becomes enfeebled in her daughter into the exquisitely ugly cult of Australian gentility. *His* realism becomes in his son, where it is uninformed by the kind of sanity which puts one into one's place in a larger, more permanent scheme, the realism of power, which in the boy's situation means petty crime and the more sordid kinds of delinquency.

There is a certain thickness of texture in the manner and idiom of *The Tree of Man* which contrasts with the intensity and neurotic fineness of *The Aunt's Story* but which is in keeping with the centrality and solidity of the common human experience it deals with. It comes out in the feeling for the land which is the sustaining support for everything that takes place throughout. It is a double feeling both for the creative force in the earth and for the homely forms and shapes that man can make it assume. Here is a passage from the beginning of the novel in which Stan Parker, faced with the power of the bush, turns upon it in a kind of loving war to make it expressive of human nature.

So they reached their destination, and ate, and slept, and in the morning of frost, beside the ashes of a fire, were faced with the prospect of leading some kind of life. Of making that life purposeful. Of opposing silence and rock and tree. It does not seem possible in a world of frost.

That world was still imprisoned, just as the intentions were, coldly, sulkily. Grass that is sometimes flesh beneath the teeth would have splintered now, sharp as glass. Rocks that might have contracted physically had grown in hostility during the night. The air drank at the warm bodies of birds to swallow them in flight.

But no bird fell.

Instead, they continued to chafe the silence. And the young man, after sighing a good deal, and turning in his bags, in which the crumbs of chaff still tickled and a flea or two kept him company, flung himself into the morning. There was no other way.

But to scrape the ash, but to hew with the whole body as well as axe the gray hunks of fallen wood, but to stamp the blood to life, and the ground thawing took life too, the long ribbons of grass bending and moving as the sun released, the rocks settling into peace of recovered sun, the glug and tumble of water slowly at first, heard again somewhere, the sun climbing ever, with towards it smoke thin but certain that the man made.

The wife too has a feeling for the natural force of the land, but in her it is shown in a preference for its products, for the cows and cabbages and the house. Her husband submitted himself wholly to the land. He accepted the omnipotence of the Australian distance but she hated the wind and the distance and the road and had for them a sort of jealousy as things she could never possess. The husband responded always to presence and actuality, but the wife could sympathise only with forms she could understand and control. She was also conscious of and frayed by what was absent. The love of the two was from the beginning flawed by this tension between them, an imperfection which makes it all the more convincingly human. In a way the wife longs for the kind of expression the man is incapable of.

So instead of telling her smooth things, that were not his anyway, he took her hand over the remnants of their sorry meal. The bones of his hand were his, and could better express the poem that was locked inside him and that would never otherwise be released. His hand knew stone and iron, and was familiar with the least shudder of wood. It trembled a little, however, learning the language of flesh.

The two passages I have quoted—especially perhaps the second, and in that particularly the phrase, 'the language of flesh'—confirm the suggestion I made before that *The Tree of Man* displays a palpable thickness of texture. It is evident primarily in the physical, substantial quality of a language which is highly appropriate in a novel intent on exploring the intimations of ordinary life, and of life, in particular, which sucks its vitality from the soil. ('Intimations', of course, include not only the steady staple, not only the corporeal, the grubby and the wretched in life, but also the poetic and mysterious which the novel testifies at every point is deeply involved in the tritest human existence.) This thickness of texture, then, shows itself at the centre of the novel in the solidity with which the characters and experience of Stan and Amy are constructed—a sculpting of resistant material—not only in their growth from ignorance to experience but also, and very beautifully, in their ageing: in the stiffening of a knee; in the way Stan's mouth becomes tight and a bit ironic when he recognises that uprooting a stone, which he could once have done with a single delighted effort, now leaves him shattered and gasping; in the transformation of motion from silky smoothness to something brittle and chalky. But it also shows itself in the densely peopled context, and in the almost Dickensian prodigality with which subordinate characters and minor movements in the novel are presented with depth and body. A swarm of characters crowds round the protagonists, each offering his own modification of a general human stuff or force, and together composing a world positively writhing with reality. There is a careless, spilling power in Patrick White's habit of putting into a corner of his novel characters which would sustain another novelist through several chapters: people, for example, like the innocent, sinuous Con the Greek; or the goitred spinster Dol Quigley and her imbecile brother Bub; or the dry solicitor Dudley Forsdyke, Thelma's husband, who was 'so used to examining reports on living that he had been made drunk suddenly by the smell of life [which] came up at him down the ploughed field and down the wet hill'; or Mrs O'Dowd, all flabby flesh and mustard-sharp speech, whose death-scene is a superb comic achievement, sardonic, accurate, immensely funny and quite unmocking. Here is one of those intensely living transients, Horrie Bourke, who had befriended and been swindled by Stan's son Ray:

> He was a fat old man with veins in his face, brimming over with the injustice that had been done him, and afraid that someday, if not soon, even tomorrow perhaps, he would have a stroke. So that mixed up with the tears that he shed for the son who was not his but might have been, a recipient of presents as well as a giver of them, was hate for the

healthy young man, whose muscles were impressive in his singlet, who stood laughing by the dung heap in a sheen of horses, and threatened him callously with a seizure.

These characters carry the strong stamp of a tradition, the tradition, in fact, of humours as modified by Dickens, to which the acute observation of the author adds the crackle and tang of Australia. But since Patrick White's observation is enlivened by what one must call a religious respect for the quality of pure being, all his characters, even the minor ones, manifest also a nature in which there is always latent the possibility of spiritual experience, so that a dimension of life seldom present in the humours tradition itself, increases and complicates the stature of his people. The exception to these remarks is the character of Madeleine, a Christabel or rather Lady of Shalott-like figure, who becomes the focus of Amy's romanticism as she rides enigmatically round the country on a splendid horse, who when she is rescued from the great fire by Stan stirs his lust (in some way, I must confess, inexplicable to me), and who finally becomes the companion of the daughter Thelma in her well-bred round. She is the one failure in realisation in the novel, the one gratuitous and unconvincing gesture.

I have referred to one literary tradition. Another and relevant one, again influencing the shape of the novel, is the tradition of the four elements of nature. The novel begins with an assertion, reminiscent of Genesis, of the power of the land; it concludes with an affirmation of the continuity of the earth's life: 'So that in the end there were the trees. The boy walking through them with his head drooping as he increased in stature. Putting out shoots of green thought. So that, in the end, there was no end.' In between there are great set pieces (although it does an injustice to what are constituents of a living organism to think of them as tableaux or extractable scenes) on the wind, on the fire and the flood. This combination of ancient cosmology and biblical drama cannot be accidental. It concentrates in a metaphor, which of course is what it is, the author's sense of the intimacy of life and land. The scope of the whole novel is enlarged and deepened by this cosmic sense, and it is something which the reader feels wholly right in that it offers a context, both a ground and background, for the author's vision of human nature. I can best describe that vision by saying that it sees life as a redemption. The presence of human life on the land itself, so nakedly exposed at the beginning of the novel, imposes on man the limitations and imperfection which constitute a kind of unwilled fall. Suffering is a function of that fall, of that existence in time and place. Stan's life dramatises both the actuality of the fall *and* the possibilities contained in human nature itself for healing and redemption. It shows the redemptive initiative coming from within human nature itself and being set in train, not by an act of the will, but by a condition, the condition of simplicity which is the unfretful working out, within some larger but mysterious pattern, of what the individual nature is, of what the individual person signifies.

Just as *The Aunt's Story* showed how neurosis could be the means to an apprehension fuller than the conventionally 'normal' one, so *The Tree of Man* shows the capacity of decent ordinariness to be transformed into a higher order of existence altogether. It requires of course a kind of genius, the genius for *becoming* in Theodora, the genius for *staying* in Stan. There was always an intrinsic fidelity between Stan's inmost nature and each manifestation of it. This loyalty, or stubbornness, when it is complete, produces a special human perfection, intensely 'natural' and in harmony with the natural rhythm of the land and the weather and the bases of physical existence which had so much to do with producing and ripening it. Natural, certainly, in this sense, and thoroughly human but also fine and capable of development into a maturity that is truly spiritual. We see the result of this faculty for persistence at a point in the novel just before Stan's death when he sits in his old man's chair on the grass in the winter afternoon. He was shrinking all the time. He no longer wanted to speak to people. He was possessed by what he saw, or was. 'His eyes had been reduced to a rudimentary shape, through which they observed, you felt, a version of objects that was possibly true.' A young evangelist, foaming with self-indulgent revivalist fervour, wants to convert the old man from his supposed indifference to salvation, although what he sees as indifference is more truly what Henry James called 'the almost helpless detachment of the short-sighted individual soul'.[1] He tells Stan melodramatic stories of the dissolute life of drinking and womanising—even coloured womanising!—he himself had been rescued from. And if he, why not the old man?

> The old man was intensely unhappy.
> When the young one had finished his orgasm, he presented the open palms of his hands and told how he had knelt upon his knees, and grace descended on him.
> 'This can happen to you too,' he said, kneeling on one knee, and sweating at every pore.
> The old man cleared his throat. 'I'm not sure whether I am intended to be saved,' he said.
> The evangelist smiled with youthful incredulity. No subtleties would escape the steam roller of faith. 'You don't understand,' he said smilingly.
> If you can understand, at your age, what I have been struggling with all my life, then it is a miracle, thought the old man.
> He spat on the ground in front of him. He had been sitting for some time in one position, and had on his chest a heaviness of phlegm.
> 'I am too old,' he said colourlessly.
> He was tired really. He wanted to be left alone.
> 'But the glories of salvation,' persisted the evangelist, whose hair went up in even waves, 'these great glories are everybody's for the asking, just by a putting out of the hand.'
> The old man fidgeted. He was not saying anything. Great glories were glittering in the afternoon. He had already been a little dazzled.
> 'You are not stubborn, friend?'
> 'I would not be here if I was not stubborn,' said the old man.
> 'Don't you believe in God, perhaps?' asked the evangelist, who had begun to look around him and to feel the necessity for some further stimulus of confession. 'I can show you books,' he yawned.
> Then the old man, who had been cornered long enough, saw, through perversity perhaps, but with his own eyes. He was illuminated.
> He pointed with his stick at the gob of spittle.
> 'That is God,' he said.
> As it lay glittering intensely and personally on the ground.
> The young man frowned rather. You met all kinds.

The old man's astounding remark is not an isolated statement which could be checked or corrected or rebutted. It is an utterance

---

[1] *Turgenev and Tolstoy*, 1897

which includes and is the climax of a life, a life lived with stubborn integrity. What the old man sees—'a version of objects that was possibly true'—is a function of what he is, and what he is enables him to see in the great glories glittering in the afternoon, and in the gob glittering intensely and personally on the ground, that quality which they and it share with God—an incandescent quality of pure being.

This is a tremendous note to finish on. Striking a tremendous note is something Patrick White has a strong predilection for. And perhaps this is not simply a personal bias but the consequence of the position of an Australian writer, or at least of one with gifts like his. He has the use of a medium, the English language, of such resource that no reach of imagination or any conceivable theme is beyond it. Patrick White has the medium, but he also has the courage of his creative power (and this is the peculiarly Australian addition) undiminished and unthinned by any failure of nerve caused by consideration of the oppressive excellence of what others in his immediate tradition have done. He joins together the advantages of the medium and the relative absence of masters or competitors. We accept 'the tremendous note', because, as I have suggested before, the ideal has been totally enclosed in a stubby, grainy actuality. Or to adapt an idiom of Henry James,[1] Stan can be 'the striking figured symbol' he is just because he is 'a thoroughly pictured creature'. And we must add to this enclosure of the symbol within the roughness of reality, the skill and patience with which the continuity of Stan's nature is elucidated. There is a ratio of proportion between the wholly transformed old man with his vision of the glittering miracles of existence from gob to God, and the wiry stripling who with an unblemished and wholly unwarranted faith sets himself to humanise the wilderness.

Mention of the wilderness leads me naturally to *Voss* which was published in 1957. *The Tree of Man* and *Voss* represent Patrick White's different reactions to what he spoke of as his panic at the exaltation of the average.

In all directions stretched the Great Australian Emptiness, in which the mind is the least of possessions, in which the rich man is the

[1] *Preface* to *What Maisie Knew*

important man, in which the schoolmaster and the journalist rule what intellectual roost there is, in which beautiful youths and girls stare at life through blind blue eyes, in which human teeth fall like autumn leaves, the buttocks of cars grow hourly glassier, food means cake and steak, muscles prevail, and the march of material ugliness does not raise a quiver from the average nerve.[1]

The Tree of Man burrows into the commonplace; *Voss* reconstructs the extreme. Patrick White describes its origins himself:

Afterwards I wrote *Voss*, possibly conceived during the early days of the Blitz, when I sat reading Eyre's *Journal* in a London bed-sitting room. Nourished by months spent trapesing backwards and forwards across the Egyptian and Cyrenaican deserts, influenced by the arch-megalomaniac of the day, the idea finally matured after reading contemporary accounts of Leichardt's expeditions and A. H. Chisholm's *Strange New World* on returning to Australia.[2]

The wilderness which was to be domesticated in *The Tree of Man* in *Voss* is to school the hero. If we use a biblical analogy, which seems distinctly appropriate to the character of Patrick White's work, we can say that *The Tree of Man* is his version of Genesis and Redemption, and *Voss* his John the Baptist. (But leading to what Christ, the reader may wonder. The answer, if there is an answer, suggested by the novel, seems to be some intrinsic or buried Christ in Voss himself.)

Voss is simply organised into three parts: the preparation for the expedition, the journey in 1845 across the continent itself, and the aftermath which consists largely of a second minor expedition to investigate the calamity of the original exploration. The first part is a remarkable 'composition' in its own right, which gives me the opportunity to notice a gift of Patrick White's I have not referred to yet, namely his sensitive historical imagination. Nineteenth-century Sydney, an English provincial city set down on the Pacific shore, with its cathedral, barracks and public gardens (a significant collocation), presses its identity upon one. White is engaged with the mercantile part of this society which lives in solid stone houses filled with mahogany furniture, books of sermons, gazeteers and almanacs, desks covered with red tooled leather, pieces of engraved

---

[1] *Australian Letters*, I, 3, 1958   [2] *Ibid*

silver, and tightly buttoned, slippery chairs. These merchants are used to fine clothes and rich food, have an almost mystical—certainly a more than economic—absorption in money, are deferential to the local gentry, and both consciously above, and genuinely under an obligation towards, their inferiors. They observe a cramped but genuine moral code and they are especially sensitive about the respectability it earns. Patrick White catches exactly the whiff of this plum-cake world of colonial gentility, strangely surrounded by mysterious gardens full of feathery bamboos, camellia bushes and scurfy native paperbarks. The people are as convincing as the setting. Massed in the middle is the strongly physical presence of the Bonner family, the complacent husband, his comfortable wife, their creamy daughter and her rubicund young officer.

Wealthy by colonial standards, the merchant had made money in a solid business, out of Irish linens and Swiss muslins, damask, and huckaback, and flannel, green baize, and India twills. The best-quality gold leaf was used to celebrate the name of EDMUND BONNER—ENGLISH DRAPER, and ladies driving down George Street, the wives of officers and graziers, in barouche and brougham, would bow to that respectable man. Why, on several occasions, he had even been consulted in confidence, he told, by Lady G—, who was so kind as to accept a tablecloth and several pair of linen sheets.

At each end of the scale of intelligence of which the Bonners are, as it were, the norm, are murmurous reminders of different possibilities. At one end is the squat pregnant maid Rose, whose baby Laura Trevelyan will eventually adopt as her own, an elemental being, close to the animals and the instinctive organic world. At the other is Laura Trevelyan, isolated in her small circle by her cool, 'Cambridge' intelligence and taste for the things of the mind. She meets Voss at a time when she is tortured by the possibility of losing her religious faith. Voss is a totally new experience for her, alien both to her conventional connections and to her own preference for moderate rationality. He was like lightning or inspiration, and inspiration, the uncalled for, the unearned experience, is important in a novel which is to be devoted in a major way to exploring the pure and abstract will: important, that is, as another

possibility or dimension in human experience. The will causes its
consequences but 'inspiration descends only in flashes, to clothe
circumstances; it is not stored up in a barrel, like salt herrings, to be
doled out'. Voss, the extraordinary German, affects her like poetry
so that she deserted when she was with him 'that rational level to
which she was determined to adhere' and her thoughts became
natural and passionate. The passivity of her existence flares into
intensity in his presence. She appreciates him in a way that no
others in her circle can but she is also still sufficiently 'rational' to
understand his nature.

> 'You are so vast and ugly,' Laura Trevelyan was repeating the
> words; 'I can imagine some desert, with rocks, rocks of prejudice, and,
> yes, even hatred. You are so isolated. That is why you are fascinated
> by the prospect of desert places, in which you will find your own
> situation taken for granted, or more than that, exalted. You sometimes
> scatter kind words or bits of poetry to people, who soon realise the
> extent of their illusion. Everything is for yourself. Human emotions,
> when you have them, are quite flattering to you. If those emotions
> strike sparks from others, that also is flattering. But most flattering, I
> think, when you experience it, is the hatred, or even the mere irritation
> of weaker characters.'

Patrick White is seldom able to keep within the limit of what is
strictly necessary to his design. He loves the pure creative play or
flourish. And yet by the end of this first movement—not, I think, an
inappropriate term—a considerable amount of the work of the
novel has been completed and the rest set in train. The dowdy town
and the easy country around it, against which the harshness of the
desert will be measured, are clearly in the reader's mind; the decent
average of the population against which the ferociously extreme
nature of Voss can be tested has been established; the relationship
of Voss and Laura has been initiated, a relationship which, since
they never meet again, is carried on in the imagination of each and
opened up to the reader by their correspondence. The members of
the group accompanying Voss have been delineated with just that
right degree of definition to mark them off as separate persons and
yet to keep them united in a single party. Above all the preliminary
work on the gigantic figure of Voss is carried firmly through.

We first see Voss—announced by the puzzled maid as 'a kind of foreign gentleman'—squirming in a social encounter with Laura, but it is rapidly borne in on the reader that his unease is not by any means a mere discomfort at unfamiliar modes of decorum. Voss is one whose powers are concentrated with ferocious intensity upon an inner life. The outer world is either a nuisance or a menace. 'All that was external to himself he mistrusted, and was happiest in silence, which is immeasurable, like distance, and the potentialities of self.' His general seediness and frayed clothes, his contempt of social niceties clothe the arrogance of an unnatural confidence. He was capable of simplicity and sincerity although it was very hard for a stranger to recognise these feelings in him. The approach of others was a threat, much more destructive to his personality than thirst or fever or physical exhaustion. The impulse of Voss's actions was not any general belief or idea but the pure shape of the will which has no content—no describable content—only force and direction. The compulsion he felt to cross the continent came from the desire to fulfil his own nature or, more correctly and more narrowly, came from the force of his will. He was placed in a situation in which the conquering of the desert might seem natural to others for reasons of economics or geography or knowledge itself, and Voss is willing to make an outward accommodation to such notions. In reality for Voss the expedition was a personal wrestling with the continent, the only opponent his pride would acknowledge as adequate. 'Deserts prefer to resist history and develop along their own lines'; they have, that is, a natural hostility to submitting to the will of man and they are therefore a proper target for Voss's colossal pride.

'Yes,' answered Voss, without hesitation. 'I will cross the continent from one end to the other. I have every intention to know it with my heart. Why I am pursued by this necessity, it is no more possible for me to tell than it is for you, who have made my acquaintance only before yesterday.'

In the second phase of the novel two lines of narrative are sustained. In one the expedition is conducted through more and more difficult, and finally brutal, country towards its disastrous end; in the other the relationship of Voss and Laura is developed in a series of meditations and (unreceived) letters. The two worlds of actuality and possibility are kept in touch and the latter, it is suggested, offers in the end a possibility of salvation to the former. There is a passage at one point in the journey in which this touching of two orders of existence is itself used as an image of the land.

> Over all this scene, which was more a shimmer than the architecture of landscape, palpitated extraordinary butterflies. Nothing had been seen yet to compare with their colours, opening and closing, opening and closing. Indeed, by the addition of this pair of hinges, the world of semblance communicated with the world of dream.

Not only in the architecture of landscape but also in the architecture of people the two worlds of semblance and dream communicate with each other.

Each member of the party obeys the logic of his own nature and responds to the sufferings of the journey in his own way. But all the physical horrors are subservient to the monstrous, Marlovian figure of Voss. He is more intent and successful than any harshness of geography or disease in searching out the weaknesses of his companions. In a situation in which life itself depends upon the naked force of will, he is seen, terrifyingly, to concentrate in himself an essential part of everyone else's humanity. Everyone's will is fused into Voss's. The question posed is whether any human situation can be just the realisation of a pure abstraction like the will. Each member of the party clings to something else, to some other standard supplied by a different life—the young man Frank le Mesurier to his poetry, Judd the ex-convict to the common kindness of a family man, Palfreyman to his science and his religion, Turner and Angus to a protective selfishness. But all in the end are consumed by the violence of Voss's burning will. 'By some process of chemical choice, the cavalcade had resolved itself into immutable component parts. No one denied that Mr Voss was the first, the burning element, that consumed obstacles, as well as indifference in others.' The aborigines are the one form of humanity which evades the absoluteness of Voss's control. Their existence is purely a passage from moment to moment, hardly directed at all by the conscious will. They drift as easily as smoke and are as responsive to the play of the physical life about them. They cannot in fact be positively separated from it, they never take on sufficient antagonist force for Voss to meet and overcome. It is 'right', in keeping with the nature of the fiction itself, that it should be these, surviving as they do by the negation of active will, who in the horrifying end, when the party has split into two fragments, destroy Voss.

If the first narrative line has to do with the world of 'semblance' or reality, the physical progress of the expedition itself, the second has to do with the world of 'dream' and the life of the spirit; and this as it is focussed in the relationship of Voss and Laura. (Not that the Voss-Laura relationship is the sole subject-matter: there is also much sharp—and comic—social observation of the colonial scene.) The only physical substratum for the relationship is the few brief meetings of Voss and Laura before the expedition leaves. On this the imagination of each, moved by deep emotional hunger, constructs a pattern of feeling of great richness, delicacy and conviction. The fact that the relationship evolves by means of an intense and reciprocal empathy causes the reader no incredulity or discomfort because he senses an essential propriety between the nature of the experience and its poetic treatment. If a writer has the creative strength, the sincerity and the tact in realisation which Patrick White shows himself abundantly to possess, he can, and the reader accepts that he can, allow himself a considerable degree of freedom from the logic of a straight-forward representational method. The relationship of Voss and Laura, then, progresses from its simple beginning by means of a sympathetic parallelism into a 'fearful symmetry'. I use the famous phrase advisedly to suggest that blend of love, terror and harmony which the relationship achieves in the moments before Voss and Laura are finally destroyed, he by the journey, she, in resonance, by a total collapse of mind and body.

The novel concludes quietly in the third section in a muted repetition and reminiscence of the positive vision—never too firmly or abstractly formulated—generated by the substance of the novel. (Having said which I must immediately correct myself: never, except at one place, where a melodramatic analogy between Christ and Voss—the spear hanging out of his side, washing the feet of his companions, kissing their sores—is clumsily elaborated. Even the fact that this is a memory of the simple-minded Judd, the only survivor of the expedition, doesn't back it with the weight and density of realised experience.) Patrick White uses the psychology of the explorer as a metaphor of man. The explorer lives at extremes, on borders and edges; he is always pushing back the frontiers of suffering, and suffering is the universal experience of extremity uniting man. Voss is the purest example of the explorer's psychology but he is saved from unconvincing super-humanity by a grubby stain of backsliding man. There is a touch of malignancy, the cruelty of vanity, in the way he treats his companions; it was very rarely that he washed their feet. This, paradoxically, makes his—conversion is too revivalist a word—illumination, which is religious in its source and derived from the acceptance which is part of his love for Laura, possible, and when it takes place, convincing. Only the sinful man can become the redeemed man. *Voss* embodies the belief or rather perception of the novelist that simplicity and suffering are the conditions for the re-making of man. The suffering is sustained and terrible; the simplicity only barely and painfully achieved at the point of dissolution.

Voss is a powerful and humane work coloured with the light and soaked with the sweat and personality of Australia. There is a Wordsworthian strength in the novel's sense of the mineral structure and the uniquely luminous quality of the landscape, which is—strangely—heightened by being made available to the reader through the sensibility of the Teutonically alien protagonist, Voss himself. The presence of the discrepant and blundering Voss makes the occasional, wilful perversities of syntax and expression never wholly absent from White's writing less exasperating than usual. In any case they are never so gross as to detract from the novel's essential humanity and the maturity of its art.

In the third section of *Voss* there occur some lines which would make an apt epigraph for *Riders in the Chariot*, published in 1961. 'It was his niece, Laura Trevelyan, who had caused Mr Bonner's world of substance to quake.' Causing the world of substance to quake is the great shaping activity working through *Riders in the Chariot*. The novel follows the favoured White pattern, a strong central conception, a broad and fairly loose design, development by means of a biographical method, and an endless multiplication of palpable detail. The world of substance exposed in the novel includes not only the hard, thick, resistant one of common life and convention but other and odder worlds too: the world of a crazy specimen of the decayed Australian gentry, the world of an unpretentious working woman, the world of a persecuted German Jew, the world of an uprooted aboriginal. In addition each of the characters in which these worlds are defined and examined gives access to one species of a fourfold variety of experience, experience of the natural world, of plants and animals through Miss Hare's nearly non-human instinct for otherness, of integral, simple goodness in Mrs Godbold, the East Anglian immigrant, of the profoundest religious experience in Himmelfarb, the saintly survivor of the Nazi camps, and of art through the painting of Dubbo, the tubercular half-caste. The four lives, their separate worlds and different orders of experience connect, or are violently knotted together, in the small, dry, dusty town of Sarsaparilla. The range, the imaginative scope is extraordinary, and the control of the varied material has that unstressed ease which comes from a total inward familiarity.

What causes the world of substance to quake is the possession by each of the quartet of a special direct, non-discursive apprehension, the apprehension of realities which the world of substance either does not recognise at all or recognises as dangerous and deserving of destruction. This faculty or organ of consciousness is independent of experience in that it is in some sense a quality of genius, a gift, but it is not at all freakish, not attached to the character like an extra limb or head. It makes its presence felt gradually like any other function of the personality and it speaks through the articulation of the characters' lives and in the idiom of action. The consciousness—of which the chariot is the symbol—resides in each of the four, Miss Hare, Mrs Godbold, Dubbo, and Himmelfarb in a form appropriate to the experience of each. But it has, too, qualities in common. This gift of insight is secret, kept and nourished in privacy, and it is recognised only by those who themselves possess it. Suffering is a necessary condition of its development. Only

H

suffering can reduce the person to that state of painfully earned simplicity which is the essential preparation for a clarified consciousness. And again it invariably provokes persecution, whether it is persecution in the home by a companion or in the factory by workmates or more monstrously in Hitler's Germany by the whole of a society.

The four lives through which the author's vision is transmitted—and vision is a strictly appropriate term for Patrick White's religious reading of life—are shown with that marvellous authenticity which comes when minute fidelity of observation is enlivened by imaginative power. The most remarkable in this respect is that of Himmelfarb. Perhaps one would expect a sensitive and sympathetic Australian to have a special feeling for the life of an aboriginal half-caste, a kind of man in which some part of the essential flavour of Australia must lurk, and one would certainly expect Patrick White with *his* background—solid, Victorian, gentlemanly—to be at home with the character and life of poor Miss Hare, who belongs to the same attenuated, genteel blood-group as Theodora Goodman in *The Aunt's Story* (just as Mrs Godbold is obviously related to Stan Parker in *The Tree of Man*). But Himmelfarb, the central figure of the book, is a wholly new creation, European, Jewish, learned, saintly, wholly new, wholly certain and wholly successful. He embodies that special combination of humanity and spirituality, that grounded and aspiring quality, which is a peculiar mark of the Jewish tradition. The ritual and the discipline of Hebrew practice convey a strong tribal and family quality, but there shines through both the remote, utterly pure spirit of the Jewish religion, and more of religion itself.

Patrick White, like Lawrence, believes that direct, intuitional consciousness at its height is religious.[1] Himmelfarb's consciousness or religious imagination, which in the last resort is shown to be

---

[1] *Selected Literary Criticism* (1955), ed. Anthony Beale, p. 105.'... the imagination is a kindled state of consciousness in which intuitional awareness predominates ... imagery is the body of our imaginative life, and our imagination is a great joy and fulfilment to us, for the imagination is a more powerful and more comprehensive flow of consciousness than our ordinary flow. In the flow of the imagination we know in full, mentally and physically at once, in a greater, enkindled awareness. At the maximum of our imagination we are religious.'

something bestowed, not earned, as the wages of effort, is nevertheless not the simple progression of a religious inheritance. It has survived, it has been dented and bruised by, the inertness and prejudice both of himself and his co-religionists, by boredom, doubt, sensuality, actual infidelity, betrayal and persecution. The living residue is a total clarity of understanding of persons and motives, relations and values which exist now for Himmelfarb (as it appears to the reader) absolutely as they are, their pure objectivity unaffected by any disturbing intrusion of self and unblurred by any mist of unconsciousness.

Himmelfarb's blemished growth to this lucidity of perception is seen by the reader, through Patrick White's strength of insight and skill in realisation, as spontaneous in prospect and inevitable in retrospect, a product of the clash of inward condition and outward influence. Sensitivity to the supernatural is shown to be the natural crown of Himmelfarb's persecuted life. Himmelfarb is himself so concretely convincing as a human being that the reader—rightly, I think—supposes Patrick White to be maintaining that openness to the supernatural is the natural conclusion to every man's development. Here, no doubt, a distinction needs to be drawn. The naturalness of the supernatural does not indeed follow from Patrick White's vision of human life, if one concentrates on the human person as an individual. Perhaps the naturalness of the supernatural really means to Patrick White the sacredness of the individual. But the human person also belongs to a community and the community in *Riders in the Chariot* reveals itself as savage and dangerous. Society, in fact, is the natural enemy of the spiritual life. The antagonism may be gross and violent as in Nazi Germany where the Jews were thought of as an abstraction to be cancelled out without a quaver of personal guilt; or it may be rough and mocking, as in the climax of this novel, where Himmelfarb, a surrogate Christ, is hung up by his workmates in a parody of the Crucifixion. The tone of this episode, which could have been an artistic outrage, is carefully calculated to make it acceptable as a realistic piece of action. The note of hearty Australian matiness is sustained throughout in tittering burlesque, in the claimed lack of personal spite, in cruelty maintained at the level of a joke. 'It was possible to practise all manner of cruelties provided the majority might laugh them off as practical jokes. And there was almost no tragedy which could not be given a red nose.' Mr Theobalds, the fat foreman who at the end, in his indolent comfortable way, helps Himmelfarb down from his cross, all the time reducing the temperature of tragedy to that of farce, explains the Australian theory of social cruelty.

'Remember,' Ernie Theobalds continued, 'we have a sense of humour, and when the boys start to horse around, it is that that is gettin' the better of 'em. They can't resist a joke. Even when a man is full of beer, you will find the old sense of humour hard at work underneath. It has to play a joke. See? No offence can be taken where a joke is intended.'

Jocular heartiness as a coat for destructive ferocity makes the episode of Himmelfarb's crucifixion tolerable as fact. But this is only the beginning of the author's intention. Its completion requires releasing a significance larger than that bounded by the limits of realistic action, namely to uncover what Henry James called 'the idea which deeply links in any vision promoted by life'. Here the idea—or concrete perception—is the conflict, ultimate in nature, recurrent in time, between the enlightened consciousness and the habitual understanding of sensible men. That the conflict is ultimate is shown in the total incomprehension of Himmelfarb shown by his workmates and in their puzzled and instinctive malice; that it is recurrent by the author's daring use of the analogy of the Crucifixion. The propriety of this is dependent on the essentially religious character of Patrick White's vision. References to the Crucifixion are deliberate and incantatory, in fact a literary form of the ritual. A ritualistic method is in place because of the fundamentally religious nature of the experience; and because the 'spirit' of religion, however much at odds it is with the 'letter', invariably expresses itself in the 'letter'; and because the 'letter' is hallowed and made effective by ritualistic repetition. Not that Patrick White has wholly avoided the danger of the explicit to which a writer of his kind is liable, particularly when he turns, as he does here, a physical fact into an emblematic rite. There is too great a degree of completeness in the ceremonial repetitiveness of the scene. One worker holds up a cloth to the crucified Himmelfarb's lips; Miss Hare sees the marble shudder and crack in her house, Xanadu; Himmelfarb is taken down from the cross into the arms of Mrs Godbold, one of the faithful women; and poor Mr Rosetree, the renegade Jew, an appealing Judas, commits suicide in his bathroom. Nothing is wanting to complete the reflection of Calvary. But the scene is carried forward by the force of the writer's imagination and by the innocent integrity of his vision. So much energy can safely carry a number of errors of tactics.

Patrick White belongs to a line of novelists whose art embodies a concentrated and dazzling vision of man. Such writers are not manipulators of plot or cultivators of a sensibility or critics of manners or chroniclers of a period. Their art is initiated by their vision and its form is determined more by a force from within than by any extrinsic scaffolding. These writers are not lacking in the capacity for the most inclusive and most significant kind of design. And while in some work of this nature minute particulars tend to melt away in the glow of vision, this is certainly not so with Patrick White, in whose novels the multiple detail is perpetually sharp and fresh. It is somewhere between imaginative power and authenticity and crispness of detail that Patrick White's work is imperfect, in the area where architectural capacity and taste are required. The failure is not in the generating concept nor in the worked-out detail—neither in the idea nor the vocabulary, that is—but somewhere between in what one might call the syntactical structure. *Voss* and *Riders in the Chariot* certainly answer this account, I believe: impressive in the constructive idea, superb in their palpable concreteness, weaker in the passages of transition and apt on occasion to offer neatness and gratuitous accretion in place of organic design. This is the other, feebler side of what I spoke of before as Patrick White's innocent integrity of vision.

One novel exempt from this weakness is *The Solid Mandala* (1966), the story of the Brown twins, shambling, simple-minded Arthur and brittle, 'gifted' Waldo. The movement between idea and material in the novel is vital and unbroken, and the complex theme is as intimate with the dense material as soul with body. The tension between abstract and concrete understanding, which Patrick White is so conscious of, is sustained throughout although it is not frozen in the neat antithesis which these words suggest, one side to each twin. The twins themselves, divided parts of one whole person, by their essentially complementary relationship draw the conflict into the centre of human nature. They dramatise it as a disturbance within man and within the single man. At the same time they act out that impure mixture of love and hate which is both a condition of the relationship of every human being to another and a condition of the attitude of the individual within himself to himself. The double theme makes the novel a tragedy of human incompleteness, and does so in a decidedly trimmer, sparer way than is usual in the earlier novels.

The Solid Mandala begins at a point in time when the two brothers, now old men and at once appealing and repulsive, stumble hand in hand along the main road from Sarsaparilla to Barranugli. They are made almost unbearably present in their hideous, pitiable humanity. The novel swoops backwards and forwards in time from this moment in a natural rhythm which has all the vitality, arbitrariness, muddle and logic of life. There is a structural tension between the tortured misery of Waldo's impotent fury at human limitation and the personal peace of Arthur's acceptance; and it is a tension which in *The Solid Mandala* is wholly enclosed in the work, and not as some of the other novels suggest, a tension unresolved in the author himself. The result is that the narrative mode of *The Solid Mandala* (which has surely benefited from the discipline of the short stories) is altogether quieter and more collected, although the material it is engaged with is principally the anguish and desperation of Waldo; and Patrick White is seldom to be caught out in this novel indulging in what he calls 'efforts to embrace some recalcitrant vastness', something indeed he is himself habitually inclined to. The clarity of the medium allows effective scope for Patrick White's singular gift for producing a richly orchestrated actuality, an actuality marked not only by accuracy of the surface but by the presence of what exists at varying levels underneath. This complexity of perception is evident not only in the treatment of the physical context but in the presentation of the neighbours and the family life of the Browns, and above all in the delineation of Waldo and Arthur.

Patrick White makes great—and functional—play in this novel with the raw, abrasive elements of Australian provincial life. They serve as a base-line against which the reader can measure the intellectual pretensions of Waldo and the direct simplicity of Arthur's goodness. Those names of people and places! Wally Pugh, Mrs Purves, Mrs Musto, Mr Mutton, Norm Croucher (even the dogs are called Scruffy and Runt); as well as O'Halloran Road, Ada Avenue, Sarsaparilla, Barranugli, Shadbolt Lane, Gibber Gunya, Mungindribble. There is an illuminating contrast between the raw ugliness these names stand for and the beautiful and mysterious space of Australia, hardly more than hinted at, it is true, in this novel but still stretching out illimitably on all sides of the suburban pocket. And there is a further contrast between the common attitude of never completely suppressed truculence on the one side, and the half-aggressive idioms in which it is expressed, the mere sounds of which suggest a jutting jaw, and on the other the openness and freedom of a society unsmothered, incredibly so by European standards, by the oppressive weight of the *a priori* and the inherited. As Mr Brown once said to Waldo and Arthur, 'There's too much you boys, reared in the light in an empty country, will never understand. There aren't any shadows in Australia. Or discipline. Every man jack can do what he likes.'

Patrick White has a strong, not always sympathetic, sense of communal life, and the members of this shadowless, self-determining Australian community appear in the novel with a solid and connected existence; and do so whether they are casual figures merely glimpsed momentarily like Waldo's colleagues in the public library (the old municipal!) or the Allwrights who keep the shop Arthur works in, or the rich local eccentric Mrs Musto; or whether they are more fully developed like the immediate neighbours of the Brown family, the dull, decent Poulters or the Feinstein family who, with their Jewish cultivation and intelligence, bring to the general British surliness a further note of comparative definition. This is even truer of the club-footed father and the willowy mother, both so English in their different ways, the one clogged 'in an impasto of nonconformist guilt', the other, before she takes to the sweet sherry bottle in old age, one of those Tennysonian figures from the English country gentry that Patrick White is so fond of, who seem in the modern urban British scene in fact quite as strange as they were in Sarsaparilla. Nourished by the most anaemic abstractions of high-minded rationalism and genteel socialism the Brown parents live a dumbly desperate life, balancing in the air—just—their hopeless aspirations, their painful memories, their present disappointments, their insoluble problems with the twins.

This is the background against which the obscurities of the twins' relationship, drawn out with a spider-web's delicate, intricate accuracy, become a lucent device for the revelation of human nature. We live in our relationships. Our individuality depends on them. These relationships are always, as they were profoundly with the twins, bedded in flesh and fact. But what they become is not a simple extension of what they were. They are never just the effects of antecedent causes. At some point they are open to the bias of a person's nature or his choice, deliberate or implicit, or his disposition or his intentions or his response to others. The relationship of the twins is genetically determined in the profoundest way but its final form is the product of the purposive will as much as the prophetic genes.

In time indeed the relationship of Waldo and Arthur becomes the opposite of what it promised to be. Waldo is the bright child, the quick boy, the promising young man. Arthur is the softheaded, slobbery-mouthed, imperfect creature. But it is Waldo's will that becomes destructive and Waldo who ends with the greater incapacity. Arthur, 'a shingle short', defective in intelligence and speech and physically incompetent, by some sweetness of nature or openness to life becomes—still with all his incapacities—a positive and protective influence. Arthur, with all the poverty of his equipment for entering into life, still fastens on enough of life to construct a rich and healing nature—a soul if not an intelligence.

Any abilities Arthur has are practical. He can milk the cow, make butter, prepare the bread and milk, he likes to work in the local grocer's, and oddly enough he had at school an uncomprehending and infallible gift for doing sums. But his slender resources include a childlike simplicity and an instinct for breaking, in however fuddled a way, into the life of others. So that he had friends and was even loved by women, by Dulcie Feinstein and Mrs Poulter, perhaps as a child, perhaps as a person, or perhaps as both. So much of life was beyond the range of his capacity. He could not understand a fraction of what Waldo mastered. But the limitation of range was accompanied during his life by a deepening, intensifying insight into what Lawrence called 'the realities' or 'the other world of pure being'.[1] The image of that limited range and focussed intensity is his 'solid mandala', the most mysterious of the several glass marbles which he fondles in his pocket and peers into entranced. Images of glass occur frequently in the novel: Arthur and his glass taws and Waldo and a mirror in which he constantly examines not only his appearance but himself and the many faceted crystal of his own mind. Waldo carries to extremity the natural bias we are all born with, that of the solipsist. Experience seems to him always a violation of his enclosed perfection, 'an assault on his privacy'. He was an 'almost' man. He almost had an affair with Dulcie, he almost wrote an essay, he almost completed a poem, his sexual experience with Mrs Poulter was that of a *voyeur*, his closest relationship with his mother was a perverse wearing of her dress after she was dead. His tragedy was that his natural solipsism was flawed from the first by the hateful presence of the other half of his self, Arthur. Even his love for and his dependence upon his brother seemed to him a rape of the self. His very existence, clogged by a twin, who is horrifyingly both himself *and* another, is a contradiction of his own crystalline perfection.

The narrative technique of *The Solid Mandala* is not Patrick White's usual steady tracking of the continuity of time. The material is still in one sense 'biographical', but the procedure here is much more one of shading and emphasis, of varying the point of entrance and sweeping backwards and forwards from there, so that *The Solid Mandala* impresses the reader as a 'composition' rather than the linear progress which is more customary with

[1] *Letters of D. H. Lawrence*, ed. Aldous Huxley, p. 405

Patrick White. This method of massing and concentration is apt for a novel in which the central experience is not drawn out in a development but given as an immediate revelation. The end is very emphatically present in the beginning of *The Solid Mandala*, which starts with the two neglected, aged men, handcuffed by love and hate, and ends—terribly—with Waldo's pure destructive malice and Arthur's terrified and unwarranted guilt. There is an unbroken circular movement connecting the old men, Waldo in his oilskin, Arthur in the old herringbone, 'sidling brittly down the path' for their walk out into the dangerous world in which people lived, and the final horror of Waldo yielding absolutely to the hatred which he had directed at all living things, destroying both himself and whatever of Arthur he is capable of destroying.

Indeed, the structure of the novel is composed of a series of similar movements or concentric circles. The outermost one is made up of ordinary people like Mrs Poulter and Mrs Dunne and the whole community of Sarsaparilla. Inside that there is the tighter circle of the Brown family, and within that again the more intense circle of the brothers, and within that again the light-imprisoning, solid mandala itself, Arthur's favourite glass marble, which becomes by the end of the novel the image, lucid and mysterious, of the depths and contradictions of human nature in every condition: as it exists in the community, in the family, in a pair of friends or lovers or brothers, or in the single individual soul that Waldo and Arthur together compose.

Simultaneity, correspondence, a common centre—these are the marks of the world seen by Patrick White, a religious, poetic and profoundly melancholy spirit. The common centre lies in a clouded paradox, the co-existence of human malice and human goodness which move in and out of one another like the folds of light and darkness in Arthur's glass taw. The co-existence is not an equilibrium: malice (not simply evil or disorder) exists as a settled condition of human life but goodness is a flickering and gratuitous visitation, a pure fluke of genius. Patrick White's writing is not at all given to the inflections of irony. His prose is too tumultuous, his thought unqualified by that complex sagacity which is able to discriminate effortlessly according to a coherent set of standards.

He is not by any means a witty writer. Nevertheless there is a deep irony in the way in which he shows a racy Australian life, physical in its energy and Philistine in its taste, embodying so medieval, or rather so biblical, a vision of man.

Biblical too, Old Testament in fact, is his habit of making the grinding ugliness of the small-town scene and the details of daily life a signal—almost a negative sacrament—of an inward condition rather in the way poverty or disease is used in the Bible. But although there is a distinctly biblical feeling about the tradition of spirituality with which Patrick White's sensibility is saturated, it would be truer to say of the positive part of his attitude towards man that it is religious rather than biblical. It is a concept of goodness which depends upon an unspoilt wholeness of the person and upon what this makes possible, an exact, unsmudged truth of relationship. This is the concrete vision quickening all the best of his work which is focussed with dazzling strength in *The Solid Mandala*. Such goodness, although it may be striven for, cannot be deserved. It is, as I have said already, a stroke of providence or a form of genius, but in any case a gift—and a gift in two senses of the word, both a donation and an endowment—and a gift most likely to be found in the possession of those commonly regarded as blemished or eccentric or disgusting or hateful. With the exception of Stan Parker, who is the saint of ordinariness, all Patrick White's most powerfully realised characters belong to the class he describes in the epigraph to his collection of short stories as 'the burnt ones, the poor unfortunate ones'.

I have been stressing the religious feeling which shines with an almost Franciscan purity and intensity through Patrick White's work. It is the principal constituent of the standard by which he tests the quality of life in individuals and in society, just as it is the main feature in the mind he attempts to project in those who embody most fully what he takes to be a necessary human wisdom. But I should mislead the reader if I seemed to be suggesting that the work exhibits a constant serenity of religious belief. Its religious expression is contorted by more contemporary grimaces and tics. He has much more than his normal share of the current awareness of the nastiness of sex. Apart from *The Tree of Man* where sex for the most part is a tranquil and organic element in the life of Stan and his wife, there is undoubtedly in Patrick White's attitude towards this side of experience a certain flinching distaste which is reminiscent of Eliot. It is a blend of quivering anxiety about the capacity of sex brutally to separate itself from tenderness, and of disgust at its physical, 'excretory' functions. Moreover, the religious quality of his vision is not, as its traditional character leads one to expect, at all sympathetic to the inherited or habitual life of the community. On the contrary he is deeply disturbed by the cruelty of communities and by their inveterate bias in favour of the average, a bias which at the first hint of danger ceases to be a merely comfortable prejudice and turns into a lust for persecution.

The cruelty in Patrick White's reconstruction of human reality is not limited to the bloodshot variety practised by communities against the odd member or the alien intruder. Within the family itself the old, in a rage of incomprehension, torture the young, the young savage the old. Men and women are locked in malice. The individual icily studies the weaknesses of his opponent, calculating where to strike. There is a Manichaean violence in Patrick White's reading of human relationships: on the one side the flow of love so brilliantly exemplified in Daise in *Down at the Dump*, in Stan Parker in *The Tree of Man*, in Himmelfarb in *Riders in the Chariot* and Arthur in *The Solid Mandala*; on the other the conversation of mankind translated as a dialectic of loathing. Rarely do the two come together as mutually confirming elements in an inclusive human order—perhaps only in *The Solid Mandala* do they do so with complete success. Patrick White is a strongly individual, richly gifted, original and highly significant writer. His powers are by any standard remarkable. His achievement is large. His art, which is an essentially poetic discipline, dense and image-ridden and sensitive to the rhythms of Australian speech, is marred by a harking after symbolic symmetry, but it is still a substantial and genuine thing.

We see in his work not only a positive but also a negative revelation. No matter how gifted a writer in Western society, even in so fresh and vital a form of it as the Australian, he cannot, it seems, help reproducing in his sensibility a certain failure of sureness or grasp in the contemporary experience of human nature. A neurotic twist or distortion, the reflection of a defect in our civilisation, forces itself into the work, even when, as with Patrick White, the writer is disposed by temperament and belief to a central and steadily traditional vision of man. An eye so justly accommodated to its object as Patrick White's inevitably brings back an image coloured with the exact stain of the society it scrutinises. Involvement is as much a matter of registration as it is of attitude. The statement of the artist can never be merely a comment; it is always in part the response of a participant. A sensibility so quick and inclusive as Patrick White's, however much it may be spiritually detached from the assumptions ruling contemporary society, is nevertheless bound, as it realises itself in art, to reflect not only the artist's individual vision but the radical disorder of the society it is turned upon.

II   A. D. HOPE

Those who know Australia, particularly certain places like the capital city of Canberra, imperceptible among the trees and overwhelmed by the sky which is so dominant a feature of the *landscape*, will have been struck by the Mediterranean quality of the light. I am reminded of this when I think of the work of the most distinguished of contemporary Australian poets, A. D. Hope. Hope is learned, passionate, sceptical—and in his work there is an insistent, almost fierce sense of a Western Latin tradition. Perhaps one is misled by the analogy of the Latin light. It may be that the creative impulse is discrepancy, an aching consciousness of the dissimilarity between the decorative density of Europe and the emptiness of the arid continent. More probably both impulses work together in the Australian sensibility, work together and work on one another, sharpening into positive existence the Latin elements —not just the linguistic ones—latent in the English language. Certainly, Hope is concerned in a most unusual way for those currently writing in English with order and coherence of feeling and with decorum and regularity in presentation. This preoccupation is a constant presence in the poetry, not always successfully realised, of course, and we have no need to go outside the verse to find a sanction for the claim I have made. But if we did we could find it in several key statements in Hope's critical writings. Hope is in fact a fine practical critic in the Arnoldian tradition. Here is a passage from Hope's remarkable volume—remarkable for assurance, urbanity and point—*The Cave and the Spring*.[1]

> This discriminating taste is the basis of the much misunderstood idea of correctness in poetry, the correctness which Pope in early youth made it his aim to bring to the practice of English verse, and which his *Essay on Criticism* is meant both to explain and to exemplify. Correctness is not primarily a matter of following explicit and ideal rules of versification but of exercising discrimination, of choices that tremble on the very limit of sensibility. Far from being a mechanical skill, it is one that depends on continual acts of judgment so little referable to any rule of thumb that they may look arbitrary to those who do not share the writer's discipline of taste. Correctness is the mastery of all that is implied in Horace's doctrine of the middle way.

This significant set of names and phrases—Pope and Horace, correctness, acts of judgment, discipline of taste, the middle way—not only point to the theme Hope is engaged with but unambiguously project a personal conviction about the artistic necessity for design and control. They also make an appropriate introduction to the poem, *The Lamp and the Jar*, I want to speak of first.

> *You are that vessel full of holy oil:*
> *Wisdom, unstirring in its liquid sleep,*
> *Hoarded and cool, lucid and golden green,*
> *Fills the pure flanks of the containing stone;*
> *Here darkness mellows what the sunlit soil*
> *To purposes unknown, for ends unseen,*
> *Produced, and labour of unnumbered men.*
> *All the unthinking earth with fret or toil*
> *Reared, ripened, buried in the earth again,*
> *Here lives, and living, waits: this source alone*
> *Distils those fruitful tears the Muses weep.*
> *And I, the lamp before the sacred ark,*

[1] Adelaide, 1965, p. 57

The root of fire, the burning flower of light,
Draw from your loins this inexhaustible joy.
There the perpetual miracle of grace
Recurs, as, from its agony, the flame
Feeds the blind heart of the adoring dark;
And there the figures of our mystery,
The shapes of terror and inhuman woe,
Emerge and prophesy; there with the mark
Of blood upon his breast and on his brow,
An unknown king, with my transfigured face,
Bends your immortal body to his delight.

The Lamp and the Jar is a remarkably contained poem, each verbal edge firmly finished off and each syntactical contour exactly defined. Two bold images, the female oil-brimmed jar and the burning male lamp are separately drawn out and then drawn together. The tranquil, mellowed richness of the first stanza, 'hoarded and cool', is put into opposition and balance with the agitation, the more personal agitation of the second. Together the stanzas, locked at once in antagonism and passion, produce the strength and scent of sexual encounter. The actual tension and embrace of love are poised above and sustained by the profound processes of organic life.

> *... what the sunlit soil*
> *To purposes unknown, for ends unseen,*
> *Produced ...*

and what

> *... the unthinking earth with fret or toil*
> *Reared, ripened, buried in the earth again ...*

The poem, keeping its varied complexities in place and in connection along a lucid argumentative line, grasps first at the physical basis of life and experience, at the oil and the earth and the calm sagacity it generates, and then touches the quick of human experience at its exquisite crisis in the mysterious meeting of love. The mystery is an essential part of the experience which the poem offers. It includes not only the joyful, physical energy of sexual love, 'the root of fire, the burning flower of light', but also a tissue of social and personal memories and images. These are both serene, 'the perpetual miracle of grace', and terrifying, 'the shapes of terror and inhuman woe'. In the poem the act of love appears as a model of all human experience which has its ancient sources buried in the earth, but which is also immediate and adapted to the light and further transformed by the imagination, itself always a carrier of a more than merely personal cargo, a conductor of both compulsion and aspiration, honour and grace.

Sexual love is a recurrent theme in Hope's work. Occasionally he celebrates it as the beneficent completion of life and personality. More frequently he is concerned with its turbidity and cruelty. He sees it as incestuous, murderous, carnivorous or absurd. Here is a poem *The Gateway* in which love is shown completing the circle and perfecting the broken, and in which Hope's characteristic energy of articulation is given a singing, aspiring quality.

> *Now the heart sings with all its thousand voices*
> *To hear this city of cells, my body, sing.*
> *The tree through the stiff clay at long last forces*
> *Its thin strong roots and taps the secret spring.*
>
> *And the sweet waters without intermission*
> *Climb to the tips of its green tenement;*
> *The breasts have borne the grace of their possession,*
> *The lips have felt the pressure of content.*
>
> *Here I come home: in this expected country*
> *They know my name and speak it with delight.*
> *I am the dream and you my gates of entry,*
> *The means by which I waken into light.*

The sense of unalloyed delight in love, spiritual as well as physical, is comparatively rare in Hope's poetry. It is true that whenever he writes of love he conveys in a masterly way the pleasure of the senses and the richness and beauty of the body. But there is always something else breaking in, something sinister or ugly or mean. Monstrous and cogent memories from the Old Testament and the classics, which supply many of the fictions used in Hope's verse, intrude on the enclosed world of lovers: reminiscences of Circe surrounded by snouted beasts, of Lot and his daughters 'crafty

from fear, reckless with joy and greed', of Susannah and the seedy
hatred of the Elders, of Pasiphae, filled with the bull's monstrous
life, of Odysseus and passion punctured by the ridiculous commonplace.

> There at the last, his arms embracing her,
> She found herself, faith wasted, valour lost,
> Raped by a stranger in her sullen bed;
> And he, for all the bloody passion it cost
> To have heard the sirens sing and yet have fled,
> Thought the night tedious, coughed and shook his head,
> An old man sleeping with his housekeeper.

The conclusion of this stanza from *The End of a Journey*, contrasting
sharply and yet following naturally on the formal eloquence preceding it (the brilliant twist of mood is completely logical) is an
example of Hope's supple virtuosity in modulation, from the
stately and measured to the casual and throwaway. It calls up the
great name of Yeats, and Hope has made no secret of his admiration
for Yeats and

> that noble, candid speech
> In which all things worth saying may be said . . .

as well as his strong preference for Yeats over Eliot. But while
Yeats is clearly a vital (and absorbed) influence on Hope, his idiom
is his own, being at once less gorgeous and Byzantine when full out
and more flatly contemporary in the lower register. Here are two
examples which separate these modes out, the first, the Yeatsian,
from a short poem called *Meditation on a Bone*, about a piece of bone
found at Trondhjem in 1901 with a runic inscription cut on it:

> Words scored upon a bone,
> Scratched in despair or rage—
> Nine hundred years have gone;
> Now, in another age,
> They burn with passion on
> A scholar's tranquil page.

The second is the beginning of *Agony Column*:

> Sir George and Lady Cepheus of Upper Slaughter
> Desire to announce to family and friends

I

> *That the death has been arranged of their only daughter*
> *Andromeda, aged twenty—Sir George intends*
>
> *To avoid undesirable pomp and ostentation:*
> *A simple ceremony, a quiet funeral feast*
> *And the usual speeches; a train will leave the station*
> *For the Virgin's Rock at four. No flowers by Request!*

An even better example of this calculatedly flat manner and one
more thoroughly charged with the macabre, the attraction of
which for Hope suggests a certain nauseated disgust with ordinary
life as part of his response to experience, is *Conquistador* in which a
certain Henry Clay 'a small man in a little way', loves an enormous
girl.

> *And afterwards, it may have been in play,*
> *The enormous girl rolled over and squashed him flat;*
> *And, as she could not send him home that way,*
> *Used him thereafter as a bedside mat. . . .*
>
> *And when, in winter, getting out of bed,*
> *Her large soft feet pressed warmly on the skin,*
> *The two glass eyes would sparkle in his head,*
> *The jaws extend their papier-mâché grin.*

Having said this—that the appeal of the macabre for Hope
testifies to some perverse disrelish for common experience—I am
immediately conscious of the need to correct or qualify it. There
is something nasty, an occasional gratuitous revelling in the
garbage-bin and perhaps also the puritan self-hatred to which this
is often a clue, in a few of Hope's poems, as for example in *Rawhead
and Bloody Bones*:

> *This Belly too commits*
> *By a strange and self abuse,*
> *Chin-chopper's titbits,*
> *Meat of his own mint, chews.*

But more often some quality in the tone, a quaver of amusement,
a glint of wit, a touch of self-mockery, even a cry of innocent
astonishment, shows that the macabre is being put to a more complicated and controlled use. It becomes an instrument instead of a
dead end, another gateway through which the poet's imagination

can enter an odd, disturbed but somehow valid world. A poem of this kind is *The Coasts of Cerigo* in which

> . . .
> *Strange sister to the polyp and the sponge,*
> *To holothurian and madrepore,*
>
> *The Labra wallows in her bath of time . . .*
> *Her ladylegs gape darkly as a cave,*
>
> *And through the coral clefts a gleam and gloom*
> *Reveal the fronded arch, the pelvic gate;*
> *Spotted and barred, the amorous fish swim in.*
> *But in that hollow, mocking catacomb*
> *Their love-songs echo and reverberate*
> *A senseless clamour and a wordless din.*
>
> *The love-trap closes on its gullible prey*
> *Despite their sobs, despite their ecstasies.*
> *Brilliant with tropic bands and stripes, they dart*
> *Through a delicious juice which eats away*
> *Their scales and soon dissolves their goggle eyes*
> *And melts the milt-sac and the pulsing heart.*

Even this short extract will be sufficient to demonstrate Hope's great technical skill in recreating the cold marvels of the submarine universe. One sees too how the manner, at once Augustan and efficiently direct, and the eye coolly intent on the object makes the biological savagery it discerns glittering and frightening. The gliding rhythm, the glassily clear imagery, the almost scientifically detached attitude themselves make 'a delicious juice which eats away' at our comfortable assumptions about life and tenderness, at once inviting our acquiescence and dissolving it with intimations of the implacable cruelty of a biologically determined life. Hope is said to be a severely traditional poet, which indeed he is in his bias towards accepted patterns and rhythms. But he has also a pointedly contemporary gift—that of conducting the permanent functions of poetry through new categories of experience and through new classes of imagery, imagery particularly drawn from the sciences of biology and psychology. The Labra is one figure drawn from such a source, the Tapeworm another. Who but Hope would conceive of celebrating this creature as one of the heroic figures of life, as he has in *The Kings*.

> The lion in deserts royally takes his prey;
> Gaunt crags cast back the hunting eagle's scream.
> The King of Parasites, delicate, white and blind,
> Ruling his world of fable even as they,
> Dreams out his greedy and imperious dream
> Immortal in the bellies of mankind.
>
> In a rich bath of pre-digested soup,
> Warm in the pulsing bowel, safely shut
> From the bright ambient horror of sun and air,
> His slender segments ripening loop by loop,
> Broods the voluptuous monarch of the gut,
> The Tapeworm, the prodigious Solitaire.

The grotesque depends on discrepancy, on a measured friction between manner and material or on discordant experiences crushed together. Both types of contrast contribute to the effect of *The Coasts of Cerigo* and *The Kings*, as they do in another startling poem in this *genre*, *The Dinner*. *The Dinner* is of unusual interest in that it adds a further note to our understanding of Hope's use of the grotesque. We see in the poem how the imagination of a poet of the grotesque hurls itself from the given situation to one at the extreme point of difference. In this violent dialectical swing the shock of the poem comes from our realising that the second stage in spite of its immense dissimilarity is really a development of the first, that it was there all the time grinning under the original elegant surface. We notice, too, how Hope arrives like a poetic zoologist at the second fiercely contrasting situation by a kind of compressed evolutionary method which appears in several poems. The reductive habit of the scientist, his concern with origins and causes, becomes in Hope's hands an instrument of poetic exploration. In *The Dinner* the lovers, risen from bed, prepare to dine:

> Delicate, young and cradled in delight,
> You take your seat and bare your teeth to bite—
> What is my courage then to suffer this

Miracle of your metamorphosis!
For in that instant I behold the jaws
Of the most terrible of carnivores
Tear at its prey; the ravening human packs
Pull down their terrified victim in its tracks;
The wit, the charm, the grace, the pride of life
Adore the bloody edges of a knife!
The nakedness I had my arms about
Was gorged with death—I see the cayman's snout
Snap the deer's nostrils as they touch the flood;
The tiger's hairy muzzle sweet with blood;
The condor, flapping from the rocky peak,
Light on the carrion, plunge his grisly beak
Into the rotting porridge; through the dark
Slides the lithe, cold torpedo of the shark.
The air, the jungle, the salt, cannibal sea
Hold no more ruthless beast of prey than she.
For her the ox falls snoring in his blood;
The lamb is butchered for her daily food;
Her exquisite mouth, that smiles and tastes the wine,
Has killed by proxy a whole herd of swine— . . .

The poem continues its backward evolutionary line and the young woman, delicate and baring her teeth to bite, becomes the world of prehistoric mankind. We see the ancestral giant and giantess,

Talking in deep, soft, grumbling undertones
They gnaw and crack and suck the marrowy bones.

I have called the technique rehearsed in this poem tracing an evolutionary line. But it is also, and perhaps more so, a method of burrowing into the image evoked in the first two lines, to release and elucidate the intimations latent there. The ravening animals, the condor plunging his beak 'into the rotting porridge', and the ancient ancestors in the cave, are the imaginative issue of the first lines of the verse paragraph I quoted earlier:

Delicate, young and cradled in delight
You take your seat and bare your teeth to bite . . .

I have referred, then, to Hope's writings in the formal Yeatsian mode, to his flatter, more markedly contemporary manner, and to work of the kind I call macabre-grotesque, although I recognise the infelicity of a term which misleadingly suggests some Gothic thrill-inducing intention on the part of the poet when the most notable thing about these poems is the control and application with which the *genre* is put to serious, indeed sombre, purposes. Use, management, the employment of a style for purposes beyond what it seems capable of is even more strikingly evident in another set of poems which look immediately to be no more than deliberate imitations. Members of this series are *Man Friday*, *The Elegy*, *An Epistle from Holofernes*, *The Cheek*, *An Epistle*, *Soledades of the Sun and Moon*. This last poem is not, Hope has told us,[1] as its name suggests an attempt to imitate Gongora, but it is strongly reminiscent of certain religious poems of the English seventeenth century.

What in the seventeenth century Hope fastened on was a composite sensibility made up of the passionate subtleties and the intellectual sensuousness of the metaphysical poets and the masculine, ironic force of Dryden. *Why* the seventeenth century should be looked to as the source has to do with the congruence between Hope's own poetic nature and the adult, ardent, almost mathematically reasoning habit of the metaphysicals: a balance further modified by another, the symmetry between Hope and his admired Dryden's gift of sensitive manliness, his way of being at once independent and level with his experience, however intricate; and modified yet again by Hope's sympathetic understanding of Dryden's skill in calling upon a range of poetic resonance within a strictly defining, disciplining pattern. Nor should we overlook that Hope had to make his choice of exemplar at a particular time and from within a certain literary tradition—not only the wider one grounded on the English language and the English literary tradition but within the local Australian one based on the altered language of his own country. It could not be a purely personal choice, although it had to be primarily a personal one, answering to the need felt in the poet's own nerves. The poet as poet is not engaged in any explicit mission to renovate a literary tradition. But of course he is involved in such an undertaking, and the more significant he is as a poet, the more profound is his involvement.

[1] *Selected Poems*, A. D. Hope, Sydney, 1966, p. 55

Hope's 'conservatism' in fact is truly radical. His poetry had to be freed from the influence of home, from a tradition still too much domesticated within the nineteenth century in which British gentility and blandness were curiously reinforced in their parochialism by an unambitious, and suspicious, Australian matiness. The seventeenth century so different, so remote from the nineteenth century in its inclusiveness and in the very assurance of its scepticism, to which poets in Britain earlier directed their attention, could be the same cleansing, tonic influence for Australia: above all if the connection were to be made by an Australian poet.

I called the set of poems which gave rise to these remarks 'imitations', and although I wanted to use the term in an active Aristotelian sense, it still carries an unfairly passive or partial connotation, quite unjust to the controlled energy of the art the poems represent. They might more aptly be called 'translations', in the sense in which Scott-Moncrieff's version is a translation of Proust, a personal and creative reproduction, with the added and powerful difference that Hope is primarily concerned to construct original poems. A technique of translation of this kind when applied by a modern Australian poet to a period as remote in time and sensibility as the English seventeenth century requires the skill to accommodate the curve of contemporary speech to the contours of another age and the ability to sink oneself in its diction and feeling. It also requires with a verse like that of the seventeenth century, depending so much on almost syllogistic structure, mastery of and intense sympathy with an alien syntax of reasoning. At the same time the poet if he is to use and not be used by his literary instruments must preserve a measure of detachment. If not, the sinking turns into a helpless drowning, the sympathy into an impotent identification. Here are two examples of this mode: the failure of the first, the success of the second depends precisely on this point of tactfully insinuated independence. The first is from *The Cheek*:

> *Here's a new Genesis; the year is One;*
> *This bed and we a world, our lamp its sun.*
> *Love to its single dark dimension bound*
> *Rules its volcano Kingdom underground:*

The feet at their remote antipodes
Twine their smooth roots; at Capricorn the knees
Nuzzle together; intershafted lies
The amplitude of firm and polished thighs. . . .

The effort at minute fidelity betrays the poet into merely mirroring shadows. Here now is the first stanza of *Soledades of the Sun and Moon*:

Now the year walks among the signs of heaven,
Swinging her large hips, smiling in all her motions,
Crosses with dancing steps the Milky Valley.
Round her the primal energies rejoice;
All the twelve metaphysical creatures and the seven
Swift spheres adore her vigour; the five oceans
　　Look up and hear her voice
Ring through the ebony vault, where Ara Celi
Flames, and the choiring stars at their devotions
　　With pure and jubilant noise
Praise and proclaim four seasons in her belly.

This stanza exhibits the fine proportion which the whole poem sustains, between, on the one side, an exactly directed historical imagination highly responsive to the original form and, on the other, the pressure of the poet's personal experience. The rhythm moves with diplomatic ease from the ceremonial stateliness appropriate to 'the choiring stars at their devotions' to the more checked and modern run of

the five oceans
Look up and hear her voice
Ring through the ebony vault,

and to the sliding glide of the star-actress-year. And to make this bold image consort without embarrassment with 'the primal energies' and 'the metaphysical creatures' in as 'metaphysical' a connection as one could conceive of is a conclusive demonstration of an authoritative and achieved art. As fine as *Soledades of the Sun and Moon*, each in its different way, are *Man Friday*, a sardonic extrapolation from *Robinson Crusoe*, and *An Epistle from Holofernes*, a grim, angry evocation of tragic love which is Roman in the strength of its despair. Both these poems are written in vigorous rhymed couplets which have something of Dryden's pace and force: Dryden's because the medium, handled by Hope with remarkable naturalness, is used as the instrument of strength rather than delicacy. Indeed the heroic couplet, employed in an easy, open way is splendidly adapted to communicate the peculiar quality of Hope's poetry which one is aware of even in his earliest, lightest pieces. This is its powerfully—almost physically—energetic character. It is muscular, quick and solid—with the relaxed poise of the gifted athlete who brings all his force to bear rhythmically and without strain. Hope is the least neurotic of poets and even when he is scrutinising the stages of his own childhood, as in one of his best poems *Ascent into Hell*, his regard is gravely objective without the least touch of narcissistic droop or any suspicion of anxious self interest. Right from the start of Hope's poetic career, the reader is aware of the formed personality beneath the finished literary character. It is positive, independent and radical in the Australian manner—in the manner of the Australian *people*, that is; the accepted Australian literary convention lacked precisely this very virtue. It is free of the fog of middle-class pretension and gentility: sharp where that was bland and harsh where that was cosy. At the same time Hope's poetry asserts a profound commitment to the great constitutive works of the Western—not just the British—tradition; and not only in poetry but also in thought and morality—accepts and asserts, namely, the principles of an intellectual aristocracy, and in doing so avoids, or ignores, the clogging dangers of Australian democracy. The result is a powerful and unfashionable maturity which joins a naked freshness of original response to a richly realised conception of an ideal order.

This is a conjunction which appears in the best of the poems I called translations, *An Epistle: Edward Sackville to Venetia Digby*, the fable of which is taken from Aubrey's *Brief Lives*. Sir Kenelm Digby when little more than a boy fell in love with Venetia Stanley, a neighbour's daughter, but the match was disapproved of and his mother had him sent abroad where he stayed for several years and was at length assumed to be dead. During this time Venetia became the lover of Sir Edward Sackville, later Earl of

Dorset, Digby's friend. The despair which is implicit in the situation and the grimness of a passionate and impossible love call to powers deep in Hope's nature and are transformed in his treatment to become the implacable conditions of tragic human life itself. It is written in language which very much obeys the prescription Hope lays down—that the language of poetry should be 'plain, lucid, coherent, logically connected, syntactically exact, and firmly based in current idiom and usage'.[1] It begins with short, stabbing, cleanly effective phrases, in a staccato rhythm and in a voice which has nothing in it but despair.

> *First, last and always dearest, closest, best,*
>   *Source of my travail and my rest,*
> *The letter which I shall not send, I write*
> *To cheer my more than arctic night.*

The poem mingling sadness and sensuousness in a strange, dry way manages unfalteringly to convey at once the coldness of present misery and the radiance of remembered passion. Not that the effect is at all romantically intimate or soft. The logical structure, the severe form and the carefully worked out syntax, both of grammar and feeling, generalise the experience into something highly organised and impersonal. So that the love passages, luminous and distant in the memory, have the refinement and the deadliness of expert swordplay, and the hopelessness and regret become positive and tense, abrasive and bleakly affecting. Here is the conclusion in which we see the particular aspiring through the lucidity of form towards a larger, general order:

> *Nature, who makes each member to one end,*
>   *May give it powers which transcend*
> *Its first and fruitful purpose. When she made*
>   *The Tongue for taste, who in the shade*
> *Of summer vines, what speechless manlike brute,*
>   *Biting sharp rind or sweeter fruit,*
> *Could have conceived the improbable tales, the long*
>   *Strange fable of the Speaking Tongue?*
> *So Love, which Nature's craft at first designed*
>   *For comfort and increase of kind,*

[1] *Selected Poems*, Sydney, 1966, p. ix

> *Puts on another nature, grows to be*
> *The language of the mystery;*
> *The heart resolves its chaos then, the soul*
> *Lucidly contemplates the whole*
> *Just order of the random world; and through*
> *That dance she moves, and dances too.*

An Epistle: Edward Sackville to Venetia Digby is a statement—but more than a mere 'statement'—about the ideal order which is implicit in, and which by means of poetry can be extracted from, the grubbiness and detritus of life. But, of course, the poet could be, and is, as concerned with the other side of the duality, with the disordered elements in their chaos. In another poem, a true translation this time, *The Twenty-Second Sonnet of Louis Labé*, he speaks of this preoccupation.

> *They would break frame and order, and disperse*
> *With random steps through a wrecked universe*
> *Like me to search, and search, like me, in vain.*

The broken frame and the wrecked universe describe very well the form under which society and the modern world appear to this tough-minded, independent poet. The search describes the general, bracing aim which keeps his observations tart, the random steps, the self-confidence of the approach. The tone of these social poems, which include some of Hope's most effective and personal work, is better seen in the beginning of *Letter from the Line*:

> *Island-hopping in the rough, the rumbustious season,*
> *The migratory poet, most solitary of birds,*
> *Having left Los Angeles with a Kyrie eleison,*
> *Repacks his baggage of carefully chosen words.*

> *For lucky Jim has given his last lecture,*
> *From the bogus mission his wits emerge alive,*
> *From a land where, despite de Tocqueville's shrewd conjecture,*
> *The liberal arts, like living fossils, survive.*

The tone here, untensed and self-mocking, is a recognition that we are all, not excluding the poet himself, 'most solitary of birds', in the same boat, or plane, and an almost amused confession of innocence—in that whatever is wrong—and so much is, both in the observed and the observer—derives from a common impersonal fault. It is the classical Western awareness—but light, wry and quite without guilt—that everything issues from a single, tainted source, an original flaw or sin. But at other times the poet collects himself into a more feline and separate contempt. *A Comminution* spits at the mass-communicating world, *Lambkin* at the malevolently stupid mob, *The Martyrdom of St Theresa* at the formal cruelties of religion, and *The Age of Innocence* straight into 'the grey eye of science'. Sometimes the tone is harsh and disgusted. *Heldensagen* savagely rejects those with all the answers,

> *Admirals with power to organise my search*
> *For Ithaca through this ten years monstrous dream:—*
> *To all Messiahs the same reply, I am*
> *Sinbad and on this Roc you build no church!*

Phallus ignominiously acknowledges the huge irrelevance of individuality, of thought and will, beside the brutal biological coercion of sex. The power and the beauty of the body roused by sex is a subject of profound importance to Hope. It has for him an absolute, intrinsic value in its natural energy, concentration and sincerity, and as a focus of experience which is completely without pretension or fake. His command of an idiom capable of expressing this reality is extraordinarily firm and clean. His attitude to it may be serious and reverent, as in the first poem I quoted, *The Lamp and the Jar*; or it may be surgically detached as in *The Damnation of Byron*, which lays bare the neurotic emptiness of the professional lover, a performer moved by fear and moving into despair. Or again it may be, as it often is in these social-satirical poems, randy and rollicking. A remarkable example of that mood is *A Blason* in which the phases of the act of love are rehearsed solely by means of an alliterative accumulation of dancing Saxon and Norman exclamations and expletives. Here are the first, preparatory stanzas of this astonishing exercise in pure verbal vitality:

> *My foundling, my fondling, my frolic first-footer,*
> *My circler, my sidler, shy-sayer yes and no,*

Live-levin, light-looker, darter and doubter,
Pause of perhaps in my turvey of touch-and-go;

My music, my mandrake, merry thought to my marrow-bone,
Tropic to my true-pole and ripe to my rich,
Wonderer, wanderer, walker-in-wood alone
Eye-asker, acher, angel-with-an-itch;

My tittup, my tansy, tease-tuft in tumble-toil,
My frisker, my fettler, trickster and trier,
Knick-knacker, knee-knocker, cleaver in kindle-coil,
My handler, my honeysuckler, phoenix-on-fire. . . .

Vastly different from this curiously innocent celebration of bodily joy, in address, tone and intention, is the maliciously analytic *Return from the Freudian Islands* (written, incidentally, as early as 1942), in which an almost impudently insinuating blandness of the deadpan, tongue-in-cheek, irresistibly Australian variety, mocks at Siegfried the Saviour for whose sake the islanders have abandoned the worship of their fathers' ghosts. The saint shocks and delights them as he brings into their consciousness 'the unacknowledged body' and forces them to see

> *How it bred night-sweats, the disease of shame,*
> *Corns, fluxions, baldness and the sense of sin,*
> *How clothes to the Analytic Eye became*
> *Fantasies, furtive symbols of the skin.*

The poem makes solemn, wicked fun of the reductive habit of the contemporary mind, of its technique at getting beneath the delusive surface in the interests of uttering some pure abstract truth. Hope combines a gravely ironic parody of psychiatric investigation with a medievally gruesome pondering on the horrors of the body, including 'a common skin disease they had called love'. Successively, clothes, skin, flesh are peeled off until the saint-sage lays bare 'the ultimate visceral reality'.

> *At the Fertility Festival that year*
> *The skinned men blushed to see the skeleton,*
> *A bone-cage filled with female guts appear*
> *Tottering before them in the midday sun.*

> *Its slats and lowering rods they saw, the full*
> *Cogged horseshoe grin of two and thirty teeth,*
> *The frantic eyeballs swivelling in the skull,*
> *The swagging human umbles underneath,*
>
> *The soft wet mottled granite of the lung*
> *Bulge and collapse, the liver worn askew*
> *Jauntily quiver, the plump intestines hung*
> *In glistening loops and bolsters in their view. . . .*

The Swift-like gravity of procedure, simultaneously recommending and undermining the modest monstrous proposal, and the hideous exposure of the skinned body are devices used in the service of a serious intention but one which can express itself in a less ferocious, more bantering species of ridicule than the master of devastation would ever allow himself. The touch of tolerant light-heartedness is confirmed by the crisply humorous conclusion. It holds out a small hope that a sense of reality is perhaps recoverable —but only as the issue of total absurdity.

> *Pimples and cramps now shed with pelt and thews,*
> *No dreams to fright, no visions to trouble them,*
> *For, where the death-wish and self-knowledge fuse,*
> *They had at last The Human L.C.M. . . .*
>
> *Here the saint paused, looked modestly at the ground*
> *And waited for their plaudits to begin.*
> *And waited. . . . There was nothing! A faint, dry sound*
> *As first a poet buttoned on his skin.*

I come now to what I see as the peak of Hope's achievement, not a great one in bulk it may be, but still substantial enough and unusually even in quality. It is made up of a handful of poems written at intervals over the period 1942-61, a fact of composition in keeping with my feeling that Hope already had a fully formed literary personality when he began to publish. His *Collected Poems*, 'those poems which I would still care to publish',[1] contains one poem written in 1930, one in 1934, two in 1938, and two in 1939. The body of the work, and the best, appeared between 1940 and

---

[1] Hope, A. D., *Collected Poems*, London, 1966, vii

1965. Perhaps there are accidental reasons in addition to those I have suggested for a situation which I take as at least partly significant about the nature of Hope's talent—the adult confident character it had from the beginning. 'I cannot remember an age at which I did not make up verses,' he writes, 'but my childish rhymes perished in an *auto-da-fé* at the age of fourteen when a friend persuaded me to burn them all and start again. Another fire, for which I was not responsible, later destroyed the evidence of prentice work up to the age of twenty-five.' 'If not symbolic, these were, I feel, at least representative fires.' The poems I have in mind are *The Wandering Islands* (1943), *Ascent into Hell* (1943-44), *The Pleasure of Princes* (1947), *Imperial Adam* (1952), *Pseudodoxia Epidemica* (1961). There are others in the cluster but these are the main lights.

The Wandering Islands is a powerful meditative poem on the theme of isolation. It makes the characteristically solid impact of Hope's best poems, seeming to have behind it the weight of personal experience which has been grasped and deeply pondered. It starts with a general statement, an announcement about human feelings which carries with it some of the certainty of a physical law, and which calmly joins the order of emotion to the geographical world of the wandering islands:

> You cannot build bridges between the wandering islands;
> The mind has no neighbours, and the unteachable heart
> Announces its armistice time after time, but spends
> Its love to draw them closer and closer apart.

It goes on in a stiffly effective way, in an idiom which is almost a combination of the language of cartography and law (the work of a dusty official working on maps in a remote office) to define the position of the unfixed islands. 'Position' may be a paradoxical term here, but it sufficiently indicates both place and nature.

> They are not on the chart; they turn indifferent shoulders
> On the island-hunters; they are not afraid
> Of Cook or De Quiros, nor of the empire-builders;
> By missionary bishops and the tourist trade

They are not annexed; they claim no fixed position;
They take no pride in a favoured latitude;
The committee of atolls inspires in them no devotion
And the earthquake belt no special attitude.

A refuge only for the shipwrecked sailor;
He sits on the shore and sullenly masturbates,
Dreaming of rescue, the pubs in the ports of call or
The big-hipped harlots at the dock-yard gates.

But the wandering islands drift on their own business,
Incurious whether the whales swim round or under,
Investing no fear in ultimate forgiveness.
If they clap together, it is only casual thunder. . . .

The Wandering Islands by nature, the shipwrecked sailor by fate, cannot share or touch another, except accidentally or momentarily; experience for them is ultimately singular and solitary. As it is, the poet suggests, for us and for the sullen shipwrecked sailor—not an admirable but certainly a real character, whose unappealing wretchedness makes him a fit figure for the common human person in this iron context. Nor is our, or the Islands', incapacity for participation any protection against suffering. The most lacerating and the most human suffering is produced by the actuality of ultimate separation and the hopeless aspiration for union. We suffer because the edge of individuality and the rigour of isolation cannot be softened, or only for an instant and by an illusion, which is itself swept away by 'the huge monotonous voices' of reality.

And yet they are hurt—for the social polyps never
Girdle their bare shores with a moral reef;
When the icebergs grind them they know both beauty and terror;
They are not exempt from ordinary grief;

And the sudden ravages of love surprise
Them like acts of God—its irresistible function
They have never treated with convenient lies
As a part of geography or an institution.

An instant of fury, a bursting mountain of spray,
They rush together, their promontories lock,
An instant the castaway hails the castaway,
But the sounds perish in that earthquake shock.

And then, in the crash of ruined cliffs, the smother
And swirl of foam, the wandering islands part.
But all that one mind ever knows of another,
Or breaks the long isolation of the heart

Was in that instant. The shipwrecked sailor senses
His own despair in a retreating face.
Around him he hears in the huge monotonous voices
Of wave and wind: 'The Rescue will not take place'.

The Wandering Islands is a strongly objective poem, written in
a mood of dry, almost grim composure, in which the settled author,
unfrayed by his own situation and its isolation, stares bleakly at
what is the case, namely the twin realities of the wandering islands
and 'all that one mind ever knows of another'. Much of the
intensity of the poem's effect comes from the simultaneous and
equal treatment of the two themes, not in a way which uses the
geographical figure as a simple analogy or parable but as an exercise
in positive ambiguity.

Australians are sometimes thought to be fustily conformist—it
is a criticism the Australians often make of themselves—but there
is also in the Australian psychology a quality of lissom independence corresponding, perhaps, to the marvellous bodily suppleness
generated by a regimen of sun, protein and sport. Only an Australian, and one of Hope's gifts—only Hope himself, I suppose—could
use the antiquarian vocabulary at the start of *Pseudodoxia Epidemica*
with such an unembarrassed lack of self-consciousness. There the
words are, his attitude seems to imply, still with a quirky flair of life
not yet quite snuffed out, as well as a degree of dubious charm. Let
me use them, therefore, taking advantage of their antique attractiveness, and consciously manipulating them in a new direction, like a
batsman who makes not simply an unorthodox but an astonishingly
original stroke, staying all the time strictly within the rules.

By acupuncture or by moxibustion
The soul repairs its vulnerable sheath;
And beetle paste is love's electuary.
True tales and false alike work by suggestion.
Cure palsy with a poison-ivy wreath
Or squeeze the devil's cherry to vamp an eye.

K

There is a checked or controlled comic impulse at work here which enables Hope to use a set of superannuated terms as though they were colloquialisms, and to employ what could easily be units of rhetoric as terms of slang. Two modes of discourse, rhetorical and familiar, run together through the poem. At one point, as in the third and fifth stanzas, the rhetorical is more strongly present; at another, as in the second and the fourth, the casually colloquial is emphasised. The half-amused, shoulder-shrugging tolerance keeps the rhetorical from becoming fustian while it gives a sardonic edge to the slang. Here are the third and fourth stanzas in which one can see the succession and friction of the two manners.

> Let reason ignore the reasons of the heart,
> Pure knowledge is a sow that eats her farrow;
> But wisdom's children may hear mermaids sing
> In latitudes not found on any chart.
> Fledged without feet, to miss the hunter's arrow
> The bird of paradise keeps on the wing.
>
> Taken full-strength, truth is a drug that kills.
> They say that when he rose, the morning after,
> Faith took a tot and felt as right as pie;
> But, having accurately checked his bills,
> Clairvoyance was found dangling from a rafter,
> All the true facts reflected in his eye.

We see too in these lines the opposition between pure reason and poetic experience which is central to the poem, a conventional enough dichotomy, it is true, but one given a personal bite in Hope's treatment since it is shown to be the structural condition of the poet's own life, which was a movement from a green youth of 'probe and test' to the 'ripe years' writing of love. The clairvoyance of reason which governed his youth gave way in maturity to poetic faith with its reviving tot. The poem has a surface inconsequence but it is supported by a spare and credible logic. Beginning with the old wives' drugs which work by suggestion, it goes on to the other side of the equation, our response, which itself exerts its influence upon what it meets. 'Our questions choose the answers they think good.' If this offends the accuracy of clairvoyant reason, it is because that mode of understanding is partial and selective, bent upon law and coherence, whereas human experience is large and thick with oddity and absurdity. Poetic power seeks for the unique and makes its rule discovering the exception. The poem, which begins with the ancient old wives' remedies, beetle paste, poison-ivy wreath and devil's cherry, and then slips through reflection, example, and the poet's own history, comes in the end in an unbroken curve to a figure taken from medieval logic, and to the exception with which the poet's (and the human being's) experience corrects the arid concept.

> *A thousand years pen-white was the tradition.*
> *There was the lake: one only had to look*
> *To see truth's emblem paddling in her snow;*
> *The black one was a joke of the logician.*
> *And yet there was a wild swan in my book*
> *Proved him a liar. But how was he to know?*
>
> *Cygnus mansuetus may be just a bird.*
> *With you my fabled swan, I give up trying*
> *To disbelieve what science cannot prove.*
> *Let ornithology find our tale absurd:*
> *The cob that sings at last when close to dying*
> *May prove at last my parable of love.*

The next two poems in this group, *The Pleasure of Princes* and *Imperial Adam* recall to me the comment with which I began about Hope's positive, almost fierce, sense of the Western Latin tradition. In the first of these poems a Roman severity outlines the Machiavellian content; in the second, another species of Latin temperament appears, mellow and disillusioned and ironically conscious. Here are the openings of both poems:

THE PLEASURE OF PRINCES

> *What pleasures have great princes? These: to know*
> *Themselves reputed mad with pride or power;*
> *To speak few words—few words and short bring low*
> *This ancient house, that city with flame devour—*

To make old men, their fathers' enemies,
Drunk on the vintage of the former age;
To have great painters show their mistresses
Naked to the succeeding time; engage

The cunning of able, treacherous ministers
To serve, despite themselves, the cause they hate,
And leave a prosperous kingdom to their heirs
Nursed by the caterpillars of the state. . . .

IMPERIAL ADAM

Imperial Adam, naked in the dew,
Felt his brown flanks and found the rib was gone.
Puzzled he turned and saw where, two and two,
The mighty spoor of Jahweh marked the lawn.

Then he remembered through mysterious sleep
The surgeon fingers probing at the bone,
The voice so far away, so rich and deep:
'It is not good for him to live alone'.

Turning once more he found Man's counterpart
In tender parody breathing at his side.
He knew her at first sight, he knew by heart
Her allegory of sense unsatisfied.

The pawpaw drooped its golden breasts above
Less generous than the honey of her flesh;
The innocent sunlight showed the place of love;
The dew on its dark hairs winked crisp and fresh. . . .

In *The Pleasure of Princes*, the stony, stoical quality and the regular edge of the verse match the author's notation of the unavoidable brutality and loneliness of life, even for one who lives it in one of its most intense forms as the possessor of power. In *Imperial Adam*, a milder but equally unquestioning regard is turned upon the myth of Genesis. In cool, strict verse the poet accepts and appreciates the grandeur of imperial Adam and the contrast between the paradisal innocence of the garden and the splendid sensuousness brought in by Eve. He registers the real humanity of the myth, the naturalness of the human experience in its animal context, and the irony by which evil is brought out of good: and Cain, the first murderer, by the union of imperial Adam and generous Eve.

. . .

It was the beasts now who stood watching by:

The gravid elephant, the calving hind,
The breeding bitch, the she-ape big with young
Were the first gentle midwives of mankind;
The teeming lioness rasped her with her tongue;

The proud vicuna nuzzled her as she slept
Lax on the grass; and Adam watching too,
Saw how her dumb breasts at their ripening wept,
The great pod of her belly swelled and grew,

And saw its water break, and saw, in fear,
Its quaking muscles in the act of birth,
Between her legs a pigmy face appear
And the first murderer lay upon the earth.

Some Australian critics have found metaphysical complexities in this poem, a view of the world and a sense of sin, particularly of the sexual sort; but to me the poem seems most remarkable for its wholeness and simplicity. A tranquil, pagan eye, not by any means without humour, is turned upon the Jewish-Christian story. This itself makes for freshness. And it is the naturalness of the events in the fable which the poet emphasises, the warmth, and goodness and human incongruity of the story; the theological implications are quite suppressed, are not in fact really there at all. If there is a view of life implicit in the poem, it is certainly not a religious or philosophical one; it is not even a psychological one in which the poet's own tensions are involved; it is, I believe, an aesthetic view, which sees the excellence of life as the shaping of experience into an objective and harmonious pattern.

If one wanted as Mediterranean but a more intimately personal and self-involved poem, one would go to *Ascent into Hell*, where the poet travels into his interior life in search of a meaning and an explanation and uses again, in keeping with that scientific habit which was part of his education, the reductive method he employed

in *The Dinner*. But while there the poet was the evolutionary bio-
logist, here he is the genetic psychologist. The difference between
Hope and the psychologist, however, is that Hope brings to bear
upon his enigmatically impalpable subject, the vaguely glimmering
beginnings of his existence, not external measuring instruments but
that most refined and disciplined of faculties, the matured poetic
consciousness. Each glimpse of, each hint about, the beginning of
his life has a poetic definition and actuality of being, and the whole
poem itself has the solidity of an event. He defines first his point of
entry, the conscious intention which is something distilled as much
by his total situation as by what he deliberately means to do.

> *I, too, at the mid-point, in a well-lit wood*
> *of second-rate purpose and mediocre success,*
> *explore in dreams the never-never of childhood,*
> *groping in daylight for the key of darkness;*

The Dantesque reminiscence reminds us not to forget Hope's
characteristic and wholly unaffected daring. But such nerve is
justified by the naturalness with which the poem starts, and the
propriety and evenness with which the body of it flows from the
opening. He next defines the location, Tasmania, where the
marsupial territories and the gum trees together with the twilight
poplars and the church pines combine the genius of Australia and
Britain, that particular blend of sensibility which is the poet's genius
too. This place, the product of two national sources, is not just an
enclosing context but an inward condition of the child's psychology. Implicit in that condition is a powerful sense of distance, of
distance as a positive and creative dimension of imagination.

> . . .
> *revisit, among the morning archipelagoes,*
> *Tasmania, my receding childish island;*
> *unchanged my prehistoric flora grows*
> *within me, marsupial territories extend:*
>
> *there is the land-locked valley and the river,*
> *the Western Tiers make distance an emotion,*
> *the gum trees roar in the gale, the poplars shiver*
> *at twilight, the church pines imitate an ocean.*

He follows the 'dwindling soul' back to where memory, no longer
a solid continent, splits into disconnected fragments and images, to
a point where the language of thought and feeling falls away into
words which are no longer supported by rational syntax. This is
the child's universe distorted by violence and terror, existing wholly
in its parts, in terrifying bits and pieces, 'the inner world of panic'.

. . .

the bayonets and the pickelhauben gleam

among the leaves, as, in the poplar tree,
they find him hiding. With an axe he stands
above the German soldiers, hopelessly
chopping the fingers from the climbing hands.

The fantasies of the young child strike the adult as deficient above
all in reality, since they seem to him to lack the essential content of
experience. But they are real in other ways: they have the intensity
of lightning and the permanence of scars; and they are real not only
as events but as influences, laying down and affecting the very cells
of personality and fastening real things and real influences into the
foundations of self.

. . .

Dreamlike within the dream real names and places

survive. His mother comforts him with her body
against the nightmare of the lions and tigers.
Again he is standing in his father's study
lying about his lie, is whipped, and hears

his scream of outrage, valid to this day.

The substance of the poem is made up of memories of violent
moments from infancy to childhood, shot through with guilt and
fear, which stand out in the poet's life as passages of naked existence
when a mysterious sense of being worked in a pure and powerful
way. The poem is, in fact, a footnote in shorthand to *The Prelude*,
in a Tasmanian rather than a North British accent. But because it is
genuinely personal and totally identified with its own conditions,
it is novel and quite underivative. And while it is not religious

or numinous in the Wordsworthian manner, it has a dimension of the same kind. The poet is aware of the unique in his experience and the mystery surrounding it. Completely conscious in an altogether contemporary way—he is after all casual, Australian and post-Freudian—he is still able to acknowledge the inexplicable in his life; and there is no absurdity in his calling upon whom he does to enforce this admission.

> Beyond is a lost country and in vain
> I enter that mysterious territory.
> Lit by faint hints of memory lies the plain
> where from its Null took shape this conscious I
>
> which backward scans the dark—But at my side
> the unrecognized Other Voice speaks in my ear,
> the voice of my fear, the voice of my unseen guide;
> 'Who are we, stranger? What are we doing here?'
>
> And through the uncertain gloom, sudden I see
> beyond remembered time the imagined entry,
> the enormous Birth-gate whispering, 'per me,
> per me si va tra la perduta gente.'

Hope is a remarkable poet, the most distinguished his country has produced. His very positive literary character is both grainily individual and strongly in the main Western literary tradition. It is, it is clear, the central tradition he adheres to: accretions, whether modish or cliqueish, he has no use, and indeed considerable scorn, for. The lucidity and correctness which he is at pains to develop in his work are qualities he admires from artistic conviction, as a humanist opposed both to romantic haze and conventional trends. But they also testify to a profound cultivation of spirit, a certain wholeness and harmony of nature, as they do too to a fine independence of literary fashion.

Hope comes at a sensitive and influential point in his nation's history, when a separate national consciousness has become clear and firm, and when the humanising influence of the arts is more than ever necessary as wealth, power and material energy increase. In Hope's poetry we sense not only the presence but also the pungency of values which are an extension of personal and national character, namely vitality, order, honesty and the capacity for not being unduly impressed. The future requires that the consciousness of the race be articulated in, and refined by, arts generated on its own soil, above all by the supremely expressive art of language, since nothing has more human reality than the savour of home. Hope has made his own invaluable contribution to this essential purpose.

CHAPTER V

KATHERINE MANSFIELD

KATHERINE MANSFIELD was born in Wellington in 1888
to a prospering business family—her father later became Sir
Henry Beauchamp. There were two older sisters and a younger
brother in the family, together with unmarried aunts and a grandmother. She was educated at a boarding school in New Zealand
and later in London. Her wealthy father made her an allowance
which continued throughout her life and she left for London for
good at the age of 19. She led a confused and wretched personal life.
There was a pregnancy, marriage to a man who wasn't the father
of the child, a miscarriage, other love affairs, and finally comparative
peace with John Middleton Murry when their life together began
in 1912. They were not able to marry until 1918. Almost from the
time she came to London her health was poor and she died of
tuberculosis at Fontainebleau in 1923. Her writing career was spent
in Europe and her reputation made there. Most of the critical
attention accorded to her—at one time it was considerable—concentrates upon her as a European writer. Very little, with the
exception of the fine essay by Professor Ian Gordon,[1] takes into
account what becomes increasingly a significant fact about her,
that she was a New Zealand writer. This is not merely a matter of
provenance but of substance. The brilliance of her innovating
contribution to the short story and her subtle mastery of its technique seems to place her firmly in the European world of the 20's
and 30's. But as time has tended to diminish the glitter of this
particular part of her reputation, or at least to give it a more purely
historical importance, we have to see that it is impossible fully to
realise the nature of her sensibility without understanding the
nature of the experience she aimed to communicate. It is not an
exaggeration to say that in her best work this is experience saturated

[1] Gordon, I. A., *Katherine Mansfield*, Longmans Green & Co., London, 1954

with the quality of the rejected country. She was a writer of a markedly autobiographical sort. She explored and used and organised what had happened to her. And in the best part of her best work she was concerned intensely with the world of childhood, or rather the world of children and adults linked together. She is indeed the poet of a family with young children. And the material of which that poetry was made was New Zealand life.

I am not thinking of muted but audible differences in the description of physical life, the strange birds, the paddocks and creeks, the tussoch grass, purple orchids and the manuka bushes, the red and white camellia trees, or the corrugated iron roof which bangs in the wind; not even locutions—'Night O' or 'Kezia thieved out the back'; but of a certain idiom of vision and style of feeling. It includes perception which is quick, candid and exact; reaction which is open and uncommitted by a cargo of presupposition: an expression which is limpid and fluent; a technique which accumulates finely registered detail with such density as to produce massive, reverberating effects; and an interest which is intimate with the past and thoroughly domestic. Let me illustrate this last point expressly, and the other points incidentally. Here is a passage from *Prelude*, one of the early, important New Zealand stories.

> . . . Old Mrs Fairfield's arms were bare to the elbow and stained a bright pink. She wore a grey foulard dress patterned with large purple pansies, a white linen apron and a high cap shaped like a jelly mould of white muslin. At her throat there was a silver crescent moon with five little owls seated on it, and round her neck she wore a watch-guard made of black beads. . . . It was hard to believe that she had not been in that kitchen for years; she was so much a part of it. She put the crocks away with a sure, precise touch, moving leisurely and ample from the stove to the dresser, looking into the pantry and the larder as though there were not an unfamiliar corner. When she had finished, everything in the kitchen had become part of a series of patterns. She stood in the middle of the room wiping her hands on a check cloth; a smile beamed on her lips; she thought it looked very nice, very satisfactory. . . . Linda leaned her cheek on her fingers and watched her mother. She thought her mother looked wonderfully beautiful with her back to the leafy window. There was something comforting in the sight of her that Linda felt she could never do without. She needed the sweet smell of her flesh, and the soft feel of her cheeks and her arms

and shoulders still softer. She loved the way her hair curled, silver at the forehead, lighter at her neck, and bright brown still in the big coil under the muslin cap. Exquisite were her mother's hands, and the two rings she wore seemed to melt into her creamy skin. And she was always so fresh, so delicious. The old woman could bear nothing but linen next to her body and she bathed in cold water winter and summer.

We see drawn in this passage the confining line within which Katherine Mansfield is able to act with remarkable spontaneity and freedom. The personal past, the known place, the home, the physical context and the chores of the household, family relationships which combine continuity and intensity and in particular the to and fro, the friction and harmony of young and old—these are the points through which the line goes. The area it encloses is narrow but capable of endless treatment. Katherine Mansfield's exquisite clarity of the eye reveals marvellously unfilmed surfaces, and her decorative sense makes brilliant patterns from the details the eye discovers. ('Discovers' because they are not faded by custom but seen in their original excitement.) Moreover, the fluency with which her vision moves releases the details from any static quality and composes them into a moving process. In these household scenes in the New Zealand stories we see none of that bitchiness and getting back at the world we feel in many of her other stories where the art, or technique, is a kind of therapy for the self used by a clever and dissatisfied personality. It is a strange thing that nostalgia which for so many writers is the occasion for indulgence is for Katherine Mansfield a discipline of remembrance. Her feelings are strong but disinterested, and the fidelity and accuracy of her observation brace and control her attitude.

Prelude, one, and one of the best, of the New Zealand stories, was written in 1916 as *The Aloe* but not published till 1930. There are three generations in it, the grandmother, then Stanley and Linda Burnell, and Linda's unmarried sister Beryl Fairfield, and the children, Isabel, Lottie and Kezia. The co-presence of the several generations was a device which enabled Katherine Mansfield to add a temporal thickness to her feeling for the light texture of immediate life. Two of the generations appear in the piece I have given above, and there is a significant contrast between the grandmother and Linda which recurs in the other stories. Grandmother is 'seen' in vivid particularity from the detail of her ornaments to the quality of her skin. Her movements in the kitchen, precise and rhythmic, her gift of conferring her civilising influence on the new, raw house, and the freshness of the whole impression she makes show a regard on the author's part which is closely attentive and appreciative but also sufficiently detached to be coolly in proportion.

Linda on the other hand, the vaguely dissatisfied, not definitely ill or well wife and mother, is not seen in the same way. She is as invisible as one is to oneself. She is the enigmatic present which is never wholly comprehended. Her feelings are misty, her identity a puzzle. She acts as the author's present consciousness which requires a dimension of distance in time to see its objects with total clarity. The grandmother represents for the daughter, and for the author, a wholesome and experienced wisdom, not passively but grittily resigned to reality. But the daughter is all the time nervously anxious to escape or evade it. Her romantic aspirations float about her, never quite grasped, but never strong enough to submerge her appreciation of the grandmother's richness. The grandmother is both Linda's ideal and her hold on reality. Retired from time, her creamy skin exquisitely fresh, able to bear nothing but linen next to her body, bathing in cold water winter and summer, she represents the value and definition which the misty, unformed Linda so much feels the lack of in her own nature.

The children, also distanced by time, are 'seen' in the same way as the grandmother. The members of Linda's generation, however, the husband Stanley and the sister Beryl as well as Linda herself, are felt rather than seen. Which is not to say that they are not substantially realised. They are, but in a different mode. The grandmother and the children are the objects of a kind of creative observation, whereas Linda, her husband and sister, are projected out of the author's shared nature and common predicament. If there is a patch of incomprehension or an unresolved knot in their nature, this belongs properly to their state of relative formlessness.

And indeed, each of them is marked by a certain arrest of development. Stanley is bustling and muscle-conscious, but flinchingly uncertain within. His peremptory casing conceals the softness of the ungrown rather than the gentleness of the experienced. Beryl's romantic fantasies, which the author reproduces with the exact nuance of self-hypnotised wonder, are punctured by bouts of frantic domestic activity and grim moments of self-recognition. But even these last are turned into passages of drama. If Stanley has failed to mature, Beryl is just (although there are hints that she may remain always so) immature. Linda herself, balancing (perhaps too neatly) the character of Stanley, achieves her purposes —but she is never quite sure what these are—through a kind of ruthless helplessness. Wavering and uncertain in action, she is concentrated and even fierce in desire. She has the selfishness of the beautiful and the spoilt, in spite of her 'three great lumps of children'.

The animating theme of *Prelude*—the theme is an event not an issue or a problem in psychology—is the Burnell family's taking-over of the new house, and their gradual soaking of it with their presence. Each generation does it in its own manner. For the grandmother it meant accommodating the new place to the rhythms she had established during her long life; it meant arranging things symmetrically and relating whatever she saw there to a significant and remoter past. When, for example, she notices the tiny corkscrew tendrils of a knotted vine she remembers the vine on the back verandah of her old Tasmanian home. When she puts the crocks away on the dresser, she does it as part of an habitual and hallowed practice. She touches the new house with her own essence. For the children the move to the new house is altogether natural, since its freshness and novelty match their own open nature with its exciting impulse to discover. The middle generation of Stanley and Linda and Beryl have a less clear-cut relationship with the new house. Just as their own rôle, at this time of their life, is more baffling than the children's or the grandmother's, so their connection with the new house is more ambiguous. Stanley is thrilled with the possibilities of a more solid and better ordered life; at the same time he has sudden terrors about possible disasters.

Beryl adores the new opportunities for fantasy, but is appalled at being shut away to rot in the country.

On Linda, the most complex of the three, the move to the new house hardly registers as such. Profounder experiences than this, like love and birth, have only brushed her in the lightest way. The novelty of a new home is too abstract an experience for her, for whom the fascination of life lies in two things, one, the fine free floating life of her own feelings and two, in her strange empathic faculty for sharing in the secret life of things. The intensity of these experiences is a function of her personality and is unaffected by a change of context. Linda is one of those whose concentration on detail leaves her unaware of the larger shape. But the detail itself has a fierce and passionate life, as well as a kind of sadness, since part of the impression it always leaves is its own limitation and imperfection.

. . . She turned over to the wall and idly, with one finger, she traced a poppy on the wall-paper with a leaf and a stem and a fat bursting bud. In the quiet, and under her tracing finger, the poppy seemed to come alive. She could feel the sticky, silky petals, the stem, hairy like a gooseberry skin, the rough leaf and the tight glazed bud. Things had a habit of coming alive like that. Not only large substantial things like furniture but curtains and the patterns of stuffs and the fringes of quilts and cushions. . . . But the strangest part of this coming alive of things was what they did. They listened, they seemed to swell out with some mysterious important content, and when they were full she felt that they smiled. But it was not for her, only, their sly secret smile; they were members of a secret society and they smiled among themselves. Sometimes, when she had fallen asleep in the daytime, she woke and could not lift a finger, could not even turn her eyes to left or right because THEY were there; sometimes when she went out of a room and left it empty, she knew as she clicked the door to that THEY were filling it. And there were times in the evenings when she was upstairs, per- haps, and everybody else was down, when she could hardly escape from them. Then she could not hurry, she could not hum a tune; if she tried to say ever so carelessly—'Bother that old thimble'—THEY were not deceived. THEY knew how frightened she was; THEY saw how she turned her head away as she passed the mirror. What Linda always felt was that THEY wanted something of her, and she knew that if she gave herself up and was quiet, more than quiet, silent, motion- less, something would really happen.

'It's very quiet now,' she thought. She opened her eyes wide, and she heard the silence spinning its soft endless web. How lightly she breathed; she scarcely had to breathe at all.

Yes, everything had come alive down to the minutest, tiniest particle, and she did not feel her bed, she floated, held up in the air. Only she seemed to be listening with her wide open watchful eyes, waiting for someone to come who just did not come, watching for something to happen that just did not happen.

Katherine Mansfield was a writer who succeeded in her best work, in *Prelude* for example, in raising a whole world on the slim basis of half a dozen members of a provincial New Zealand family. She was able quite unportentously to suggest the human universality implicit in the Wellington household. Taking over a new house is itself an instance of the way in which domestic commonplace becomes more largely significant since it is a natural extension of the human impulse to turn impersonal things in the direction of humanity. The conditions of success required by Katherine Mansfield for making the brilliantly pictured particular expressive of substantial human nature were the creative action of memory working in a setting with which she was intimate without strain, a set of characters in whom lurked all the actualities of her own past and a nest of relationships which were rich and ancient but also thronging with possibilities of development and contrast; and as well as these, a general sense, not by any means present in most of her stories, the sense that Beryl has intermittently in *Prelude*— that 'life is rich and mysterious and good. . . .' The goodness comes from the coherence of value and attitude which supports the life of the family and its society; the richness from the emotionally grounded and significantly interesting and worthwhile life its different members live, in which variety is sustained by the strength of the family union; the mysteriousness from the writer's power to reproduce the radiant and inexplicable in human experience. (Linda's version of this mysteriousness appears in the passage I have just quoted.) In these New Zealand stories Katherine Mansfield's sympathetic imagination is controlled by a gift for allowing freedom to the subject so that an extraordinary sureness of touch goes with a remarkable absence of manipulation or forcing of the material.

And the world represented in the New Zealand stories is almost completely uncramped by inherited rigidities. It is open, aerial, unfoggy, lucent. Not that it is without its blemishes of prejudice, like Beryl's icily superior behaviour to the servant Alice in *Prelude*, or the adults' stiff imperviousness to the feelings of the bereaved working class family in *The Garden Party*. But these are, perhaps, more defects of personal sensibility than the formal coldness of class. The Wellington world may not be class-free but class is not the principle on which it is based. Nor is class anything like so strong in its hold on society as family. The divisions of this society are vertical, from family to family, rather than horizontal, from social layer to layer. Within the family the ideal lies in the combined keeping of the very old and the very young. The old, like the grandmother in *Prelude*, offer a standard of life which combines in a surprising but harmonious way the virtues of the well-bred with the qualities of classlessness. The young, on the other side, show vitality unqualified by the bias of *a priori*. Their innocence is not merely negative but a living capacity for experience. The old represent experience carefully gathered up and modestly preserved; the young the intensity with which we live. Between them are the puzzled adults, much less sure of themselves than the very young, much more puzzled about what they aspire to than the old. It is an open universe full of air and freshness. But there runs through it, too, saving it from becoming a nostalgic paradise, a vein, not so much of personal evil, as of natural harshness and even cruelty. We feel the existence of this in the scene in which the good-hearted servant Pat cuts off the heads of the ducks for the amusement of the children in *Prelude*, or where Linda thinks of her husband as an animal, often a nuisance, on occasion a savage, hunting dog. The image of this unavoidable condition of existence, a kind of grimness of reality, is the aloe.

. . . Nothing grew on the top except one huge plant with thick, grey-green, thorny leaves, and out of the middle there sprang up a tall stout stem. Some of the leaves of the plant were so old that they curled up on the air no longer; they turned back, they were split and broken; some of them lay flat and withered on the ground.

Whatever could it be? She had never seen anything like it before.

L

She stood and stared. And then she saw her mother coming down the path.

'Mother, what is it?' asked Kezia.

Linda looked up at the fat swelling plant with its cruel leaves and fleshy stem. High above them, as though becalmed in the air, and yet holding so fast to the earth it grew from, it might have had claws instead of roots. The curving leaves seemed to be hiding something; the blind stem cut into the air as if no wind could ever shake it.

Not all the stories have the rich, many-levelled seriousness of *Prelude* or *At the Bay*, which I shall turn to shortly. There are some, a few no more than sketches, where the strain of impersonal, harsh reality, figured in the aloe, would in fact be out of place. One such is *Her First Ball*, another *Taking the Veil*. Both register with great rapidity the ecstatic, momentary moods of adolescence, and its gift for arguing itself into, and out of, a theoretical despair. Katherine Mansfield in her best New Zealand stories disciplined the expression of self, subduing it to the composition and content of the fiction. In the stories of adolescence this shows itself in an ironic crispness which sympathy keeps just on this side of cool amusement. But the suspension of self-intrusiveness is most evident in the stories about children, in *Prelude* itself, *Susannah*, *How Pearl Button was Kidnapped*, *The Little Girl*, *Sixpence*, *The Wind Blows* and *The Doll's House*. Childhood at one end of the scale like age at the other offered Katherine Mansfield less temptation than more contemporaneous themes to project her own dissatisfaction and tensions into it.

In these stories an attitude of personal detachment supports a subtly perceptive insight. A stance of objectivity and a gift of empathy combine in her technique of modulating the narrative voice at every point into one exquisitely suited to the character and feeling of the moment. Whether it is the very young, as with Kezia in *Prelude*, or the irritated schoolgirl voice of Matilda in *The Wind Blows,* the tone and idiom are exactly right and the transition from author to character conducted with the tact of perfect control. Here are some lines from *The Wind Blows*:

> She has a music lesson at ten o'clock. At the thought the minor movement of the Beethoven begins to play in her head, the trills long and terrible like little rolling drums. . . . Marie Swainson runs into the

garden next door to pick the 'chrysanths' before they are ruined. Her
skirt flies up above her waist; she tries to beat it down, to tuck it
between her legs while she stoops, but it is no use—up it flies. All the
trees and bushes beat about her. She picks as quickly as she can, but
she is quite distracted. She doesn't mind what she does—she pulls the
plants up by the roots and bends and twists them, stamping her foot
and swearing.

'For heaven's sake keep the front door shut! Go round to the back,'
shouts someone. And then she hears Bogey:

'Mother, you're wanted on the telephone. Telephone, Mother. It's
the butcher.'

How hideous life is—revolting, simply revolting. . . . And now her
hat-elastic's snapped. Of course it would. She'll wear her old tam and
slip out the back way. But Mother has seen.

'Matilda. Matilda. Come back im-me-diately! What on earth have
you got on your head? It looks like a tea-cosy. And why have you got
that mane of hair on your forehead?'

'I can't come back, Mother. I'll be late for my lesson.'

'Come back immediately!'

She won't. She won't. She hates Mother. 'Go to hell,' she shouts,
running down the road.

The maddened, and I think calculatedly inaudible, 'Go to hell'
suggests in a certain sense the gulf between the generations. But
much more the words convey, not the uncrossable gap between
youth and maturity, but, rather, their paradoxical connection.
Friction is as close, perhaps even more searchingly intimate, and
certainly more constant than amiability. If this is the negative
testimony to the continuity between the ages, the positive evidence
is the unimpeded flow of mutual understanding between very
young and very old, as in the attachment between Kezia and her
grandmother in *Prelude*.

Alert as Katherine Mansfield was to the continuity of childhood,
to the mysterious ongoing rhythm which carries it forward, she
was equally sensitive to its uniqueness and autonomy. She understood the absolute world of the child, in which things and feelings
are there or not, brilliantly in the foreground or vanished altogether,
in which the present is dominant and neutrality intolerable. She
felt the bitter sense of injustice which children frequently suffer
from, like poor Kezia in *The Little Girl*, whipped for tearing up

her father's speech to fill a pin-cushion she was making as a present for him, or the cruelty practised against them by mealy-mouthed or merely foolish adults, like Mrs Spears and Mrs Bendall in *Sixpence*.

'Oh, my dear,' said Mrs Spears, and she laid her sewing down. 'I don't wonder Dicky has these little outbreaks. You don't mind my saying so? But I'm sure you make a great mistake in trying to bring up children without whipping them. Nothing really takes its place. And I speak from experience, my dear. I used to try gentler measures'— Mrs Spears drew in her breath with a little hissing sound—'soaping the boys' tongues, for instance, with yellow soap, or making them stand on the table for the whole of Saturday afternoon. But no, believe me,' said Mrs Spears, 'there is nothing, there is nothing like handing them over to their father.'

She had a sense of the tip-tilted and melodramatic universe which children inhabit, and of their need to turn objective events into personal crises. She conveyed quite beautifully the way in which for the very young child life is based on a series of incidents, inexplicably unfolding and changing. She saw, too, more intimate things like the significance of touch in the life of the very young, as the essential means by which they break into the world of otherness, and are reassured of its existence and goodness. Think of the deep, the powerful comfort Kezia finds in the touch of her grandmother in *Prelude*, or from her father in *The Little Girl* after a nightmare—the same father, incidentally, who had appeared a ponderous, uncomprehending enemy earlier in the day. She grasped the part sheer size played in the consciousness of children, the menace of what was too large, the delight in manipulating the tiny. What a relief for Kezia again in *The Little Girl* when the immense figure of her father departed after a perfunctory kiss. 'He was so big—his hands and his neck, especially his mouth when he yawned. Thinking about him alone in the nursery was like thinking about a giant.' Or how clearly we see the pleasure of Kezia, in *Prelude*, in arranging the minute bits and pieces of the surprise she is going to make for her grandmother.

... She looked down at the slope a moment; then she lay down on her back, gave a squeak and rolled over and over into the thick flowery orchard grass. As she lay waiting for things to stop spinning, she decided to go up to the house and ask the servant girl for an empty matchbox. She wanted to make a surprise for the grandmother. . . . First she would put a leaf inside with a big violet lying on it, then she would put a very small white picotee, perhaps, on each side of the violet, and then she would sprinkle some lavender on the top, but not to cover their heads.

All the perceptions I have abstracted flow together in the elegant, strong story, *The Doll's House*. At the centre of this 'composition' stands the doll's house, making an emphatic and solid impact; its colours are thick and bright, and its sharp definition and bold actuality insist on the importance it has for the children. Its diminished size and the minuteness of its appointments show reality reduced to a controllable size, a model of the way the children would wish existence to be.

There stood the doll's house, a dark, oily, spinach green, picked out with bright yellow. Its two solid little chimneys, glued on to the roof, were painted red and white, and the door, gleaming with yellow varnish, was like a little slab of toffee. Four windows, real windows, were divided into panes by a broad streak of green. There was actually a tiny porch, too, painted yellow, with big lumps of congealed paint hanging along the edge.
But perfect, perfect little house! Who could possibly mind the smell. It was part of the joy, part of the newness.
'Open it quickly, someone!'
The hook at the side was stuck fast. Pat prised it open with his penknife, and the whole house front swung back, and—there you were, gazing at one and the same moment into the drawing-room and dining-room, the kitchen and two bedrooms. That is the way for a house to open! Why don't all houses open like that? How much more exciting than peering through the slit of a door into a mean little hall with a hat-stand and two umbrellas! That is—isn't it?—what you long to know about a house when you put your hand on the knocker. Perhaps it is the way God opens houses at the dead of night when He is taking a quiet turn with an angel. . . .

It becomes a great thing in the children's lives, a dream realised. It is the rage at school, the one subject during dinner-hour when the children sit under the pine trees eating the thick mutton sandwiches and big slabs of johnny cake spread with butter. The Burnells who own it glow in its reflection and all their relations with the others are modified by their status as owners. Access to it marks the division in the school between those who belong, like the Burnell children and their friends, and the others like Lil and Else Kelvey, who for lunch 'chewed their jam sandwiches out of a newspaper soaked with large red blobs'.

> . . . It was the only school for miles. And the consequence was all the children of the neighbourhood, the Judge's little girls, the doctor's daughters, the store-keeper's children, the milkman's, were forced to mix together. Not to speak of there being an equal number of rude, rough little boys as well. But the line had to be drawn somewhere. It was drawn at the Kelveys. Many of the children, including the Burnells, were not allowed even to speak to them. They walked past the Kelveys with their heads in the air, and as they set the fashion in all matters of behaviour, the Kelveys were shunned by everybody. Even the teacher had a special voice for them, and a special smile for the other children when Lil Kelvey came up to her desk with a bunch of dreadfully common-looking flowers.

This is one of the most explicit of Katherine Mansfield's comments about class in New Zealand, although to a British reader it has a certain gentleness and lightness about it which one would not find in a society more strenuously committed to class. The judgment that 'the line had to be drawn somewhere' points more to a desire for differentiation—of dress and behaviour, perhaps—than the plain recognition of it one would get in a society irremediably involved with class. But in whatever way class existed in Wellington, the doll's house was the occasion for its intrusion into school in the fiercer and less compromising way it takes with the young. The purity of the children's attitude to the doll's house is muddied as the toy becomes a piece in the political game of in-and-out. Fascination becomes hysterical excitement, then impersonal cruelty as the children turn on the outsiders, Lil and Else. Here is a case where the children's merciless satisfaction in playing with their victims is sanctioned by the authority of adults, for whom the freakishly clothed, near-idiot Lil and Else, standing for everything 'common' and graceless, are the fit objects of respectable distaste.

> Lil . . . a stout, plain child, with big freckles, came to school in a dress made from a green art-serge tablecloth of the Burnells', with red plush sleeves from the Logans' curtains. Her hat, perched on top of

her high forehead, was a grown-up woman's hat, once the property of Miss Lecky, the postmistress. It was turned up at the back and trimmed with a large scarlet quill. What a little guy she looked! It was impossible not to laugh. And her little sister, our Else, wore a long white dress, rather like a nightgown, and a pair of little boy's boots. But whatever our Else wore she would have looked strange. She was a tiny wishbone of a child, with cropped hair and enormous solemn eyes—a little white owl. Nobody had ever seen her smile; she scarcely ever spoke. She went through life holding on to Lil, with a piece of Lil's skirt screwed up in her hand.

Only two children, the single-minded Kezia, the youngest Burnell, and the simple-minded our Else (for her sister Lil with her foolish smile and weird, grown-up hat is a soft, co-operative victim, accepting her subordinate station) escaped the general infection, an image, this, of the wider corruption outside. They are saved by the rapt intensity of their self-forgetting attitude to the doll's house.

... The Kelveys came nearer, and beside them walked their shadows, very long, stretching right across the road with their heads in the buttercups. Kezia clambered back on the gate; she had made up her mind; she swung out.

'Hullo,' she said to the passing Kelveys.

They were so astounded that they stopped. Lil gave her silly smile. Our Else stared.

'You can come and see our doll's house if you want to,' said Kezia, and she dragged one toe on the ground. But at that Lil turned red and shook her head quickly.

'Why not?' asked Kezia.

Lil gasped, then she said, 'Your ma told our ma you wasn't to speak to us.'

'Oh, well,' said Kezia. She didn't know what to reply. 'It doesn't matter. You can come and see our doll's house all the same. Come on. Nobody's looking.'

But Lil shook her head still harder.

'Don't you want to?' asked Kezia.

Suddenly there was a twitch, a tug at Lil's skirt. She turned round. Our Else was looking at her with big, imploring eyes; she was frowning; she wanted to go. For a moment Lil looked at our Else very doubtfully. But then our Else twitched her skirt again. She started forward. Kezia led the way. Like two little stray cats they followed across the courtyard to where the doll's house stood.

The children's trance of contemplation in front of the doll's house, and especially before the tiny lamp which sums up all its perfections, is splintered by the cold, proud voice of Aunt Beryl (the shift from child to adult and back to child is managed with silken ease) who represents the adult world they are attempting to deceive. She berates them viciously, brutally shattering their dazed felicity. The ugly and clinically observed thing here is that Beryl's anger is not really genuine, in the sense of being directly provoked by the children's disobedience. She is using them as the means of relieving her own tension. 'The afternoon had been awful. A letter had come from Willie Brent, a terrifying, threatening letter, saying if she did not meet him that evening in Pulman's Bush, he'd come to the front door and ask the reason why! But now that she had frightened those little rats of Kelveys and given Kezia a good scolding, her heart felt lighter. That ghastly pressure was gone. She went back to the house humming.'

In the volume *The Dove's Nest* (1923) in which *The Doll's House* appeared, Middleton Murry quoted from Katherine Mansfield's *Journal* (*Journal*, as he called his arrangement of what was more a rather haphazard Note Book) under the heading *Stories for my New Book*: 'N.Z. At Karori: The Little lamp. I seen it. And then they were silent'. Out of this glimpse of its ending the story shapes itself with buoyant certainty, beautifully exemplifying the wish which appears under another *Journal* entry for July 1921. 'I want to be nearer—far nearer than that. I want to use all my force, even when I am taking a fine line.'

I turn now to a group of stories, published in a number of volumes, which seem to me to go naturally together. These are *The Garden Party*, *An Ideal Family*, *The Voyage*, *Six Years After*, *The Stranger*, and *The Fly*. All but *The Fly* have a New Zealand ambience, and even in this, as Ian Gordon[1] points out, the two protagonists express different aspects of the father-figure, Burnell. These stories have three things in common. They concern themselves with a variety of family relationships spread over a full lifetime. In all of them we are aware of death as a presence or a

[1] Gordon, I. A., *Katherine Mansfield*, Longmans Green & Co., London, 1954, p. 16

threat or as the initiator of action. And each of them exhibits the combination spoken of in the *Journal* of force and a fine line. There is no unabsorbed wash of feeling in them. They are defined by a line which is delicately sinuous, tracing each modification of the narrative contour, but also sure and strong. And at key points they come to considerable, almost painful, intensity.

In *The Voyage* the young girl Fenella, whose mother has just died, is seen off by her father (another solid and nervous member of the Burnell species) on a voyage on the Picton boat with her grandmother, with whom it is suggested she is going to live. The dramatic clarity with which Katherine Mansfield evokes the dockside, the embarkation, and as they arrive, the landfall, brings out the peculiar island-consciousness of the New Zealanders; and the meaning of the ship in the people's lives is felt in its being not another form of transport but a different kind of home, with a saloon for a sitting-room and bunks instead of beds. The little girl is disturbed but not distraught and her grandmother, although agitated at leaving her bereaved son, has learned to sway with the blows of life. The grandmother is beautifully realised, dry and withered but also energetic, efficient and brimming with vitality. She is the natural focus for touches of something I have not spoken of yet, Katherine Mansfield's gift of a serenely mellow good-humour.

> . . . An immense basket of ham sandwiches caught her eye. She went up to them and touched the top one delicately with her finger.
> 'How much are the sandwiches?' she asked.
> 'Tuppence!' bawled a rude steward, slamming down a knife and fork.
> Grandma could hardly believe it.
> 'Twopence *each*?' she asked.
> 'That's right,' said the steward, and he winked at his companion.
> Grandma made a small, astonished face. Then she whispered primly to Fenella, 'What wickedness!'

The domestic scene is given all its fullness and value in grand-mother's undressing in the tiny cabin, in Fenella's washing at the basin.

> The hard square of brown soap would not lather and the water in the bottle was like a kind of blue jelly. How hard it was, too, to turn

down those stiff sheets; you simply had to tear your way in. If everything had been different, Fenella might have got the giggles.

This richness of the domestic interior, a poetic homeliness, meets
them also when they arrive at grandmother's house where 'lying
to one side of an immense bed, lay grandpa. Just his head with a
white tuft and his rosy face and long silver beard showed above the
quilt. He was like a very old, wide-awake bird.' This slim, or rather
wiry, story has complete honesty and real power and it is quick with
implications of the rhythm of life. The desolation surrounding the
child is there—'Oh it had been so sad lately.Was it going to change?'
—but it is seen as part of a more encompassing movement which
includes promise and comfort as well as death. Its fascination lies
in the way in which life here belongs to the aged, the tiny grandmother and the ancient, gay grandfather.

In *The Garden Party*, life is with the young, with the unformed
and generous Laura. The story depends on the gap which exists
between two worlds: Laura's, where the gardener is up since dawn
sweeping the lawns in preparation for the garden party, where
friendly workmen consult her on where the marquee should go,
and where florists bring trays of crimson-stemmed canna lilies, a
world of Godber's cream puffs, cooks, icing and gorgeous hats;
and on the other side, a world of mean cottages where the garden
patches hold nothing but cabbage stalks, sick hens and tomato
cans, swarming children and minute birdcages. 'When the Sheri-
dans were little they were forbidden to set foot there because of the
revolting language and of what they might catch.' These alien
worlds are joined at one point and by one person but through two
opposing forces; life which brims in Laura, and death in the fatal
accident to one of the workmen from the cottages. When this event
breaks into the beautiful morning Laura's reaction is total. She
wants the garden party cancelled. But the family's cool, superior
common sense muffles the force of her response. She is sent in what
is a gesture towards her to the cottages with a basket—a basket!
—of remnants from the party. When she arrives at the stricken
house she finds the mystery of death set about with cheapness and
ugliness and oily neighbours and with just as much convention as
surrounded the garden party at home. There are two absolutes

in this story, life and death, but they are conveyed without the least hint of abstraction in the rapture of Laura's morning and in the remoteness of the young man dead in the cottage. There is not a false or contrived moment in the piece, whether in feeling, character, construction or transition. What the words promise *is* there, even if this is inarticulate or evanescent, like Laura's nearly dumb, deeply felt sense of communication with her brother, Laurie.

In two other stories in the series, *Six Years After*, and *The Stranger*, life is more worn and the faces more ravelled. These too have to do with ships, that constant in New Zealand life. In them both death is the separator—but of the living. In *Six Years After* a mother remembers her son killed in the war as she stares through the rust-spotted railing of the ship at the gulls flying listlessly by: 'they looked cold and lonely. How lonely it will be when we have passed by, she thought. There will be nothing but the waves and those birds and rain falling.' A deeply romantic nature feels even this intolerable grief in a romantic form, as some vague presence calling out to her from the sea. Her nature and its burden had in fact made it impossible for her to grasp the present experience for what it is, and this light impenetrable veil stands between her and her vigorous, but dependent husband. In *The Stranger*, Mr Hammond, again a Burnell type, immensely active and confident but worried, too, and avidly possessive, waits on the dock for his wife's ship to arrive. The harder he tries to get closer to her the more inwardly remote she becomes. And again it is death, not love or life, which is the divisive force. A stranger at sea had died in her arms.

'You're not—sorry I told you, John darling? It hasn't made you sad? It hasn't spoilt our evening—our being alone together?'

But at that he had to hide his face. He put his face into her bosom and his arms enfolded her.

Spoilt their evening! Spoilt their being alone together! They would never be alone together again.

In both these stories one has the impression of observation rather than participation. The author is looking on and reporting back with disciplined fidelity. Death she sees as a force subtly intruding upon and modifying the nature of the living in accordance with the bias of their being.

Where the mood in *The Stranger* was melancholy and in *Six Years After* plangent, in *An Ideal Family* it is bleak, the cold recognition not so much of the laceration of old age as of the onset of death. Old Mr Neave is not really ill or feeble but he is becoming aware—in bones, nerves and soul rather than mentally—of the mutter of mortality. The irony of the title comes from the division between the family reputation—'You are an ideal family, Sir, an ideal family. It's like something one reads about or sees on the stage'—and the vulgar actuality he meets on returning to his house, the fractious family, the bright social chatter, the suave son, the spoiled daughters, the tennis parties, the dressing for dinner, the smart clothes and the frivolous quarrels. All this was too much for old Mr Neave's thinning blood and diminishing appetite. But it is not so much that he embodies a finer spirit than his coarser family as that their vulgarity speaks of life flooding in them, ebbing in him. Another expression of that difference enlivens the splendid first paragraph describing old Mr Neave's encounter with Spring. It was the swirl of life in the Spring which confused and numbed him.

> He stumped along, lifting his knees high as if he were walking through air that had somehow grown heavy and solid like water. And the homeward-going crowd hurried by, the trams clanked, the light carts clattered, the big swinging cabs bowled along with that reckless, defiant indifference that one knows only in dreams. . . .

In the same way, more profoundly antipathetic than his family's suburban commonplace, is the vitality, the life which is suggested by his wife's 'warm, plum-like cheek' or his daughter Ethel's bright hair, or Lola's violent responses. 'They were too . . . too . . . But all his drowsing brain could think of was—too *rich* for him. And somewhere at the back of everything he was watching a little withered ancient man climbing up endless flights of stairs. Who was he?' Nor is there anything particularly stoic or noble about poor Mr Neave's experience. The quality of his coming death is shaped, like the quality of his life, by his own thin nature. When he sees himself in the detached telescopic way of one slipping away from life, what he sees is 'that little ancient fellow . . . climbing down endless flights that led to a glittering, gay dining-room. What legs he had! They were like a spider's—thin, withered'; and what he hears is 'the wind of evening [shaking] the dark leaves to a thin airy cackle'.

In the scale of grimness made up by the series of stories I have just been considering, *The Fly* is the most savagely mordant. Its setting could be any British city. But the two elderly men meeting in the boss's office are two faces of Katherine Mansfield's New Zealand male, the Burnell father-husband, the one before, the other after the crisis of finally giving up work. Old Woodifield, the retired employee, stares almost greedily at the boss, sitting rosily in his chair, and deriving deep satisfaction from the frailer, muffled figure before him. There is a great business of a glass of whisky given and accepted which conveys not simply pity from the active to the inactive but even a half-submerged fear at what is about to happen to oneself. A visit to Belgium brings up the subject of the boss's son, killed in the war six years ago. (Here again is that echo from Katherine Mansfield's personal life, the beloved brother lost in the war.) The puzzled boss discovers that he now feels no grief, that in fact he feels nothing. At this point he notices a fly in his inkpot, feebly trying to climb out. He rescues the fly out of admiration for its courage, and in a detached, dreamy way he drops a blob of ink on it, giving himself a chance to admire its pluck again; and he does it once more after it has painfully cleaned its legs, and then again.

> He leaned over the fly and said to it tenderly, 'You artful little b . . .' And he actually had the brilliant notion of breathing on it to help the drying process. All the same, there was something timid and weak about its efforts now, and the boss decided that this time should be the last, as he dipped the pen deep into the inkpot.
>
> It was. The last blot fell on the soaked blotting-paper, and the draggled fly lay in it and did not stir.

The paradox of the story is that the living man, not the dead boy, is the representative of death. The dead boy was alive when he died. The old man with his inky fly is simply embalmed. It is a cold, terrifying story and it speaks for the stony, impersonal quality, the indifferent process of life which is a theme running through many of the stories, and which was present in a more generous context in *Prelude* in the shape of the aloe that held 'so fast to the earth it grew from, it might have had claws instead of roots'.

A Katherine Mansfield story is a complex, subtly woven organism, making its point, or its several points, by a blend of implication, imagery, contrasting half-tones and the manœuvring of distinct but chiming voices, each voice and each viewpoint melting without grating or jar into the next. It is, that is, a poetic technique with the characteristic of such, a capacity to stay transparently faithful to the author's vision and also to take on colour, whether it be subdued or strong, perfectly fitted to the theme at any given moment. That this is the mode natural to Katherine Mansfield's genius is clear if we look at two stories, the one a failure, the other not her finest, where a prosaic is contrasted with a poetic technique. *The Woman at the Store* is violent and clever in an obvious way. There is in it no throb of personal experience or history, and certainly no sanction in the self. It is a plotted, too carefully plotted, sequence of events with a calculated crisis and a neat twist. A gang of sweating muscular workers are riding between jobs on their way to the store, randily in hope of game, and they are met by a scrawny woman, deserted and whining, and her moronic child. This youthful exercise in the wild colonial boy manner labours on its predestined route to a predictable climax: a mean, chemical kind of sex between the woman and one of the men provokes the child's spite at being excluded from its mother's bedroom. It puts its only talent to service by drawing a picture of the forbidden subject, the mother shooting and burying the father. Any value the story has comes from its indignant sense of the female exploited by the rapacious and fundamentally indifferent male, and from the way in which the scene and the weather are made to echo the mood. But the melodramatic seeps in here too. 'There is no twilight in our New Zealand days, but a curious half-hour when everything appears grotesque—it frightens—as though the savage spirit of the country walked abroad and sneered at what it saw.'

The same theme, the used woman, and the same device, making mood resonant in scenery, appear in *A Birthday*, which for all its

German names and its publication in the volume *In a German Pension* is distinctively New Zealand. The theme and the device, however, are very much more sensitively handled. The connection with the physical world is more obliquely made and the feminine theme is realised solely through the consciousness of the husband. One notices particularly, too, how time, which was used in *The Woman at The Store* as a successive medium, in which each event is provoked by and provokes another, is in *A Birthday* much more characteristically simultaneous. Time is a wavering direction and its tenses have no absolute status. They are qualified by feeling and by intention and they waft back and forth as the fiction requires. Andreas Binzer, one more male member of the Burnell species, whose wife is in labour; the doctor, a hearty man protected by certainty and conceit; and the maid dramatically ready to yield her allegiance at the slightest encouragement, are all vividly delineated and marked off from one another, perhaps more sharply than is the case in her subtler stories. Andreas is physically tough but infinitely vulnerable, above all to any pain of his own, even when this is induced in him by the sounds of his wife's labour. He reveals himself in that kind of analysis in which self-deception is more revealing than sincere confession. Monster as he is in some ways, he is monstrous in a genuinely human way. We can all grasp and share in the macabre drama which goes on behind Binzer's set, social face. In this story character shades into place—the neglected street in the small sordid town—and feeling into atmosphere, 'Suddenly he realised that the wind had dropped, that the whole house was still, terribly still. Cold and pale, with a disgusting feeling that spiders were creeping up his spine and across his face, he stood in the centre of the drawing-room, hearing Doctor Erb's footsteps descending the stairs.' His wife's suffering presents itself to Andreas as a form of cruelty, and this inversion of reality is completely acceptable, and, we realise, universal. This perception of the collision, or rather conflation, of the categories of experience, produced by stubborn human self-centredness, is made with telling, ironic economy in the last lines, where death and birth themselves are rolled together.

He saw Doctor Erb come into the room; the room seemed to change into a great glass bowl that spun round, and Doctor Erb seemed to swim through this glass bowl towards him, like a goldfish in a pearl-coloured waistcoat.

'My beloved wife has passed away!' He wanted to shout it out before the doctor spoke. . . .

'Well, she's hooked a boy this time!' said Doctor Erb. Andreas staggered forward.

'Look out. Keep on your pins,' said Doctor Erb, catching Binzer's arm, and murmuring, as he felt it, 'Flabby as butter.'

A glow spread all over Andreas. He was exultant.

'Well, by God! Nobody can accuse *me* of not knowing what suffering is,' he said.

True, and effective, and comic as this is, I still think the man versus woman concern in *A Birthday* is just one degree too generalised, just as the characters, grossly husbandly husband, hearty doctor, foolish maid, seem a shade too firmly defined or outlined. Nobody could have this feeling about the thoroughly penetrated material of *At the Bay*. In this story, as in *Prelude*, Katherine Mansfield possesses perfectly, and uses marvellously, the kind of knowledge Henry James spoke of in his essay on Flaubert, 'the knowledge by which he was subsequently to measure everything, appeal from everything, find everything flat'. This was the ultimate premise of Katherine Mansfield's work, a knowledge which was the assimilated, mastered experience of family, home, New Zealand. The story itself is composed of twelve separate pieces, each one marking a certain phase of the day. There is a faint temporal connection from section to section. The first one begins 'Very early morning', the second 'A few moments later'; and so on. The central impression, however, is not of the successiveness of time but of its presentness, an immediacy in which there is nothing hard or fixed. The moment contains, as it were, an incurving space in which the forms of people and events appear, act and turn away. Each piece combines the mysteriousness of existence with the homeliness of actuality. When her attention is turned to the physical world, a tentative contingent note, and the feeling of the senses concentrated, even strained, in recording it imply, not uncertainty, but a discipline of accuracy. How far? She asks at one point, and a little later, What was it?—Questions which by limiting and defining ratify the fidelity of the recording instrument and establish more firmly the existence of the place—or rather the event which is what her response turns place into. The introductory section evokes the misted, edge-dissolving morning,

> It looked as though the sea had beaten up softly in the darkness, as though one immense wave had come rippling, rippling—how far? Perhaps if you had waked up in the middle of the night you might have seen a big fish flicking in at the window and gone again. . . .

This cloudy context is interrupted by the passage of the sheep—'their thin, stick-like legs trotted along quickly as if the cold and the quiet had frightened them', by the sheep-dog, and then by the shepherd,

> He was a lean, upright old man, in a frieze coat that was covered with a web of tiny drops, velvet trousers tied under the knee, and a wideawake with a folded blue handkerchief round the brim. One hand was crammed into his belt, the other grasped a beautifully smooth yellow stick. And as he walked, taking his time, he kept up a very soft light whistling, an airy, far-away fluting that sounded mournful and tender.

This use of a liquid, lapsing movement together with the presentation of exact, absolutely immediate actuality, the first the medium in which the second has its brilliant, complete existence, fits both the sensibility of the author, which works by combining lucidity and suggestiveness, and also the nature of her purpose, which is to extract from minor occurrences the essential dimensions of reality. Memory, in Katherine Mansfield's work, consecrates the commonplace and particularly the routine of family life, not in any muffling or mystical way, but in a manner which made it capable of revealing the intricate, amazing richness of the ordinary.

She reveals, for example, the unexpected folds which lie beneath the simple, straight lines of routine family behaviour, the malice felt towards the close relative who invades one's privacy by sharing the ocean with one at eight o'clock in the morning, incidentally betraying to oneself one's raw susceptibility to his maddening intrusiveness; or the significance in the family context of *not* passing the sugar at the breakfast table. 'What did this mean? As Stanley helped himself his blue eyes widened; they seemed to quiver'; or the pleasure of the women when the man leaves in the

M

morning. 'Oh, the relief, the difference it made to have the man out of the house. Their very voices would change as they called to one another; they sounded warm and loving and as if they shared a secret.' There are subtler observations of the truth of family relations than these. There is the portrait of Linda Burnell in a romantic posture, dreaming the morning away under the manuka tree while the baby lies beside her on the grass and then the shock of realising while she poses in a setting clearly designed for a more traditional emotion, her indifference to the baby, and to all her children. Half her life is spent in the dread of having children, and the other half in disliking the ones she has had. The relationship of the husband and wife, Stanley and Linda, apparently so calmly conventional, is really agitated and ambiguous. His fury at her unoffered sympathy is balanced by his unrecognised punishment of her.

> 'Stick, dear? What stick?' Linda's vagueness on these occasions could not be real, Stanley decided. Would nobody sympathise with him? . . .
> Stanley waved his arm to Linda. 'No time to say good-bye!' he cried. And he meant that as a punishment to her.

The Stanley Linda had married, 'timid, sensitive, innocent Stanley, who knelt down every night to say his prayers, and who longed to be good', this Stanley is now wrapped in activity and buried in the business man. It was very seldom she saw *her* Stanley.

> There were glimpses, moments, breathing spaces of calm, but all the rest of the time it was like living in a house that couldn't be cured of the habit of catching fire, or a ship that got wrecked every day. And it was always Stanley who was in the thick of the danger. Her whole time was spent in rescuing him, and restoring him, and calming him down, and listening to his story.

This relationship is an example of the intimacy which divides; there is another of the remoteness which draws together. The relationship of Kezia and her grandmother is the purest and most disinterested of the many explored in the story—a positive abundance, in fact, in view of the limitation of the form. It is one in which each party is totally concerned with the other and the flow of feeling between them is completely free and undisturbed by any subjective twist or knot. An image of this wholesome simplicity is supplied by the very furniture of the room in which the little girl and the old woman are taking their siesta together.

> This room that they shared, like the other rooms of the bungalow, was of light varnished wood and the floor was bare. The furniture was of the shabbiest, the simplest. The dressing-table, for instance, was a packing-case in a sprigged muslin petticoat, and the mirror above was very strange; it was as though a little piece of forked lightning was imprisoned in it. On the table there stood a jar of sea-pinks, pressed so tightly together they looked more like a velvet pin-cushion, and a special shell which Kezia had given her grandma for a pin-tray, and another even more special which she had thought would make a very nice place for a watch to curl up in.

Kezia and her grandmother are talking of Kezia's Australian Uncle William, and it is fascinating to see how the grandmother instinctively pares off every adult accretion and irrelevance from her account, and how this is translated in Kezia's mind.

> 'Well, what happened to him?' Kezia knew perfectly well, but she wanted to be told again.
> 'He went to the mines, and he got a sunstroke there and died,' said old Mrs Fairfield.
> Kezia blinked and considered the picture again. . . . A little man fallen over like a tin soldier by the side of a big black hole.

This relationship contrasts in its clarity with the obscure one existing between Linda and her own children, and in its candour with the equivocal one between Beryl and Mrs Kember, 'a long, strange-looking woman with narrow hands and feet', who looks at Beryl as they undress to bathe in a bold, pawing way. It contrasts, too, in the perfect satisfaction Kezia and her grandmother get out of it, with the vague bond—no more than a common sense of failure—which unites Linda and her brother-in-law, Jonathan, a character who seems faintly to dissolve in the aura of romanticism surrounding Linda and who is hardly seen as a person in his own right. It contrasts, finally, in what I can only call its reality, with the fantasy of Linda's relationship, uneasily longed-for, violently rejected, with the dissolute Mr Kember.

'Reality', I agree, is an off-putting word. But it is difficult to avoid it, portentous as it may be, when one attempts to define the nature of Katherine Mansfield's achievement. Not that she hadn't her failures. Her art was frequently impure, distracted by cleverness or softened by sentimentality or clouded by being used as a kind of personal therapy; and why not in her time at her age with her disease, troubled with the terror of death? But in the New Zealand stories where she has a rich subject and a deep personal engagement, where the best of her capacities are used at the pitch of their force, and where there is a genuine subordination of self to the work, she succeeds quite beautifully in communicating the plural quality of human experience and the several levels on which our lives are conducted. I have referred to the mingling of generations, natural in the family setting, which makes human experience in these stories a concert of time and character, merging tenses and moods. Her mobile conception of experience is realised in the light, rapid run of the prose. Or, since the athletic figure hardly fits the smooth continuity of the medium, perhaps I should say, realised in something more like the flow, the wavy motion, of the prose—which may also suggest its sensitive obedience to every current of feeling and every turn and impulse of action.

And the sensitivity of the medium, also, to the forms and flux of physical life, whether this is the land itself in its own unqualified existence or the landscape as it is modified by human action. Here are some lines from the start of *At the Bay* in which we see the shift from a naked, solitary world to one affected by listening, watching, human presence.

> Ah-Aah! sounded the sleepy sea. And from the bush there came the sound of little streams flowing, quickly, lightly, slipping between the smooth stones, gushing into ferny basins and out again; and there was the splashing of big drops on large leaves, and something else—what was it?—a faint stirring and shaking, the snapping of a twig and then such silence that it seemed someone was listening.

Katherine Mansfield had an exquisitely sure sense of the fine gradations of existence and the passage between them. 'The breeze of morning lifted in the bush and the smell of leaves and wet black earth mingled with the sharp smell of the sea'. But one also finds the beach when it is 'strewn with little heaps of clothes and shoes [and with] big summer hats, with stones on them to keep them from blowing away . . . it was strange that even the sea seemed to sound different when all those leaping, laughing figures ran into the waves'. Or again she shows the garden as land deeply interfused with human influence, occupied in the morning by Linda Burnell, stared at excitedly by Beryl at night. 'But the beautiful night, the garden, every bush, every leaf, even the white palings, even the stars, were conspirators too.' Then she reconstructs those forms of physical life so thoroughly modified by human action that they become expressive symbols of character, like the furniture in grandma's room or the washhouse in which the children played in the evening.

> It was a small tin shed standing apart from the bungalow. Against the wall there was a deep trough and in the corner a copper with a basket of clothes-pegs on top of it. The little window, spun over with cobwebs, had a piece of candle and a mouse-trap on the dusty sill. There were clothes-lines criss-crossed overhead and, hanging from a peg on the wall, a very big, a huge, rusty horseshoe.

And in certain key passages, like this in section nine, she rehearses the process by which each category of existence supports and shades into the next.

> And now the quick dark came racing over the sea, over the sand-hills, up the paddock. You were frightened to look in the corners of the washhouse, and yet you had to look with all your might. And somewhere, far away, grandma was lighting a lamp. The blinds were being pulled down; the kitchen fire leapt up in the tins on the mantel-piece.

Katherine Mansfield's gift for summoning in her art the manifold differences of being in the physical world has its equivalent in the human one, where it shows itself as the nimblest skill in discriminating the various planes and levels of life. In *At the Bay*, *Prelude*, *The Garden Party*, *The Doll's House* we find the *personae*, each in an appropriate tone and idiom, and without the least sacrifice of an unaffected realism, contributing to a lucid system of contrasts, and composing together a scale of experience differentiated according to the degree of 'spirit' or delicacy of being. It is not an hierarchical array where Katherine Mansfield's admiration, as one might perhaps expect of someone with her nature, is accorded to the characters most closely mirroring her own painful strivings after spirituality. It is very much more an objective recognition of the qualitative variety of human life. Nor should one think of it in a straight-forwardly cognitive way as an arrangement of different kinds of knowing, from the highly intelligent to the lively, from the conventional down to the stupid. This would be to overlook the author's sense of the plurality of being which is actively productive here, and her fascination with the rich oddity of human nature. In *At the Bay* Linda's mysterious aspirations and Jonathan's puzzled gropings speak of one part of our nature. The liveliness of the children, their perfect adaptation to the moment and the marine environment ('On the other side of the beach, close down to the water, two little boys, their knickers rolled up, twinkle like spiders') express a vitality balanced between the refined but somehow impoverished quality of Linda's consciousness of life, and the toughness of Stanley Burnell's, at least of the usually visible Stanley Burnell.

> A few moments later the back door of one of the bungalows opened, and a figure in a broad-striped bathing-suit flung down the paddock, cleared the stile, rushed through the tussock grass into the hollow, staggered up the sandy hillock, and raced for dear life over the big porous stones, over the cold, wet pebbles, on to the hard sand that gleamed like oil.

A position on a different part of the range of human existence is taken by Mrs Stubbs, Alice's shopkeeper friend. She embodies the heavy, corporeal element at the furthest distance from Linda. This episode is narrated with Dickensian gusto and a humorous relish for our thick, commonplace—but how appealing!—flesh.

> 'Draw up your chair, my dear,' said Mrs Stubbs, beginning to pour it. 'Yes,' she said thoughtfully, as she handed the tea, 'but I don't care about the size. I'm having an enlargemint. All very well for Christmas cards, but I never was the one for small photers myself. You get no comfort out of them. To say the truth, I find them dis'eartening.'
> Alice quite saw what she meant.
> 'Size,' said Mrs Stubbs. 'Give me size. That was what my poor dear husband was always saying. He couldn't stand anything small. Gave him the creeps. And, strange as it may seem, my dear'—here Mrs

Stubbs creaked and seemed to expand herself at the memory—'it was dropsy that carried him off at the larst. Many's the time they drawn one and a half pints from 'im at the 'ospital. . . . It seemed like a judgmint.'

Alice burned to know exactly what it was that was drawn from him. She ventured, 'I suppose it was water.'

But Mrs Stubbs fixed Alice with her eyes and replied meaningly, 'It was *liquid*, my dear.'

Liquid! Alice jumped away from the word like a cat and came back to it, nosing and wary.

'That's 'im!' said Mrs Stubbs, and she pointed dramatically to the life-size head and shoulders of a burly man with a dead white rose in the button-hole of his coat that made you think of a curl of cold mutton fat. Just below, in silver letters on a red cardboard ground, were the words, 'Be not afraid, it is I'.

'It's ever such a fine face,' said Alice faintly.

The pale-blue bow on the top of Mrs Stubbs' fair frizzy hair quivered. She arched her plump neck. What a neck she had! It was bright pink where it began and then it changed to warm apricot, and that faded to the colour of a brown egg and then to a deep creamy.

'All the same, my dear,' she said surprisingly, 'freedom's best!' Her soft, fat chuckle sounded like a purr. 'Freedom's best,' said Mrs Stubbs again.

I do not want to suggest that the array of differences I have been pointing out is set in some formal, abstract structure. These distinctions are implied; they run under an unbroken surface. Perhaps the strongest impression one gets from *At the Bay* is of a distinct sensibility fluently bending this way and that, and endlessly capable of assimilating without destroying diversities of experience. The manner in this and other New Zealand stories is neither sweetening nor souring. There are none of those infusions of sentimentality and cynicism common enough in the European stories, particularly the 'clever' ones. Nor does the individuality of the style or the idiosyncrasy of rhythm force or twist the material. There is a kind of sensitive neutrality in the medium and it is notable for what I should like to call its non-interference with the subject. A manner making for accuracy and an attitude allowing for respect: these two things witness to the power of the whole New Zealand theme and to Katherine Mansfield's full and controlled response to it. All the poetry of her nature is enlisted, as well as her observer's unblinking attention to the symptom and the illustrative detail, to the wrinkle on the face, or the vein on the pebble, or the fleeting evidence of even not quite articulated feeling.

The world reconstructed with such fidelity—and warmth—in these stories is physically and morally attractive: beautiful in its blend of the Pacific and Western scene, fundamentally decent in its code, and humane in its aspiration. It sustains a mode of life in which children can live imaginatively and adults freely, in which there is a reasonable openness of communication between the sexes and between the different parts of society, and in which the frictions and imperfections, of which there is a full measure, are inward and universal, the products of a substantial, permanent human nature. The figure in which the virtues of this society are collected is the grandmother, Mrs Fairfield. She stands outside the action, mild, firm, tranquil, weathered, having about her an air of bodily sweetness and sober radiance. She has won through to a point of equilibrium between the unavoidable accommodations and the necessary resistances to the rhythms of life. She is saved from any touch of old lady sentimentality by—not a stiffness or severity—but a certain angularity of temperament; and as her exquisite and luminous relationship with her granddaughter Kezia shows, she has, though worn, kept the capacity for true, spontaneous feeling. This relationship stands for all that her New Zealand life meant to Katherine Mansfield herself. It was the ground, the standard, the subject and the nurse of her best art.

CHAPTER VI

MORLEY CALLAGHAN

IT would be hard to find a writer who contrasts more vigorously with Katherine Mansfield than the Canadian Morley Callaghan, whom I wish to consider now. For one thing he works at a much greater psychic distance from, and with a considerably lower degree of sympathy for, the English literary tradition, in which Katherine Mansfield felt so intimately at home. For another, there is in his work, as in that of other Canadians writing in English, a further strain, an implicit sense of oppression by the powerful tradition of the United States. Moreover, Morley Callaghan is a writer whose intentions are simpler than those of Katherine Mansfield, and whose achievement is more restricted—a difference manifested in the contrast of their prose styles: where hers is poetic and suggestive, his is crabbed; where hers is light and gliding, his is stiff. And how extraordinarily discrepant are the materials they treat and the worlds they construct. The world evoked in Morley Callaghan's work is a bleak, industrial one, and its gritty presence rubs off even on the countryside. It is a shut-in, remorseless place in which the individual person even when he lives in a family is painfully isolated. Morley Callaghan's characters in the short stories, with which I shall begin, are mostly drawn from the middle and lower reaches of society: the bereaved poor, the workman, the forsaken wife, the widow, the hard-up young man, the nervous curate and the elderly parish priest, the part-time pugilist, the small girl with a dying mother, the amateur criminal, the drug-store keeper, the apprentice reporter, the cocky young man, the pianist in the tavern. His style is plain to the point of drabness and often painfully clumsy, and yet, in spite of the raw, northern world, the graceless manner and the dreary ordinariness of the characters, the reader is increasingly conscious of an awkward, stubborn and unfashionable conscience, and of a bluntly honest endeavour to dig out and to hold on to some evasive human truth.

'To dig out': as I use the phrase to convey something of Morley Callaghan's hard, blow-by-blow prose, it comes to me that the words say more about him than I had thought. They carry with them a sense of investigation and reporting, and Callaghan's stories strike one precisely as reports—as reporters' reports, in fact. They give the feeling of pre-1914-18 provincial newspaper chronicles, and sometimes of provincial newspaper prose, too. (In fact, Morley Callaghan began his career as a reporter on the *Toronto Star* when Ernest Hemingway was working on the same newspaper.) The storyteller's function as Morley Callaghan practises it is in keeping with this bias in his work. It is to impose an arrest upon time, and to outline for a moment an interruption in the flow of life, which, it is clear, continues as before once the observer's eye is withdrawn. His is a restrictive, framing technique. He is concerned with events, which are shown as instances and images of experience, while the people involved are planed down to an extreme simplicity. A Morley Callaghan story presents a special combination of realistically rendered happening and of people denuded of complication, who are seen as strangers are seen in the street in a single concentrated glance, as types and illustrations. Realism, and a somehow surprising strain of formality, blend in a drily personal way. Indeed, as the reader begins to find his way about the stories, he becomes gradually aware—the effect is slow and cumulative—of an authentic individuality strong enough to show through the plain prose and the straightforward narrative technique.

The reader's sense of that presence is arrived at by continuous application. The unremarkable medium, which has none of the literary sophistication of Hemingway, one of Callaghan's early heroes, takes time to make its mark. And yet it is exactly suited in its unpretentiously humdrum way to the intention on which all this work is sprung, the effort at scrupulous fidelity to the facts of the case. And the 'case' in these stories is the mysteriousness of the ordinary, the inexplicable sequences of feeling, the bewildering discrepancies of human fact, *and* the logic, 'as severe as it is fleeting' as Coleridge has it, which the imagination can elicit from these frictions and inconsequences.

Short stories by Morley Callaghan appeared in 1929 (*A Native*

Argosy,) 1931 (*No Man's Meat*) and 1936 (*Now that April's Here*), and in the two-volume collection (*Morley Callaghan Stories*, 1959). Most of them are strikingly uniform in quality and even a random choice provides the characteristic Callaghan combination, an undistracted concentration on essentials, a rather grouchy but unquestionable honesty, a grave sobriety of mood and treatment and a naturally discriminating moral imagination. Let me look for a moment at the first story, *All the Years of her Life*, in the 1959 collection. The dim and oddly innocent Alfred Higgins is caught by his employer pilfering from the drugstore in which he works silly little objects which he sells for spending money. From this thin, commonplace situation there springs a movement towards complexity, not through analysis but by the natural growth of the action. Alfred's crime, at first denied, and then admitted, becomes an event, a phenomenon, which is gravely scrutinised by Mr Carr, the employer, Alfred himself, who from now on is the registering instrument rather than an active protagonist, and Mrs Higgins, Alfred's mother. She is large and plump with a little smile on a friendly face and seems an intensely positive person beneath her deference. The employer is dislodged from his position of moral superiority, which he had indeed begun to enjoy. Alfred realised that 'Sam Carr was puzzled by his mother, as if he had expected her to come in and plead with him tearfully, and instead he was being made to feel a bit ashamed by her vast tolerance. While there was only the sound of the mother's soft, assured voice in the store, Mr Carr began to nod his head encouragingly at her. Without being alarmed, while being just large and still and simple and hopeful, she was becoming dominant there in the dimly lit store.' The mother's contained strength deflects the angry proprietor. His expression of regret at what happened is almost an apology to her. When Alfred and his mother return to their home he begins to see that the force she showed in the shop was not what it seemed to be. It was not some intrinsic strength of character but a force which issued out of a passion for protection, and once home, with the crisis over, it collapses. As she drinks her tea her hand is trembling and she looks very old. 'He watched his mother, and he never spoke, but at that moment his youth seemed to be over; he knew all the years of her life by the way her hand trembled as she raised the cup to her lips. It seemed to him that this was the first time he had ever looked upon his mother.'

A moment of consciousness—of true recognition, not the usual routine registration—is necessary to clinch the existence of an event, like Alfred's petty crime, or a state of feeling like the mother's weary anxiety, and as it were, to sanction the disturbance it will produce. Or the point of awareness may be necessary to conclude the existence of something long supposed to have been operative: as in the story *An Old Quarrel* where two old ladies, whose nervous trembling age is established with quiet, unsentimental firmness, meet again after many years, one of them under the impression, the illusion as it turns out, that her friend, like her, has spent her life grieving at a bitter, unnecessary quarrel. ' "You shouldn't go on like that, then," Mrs Massey said, fretfully. But she, too, felt her eyes moistening. "Oh, dear, oh, dear." She tried bravely to smile, but it no longer seemed important that they had once quarrelled bitterly, or that her life had been full and Mary's quite barren—just that once they had been young together. A great deal of time had passed, and now they were both old.' But it is never a final revelation, never anything approaching a beatific vision, since it begins at once to be incorporated into a new system of ordinariness. It is this double disappointment which gives a raw reality to several of the short stories, like *Rigmarole* and *Magic Hat*, which have to do with marriage. First the wonder, then the routine, then the recognition, then the new situation and its new unsatisfactoriness, which is sometimes wholly exposed and sometimes merely promised.

Frequently the stroke of realisation brings out that the natural extension of a current state of affairs is, in fact, its contrary. This is so, for example, in *The White Pony*, in which a small boy, ecstatic at the thought of being allowed to attend a circus pony, is led on by a big, freckled, blue-eyed giant of a trainer to carry heavy pails filled with water-soaked sponges, but then brutally excluded when he has done his job.

'No kids in here,' the red-head said brusquely, taking the pails.
'Gee, Mister,' Tony cried. But the door had closed. Tony stood there

with his mouth open, feeling almost sick at his stomach, still seeing the
red-head's warm, magnificent smile. He couldn't understand, if the
red-head were like that, why the pony loved to swing its head to him.
Then he realised that the big fellow had simply used him, that that
was the kind of thing they took for granted in the world he had
wanted to grow into when he had glimpsed it from the garage
window.

'You big red-headed bum!' he screamed at the closed door. 'You
dirty, double-crossing, red-headed cheat!'

The same development by contrariety occurs in *The Shining Red
Apple*, in which the powerful, hairy Joe Cosentino, the green-
grocer, teases and lures the skinny kid who is hanging about waiting
to steal one of the big, juicy-looking apples. Every ounce of energy
and calculation is used to trap the boy, who is suddenly terrorised
as he grasps what is happening. He runs, and Joe is left desolated
that the boy will not succeed in stealing his apple. 'Joe stood on the
sidewalk, an awful eagerness growing in him as he stared at the
shiny red apple and wondered what would happen to the kid he
was sure he would never see again.'

There is a kind of dialectic in human feeling which makes it
swing violently from moment to moment into complete opposition. This movement brings a note of dramatic intensity into
Morley Callaghan's glum and narrow world, making its conflicts
domestic and intense. Turbulence in such a cramped, spiritual
universe—and, incidentally, in such a confined space (the stories
are hardly ever more than a few pages long)—conveys a sense of
unexpected energy: something one feels, too, in Morley Callaghan's
endless inventiveness inside such a limited medium. He has a
particular gift for defining the differing lines of family relationship
and the ugly knots which abruptly interrupt its continuity. There
are of course larger dimensions in his territory. He has a near
Marxist sense of grinding economic law and of the cage of poverty
and unemployment in which many of his subjects are trapped. The
passivity of the poor, an attitude bred by a careful accommodation
to external brutalities, is a favourite theme. At the same time he
shows a certain warmth and sweetness and directness of access to
human feeling which saves the stories from any diagrammatic
coldness.

This is particularly evident in his sensitive treatment of children, where his habit of making the explicit emotional comment appears more naturally than in the adult stories. In *The Little Business Man* the orphaned twelve-year-old Luke lives with his Uncle Henry in a house on the stream by a sawmill. Uncle Henry is a burly man who has mysterious pains which puzzle the doctors, and—fittingly, somehow—an obsessive concern with efficiency and practicality. He decides that the boy's eleven-year-old collie who can hardly see or eat should be put down, not maliciously but simply through motives of efficiency and the economic use of resources. There is nothing personal in his decision —which makes it even more dreadful to the child. The boy saves the dog from being drowned and, using the uncle's character against him, offers to earn and pay seventy-five cents a week for his keep. 'I want to make a practical proposition, Uncle Henry.' Uncle Henry tries desperately to turn his uneasiness and his shame at being weak when he agrees to the boy's keeping the dog into 'a bit of good useful common sense', and he accepts the proposition. ' "I am accepting it because I think you will learn something out of this," he went on ponderously.' The story poses in opposition, disinterested love and practical use, and the subtlety comes in the revelation of how the boy learns to defend the first by adopting the technique of the second. But this triumph is also in a sense an ironic comment on his education because it teaches him that 'love' must be flawed by 'use', and the intrinsic value if it is to be preserved in a world set to destroy it, cannot avoid being infected by the efficient means.

In another story of this kind, *A Cap for Steve*, Morley Callaghan again uses the child's ritualistic nature, the way in which his feelings coalesce overwhelmingly in an object, as the motive of the action. Steve, a games-loving boy, is given a cap by a famous athlete, and the sweaty thing is hallowed for him by an almost numinous glory. He is in despair when it is lost, and all his energy is concentrated on recovering it. When it is found in the possession of a rich man's son, Steve and his father visit the house to reclaim the cap. The scene here is beautifully played out: Steve avid for the cap, the father indignant on his son's behalf, the rich man shrewdly calculating the cost of keeping the cap for his own boy. His mounting offers of course trap Steve's father. The mutual resentment of father and child is developed with clarity and economy. The boy feels that *he* has been sold, the father that *he* has been caught through his son's fault in a web of another man's cunning and his own unfair poverty. The relationship of father and son has a remarkable depth and accuracy and it keeps in play a whole pattern of elements, their circumstances and attitudes, their aspirations and their limitations, their tentative, flinching hopes, their common feeling of betrayal, their fumbling efforts at reconciliation.

The capacity which could produce these clipped, significant stories is not very evident in the early novels, *Strange Fugitive* (1928), *It's Never Over* (1930) and *A Broken Journey* (1932) which are muddy in texture and melodramatic in action. It revealed itself first in *Such is My Beloved* (1934), a novel of which the whole air and idiom belong to the 'thirties, not, that is, the literary 'thirties, but the 'thirties of the depression, of insecurity, unemployment, malnutrition, meanness. Father Stephen Dowling is an assistant priest at a Cathedral—down-at-heel, North American Gothic in a district rapidly crumbling into slumdom. He shines with a special bloom of innocence, health and sincerity. He performs his priestly duties with an eager devotion. He is rapt at the altar, patient in the confessional, conscientious in visiting, eloquent in the pulpit. 'Last Sunday, for instance, at the ten o'clock mass, Father Dowling had preached a sermon on the inevitable separation between Christianity and the bourgeois world, and he spoke with a fierce warm conviction, standing in the pulpit and shaking his fist while his smooth black hair waved back from his wide white forehead and his cheeks were flushed from his glowing enthusiasm. After that sermon, Father Anglin had wanted to argue with the young priest, but he was afraid he would reveal too easily his own lack of faith in any social progress, so, instead of arguing, he merely stared at him with his pale blue eyes and shrugged his shoulders as a kind of warning.' But Father Dowling is also a priest of Irish extraction in a modern industrial society and he likes a good cigar, a ranging conversation with his agnostic friend, a well-cooked meal, a glass of wine, and bridge with the ladies of the parish.

The separation of the two worlds, Christian and bourgeois, is the initiating contrast of the novel. Father Dowling speaks of it in his sermon in a lofty, generalising way. The novel shows it becoming biting and personal—'inevitable' in this way—in his own life. For all his spiritual and social conviction, and in spite of his working-class origins, he himself, because of his education, his status, his looks, his popularity with the parishioners, has a recognised position in the bourgeoisie. Officially he is on the side of religion against bourgeois convention; in reality he has at least one foot in both camps. The point at which the antagonism of the two orders becomes incorporated into his own life, the point at which he starts to be harrowed by the necessity for deciding between them, comes when he meets the two young prostitutes, Ronnie and Midge. One winter night as he walks home from visiting the sick, the two girls solicit him, not realising what he is, and he hurries on in alarm and confusion. But his natural generosity turns him back. From this moment his life is entangled with that of the girls. He visits them in their seedy hotel, ignoring the leers of the proprietor, Mr H. C. Baer. He gives them money and clothes, he begs for them, he tries to find work for them. Above all he becomes their friend, and the girls after their first suspicions and their bewilderment at his motives, recognise his genuine concern and respond to his warmth and sincerity.

The girls' suspicions—the reaction of anyone in their rôle—correspond to Father Dowling's ostensible purpose—his official aim to convert them from their dissolute lives. But the relationship on both sides moves on from this stereotyped posture. Prostitution is only part of the girls' lives, their work, and hard, ill-paid, dirty, dangerous work at that. But it cannot, Father Dowling gropes to realise, be right to identify the person with the function and so to cancel out the girls' essential humanity. On his side, his professional concern with the girls' sinfulness, and his anxiety to redeem them from it, is, at its finest, his own interpretation of a more profoundly human preoccupation, his will to make a human presence available to them. The distinction between the religious and the bourgeois orders, which was implicit, but so ambiguously, in Father Dowling's consciousness at the beginning of the novel, is explored in the light of a similar perception. The point of religion is the expression and refinement of humanity. But many of its attitudes are only ritualistic endorsements of bourgeois prejudices. In the same way, the bourgeois world itself is seen to be larger than a system supported by middle-class morality and comfortable plushness. It stands, indeed, for what is worldly and immoral in a human sense and its membership is by no means limited to the middle classes. Its norm may be the wealthy parishioners Mr and Mrs Robison, its freer, more liberal side may exist in Father Dowling's friend, Charlie Stewart, but it also includes its formal spokesman in the conventional clergy, and a great range of others stretching from the more dubious functionaries necessary to sustain it, like Mr H. C. Baer, or the ghastly Lou, pimp and boy-friend of Ronnie, all the way up to its most eloquent voice, the subtle and impressive Bishop. Religion, during the course of the novel, becomes fined down to a single representative, Father Dowling, whereas the bourgeois world expands to include the proletariat and the aristocracy.

Immediately I write this I find myself, in trying to report on my response to the novel, wanting to correct what may give a misleading impression of neatness. The two worlds, religious and bourgeois, do not fall apart in this absolute way. The standard of human goodness embodied, or painfully achieved, in Father Dowling, is not totally separated from the grubby life of which it is the measure. Just as in Father Dowling himself there is, as I suggested, a clogging residue of bourgeois beliefs, so in the members of the bourgeoisie—in the larger sense—there lurk hints and distorted manifestations of the ideal which burns in Father Dowling. That this should be so, that there should be a distribution of quality over the whole human range, fits the manner of a novel which is governed not by natural law—certainly not that, nor by any Marxist dialectic—but by an economy of naturalness. The partial, uncertain life of the ideal, existing most fully in Father Dowling, may be glimpsed in the timid charity of the pompous Mr Robison, even in the puzzled uneasiness of Lou trying to see what lies behind the priest's actions; or it may be seen in the more complicated struggles of the Bishop's conscience and the irritability with which he applies his analytical intelligence to Father Dowling's situation.

N

'Father Dowling made a fool of himself. It became a kind of arrogance in him. Who does he think he is to win those girls over just by his presence?. . . . If I had it to do over again, I would face the problem in exactly the same way, he thought firmly. What on earth is bothering me then? He was an honest man who committed himself to a piece of folly that can't be tolerated, that's all there is to it.'

The economy of naturalness—which is a reconstruction of movement rather than a Zolaesque realism of detail—is best realised in the principal relationship of the novel, that between Father Dowling and the prostitutes. Its growth, like that of all complex human feeling, is checked, troubled, backsliding, never wholly smooth or continuous; and yet it moves irresistibly onward, obeying and balancing an inward initiative as well as outer circumstances. At first it is sympathetic but embarrassed on one side, suspect and then irritated on the other. 'Ronnie waved her long thin arm threateningly. "Look here. We've got our own way of living just as you've got yours." ' The girls see Father Dowling's intervention as a threat to a whole way of life. They are not persons aware of guilt but resentful of intrusion.

> 'Isn't it better to starve than lose your. . . .'
> 'If that's what's worrying you and if it will buck you up and make us seem like tin saints, we're just about starving now. Look around this dump. See all the silks and satins. What do you see? See that old brown coat of mine over there? I've been wearing it for three years. I have to take it off like it was tissue paper or it'll fall to pieces. Isn't this a lovely room? Don't you hate to put your wet boots on that lovely rug? It's filthy, filthy, filthy. But I'd rather be here than out there,' she said, pointing to the window. The little dark girl was pouring the words out of her as if she had become full of hate. 'We're not even high-class whores, see,' she said. 'We take what comes our way and mighty glad to get it.' She was speaking with all the fury of an indignant, respectable woman and the mingling of her strange humility and her passion was so convincing that Father Dowling began to feel doubtful, as if there might be many things he did not understand. He could see the twisted heels on Ronnie's shoes, the broken toe-cap, and the stockings with the sewn-up runs. A long time ago he had heard a Redemptorist priest preaching a sermon about the luxurious life of vice which was always a temptation to poor girls.

Somehow, he himself had always thought of vice as yielding to the delights of the flesh, as warmth and good soft living and laziness. But as he looked around this room and at these angry girls he felt close to a dreadful poverty that was without any dignity. He felt, too, that Ronnie and Midge worked far harder than almost any young women he knew.

As the priest begins to understand the economic forces beating on the young women ('. . . there was a whole economic background behind the wretched lives of these girls. They were not detached from the life around them. They had free will only when they were free'), his attention is less firmly concentrated on the rescue from prostitution and more on bringing a spontaneous human response from them. ' "Midge, would you do a small favour for me? Come around to the church some time. Just of an evening when the church is full. Will you do that?" "I guess so," she said, looking upset and a bit resentful. He loved to have this response and see that indignant expression. It made him feel there was a depth to her that could be touched, some kind of feeling, even if only resentment, and he was much encouraged. "There's passion still there," he thought.' He wants to come face to face with them as person to person instead of as physician to malfunction. But the girls are what they are, and it is hard for them not to believe that Father Dowling might actually be in love with them. They would encourage him, sit on his knee, put their arms around him, be puzzled when he pushed them away. They could not believe that sooner or later he would not want one or other of them. Father Dowling himself is a full-blooded man and there are moments when he feels the sensual attraction of the young women. 'I ought not to be ashamed of being tempted,' he thought. 'I am not a eunuch. The Church will not accept a eunuch for a priest. I'm a normal man and I wouldn't be normal if I wasn't tempted. But I'll never be tempted like this again.'

Father Dowling's estimate of himself is modest and accurate. He *is* a normal man with the customary ration of sensuality and other faults, but there is also a lambent quality in his nature, a glowing capacity for love, or for charity in theological terms, which slowly burns its way through his ordinary human shabbiness to make its presence felt by others. Even the dim and the malicious become aware of it, even the least sympathetic answer to it. It shows itself not in any extreme spirituality or other-wordliness, but in the power to enter into the lives of others. When he walked about the streets on a mild evening with the snow nearly gone, and freshness in the air 'he passed a young man and a girl walking very close together and the girl's face was so full of eagerness and love Father Dowling smiled'. And it is with Midge and Ronnie, the extravagantly inappropriate whores, the ones at the remotest distance from him, that this gift flowers. Its essential achievement is not to 'save' the girls, who will, it is clear, never leave their profession, not to mediate to them the grace of religion but more miraculously still to communicate the grace of life. 'He felt very happy to have thought of the dresses. It seemed that for a long time he had been groping and scraping away at old reluctant surfaces and suddenly there was a yielding life, there was a quickening response. He sat there hardly smiling, looking very peaceful.'

The contradiction between the donors and the deniers of life is at the heart of *Such is My Beloved*. It is the conclusion to which the original division between the religious and the bourgeois worlds finally leads. Father Dowling in his efforts to be as richly a donor as he can becomes a scandal to the deniers. The novel makes it quite clear why; and not only clear but convincing. It has nothing to do with any sentimental falsification of the girls or of prostitution. The angular Ronnie with her hopeless dependence on her hideous lover, Lou, and the soft, neurotic Midge are thoroughly credible, whether 'loafing or hunting'; and their mechanical promiscuity appears as a flat denial of a fundamental law of life. Father Dowling's offence is caused by a nature with a genius for generosity which can be satisfied only with an immediate, personal relationship with the prostitutes, and which, as a condition of that relationship, acknowledges in the girls an uncrushable human quality; and acknowledges it the more positively the more he gets to know *them* rather than just their shiftless, disorganised lives. The offence is to go outside the routes for treating with such people sanctioned by the Church and the State. The approved institutional modes are those of rescue, punishment, and, in the last resort, banishment. Their common note is one of detachment from an object, kindly or severe or even ruthless as the circumstances require. But Father Dowling's vocation by nature and profession is to personal engagement with a subject. By the end of the novel the two attitudes have been completely exposed and opposed in an angry antinomy. The resolution is uneventful and muted, a quiet, ordinary close to the agitation. A word from the Bishop to Mr Robison, and from Mr Robison to the authorities—all, it must be said, acting with a kind of social sincerity in defence of public propriety—and the police bring the girls before a tired, not inhuman magistrate, who again with much sincerity and even a degree of kindliness, banishes them from the city. Father Dowling, too, suffers his own banishment. In his case it is an internal one, banishment from self and reason. He has a total mental collapse which leaves him only an occasional interval of sanity, and this he promises will be devoted to writing a commentary on *The Song of Songs*: a nice example, this, of a simplicity of character becoming an irony of situation.

As a composition *Such is My Beloved* has the benefit of several qualities not always evident in Morley Callaghan's work. It is a supple and articulate novel. Father Dowling's innocence is connected with spirituality and not with stupidity. He is an intelligent, eloquent man with a taste for analysing his problems. The two girls, Ronnie and Midge, have a quick, feminine expressiveness which makes them lively partners in conversation. So that the language of reflection is more refined, the dialogue nimbler and more vivid than we find either in the short stories or in several other novels. The idiom of this novel is more fluent, the movement less crabbed, and the density less oppressive than in the staple of his work. The minor characters are drawn with just, and no more than, that degree of depth required by a design strongly based on a single central figure and clear leading theme. If novels move between the poles of poetry and journalism, and if Morley Callaghan stands habitually nearer to the journalistic end, then this novel is the exception on the other side. I think this must be because of a natural consonance between talent and theme, because of the inwardness with which the nature of Father Dowling's dilemma is understood and because of the natural human significance which Morley Callaghan is able to extract from a system of religious reference. The religious conception, poetically treated, implicit in the structure of the novel is made to seem luminously relevant to the understanding —not the solution: there is no solution—of a permanent human predicament.

Poetry and religion have a universalising effect in *Such is My Beloved*, making it appear to the British reader more accessible and less off-puttingly embedded in alien ground than, say, *More Joy in Heaven* (1937), which wears an aspect—I can only put it like this— of continental parochialism. *More Joy in Heaven* is irremediably indigenous, North-American in a limiting way. It is the story of a paroled criminal's effort to re-enter the society which has first punished and then forgiven him. Behind it stands an ethos of violence and the myth of the heroic gangster. Its setting is the brutal North-American city, ugly and unhistorical and very much 'a machine for living', the sense of which is conveyed with confident incisiveness.

> The Coronet Hotel near the university was a four-storey, brick hotel used mainly by the second-class sporting trade. Across the street was a public dance hall. The hotel-keeper, Harvey Jenkins, wrestling and boxing promoter, had a string of wrestlers of his own. Squat, tin-eared, short-necked, heavy-shouldered men with bald heads were always going in and out of the Coronet. In the lounge there was always a group of young fellows gathered around some local light-weight who was promising to beat the ears off an imported punch-drunk third rater. During the racing season the hotel was crowded with men from far-away tracks with fine names like Blue Bonnets, Hialeah, and Tia Juana, who had been coming to the Coronet for years. Every day a special bus carried them out to the track and brought them to the hotel at night, or they could make their bets right in the hotel, for there was a wire direct to the track. With a dance hall just across the street, all the little tarts in town used to hang around there in the racing season.

The style of the characters is just what this *milieu* prepares one to expect: the local political boss, Senator McLean, 'investment banker, mining magnate', and his spoilt grasping daughter; the

central figure himself, Kip Caley, in whom there struggles some
Rousseauistic worth the progress of which is blocked, the novel
suggests, by an uncomprehending society; Caley's dying mother
and his prim lawyer brother who has changed his name in order not
to have his career destroyed by his relationship with a notorious
gunman and bank robber; two or three local gangsters and near-
criminals, including the fat, sinister hotel-keeper, a warm-hearted
all-in wrestler and a ferret-like Iago who is appalled by the idea of
Caley's falling for the good life and who hopes against hope that his
transformation is all a front; another rather dim good girl, Julia,
who is working as a waitress but is really a model resting—a
conventional combination of jobs, this; and inevitably 'the big,
raw-boned, sandy-haired prison chaplain'. One's expectations
about the characters in this novel comes not only from the *milieu*
but, one realises on reflection, from a succession of American films
of the 'thirties and 'forties. And how positive and important in
shaping expectations was the cinema for those growing up in this
period. Its images seemed to them to represent reality with a
peculiar point and fitness, its themes and situations to be exactly
level with their experience. The paradox of one's reaction to *More
Joy in Heaven* is that while its pure Americanism is so remote (it is,
it seems to me, markedly more American than Canadian, unlike
Such is My Beloved) its cinematic conception, technique, imagery
and characterisation are intimately familiar, part indeed of the
history of one's own life. So much so that it is impossible to think
about *More Joy in Heaven* without seeing it as a film and without
casting its characters from those familiar names: Victor McLaglen,
William Bendix, Janet Gaynor, Veronica Lake, Humphrey
Bogart, Richard Widmark, Sidney Greenstreet, Franchot Tone,
Edwin Arnold, Edward G. Robinson. *More Joy in Heaven* would
make—perhaps, for all I know, it has already made—a superb film
script. It begins abruptly with Kip Caley's release from prison, it
ends shockingly with his death after a battle with the police. In
between there are two distinct movements or sequences, one which
records his effort to re-enter the normal world, not just as a rescued
criminal but as a man with a new, positive function to interpret the
criminal to society and to ease his return to it; the other records the

process of Caley's realisation that society rejects his rôle as absurd and dangerous.

The clean-cut simplicity of design goes with an abundance of sharply photographed detail. The author maintains his customary unobtrusiveness. He is the registering camera, and the novel's effects are gained by swiftly tracking from point to point or by panning out over a wider prospect before focussing in to concentrate on a single feature. Here is an example of the latter tactic in a scene where Kip Caley watches the hard-up waitress Julie being cruelly teased by two young customers.

> 'Look, lady,' the fair boy said. He tossed the silver up and down. In spite of herself she half turned, her head down, watching the coins in his palm, and everything that Kip had ever wanted seemed at that moment to be held in the boy's palm, all the things he had wanted when he used to lie awake in his cell dreaming of nights of freedom when freight trains rumbled through the hills. And he whispered to himself, 'Go on, son. Give it to her.'

This concentration on a single, tiny, expressive area, in this case the hand tossing the coin, is an instance of an essentially cinematic technique. This is one variation that can be played against the base of the camera's gravely objective scrutiny. Another is to use its distorting power to produce a frantic nightmare unreality. There is a scene worked out in this manner when Kip Caley at a party at an ice-rink is suddenly appalled amid the metallic music and the capers on the ice, by the inhuman monkey-like curiosity of the company.

> When they shook hands with him, he became startled and backed away. Worried, he swung around, looking for a passage to the exit. But a little crowd had gathered in the aisle. They smiled and whispered. The tightness in him was becoming unbearable and spoiling this world for him. All their faces seemed to belong to the glistening ice, the violet lights, the stiffly jumping horses. These faces were bright masks. The Senator's mask was pink and white. Ellen had on a sharp, pretty little frozen-faced mask. Kip felt he was incredible. They gaped up at him as if he were a great crag of basalt.

This technique is supported by a characteristically American use of language in the cinema, by tersely rapping dialogue and by bare and bony speech for narrative, speech which seems to require the accompaniment of realistic acting if it is not to seem grimly thin and dry. The main relief, as in most American film speech, is the harsh wisecrack and the ethnically derived joke. As Kip enters the hotel, where as a famous converted criminal he is to be a draw, he calls out to the Senator:

'I saw the Mayor,' he said. 'He was swell. He wants me to go and see him. What do you know about that?'

'He wouldn't be smart if he didn't,' the Senator said. 'You're his whole social program walking around the streets.'

And then a round, rosy-faced Greek restaurateur with big black moustaches, bounces over to him shouting:

'Tomorrow I make a special sandwich. I call it the Kip Caley sandwich—a gesture for peace, freedom—international, see? How's that?' he asked grandly.

What Morley Callaghan's cinematic method is successful—in a qualified way—in doing in *More Joy in Heaven* is two things. One, to present characters, or rather one character, since Kip Caley's is the only one that counts, which can be felt by sympathy although not entered into by intelligence. The other is to convey a sense of life as energy, as an embodied force flowing this way or that. To point to this achievement is also to expose the essential and double problem of this novel which is both moral and artistic. Kip Caley's is a thick-set block of a character, one of a tribe of the nearly articulate, towards whom Callaghan feels a special sympathy. When Caley thinks or reflects or puzzles about his predicament, his mind creaks; the reader is aware of the clumsy stretching of unused muscles. Caley's thoughts are incapable of escaping from their deep immersion in his moods, from the euphoria with which he leaves prison on his mission to speak for the criminal to society, and from his despair when he finally grasps that in the eyes of society his rôle of interpreter is ridiculous and dangerous. He has the will to move to a moral level of existence without the capacity to make his will effective, or that lucidity of consciousness which is the condition of self-knowledge. Enfranchised from the Kingston Penitentiary Caley may be, but he remains caged in the prison of his own clogged nature.

I speak as though Caley's problem were a real historical event. But of course *this* problem, the inability of the protagonist to move in the direction which the formal transformation of his character requires, is an artistic problem. It is Callaghan's problem and an unsolved problem, too. It is the failure of the author to endow his protagonist with a dimension of possibility—the latent part of Caley's nature is too thin—and at the same time a fault in the author's eyesight which stops him from discerning this deficiency. Callaghan is asking from a character conceived in a certain mould more than it has in it to give. The moral problem in the novel is of a similar sort. It also comes from an uncritical or disproportionate expectation of what a given conception may be able to develop into. As with the character of Caley, so with the idea of experience implicit in the novel. Life is taken to be an expenditure of energy; some forms of it may be regrettable, others not. But it is judged in a pragmatic way solely by criteria within itself. It is impossible for life conceived of in this way, simply as energy, sometimes flowing, sometimes checked, to be the material of moral experience—which is what the author of *More Joy in Heaven* is asking of it in his fiction. Kip Caley's death in a welter of pointless violence is in keeping with the frantic, meaningless activity of his early life as a criminal. But it is also in keeping, it seems to me, with the interval, the period the novel deals with, during which he is, at first with the sympathy, and then against the hostility, of society, apparently undergoing a moral experience. It is in keeping because of the limitations imposed by the brutal convention in which the novel is written, where all human experiences, even as in this case the struggle for moral experience, appears as an outflow of force, another species of violence.

I have stressed what I take to be the essential failure in *More Joy in Heaven* but it remains a strong piece of work and an impressive example of its *genre*. It is solid, vigorous, lean and precise, the product of a serious mind. It has more weight than the documented but insubstantial study of a university institution, *The Varsity Story* (1949), more bite than the more vaguely organised *A Passion in Rome* (1961). *More Joy in Heaven* is a member of the group of novels which includes *Such is My Beloved*, *The Many Colored Coat* (1960), and *The Loved and the Lost* (1951) to which I turn now. These novels, different in theme and setting, have in common a preoccupation with what I should like to call self-preservation, as long as I may remove from the term any hint of selfishness or over-personal concern.

Morley Callaghan is fascinated by what Henry James in the Preface to *What Maisie Knew* called a character's 'truth of resistance', the gift or genius that some have for preserving intact the lineaments of their nature. It is a power which has at its heart a certain insistent simplicity: not self confidence but trust in self. In Father Dowling it shows itself as a steady flame of goodness impervious even to the most high-minded opposition, in Kip Caley as the persistent, and finally desperate, thrust of an abrasively independent identity. In *The Loved and the Lost* it is the girl Peggy Sanderson who possesses this faculty. It reveals itself in conduct which ignores or evades—rather than defies—the acceptable canons of behaviour in her world. The well-disposed think her capricious, the suspicious perverse. Her strangeness lies in her unpredictability, in her assumption that she is not caught in the same net as everybody else. She is described by his friend Foley to James McAlpine, a University teacher and would-be newspaper columnist, who is our source of awareness during this novel, in a fumbling conversation which tries to define her strangeness, as a blue jay, a bird which flies off at crazy and unpredictable angles.

The substance of the novel is the search for the true nature of the girl's odd, disconcerting individuality. It is conducted against the quietly insinuated but effectively established presence of Montreal. In no other novel of Morley Callaghan is the city context so significantly part of the story and—at least to a British reader—so attractive. Incidentally, unobtrusively and, at every point, relevantly, the dimensions of the city appear, from the mountain with wealth clustered round its sides, the river and the boats whistling all night long, to the North-American towers and hotels, the antique stone office buildings and the old French town and its church steeples spreading eastwards, down to St Henri's along the canal where Peggy Sanderson lives in a bare room in a run-down apartment house, and St Antoine, the Negro quarter crammed with tawdry taverns and cafés, pool parlours, delicatessen stores, cleaning establishments, railway yards. The detail carries with it a pure Canadian quality. One has a sense of a city, neither American nor European, with an authentically separate style of its own, of a place in which a complete human life can be lived and where an immense range of experience is available. It is the universal language with a unique accent. From a rapid touch here and there—there is little extended description—comes a sense of the form and condition of the place: space, snow, and air heavy with unbearable cold, the sound of church bells and sleigh bells, the varying manners of different races and nations and their tense relationships, the chime of different languages, the characteristic bluish winter light, the typical great occasion like the ice hockey match, the glimpses of a fastidious French-Canadian priest helping his sister from a taxi, a fat Jewish tavern keeper, Negro jazz players, a rich man contemplating his Renoir, a University professor with his marbles-in-the-mouth accent.

It is in the freshly realised setting of Montreal, then, that the search for a definition of the girl's identity is undertaken. There is a kind of symmetry between the exact notation of the city and the effort more and more precisely to reveal the quality of her individuality, although, I must add, the symmetry is unusual in that what is explicit and achieved on the side of the city, is suspended and enigmatic on the side of the girl. The instrument of exploration is the consciousness of James McAlpine which becomes, as the novel progresses, the mind and the approach of the reader. McAlpine is well suited to be the honest searcher and, in his normality, to stand for the engaged reader. He is open-minded, intelligent, sensitive and warm-hearted, with a rather obvious ambition to which he is consciously inclined to allow more weight than his fundamentally generous nature warrants. At first puzzled and then fascinated, and at last uneasily in love with Peggy, his feelings at each stage have in them an element of wonder at the girl's originality—an originality which is shown, ironically enough, to be no more than an intimate fidelity to her own nature. Other people in the novel live, as it were, at a distance from themselves, under the influence of principles, prejudices, conventions, formalities, imposed from outside. Most of their conduct and their feelings are imitated, not self-initiated: they are shown as activities and functions set in motion from the outside. But Peggy Sanderson has the strange power of being—herself. She is the standard, a mild, quiet, rather humble standard (remembered by her university teachers as merely a mediocre student) by which we judge the other characters; and so strong is the sense of general human truth in this novel, the standard by which we judge ourselves.

Peggy Sanderson lives directly from her own centre, and in a world where most live indirectly or deviously, this makes her an object of bewilderment and hostility, and since she is an attractive young woman, attitudes towards her are also clouded with sexual desire or sexual envy. The genuine goodness in her nature, hinted at in a variety of forms, and yet teasingly suspended as to certainty till the end of the book, leads her to seek out the poor in whom she feels the response her temperament naturally requires. The poorest in Montreal are the Negroes. She seeks them out not to do them good but simply to be with them. So that there hangs round her the dubious reputation of a woman with perverse sexual tastes, a reputation which is a projection of perverse white feelings, and all the stronger for being a matter of guess and inference. She has the same reputation among Negro men and women, too: among the men because they half-share the feelings of white society, among women because they see their men turning from them to her. Her Negro-haunting life costs her a respectable job—she is now working in a miserable textile factory and is known to James McAlpine as Peggy the Crimp—costs her as well her friends and reputation and ultimately her life. She is raped and murdered by a degenerate white man. The reasons for the shape of her life are partly that the Negroes are what they are in Montreal, and partly the events of her own past. She had loved, as the repressed child of a grim Methodist minister, a Negro family where the gaiety matched the poverty and where she had her chief experience of human warmth. She also had had her first sexual pang at the sight of a nude Negro boy. But these sociological and genetic circumstances, while their importance is recognised, are never offered by Morley Callaghan as total explanations or causes. They are occasions and conditions of spontaneous feeling. There is always in his account of the girl's motives a shaded ambiguity which, while it may be lacking in abstract logic, is, one feels, closely in correspondence with the complications of reality.

The last point suggests something of the technical achievement in *The Loved and the Lost*, Callaghan's success in treating a difficult and serious theme in a casually conversational medium. The writing has little local richness or intricacy; it is bare in metaphor and not at all remarkable in phrasing or wit. But it is always lucid and apt, it has an easy natural run, and the kind of subtlety of inflection more often found in the intimacy of speech. Not that Callaghan hasn't his own ways of using his low-toned medium to good effect: in particular, great skill in the sudden small shock of contrasting sequences, sometimes of personality, sometimes of location. In this novel he makes effective use of the contrast between the space of the city and vividly pictured interiors, between, for example, the rearing mountain and a brilliantly lit shop window showing a single carved leopard, or between the flowing expanse of the streets and the confined, nun-like severity of Peggy Sanderson's room, or a smoky ground-floor club occupied by rapturously intent jazz musicians. One notices even more the attitude of the writer, an air of relaxed restraint, which comes from his confidence in his capacity, certainly not to force, not even to persuade, but rather to allow, a profoundly significant theme to appear at critical moments and with complete naturalness from its immersion in the coolly observed detail.

It is this triple set of medium, theme and attitude, which distinguishes *The Many Colored Coat*, one of the finest of Morley Callaghan's novels, and the one I take to represent his latest, most developed work. The medium is in the same mode, quiet, unpretentious, close to speech in movement and with much of the flexibility and versatility of the spoken language. The medium, at once masculine and unpretentious, is in accord with Morley Callaghan's attitude, which is, characteristically, both self-effacing and positive. The theme of *The Many Colored Coat* is that of Joseph, the gifted and beloved young man. The novel rehearses the theme of the fortunes of the fortunate man. The biblical reference comes

through, as the novel unfolds, without the least touch of impro-
priety or tactlessness, and it testifies to the steadiness Callaghan sees
in human nature and to his perception of the permanent content of
the varying crises it has to face. At the same time the pretentious
absurdity of the hero's job, Public Relations man to a distillery, an
ambassador of alcohol, in fact, has an almost clinically exact contemporary flavour, that of business modified to suit the entertain-
ment industry and surrounded by a mist of dubious scientific
management.

The novel has a pleasingly simple shape. It falls into two parts,
each of which concludes in a critical and brilliantly conducted
court scene. In the first we see Harry Lane as Joseph the blessed,
blooming with health, beauty, riches, success, courage—he is
modest about his fine war record—popularity and love. He deals
with radio and television people, speaks at banquets, organises
golfing tournaments, spends his employers' money right and left
to sell whisky. Why then didn't all the phoniness rub off on him?
It was because he radiated an essential air of well-being. People
lived off him, but they loved to live off *him*. 'He had always had a
talent for generosity . . . and his good natural talent was now
flowering outlandishly. . . .' Scotty Bowman, a middle-aged,
middle-class bank manager, a solid decent man, who is deeply
drawn to him, notices two things about him: one, 'that unbelievable
luck which was like a magical adjustment between himself and the
world', and two, that he had, as Scotty said, '. . . a bad flaw. He's
a kind of innocent guy.' Only the old or the twisted feel alien to
him, like his girl's father Judge Morris, for whom his popularity
was 'the whole corrupting essence of this thing', and for whom
his attractiveness was terrible and criminal, 'his occupational
weapon'; or Mike Kon, Scotty Bowman's friend, an ex-boxer with
a passion for respectability, who is jealous of Harry's effect on the
friend to whom he owes everything. To Kon, Harry is a smooth
and superficial man. To Francis Ouimet, a Catholic lawyer with a
spinsterish aloofness from any kind of self-indulgence, the grace
and charm to which Harry's friends yield is 'the corrupting pressure
of friendship'. The astonishing achievement of Callaghan's here is
to make us feel the sweetness and wholesomeness, too easily

accepted by Harry himself perhaps, but completely genuine, of the nature involved in this idiotic commercial confidence work. Callaghan can do this because he never sees the character as an abstraction, never takes it to be an arrangement of qualities but always a dense and complex pattern. He has an insight, which is both realist and mature, into the mixture of motives, the flawed surface and the clouded quality of human substance. There are discrepancies, aberrations, snags and twists in the material. But it impresses us always as real and not synthetic.

Harry's golden years are shattered when a friend, out of gratitude, offers him the chance of making a fortune in oil shares. He needs to borrow money to buy them and the banker, Scotty Bowman, persuades him to arrange a large loan at Bowman's bank. The consideration, the banker suggests, will be some shares for himself. The disconcerted Harry has brought home to him what has already been tellingly indicated to the reader, that Bowman has rapidly succumbed to the financial morality of the world around Harry. Harry agrees, the money is passed over, the shares turn out to be worthless, and the bank manager is tried for fraud since he had, although Harry had not realised this, insufficient cover for the loan. He is found guilty in a trial scene which has all the elegance of a ballet and the excitement of a film. The damage to Harry's reputation is done by Mike Kon, Bowman's devoted friend, whose testimony in defence of Bowman makes Harry out the chief though not legally responsible culprit. The disgust with which all his friends now look at Harry turns to horror when Bowman, who to all appearances was duped into committing a crime by the sophisticated Harry, kills himself in prison.

The second part of the novel traces, with an unemphatic, wandering but expressive line, the dissolution of personality worked in Harry Lane by his loss of reputation. The process, a passage from incredulous fury when his innocence is not recognised, through self-pity and disorientation to despair and revenge, is one partly of drift, a flinching accommodation to circumstances, partly of defiant self-destruction. Callaghan has the realist's talent for rendering the densely conditioned movements of life and their peculiar combination of limpness and drive. In *The Many Colored*

Coat the characteristically solid evocation is strengthened and filled out by a second parallel movement, the break-up of Mike Kon who in his truculent, dumber way, mimics the disintegration of Harry Lane. The finesse of the design lies particularly in the combined parallelism and friction of these two movements. Mike's decline, desertion by his friends, failure at work, a bad name, a disordered personal life, repeats Harry's; and yet each sees the other as the malevolent force which keeps the original cause of his disaster, Scottie Bowman's suicide (which means to Harry, Bowman's guilty silence, and to Mike his undeserved disgrace), continually operating as a malign influence in his own life. Each, once he is ousted from what he sees as his normal 'pre-lapsarian' state, has his own way of making the other suffer. Harry's is more consciously cruel, Mike's is more angrily bull-like.

The twisted logic of the novel's design fits the perverse will, itself the function of a distorted consciousness, which in each of the two men turns persecutor into victim, victim into persecutor, and makes punishment and crime change places. The irrational assumptions revealed in Harry's frantic conduct lead some to believe that his trauma has made him mad, 'You've changed,' his lover Molly says to him. 'Your whole personality has changed. This . . . this exploration of your innocence, I think you are out of your mind. . .' But a friend shrewdly comments on this, 'No, not mad at all. Harry Lane's thumbing his nose at the world.' What does become clear is that Harry's obsessive concentration on his suffering damages his capacity for human connection. 'When a man clings to his suffering,' Molly says to him again, 'he violates all human sympathy and without that human sympathy what he does has no meaning. All you're doing with your antics is cutting yourself off. . . .' The love between Harry and Molly becomes tense and finally impossible, and the same infection invades the devotion of his alter-ego, Mike, to his father, a paralysed old man, the whole of whose intelligence and affection is concentrated in his one good eye (both these relationships are realised with accurate, moving sympathy). Harry believes that he is carried along solely by the conviction of his own innocence. But what is even clearer is that his more constant feeling is one of 'a sense of foolish, endless humiliation'.

o

'Humiliation' is indeed the key word. Harry is fascinated by 'the blind and perfect selfishness of Bowman's despair that could let him make Harry his victim again. Oh, the monstrous egotism of despair, he thought, sighing.' But as an old mumbling priest, whose confessional he uneasily enters one night, not to confess but to ask for advice, points out as he complains of the injustice done to him, 'The more you suffer from injustice, the deeper the wound to your pride . . . a man killed himself, surely not to spite just you. What awful egotism of you to think so. . . .' Harry's bitter sense of injustice, his anguish at the guilt so unfairly imputed to him, turns out to be a disguise for the rage of wounded pride.

The importance attributed to pride, not in any doctrinal way but by suggestive, concrete pointing, is justified not only by the facts of the case in this novel and the intelligent psychological investigation of them, but by a certain habit of sensibility in Morley Callaghan himself. He has, as Edmund Wilson point out in a perceptive and sympathetic essay,[1] 'an intuitive sense of the meaning of Christianity'. 'Though [the novels] depend on no scaffolding of theology, though they embody an original vision, they have evidently somewhere behind them the tradition of the Catholic Church. This is not the acquired doctrine of the self-conscious Catholic convert—of Graham Greene or Evelyn Waugh.' The human vision of these novels depends on a Christian style of feeling, of a particular tradition of religious sensibility which is present not as dogma or metaphysic but as a mode of perception and reaction.

This Christian touch—it is as silent and precise as that—is present particularly in the quiet close of the novel. ('Climax' would be too heightened a word for work which, as Edmund Wilson in the same essay said, 'avoids convulsions and . . . allows itself no outbreak in tirades'.[2]) Mike Kon, maddened by Harry's harrassment and his refusal to back down, does serious violence to him, is arrested and put on trial in a scene which has all the acrid sharpness and the shaped definition of the earlier trial. Harry, who in hospital had

[1] Edmund Wilson, O Canada, London, 1967, p. 20
[2] Op. cit. p. 31

been calculating his revenge, unaccountably fails to appear to give evidence against Mike, and he is acquitted. With equal unpredictability, Mike Kon suddenly admits in court that he was unjust to Harry Lane in his original testimony. There is a gratuitous, unprepared note in these two actions which corresponds to, or is the outcome of, the unforeseeable visitations of grace, the sense of which is the positive side in Callaghan's economy of Christian response, of his feeling for guilt and negation.

I speak of Callaghan's Christian response, but, of course, that response and the whole economy of feeling of which it is a part, are sunk deep in the constitution of the novelist. If Callaghan is a Christian novelist, this is the way in which he is one. He is not the spokesman of religion, but the artist who possesses it as part of his personal nervous equipment. This traditional steadiness blends in Callaghan with that acute feeling for contemporary society, which, to a European at least, seems very natural to an artist working in the New World, and the combination makes him a novelist of an impressively serious quality. The contemporary flavour appears everywhere in his work, in themes, situations, characters and procedures. A single notable example of it in *The Many Colored Coat* is his treatment of the life of the streets. The street in a modern industrial society presents itself to him as an image of that society and its experience. His skill in rendering the flow of life through the street, the brutality and ugliness, the glimpses the street provides of other, less tangible experiences, the altercations, the moments of communication, show the street not only as a place but as the analogue of human vitality and representativeness. 'That night,' he writes of Harry Lane after his fall, 'he walked through the streets for hours feeling he was wandering through his own life.'

I end by quoting the concluding paragraphs of *The Many Colored Coat*, a novel which strikes one very much as a walk through the streets of life (and one, too, in which Callaghan allows himself the unaccustomed liberty of an explicit comment). It brings out, I think, the serenity and balance of a writer whose religious sense is part of his grip on reality, and the quality of one who, as he puts it, appreciate's people's capacity to 'handle their lives and be comfortable together' but who also sees the point of lives of a different sort, those who are 'alone, knowing the terror of their innocence'.

It was the hour when the neighborhood came alive for the night. People wandered along the boulevard seeking pleasure or excitement or just new sights, or new merchandise in the store windows. No one paid any attention to him. He was a stranger to them. Loafing along in the crowd he found himself looking with interest at the passing faces. A plain plump woman with her thin husband bumped against him. Three young men, hatless, their thick shiny black hair carefully combed, stared at him coldly. A taxi stopped at the curb and three men and three girls scrambled out and rushed at a doorway to a dance hall and went running and pushing each other up a long flight of stairs. He could hear the clatter of their footsteps and their laughter on the stairs. It was a fine clear evening. As he passed a dingy little candy store where the prostitutes were allowed to sit undisturbed, one of the girls smiled at him, then saw someone she knew on the street and got up eagerly. An old Jew with a beard and grave eyes passed by, then a tired old man, then a boyish-looking seminarian, plump-cheeked and clean, his eyes cast down, then a pretty girl with her stern watchful mother. An opulent fat man, a rich drug peddler who held court every night at a table by the dance floor in the biggest beer hall in the neighborhood, got out of a new car with three obsequious young fellows. The opulent-looking man had an evil face, Harry thought.

It was a tough neighborhood of ordinary people. Kids with long smooth hair and leather jackets, workmen, a lawyer taking a stroll, a serene-faced old man, girls in sweaters and short straight hair, and middle-aged men with pale hard faces and shifty eyes—they all brushed against him on the way to their cafés.

But on this wide crowded boulevard at that hour were all the faces of the world; some were evil, some pious, some greedy, some just didn't care, and some no doubt avowed their sins, suffering whatever torments. Yet they looked as if they could handle their lives and be comfortable together. There would be some though, he was sure, who would really be alone, knowing the terror of their innocence.

INDEX